WITHDRAWN

THE YALE EDITION OF THE

SWINBURNE LETTERS

IN SIX VOLUMES

I

WB.S. Jan^y & Octr 1860.

THE

SWINBURNE

LETTERS

EDITED BY CECIL Y. LANG

VOLUME 1

1854 - 1869

New Haven: YALE UNIVERSITY PRESS, 1959

To

PAULL FRANKLIN BAUM

HOWARD MUMFORD JONES

HENRI PEYRE

FRANK E. BROWN

and *In Memoriam*

HYDER EDWARD ROLLINS

νῦν δ' αὖ μνησάμενον γλυκύπικρος ὑπήλυθεν αἰδώς,
οἷα τυχὼν οἵου πρὸς σέθεν οἷος ἔχω· . . .
οὐ γὰρ ἔχω, μέγα δή τι θέλων, σέθεν ἄξια δοῦναι,
θαπτομένου περ ἀπών· οὐ γὰρ ἔνεστιν ἐμοι·

ACKNOWLEDGMENTS

THIS BOOK was written under the shelter of academic bowers, with every convenience but amidst distractions that seem to me the very antithesis of the soft obscurities of retirement. It could not have been completed without the assistance of the learned and the patronage of the great.

Much as I should like to thank by name all the owners of letters who have so kindly allowed me the use of their property, I am required to limit myself to a general expression of gratitude here and to specific acknowledgments in the appointed places. "Beggar that I am," as Hamlet remarked, "I am even poor in thanks, but I thank you." Librarians and library staffs everywhere (or so it seems) have been unfailingly generous with their time and resources, but it is the magnificent Library and the magnificent librarians of Yale University that have made this book possible. I am especially indebted to Donald Gallup, Robert Metzdorf, Barbara Simison, Jean Smith, and Marjorie Wynne, all of whom have aided me not merely above the indicatives of duty but beyond the imperatives of friendship. I am also under most pleasant obligation to Dudley and Jean Bahlman, Harold Bloom, Talbot and Christine Donaldson, Edgar S. Furniss, Gordon Haight, Sue Hilles, David Horne, Louis Martz, James Osborn, Norman Pearson, Frederick and Marian Pottle, Charles and Ruth Prouty, Richard Purdy, Elizabeth Swift, C. B. Tinker, Janet Camp Troxell.

William A. Jackson and William H. Bond have helped me in many indispensable ways for well over a decade. And for various favors I am obliged to Helena Baum, Ronald Berger, Harold Chase, S. C. Chew, M. N. Cohen, Ben Cornelius, David Davies, Edwin and Jean Fussell, John Gordan, Richard Gross, Anne Henry, C. L. Lambertson, Leslie and Marion Marchand, Robert Mason, Philip Neufeld, Gordon Ray, Mark and Martha Reed, Bernard and Susan Schilling, Edgar Shannon, David and Annette Smith, Mabel Steele, Wilfred Stone, Richard Swift, Robert Taylor, Benjamin Townsend, Charles Weis, and John Seelye.

In Great Britain and on the Continent I owe thanks to Alan G. Agnew, Louis Bonnerot, R. N. Carew Hunt, John Carter, Sir Sydney Cockerell, Laura Dallapiccola, Irene Cooper Willis, Evelyn Courtney-Boyd, D. Cox, Bonamy Dobrée, A. J. Farmer, Philip Gosse, Roger Lancelyn Green, Marthe Guérin-Lésé, Ethel C. Hatch, Gwyn and Alice

Jones, Dorothy Kilgour, Eileen LeBreton, R. D. Macleod, Andre Maurois, Nancy Mitford, Henri Mondor, Sir Harold Nicolson, the late Paul Oppé, B. S. Page, James Pope-Hennessy, John Pope-Hennessy, Harold Raymond, Alan Redway, J. S. Ritchie, Angela Thirkell, Cecil J. Travers. My gratitude to John Hayward is profound. I am also indebted to Peter Calvocoressi, Director of Chatto and Windus, Ltd., and to A. S. Frere, Chairman, William Heinemann, Ltd., for permission to reprint copyright material.

For help with family relationships and for delightful reminiscences, as well as for a guided tour of Capheaton, the Swinburne seat in Northumberland, I owe thanks to Lady Swinburne and to Captain and Mrs. Browne-Swinburne. A few miles away at Wallington, which for a while was almost a second home to Swinburne, Sir Charles and Lady Trevelyan showed me every hospitable kindness and rendered me every service, placing at my disposal all the rich stores of family correspondence that had any relevance to my undertaking.

Clyde Kenneth Hyder has been large-hearted and open-handed with his personal and expert assistance, and his invaluable study, *Swinburne's Literary Career and Fame,* has been consulted at every turn. Lowell Kerr has sent me photostats of manuscript letters in his fine collection, and has most generously helped me solve problems in them. The name John S. Mayfield appears so often in these volumes that the size of my debt to him ought to be obvious. He has not only allowed me to include all the manuscript letters in his extensive Swinburne collection, but over and over again has drawn my attention to helpful information and, with his intimate knowledge of Swinburniana, has repeatedly caught me out in errors of fact and fancy, omission and commission. Without his friendly counsel this book would be far faultier than it is.

My opening allusion to the "patronage of the great" was not idle. A year's residence in England in 1951–52 was made possible by grants from the Fulbright Commission and the John Simon Guggenheim Memorial Foundation, and subventions from the Guggenheim Foundation and the Morse Fund at Yale have helped defray some of the staggering costs of publication.

I have not been hurried by eagerness to the end, but though I have protracted my work, I will not protract this preface. With one paralyzing exception, those whom I most wish to please are alive and in the prime of life, and I await their judgment with anything but Dr. Johnson's "frigid tranquillity."

C.Y.L.

May 1959

viii

CONTENTS

Frontispiece: Swinburne, aged 22. From an
    etching by William Bell Scott, 1860

Facsimiles of Swinburne's handwriting appear
    on pages 24, 119

SHORT TITLES

AOP Algernon Charles Swinburne, *Astrophel and Other Poems,* 1894.

Bonchurch Sir Edmund Gosse and Thomas James Wise, eds., *The Complete Works of Algernon Charles Swinburne,* 20 vols., 1925–27. The Bonchurch Edition.

CPOP Algernon Charles Swinburne, *A Channel Passage and Other Poems,* 1904.

CR Algernon Charles Swinburne, *A Century of Roundels,* 1883.

DNB *Dictionary of National Biography.*

Early Letters *Early Letters from Algernon Charles Swinburne to John Nichol* ("Printed for Private Circulation"), 1917.

ES Algernon Charles Swinburne, *Essays and Studies,* 1875.

Lafourcade, *Biography* Georges Lafourcade, *Swinburne: A Literary Biography,* 1932.

Lafourcade, *La Jeunesse* Georges Lafourcade, *La Jeunesse de Swinburne 1837–1867,* 2 vols., Paris, 1928.

Leith Mary Charlotte Julia (Gordon) Leith, *The Boyhood of Algernon Charles Swinburne; Personal Recollections by His Cousin, Mrs. Disney Leith, with Extracts from Some of His Private Letters,* 1917.

MHOP Algernon Charles Swinburne, *A Midsummer Holiday and Other Poems,* 1884.

PB1 Algernon Charles Swinburne, *Poems and Ballads,* 1866.

PB2 Algernon Charles Swinburne, *Poems and Ballads,* Second Series, 1878.

PB3 Algernon Charles Swinburne, *Poems and Ballads,* Third Series, 1889.

PMLA Publications of the Modern Language Association of America.

Pope-Hennessy James Pope-Hennessy, *Monckton Milnes: The Flight of Youth, 1851–1885,* 1951.

Rossetti Papers William Michael Rossetti, comp., *Rossetti Papers, 1862–1870,* 1903.

SBS Algernon Charles Swinburne, *Songs before Sunrise,* 1871.

SPP Algernon Charles Swinburne, *Studies in Prose and Poetry,* 1894.

STN Algernon Charles Swinburne, *Songs of Two Nations,* 1875.

TLOP Algernon Charles Swinburne, *Tristram of Lyonesse and Other Poems,* 1882.

INTRODUCTION

SWINBURNE has long been out of fashion. Of the great English poets he remains the most unappreciated, and the reasons are not hard to find. Born in 1837, he lived till 1909, surviving by eight years the queen who had acceded to the throne in the year of his birth. His virtuosity was dogma, but his strength had become labor and sorrow, and the glow was gone. The shifting and resettling of taste was seismic, as it had been at the beginning of the nineteenth century, and those who seemed to follow his tracks only drew attention to the change. Among the contemporaries whose genius he had honored none remained but Meredith, whose death followed his own by a month. Hardy, though only three years his junior, belonged to a new generation. Swinburne was unresponsive to his poetry, and the last of the novels had appeared many years earlier. Tennyson had been dead for seventeen years, Browning nearly twenty, Arnold twenty-one. Gabriel Rossetti, for fifteen years his most cherished friend, had died in 1882 (their intimacy had come to an unhappy end ten years before), William Morris in 1896, Burne-Jones in 1898. (Even Bertie Mason, whose childhood he had celebrated with so many verses, was already in the middle of the journey.) New friends had come and gone without taking the places of those who had known Swinburne in his springtime, and of the latter only four lived on after him—a sister, a cousin, William Rossetti, Watts-Dunton. Three months before his death, in the last letter that we have from his pen, he referred to himself as an " 'idle old man,' like King Lear," and in view of the circumstances the allusion is revealing and symbolic, if not actually self-conscious and deliberate. He had no impulse to manage still "those authorities" that he had given away. He did not rage against the dying of the light. Nothing could emphasize more starkly the fate that had overtaken him while still alive than a letter written by Ezra Pound less than a month before Swinburne died. "I am not doing society, ye knaow," he wrote to his father. "I am engaged in that gentler pursuit, meeting the people I want to know. Swinburne happens to be stone deaf and with a temper a bit the worse for wear, so I haven't continued investigation in that direction."

The reaction was as much against the imitators of Swinburne as against Swinburne himself, and a lover of paradox could argue that Swinburne might properly be termed the stepfather of modern poetry. T. S. Eliot's well-known strictures against Gilbert Murray's translations of Euripides were directed, precisely, against the "vulgar debasement of the eminently personal idiom of Swinburne," and he named as harbingers of the new order "H.D." and Ezra Pound. To the extent that modern poetry has grown out of the translations of "H.D.," Pound, and the others, it may be said (perversely) to have grown out of Swinburne. Any thorough study of its origins would have to reckon with the literary consequences of the poet's long friendship with Benjamin Jowett—the translator of Plato, Master of Balliol, and (like Gilbert Murray, years later) Regius Professor of Greek—in whose company Swinburne, for so many years, exercised a personal and direct influence on the "Benjamin Jowett Brotherhood."

Oddly enough, at the same time that the makers of modern poetry were reacting against Swinburne by revolting against his imitators, his reputation also suffered from the decline of classical learning (a decline that seems to have exiled his revered Landor to permanent oblivion). Except for Milton, Swinburne was the most learned of all the major poets, and with the possible exception of *Samson Agonistes* (in a structural sense) his *Atalanta in Calydon* and *Erechtheus* are undoubtedly the most Greek works in English dramatic poetry. His Hellenism—not simply in a formal sense, as in the two dramas, the odes, the translations, but, more importantly, in the allusiveness of all his verse—has told against him.

There is another charge. The "garland of red roses" dropped "about the hood of some smug nun," of which Hardy wrote, stimulated the admiration of a whole generation, as any reader of Hardy's novels could testify. Imitations and imitators aside, the frequency of the allusions to Swinburne in the works (say) of Jack London, Scott Fitzgerald, Gide, O'Neill, is symptomatic of a literary fashion that bore the seeds of its own destruction. But no man bathes twice in the same stream. The necessity for change, novelty, shock has made itself felt, and the present editor himself, for example, could no more rid his pulses of a hundred lines and phrases in the "eminently personal idiom" of Mr. Eliot than, in an earlier generation, Buck Mulligan could look at the ocean without recalling "the grey sweet mother," the "snotgreen sea."

Few signs have appeared of a revival of interest, but Swinburne has much to say to the modern mind, and a little reflection on the primary sources of his inspiration, of which so much evidence appears in his letters, will show how often his sustenance was that of the early moderns. No poet has been more immersed than Swinburne in the Greek classics, a foundation of so much of the best English poetry. Of the seven poets specially recommended for study, a generation ago, in the once-famous manifesto of Flint and Pound, only Heine would have been struck off Swinburne's own list. Four of the others, Sappho, Catullus, Villon, and Gautier, he had studied, absorbed, paid tribute to as well as any man in history. The remaining two, Dante and Chaucer, were scarcely part of his very fiber like the others, but his repeated allusions to them reveal a deep and enduring love.

Taste, fashion, shifting sensibility, the modern temper, and other theoretical considerations apart, Swinburne has many virtues that have never been adequately recognized. As a translator, for instance, he could have ranked with the great masters. Passages from Sappho, Aeschylus, Euripides, Leopardi, Baudelaire, are woven into the fabric of his poems, and selections from Aristophanes, Hugo, Sade, and (above all) Villon were presented separately. He never undertook a sustained piece of translation, however, except for the renderings of Villon, and even these, though they have wrung admiration from practically all critics, including that most exacting master, Ezra Pound, still seem to be all but unknown. The fact that he translated so little is a double loss to letters, for in such work he found a kind of discipline that nothing else, except actual imitation, seemed able to impose. Not the sonnet or the roundel or the sestina was able to confine him. A translation by Swinburne of Catullus and Baudelaire, both of whom he revered and with both of whom he had such an affinity, would have rendered an inestimable service to three great poets and to posterity.

As a parodist, Swinburne has received a certain amount of recognition but hardly his due. No careful reader of *Specimens of Modern Poets: The Heptalogia* could fail to concede that he is, quite simply (to use his own kind of phrase), the greatest parodist who ever lived. His absorption of the manner, his reproduction of the mannerisms—and his genius for making the two things appear one thing—of Tennyson, Browning, Mrs. Browning, Coventry Patmore, "Owen Meredith," and Gabriel Rossetti are a kind of miracle of "negative capability." Only Swinburne could have followed Tennyson's poem "Despair" with "Disgust; A Dramatic Monologue" a month later, and only he would have revised "John Jones" to "John Jones's Wife" as Browning had altered his own poem "James Lee" to "James Lee's Wife." "Nephelidia," beyond all comparison the finest self-parody in the language, is so cunning and pitiless that it seems almost autoerotic, and "Poeta Loquitur," unprinted until 1918 and thus hardly known at all, is only less self-analytical:

> In a maze of monotonous murmur
> > Where reason roves ruined by rhyme,
> In a voice neither graver nor firmer
> > Than the bells on a fool's cap chime. . . .
>
> Mad mixtures of Frenchified offal
> > With insults to Christendom's creed,
> Blind blasphemy, schoolboylike scoff, all
> > These blazon me blockhead indeed. . . .
>
> In my poems, with ravishing rapture
> > Storm strikes me and strokes me and stings:
> But I'm scarcely the bird you might capture
> > Out of doors in the thick of such things.

No man with such talents in *pastiche* as Swinburne's—he could be a perfect chameleon when he chose—could have missed greatness as a parodist, and this facility must have been a burdensome problem in the fifties and sixties when he was working toward a style of his own.

Swinburne also had satiric and epigrammatic gifts of a high order. He was not a Martial lost in Putney, and he published little that could properly be termed satirical, but if he had set his sights in that direction, he might have won a reputation. Here again he seems to have profited from the discipline of form, in compression of thought, concreteness, clarity, instantaneousness of effect. Some of his quatrains seem to deserve a phrase of the purest Swinburnese—"simple perfection of perfect simplicity":

> Which is most worthy the rod
> > That justice wields when she can;
> Man, the creator of God,
> > Or God, the creator of man?

Though the surviving examples of his work in this mode—"artistic release from the nausea of the absurd," as Nietzsche termed it—tend to be too rigidly occasional, and even personal, to justify great claims, they reveal an authentic flair. The quality is high enough to repay investigation, and it is another consequence of the general neglect that his satiric poems have never been collected, not to say accurately printed and properly edited.

As a critic, Swinburne seems to be known and recognized but not often read. It could be said of him, as Boswell said of Johnson, that "no man had a more ardent love of literature, or a higher respect for it," but much of his work was done in a field so exclusive that no one not a specialist in the third- and fourth-rate seventeenth-century dramatists (or in Swinburne himself) could feel involved in it, and his standing today would be immeasurably greater if he had employed his limitless energies in propagating only the best that was known and thought in the world rather than in hierarchically ranking forgotten playwrights.

The absurd prose style of his later period requires no comment beyond Edward Thomas' observation that if De Quincey and Dr. Johnson had "collaborated in imitating Lyly they must have produced Swinburne's prose." Yet his early prose was an instrument of beauty. I think he must have learned much from Gautier. That he gave something to Pater he himself recognized ("Swinburne of course invented him," Watts remarked to William Rothenstein), but he never admitted, nor has anyone demonstrated, how much he gave. Still, in a passage like the one that follows from the essay "Notes on Designs of the Old Masters at Florence," one can only say "The voice is Jacob's voice, but the hands are the hands of Esau." Swinburne is speaking of some drawings by Michelangelo, which he compared with the work of Aeschylus and Shakespeare:

> The least thought of these men has in it something intricate and enormous, faultless as the formal work of their triumphant art must be. All mysteries of good and evil, all wonders of life and death, lie in their hands or at their feet. They have known the causes of things, and are not too happy. The fatal labour of the world, the clamour and hunger of the open-mouthed all-summoning grave, all fears and hopes of ephemeral men, are indeed made subject to them, and trodden by them underfoot; but the sorrow and strangeness of things are not lessened because to one or two their secret springs have been laid bare and the courses of their tides made known; refluent evil and good, alternate grief and joy, life inextricable from death, change inevitable and insuperable fate.

Despite learned discussions pointing out the error, the idea prevails that Swinburne was an "impressionistic" critic of literature (as he was of *art*) or an "aesthetic" critic, as he seemed to be initially. But no poet who praised Hugo, Shelley, and Aeschylus as Swinburne praised them could have been an "aesthetic" critic, and no critic who applied standards as consistently as he applied them could have been an impressionist.

Swinburne's criticism has rendered several distinct services to literature, and the study of his complete correspondence will make clear for the first time the intimacy of his involvement and the depth and range and sureness of his learning. He was a vigorous and crusading champion of Shelley. By no means blind to Shelley's faults, he remains to this day one of Shelley's best critics. He rescued Blake. The work on Blake is on the whole dated, but its historical importance can scarcely be overestimated. Swinburne spoke out loud and bold about his contemporaries: Carlyle, Tennyson, Browning, Arnold, the Brontës, FitzGerald, Rossetti, Meredith, Morris, Dickens, Wilkie Collins, Charles Reade, Whitman. With remarkable tact, he could separate the good from the bad, the weak from the strong. "In the whole range of literature covered," T. S. Eliot once wrote of the essays on the Tudor and Stuart dramatists, "Swinburne makes hardly more than two judgments which can be reversed or even questioned." The same claim, with not much more qualification, might be made of the whole *corpus* of his criticism. Swinburne lent all his prestige, all the power of his prose, all his antiquarian learning, to the Elizabethan revival, in which he was a pioneer. And his was the clearest, surest voice in England directing English attention to French literature: Villon, Hugo, Dumas, Gautier, Baudelaire, Musset, Banville, Vacquerie, Mallarmé. Among his friends he evangelized tirelessly for Balzac and Flaubert. The study of his letters will aid immensely in helping to establish for Swinburne the rank to which he is entitled as a critic—not merely in these areas and with these specific names but with a host of others: Landor, Poe, Leopardi, Zola, George Sand, Laclos, the Kingsleys, Dobell, Clough, Meinhold, P. J. Bailey, P. B. Marston, Sheridan Le Fanu, Newman, Hardy, Léon Cladel. Swinburne, in fact, leaves the impression that he had read *all* of English and French literature and most of Greek, Latin, and Italian.

But these are all peripheral attributes, and Swinburne's reputation will not rest upon his standing as translator, parodist, satirist, critic. His return must wait on a recognition of his solid qualities, independent of shifting taste. The central fact about him is that he was a poet and wrote great poems, and the central fact about Swinburne criticism is that he has never been judged solely by his best poems. (What would Wordsworth's reputation be today if it depended upon enthusiasm for *The Excursion?*)

Appreciation has always been clouded over by two criticisms of his work made in his own lifetime. Each remark was made by a friend, and each has been elevated by later generations to the status of something gnomic or oracular. "I don't see any internal centre from which springs anything that he does," Meredith once wrote to a friend, but the fact that he wrote this in 1861, speaking of *La Fille du policeman,* is usually overlooked, critics having found it a convenient peg on which to hang an indictment of *Poems and Ballads.* William Morris' criticism has proved even more useful. "I never could really sympathize with Swinburne's work," he wrote in 1882. "It always seemed to me to be founded on literature, not on nature." An odd remark for the author of *Jason, The Earthly Paradise, Sigurd the Volsung*—and curiously imperceptive. For it is becoming increasingly clear that Swinburne's best work was founded on nature, not on literature, that his "internal centre" was not books, liberty, progress, but, as in so much distinctively romantic poetry, his own ψυχή, that his poems of enduring appeal nearly always endeavor to explore (the word applies also in its etymological sense) the relationship between this *natural* experience and the external world. It is almost impossible, for example, to avoid the inference that his "reformation" in 1879 was in some way made possible by the death of his father in 1877, was, in fact, an emancipation, and it is simply astonishing that readers of this day and age could persist in the belief that the *personal* element of *Atalanta, Erechtheus,* "The Tale of Balen," even of "Tristram of Lyonesse," is not rather intrusive than inexistent.

Swinburne was a thinker. Tennyson, describing him as a "reed through which all things blow into music," failed to point out that in the best poems all things also blow into meaning. These poems nearly always embody "fundamental brainwork," as Rossetti called it, and it is inaccurate and unjust to say that in them the sound obscures the sense: *Atalanta in Calydon; Erechtheus;* "The Triumph of Time," "A Leave-taking," "Itylus," "Anactoria," "Hymn to Proserpine," "Ilicet," "The Garden of Proserpine," "Hesperia," and a few others in the first *Poems and Ballads;* the "Prelude," "Super Flumina Babylonis," "Hertha," "Genesis," "To Walt Whitman in America," "Siena," and one or two more from *Songs before Sunrise;* nearly all of *Poems and Ballads,* Second Series, the finest of his volumes of poems; "Thalassius" and "On the Cliffs"; "By the North Sea"; "Tristram of Lyonesse" and "Adieux à Marie Stuart"; several of the exquisite *Century of Roundels;* "A Midsummer Holiday" and "A Ballad of Sark"; "To a Seamew," "Neap-Tide," and all the Border Ballads; "A Nympholept," "A Swimmer's Dream," "Elegy" ("Auvergne, Auvergne"); "The Tale of Balen"; "A Channel Passage" and "The Lake of Gaube."

Joseph Warren Beach has long since defined Swinburne's position in the main stream of nineteenth-century philosophic poetry, summing up the doctrine in one sentence (as Swinburne himself, who put into "Hertha" the "most of lyric force and music combined with the most of condensed and clarified thought," summed it up in the one poem): "Everything is in nature,—good and evil, body and spirit, objective and subjective, the fact and the judgment passed upon the fact, man and man's God." Much of this could have been said of the early Wordsworth, who in all things saw "one life," or of Coleridge, who sang of "The one Life within us and abroad," and more easily than almost any other English poet Swinburne could have understood Wordsworth's inability, at times, "to think of external things as having external existence"; or Thoreau's desire to dwell near "the perennial sources of our life"; or Colette's passionate "Il n'y a qu'une bête! Tu m'entends, Maurice, il n'y a qu'une bête." Unlike Wordsworth, Swinburne did not abandon the "religion of naturalism." His point of view was always more coherent and more "logical" than Wordsworth's ever was, but it was a point of view to which Wordsworth had led the way.

He has never achieved recognition as a poet of nature. Yet from his earliest letters to those of the nineties he reveals a turn for the observation of natural scenery and an uncommon faculty for describing it, and over and over again one can detect in a letter the seeds of a poem. Usually, he was not attracted by the snowdrop or the small celandine, preferring the grandeur of cliff-encircled bays or of wild mountain fastnesses. In time, he came to be much preoccupied with decay and dissolution, and nothing was likelier to quicken an inspiration than a vista of the sea encroaching upon land, the "wrathful woful marge of earth and sea," reclaiming what had been wrested from it and put to other uses, an old cathedral, a forsaken garden, the "wall and tower" and the "wrecked chancel by the shivered shrine."

Visiting Auvergne in 1869, he wrote to his mother that the cathedral of Le Puy is "adapted with almost a miraculous instinct of art to the tone of the landscape and character of the country about. . . . there is nothing but alternately brown and grey mountain-land ending in a long and beautifully undulating circle of various heights and ranges. These mountain colours are most delicately repeated in the alternate stripes of the cathedral front." Such description is not far away from the kind of landscape described in "Tintern Abbey," with its perfect blending of man and nature. "Steep and lofty cliffs" always impressed on Swinburne "thoughts of more deep seclusion," and in his mind they connected "the landscape with the quiet of the sky." The imagination that conceived of "ships, towers, domes, theatres, and temples" that "lie open unto the fields, and to the sky" or said that Nature includes "in her wide embrace City, and town, and tower, and Sea with ships Sprinkled" (*The Excursion,* Bk. IV, 1196 ff.) had something in common with the mind that could say of Genoa that it "certainly lies open beautifully to the salt lake." The opening stanza of "The Lake of Gaube" has merely made the imagery, and the technique, explicit:

> The sun is lord and god, sublime, serene,
>   And sovereign on the mountains: earth and air
> Lie prone in passion, blind with bliss unseen
>   By force of sight and might of rapture, fair
>   As dreams that die and know not what they were.
> The lawns, the gorges, and the peaks, are one
> Glad glory, thrilled with sense of unison
> In strong compulsive silence of the sun.

Swinburne was much more nearly a Wordsworthian, and not merely in the descriptive mode, than he himself realized or than his critics have acknowledged. After his early years the correlation between his letters and descriptive passages of his poems is remarkable. In the "Elegy" written after the death of Richard Burton to commemorate their visit in Auvergne together, more than twenty years earlier, Swinburne, so retentive was his memory, seems to have before his eyes the very letters that he wrote in 1869. He had no need to consult a sister's journal for details, least of all his own letters, and yet there is nothing in Wordsworth, not even the transfer of the description of the daffodils from Dorothy to William, quite so striking as the comparison between "A Ballad of Sark" and his Letter 741, dated May 15, 1876, describing the island and written the day after his visit. That Swinburne himself took pride in the literal accuracy of the natural scenes limned in his poetry is revealed time after time in his letters. Even in unlikely places there are many bits of almost Pre-Raphaelite detail and evidences of close observation.

Theologically speaking, Swinburne remained agnostic to the end of his life, but philosophically a progression is clearly visible in his poetry even from *Poems and Ballads* (1866) to *Songs before Sunrise* (1871). Sandor Ferenczi's monograph, *Thalassa, A Theory of Genitality* (Albany, N.Y., 1938), seems to explain a good deal about the psychological mainspring of the bitter, cynical death-wish in the former volume, where Swinburne could have said, with Nietzsche's Silenus, that the best is "not to be born, not to *be,* to be nothing. But the second best . . . is quickly to die." But the most perceptive *literary* comment was perhaps made by Maud Bodkin (whose specific concern was a poem by Arnold) in the second chapter of *Archetypal Patterns in Poetry* (1934):

> By the neurotic, medical psychologists tell us, death is en-visaged, not objectively, as "normal people" are expected to view it—as the end of life, an event with social, moral, and legal implications—but as "a quiescent resolution of affective excitement"; "the tendency to it is an effort of the organism to restore the quiescent equilibrium," realized once (it is sup-posed) at the beginning of life, within the mother's womb. Like the neurotic, the poet or his reader, dreaming on the river that breaks at last into the free ocean, sees in this image his own life and death, not at all in their social and legal implica-tions, but in accordance with a deep organic need for release from conflict and tension.

Of the religion of man as "the master of things" in *Songs before Sunrise,*

> With all her tongues of life and death,
> With all her bloom and blood and breath,
>   From all years dead and all things done,
> In the ear of man the mother saith,
>   "There is no God, O son,
>   If thou be none,"

enough, perhaps more than enough, has already been recorded. Swin-burne's own familiar remark, "My other books are books; that one is myself," is a convenient (and telling) label for what Tennyson called the stepping-stone of a dead self. After sunset, however, the emphasis shifted to a resting-place approximately halfway between the two books—to what he termed, in another connection, "cheery stoicism." In his poetry the stress falls on the second word, in his letters on the first.

No other poet has sung with such consistent and persistent melan-choly the pain of existence. His outlook has a Greek or even Oriental quality. All his great themes and symbols, birth and death, growth and decay, pleasure and pain, unity and division, the mother-son re-lationship, the seasons, water, roses, birds, dreams are rooted in this preoccupation, and his imagery and symbolism will reward investiga-tion as amply as those of any poet in the language, for in them is the very substance of both the man and the poet. How often, in his letters and in his poems, is he drawn, so strangely drawn, to a cliff by the shore, to high downs leaning to the sea, especially to a quiet bay encircled by sheltering rocks:

> The heavenly bay, ringed round with cliffs and moors,
> Storm-stained ravines, and crags that lawns inlay,
> Soothes as with love the rocks whose guard secures
> The heavenly bay.

Thomas Gray, seeing the Grande Chartreuse for the first time, reported to Richard West in a famous letter that "not a precipice, not a torrent, not a cliff, but is pregnant with religious poetry. There are certain scenes that would awe an atheist into belief, without the help of other argument." No Grande Chartreuse, with or without argument, would have awed Swinburne into orthodoxy (any more than it converted Wordsworth or Arnold), yet his response to nature was quite as religious as Gray's, considerably less conventional, far more instinct with meaning. Of a swim in the Channel at Lancing he wrote to one of his sisters: "The whole sea was literally golden as well as green—it was liquid and living sunlight in which one lived and moved and had one's being. And to feel that in deep water is to feel— as long as one is swimming out . . .—as if one was in another world of life, and one far more glorious than even Dante ever dreamed of in his Paradise." Pre-Freudian language could scarcely be more explicit; nor could a neater pattern, a more striking "symbolic action," a more precisely weighted counterbalance have been wished into being than the long letter to a cousin in which Swinburne describes how, as a boy of seventeen, emerging naked from the sea, he dressed and then scaled the perilous face of Culver Cliff, joining his "brothers and sisters," the sea-gulls, near the top. In this context his nature poetry, his philosophical outlook, his symbols, conscious and unconscious, reveal a depth of feeling and a dimension of meaning with which they are not always credited and which have more in common with the modern temper than hostile critics have hitherto supposed.

"The history of his mind as to religion" is, as Boswell wrote of Johnson, "an important article." So tightly woven was the fabric of his thought that, as with the youthful Wordsworth, his "religion" can hardly be separated strand by strand from his politics or his attitude toward nature. As his letters show, in 1854 and 1855 he was as orthodox as the most doting mother, the most exigent father, could have wished, and the boyish pleasure that he derived in April 1854 from having Holy Communion on his father's birthday, together with his pious wish, fifteen months later, that "some day all [the sects] will be able to worship together and no divisions and jealousies 'keep us any longer asunder' " contrasts vividly with the weird, jeering letter to William Rossetti in January 1904 in which, considering the circumstances, his jibes against the "criminal lunacy of theolatry" verge on indelicacy. Like many others, Swinburne cast off his theology in college. For the remainder of his life his antitheism was absolute, and from this particular point of view his letters show no development, no retreat, no wavering, no *arrière-pensées* whatever. As an antitheist he was perfectly consistent.

In a broader sense, however, he underwent considerable change, and having shed his sickness (Lawrence's phrase) in a book, *Poems and Ballads,* he was ripe for conversion. And he *was* converted. "After all, in spite of jokes and perversities," he wrote to William Rossetti in October 1866 in connection with "A Song of Italy," ". . . it is nice to have something to love and to believe in as I do in Italy. It was only Gabriel and his followers in art (l'art pour l'art) who for a time frightened me from speaking out; for ever since I was fifteen I have been equally and unalterably mad—tête montée, as my Mother says—about this article of faith; you may ask any tutor or schoolfellow." His love for and belief in Italy, dating (as we see) from about 1852, would seem to have led him straight to Mazzini in 1867, and thence to a philosophy that had much in common with positivism. In August 1874, when John Tyndall's inaugural address to the British Association for the Advancement of Science on the relations between science and theology was reported in the papers, Swinburne wrote:

> My mind is very full just now of Tyndall's magnificent address, which I have read with great care and greater admiration. Science so enlarged and harmonized gives me a sense as much of rest as of light. No mythology can make its believers feel less afraid or loth to be reabsorbed into the immeasurable harmony with but the change of a single individual note in a single bar of the tune, than does the faintest perception of the lowest chord touched in the whole system of things. Even my technical ignorance does not impair, I think, my power to see accurately and seize firmly the first thread of the great clue, because my habit of mind is not (I hope) unscientific, though my work lies in the field of art instead of science; and when seen and seized even that first perception gives me an indescribable sense as of music and repose. It is Theism which to me seems to intro-

duce an element—happily a factitious element—of doubt, discord, and disorder.

Two of Swinburne's attitudes perhaps call for special comment here. One is his view of Christ. It is not entirely certain that the headstrong, impetuous, self-conscious rebel of the early and middle sixties conceded to Christ the same reverence that, before all other poets, he offered so willingly and humbly to sages, great ethical teachers, or merely elderly men of his own time, but it is clear that thereafter his attitude, within these narrow confines, was not merely decorous but exemplary. "Ever since I knew him," he wrote to his sister in June 1903, referring to Mazzini, "I have been able to read the Gospels with such power of realizing and feeling the truth of the human character of Christ as I have never felt before."

On the question of immortality Swinburne seems to have been at odds with his own instincts. He remained skeptical, but in his letters one seems to perceive a yearning for a kind of commitment that intellectually he could not allow, and every single allusion to the problem leaves one with an impression of cautious fingers searching among broken glass. After Gabriel Rossetti died in April 1882, Swinburne sent to W. B. Scott a copy of a sonnet, "A Death on Easter Day":

> You know, I am sure, that I am incapable of dealing at such a time and on such a topic in poetical insincerity or sentimental rhetoric: so perhaps I need hardly add that I do now— on the whole—strongly incline to believe in the survival of life —individual and conscious life—after the dissolution of the body. Otherwise, I would not on any account have affected a hope or conviction I did not feel. The glorious and desperately unorthodox verses written in sight of death by Emily Brontë express my creed—or rather my creedless faith—better than any words I know.

But a strong inclination is not actual belief. The occasion being, in a way, a double crisis, the death of the most intimate friend he had ever known occurring on Easter Day, the emotional pull of the latent symbolism perhaps allured him into assenting poetically to a doctrine that his intellect rejected. For it is a fact that Swinburne never again made such a statement. Even in May 1885, writing to his mother about the death of Victor Hugo, Swinburne averted his gaze from eternity:

> When I think of his intense earnestness of faith in a future life and a better world than this, and remember how fervently

Mazzini always urged upon all who loved him the necessity of that belief and the certainty of its actual truth, I feel very deeply that they must have been right—or at least that they should have been—however deep and difficult the mystery which was so clear and transparent to their inspired and exalted minds may seem to such as mine. They ought to have known, if any man ever did: and if they were right, I, whose love and devotion they requited with such kindness as I never could have really deserved, shall (somehow) see them again.

It is possible, and even tempting, to read Swinburne in his later phases as a kind of existentialist, but he cannot be made over into a Christian. The last letter in these volumes is followed by a brief record of the squabble between his sister and his heir and executor over the funeral rites (and rights) that, irreverent though the comparison may be, barely escapes parodying Sophocles. Watts-Dunton on his sickbed dons the mask of Creon, and Isabel Swinburne, like Antigone, demands traditional services for her dead brother (Mrs. Leith qualifies admirably as Ismene): "If he had made a slight matter of his antagonism against Christianity, as so many free thinkers do, it would have been different," Watts-Dunton wrote to her, "but with him it increased with his years and at the last . . . it was bitterer than ever."

The truth is that though, philosophically, Swinburne receded as far from the quasi-positivism of *Songs before Sunrise* as he had earlier moved in order to attain that position, he did not revert to his youthful Christian orthodoxy. His fourth (and final) "period," indeed, was far closer to his second than to the first or third—with the difference that pessimism had become melancholy, withdrawal had replaced resignation, and endurance had supplanted the blind quest for oblivion of the middle sixties. He summed up his own philosophy, as we have seen, in a phrase borrowed from Carlyle, "cheery Stoicism," and like Epictetus, whom, surprisingly, he ranked so high in his hierarchy of literary treasures, he was guided by two words, ἀνέχου and ἀπέχου, "endure" and "abstain." This is the background that invests with dignity and nobility the finest poems of Swinburne's last, and longest, period, of which the beginnings are perceptible long before Putney, even as early as 1875—from the ever-memorable "A Forsaken Garden" or "A Vision of Spring in Winter" with its moving conclusion,

> The morning song beneath the stars that fled
>   With twilight through the moonless mountain air,

> While youth with burning lips and wreathless hair
> Sang toward the sun that was to crown his head,
> Rising; the hopes that triumphed and fell dead,
>   The sweet swift eyes and songs of hours that were;
> These may'st thou not give back for ever; these,
>   As at the sea's heart all her wrecks lie waste,
>   Lie deeper than the sea;
> But flowers thou may'st, and winds, and hours of ease,
>   And all its April to the world thou may'st
>   Give back, and half my April back to me,

to "The Lake of Gaube," perhaps the greatest poem of his later years. He was never more remote than in these later years from "the things of the Spirit of God" of which Paul wrote. They were in fact "foolishness" to him.

Swinburne's political development is too well-known to require detailed comment. From the heights of republicanism he fell into a kind of quicksand of political heresy. The more he struggled, the deeper he sank. His vision became obscured, partly with mud from his own floundering; words came to mean for him, as for Humpty-Dumpty, what he chose them to mean. He came perilously close to infection by the fault that he hinted of Matthew Arnold, "the theologian's habit of using words and phrases in a special and extranatural sense which renders their message impervious, their meaning impenetrable, to all but the esoteric adept." And it is hardly an exaggeration to say that during the last three decades of his life he elected, in terms of his own earlier principles, the "wrong" side of every important political issue that arose. On the question of Home Rule he was scarcely less violent than Parnell himself, and Gladstone presiding over the liquidation of Her Majesty's empire became for him in the eighties very nearly what Napoleon III had been until 1873. When Richard Pigott was exposed as a perjurer and forger in 1889, Swinburne's only response was the petulant, clever "A Logical Ballad of Home Rule." In 1896 he expressed regret "for the Italian reverses" at Aduwa in Abyssinia. In 1899 he made it plain, in verse and prose, that his sympathy did not lie with "that unspeakable old villain Paul Kruger and his lying thieving murdering Boers" or with his own government for "not giving the rascals shorter shrift." Even Karl Blind, whose support had been invoked in the matter of Home Rule, parted company with him on the South African question.

Nevertheless, some of Swinburne's finest letters had a political inspiration, and not many poets in history—one has to turn to Pindar for an adequate comparison—could have dashed off, at a white heat, an "Ode on the Proclamation" of any republic, following it with such a letter as he wrote to William Rossetti on September 7, 1870, headed "Gloria in excelsis Republicae et in terrâ pax hominibus bonae voluntatis" and spilling over the margins with quotations from (among others) Whitman, Carlyle, Browning, Dante, Judges, Isaiah. "An Ode literally burst out of me," he wrote:

> I am nine-tenths out of my mind with joy and pride in Paris. Now, it may be razed to the ground and sown with salt and the last child killed in the last Frenchwoman's womb, but shame cannot touch it. If the Republic die tomorrow choked in blood and ridden down by brute force of horsehoofs, it has lived this divine hour, worth aeons of empires. I do think the rejoicings and salutations, tears and embraces of the people at such a time, in the jaws of ruin *and* in sight of the Republic, the most glorious thing in democratic history (barring Rome and Venice) since the old days.

The trajectory that began with an "Ode on the Proclamation of the French Republic" in 1870 and curved through a decade and a half to such poems as "The Commonweal. A Song for Unionists" (1886), "The Commonweal" (printed as "The Jubilee" in 1887), and "The Armada" (1888) has been well described by Georges Lafourcade and others. One aspect, however, has not yet been sufficiently emphasized, no doubt because it is unmistakably visible only in the collected letters consecutively read. The very title of an essay published in 1876, "Note of an English Republican on the Muscovite Crusade," seems premonitory. For the essay was not a note. Whatever it was, it was not by a republican. There was no "Muscovite Crusade." Of the five operative words only the second is accurately employed, and this word is significant. For it was Swinburne's insularity, his very *Englishness,* that came to dominate his political thinking. The most cosmopolitan of English poets was transformed into the most parochial and chauvinistic of British jingoes. The republican-turned-"English Republican" became English first and last, and remained republican only by a semantic sophistry that would be as much at home in *1984* as in *Through the Looking-Glass.* "People nowadays seem to forget . . . ," he wrote to his mother in 1886, "that the first principle of a Republican is and must be Unity (without which liberty can only mean license—or pure anarchy—or pretentious hypocrisy) and that Republicans ought in common consistency and honesty to the first to protest against a party

xxviii

of anarchists and intriguers whose policy is to break up the state." Whether the first principle of an Irish peasant, an Abyssinian, a South African ought to have been unity seems not to have occurred to him, any more than it occurred to him that by uttering these words he convicted himself of precisely the same crime for which, years earlier, he had arraigned Carlyle in the little essay "Of Liberty and Loyalty." "Men create oppositions which are not," wrote Bacon, "and put them into new terms so fixed, as whereas the meaning ought to govern the term, the term in effect governeth the meaning."

In a letter to the editor of the *Pall Mall Gazette* in January 1886, Swinburne responded to an invitation to name the "hundred best books" with "the list of a student whose reading has lain mainly, though by no means exclusively, in the line of imaginative or creative literature." The date is significant, for the list, from which "living names" are excluded, is assuredly not what it would have been two decades earlier. But among all its curiosities of inclusion and exclusion nothing is more striking than the fact that of a hundred names, assembled with some care by "the most cosmopolitan of English poets," seventy-two (counting the Bible and FitzGerald's *Rubáiyát*) are British.

Swinburne came to prefer English scenery above all scenery he had observed. He lauded English sea-bathing, English weather, English flowers, English ale, English courage, even the English queen, whom he had so wickedly derided in *La Fille du policeman* and *La Sœur de la reine:*

> And now that fifty years are flown
> Since in a maiden's hand the sign
> Of empire that no seas confine
> First as a star to seaward shone,
> We see their record shine.
>
> A troubled record, foul and fair,
> A simple record and serene,
> Inspires for praise a blameless queen,
> For praise and blame an age of care
> And change and ends unseen.

Concurrently, Swinburne's literary interests (except his passion for Hugo, which remained unabated) became focused almost exclusively on the Elizabethans. Apart from an undergraduate piece and one article on John Ford, every one of his essays on the Tudor and Stuart dramatists, nearly three dozen in all, postdates *Songs before Sunrise*.

His very choice of subjects, as in "Tristram of Lyonesse," *Locrine,* "The Tale of Balen," "The Armada," "Astrophel," is revealing. It seems clear that a connection exists between his political outlook of the eighties and nineties and his self-immersion in England's past, especially the heroic Elizabethan era, and this aspect of his development would reward investigation.

In some ways, Swinburne's collected letters may be read not only as a portrait of himself but also as a portrait of an age. He was first and last a poet, but for a practitioner of what Carlyle denominated the "idle trade," he shows for more than half a century an enormous, even a consuming interest in a great variety of subjects. He read (and wrote to) the newspapers assiduously; and no strain in these letters is sounded more often than his plaintive plea that the papers and magazines be regularly forwarded to him in the country.

Politically, as we have seen, no issue escaped him. Though it would be wildly immoderate to claim that a political history of Italy during two or three decades could be inferred from Swinburne's letters, still he observed, thought about, wrote about an astonishing number of events. Similarly, not the slightest act of Napoleon III went unnoticed, nor did the Franco-Prussian War, the Third Republic, the Commune, or subsequent events. Ireland and Home Rule were an obsession. Crete, the American Civil War, the Eastern Question, the proclamation of Victoria as Empress of India, the assassination of the Czar, the Jubilee celebration, the rise of Germany, the Boer War all find their reflections here. Of the Russo-Japanese War he wrote:

> "The still small voice is a-singing comic songs within me" every day that I read of a Russian reverse. Can it be possible that we shall live to see a revolution which will eclipse the French—in its beneficent and necessary result, even if the worst of the Terrorists should (naturally) be eclipsed by the Carrierowsky, the Herbertoff, and the Lebonski of the future?

On other levels, his interest was stirred simultaneously by the latest Parisian criminal and the death of George Peabody. The meeting of the Ecumenical Council in Rome to proclaim the infallibility of the Pope is counterpointed against that of the Anti-Catholic Council of Naples. The whole question of the Tichborne Claimant, and many other law suits, held him in thrall, the Society for the Suppression of Vice aroused his ire. When Matthew Webb swam the Channel in 1875, he wanted to write a Pindaric ode. The Governor Eyre controversy moved him to anger. Most unmusical of men, he attended Clara Schumann's concerts, he sought out and turned to account the music of Wagner, which, he said explicitly, "stimulated" him in composing "Tristram of Lyonesse." He came to loathe the theater, partly as a result of encroaching deafness, but maintained his contact with it through Henry Irving and William Poel. He was passionately interested in art and if he had so willed could have been a significant art critic. His essay "Notes on Designs of the Old Masters at Florence" is a first-rate piece of pioneering, and the remarks on art and artists in his letters reveal a breadth of learning and a delicacy of sensibility unapproached by any other major poet. He not only read about archaeological excavations, he met Heinrich Schliemann himself in the home of Karl Blind. In sum, for a poet who never wandered long outside the confines of literature, his letters reveal an altogether surprising range of curiosity and interest, a sensibility responsive to a remarkable variety of stimuli, a hunger for the world about him almost as avid as his celebrated appetite for certain glorious eras in the past.

About two thousand letters will be printed in these volumes. The manuscripts have been assembled from nearly three dozen libraries and about fifty private collections, and in addition I have reprinted letters, of which the holographs have not been found, from several dozen books and periodicals. Among the libraries the British Museum and Yale University together own a total of about five hundred letters, and at the moment I write these words it is not possible to say which collection is numerically superior. Rutgers University is third with just over a hundred letters, the National Library of Wales fourth with just under a hundred, and the Brotherton Library, Leeds University, follows with about six dozen. Among private collections the magnificent series of fifty-seven letters to Richard Monckton Milnes (Lord Houghton), owned by the Marchioness of Crewe, is the largest known to me.

During the past ten years I have had the pleasure of visiting personally most of the well-known libraries in the United States and Great Britain, and I have of course met a vast number of people I would not otherwise have known. Many new friends and a few antagonists have been the result. In the line of duty I was on one occasion the victim of a most elaborate and plausible piece of cozenage, once I was all but swindled, and I have been insulted privately and abused publicly in language that only Swinburne himself could have bettered. All these things I have enjoyed greatly and I have suffered not at all. It has been exciting to bring together letters from Inverness, Cardiganshire, Sussex, from New England, Texas, California, from Venice and Rome; to search for them in Madrid and Lisbon and in the major libraries and collections in and near Paris. And compared with the thrill of discovery, with the fascinations of transcribing and dating, calendaring, annotating, with the delights of stumbling upon unexpected interrelationships and the inquietude of suspecting how many have been overlooked, it is indeed dull to pause, to make an end.

This edition, more than four times larger than any earlier compilation, is the first collection of Swinburne's letters to aim at completeness. The goal is clearly beyond reach, restricted as it must be to the letters still extant or, more narrowly, to those *known* to be extant, but these six volumes, however much they fall short of their aim, include not only all letters previously printed in any form whatever but also a great many additions to the canon.

Swinburne's cousin, Mrs. Disney Leith, edited the first considerable collection, *The Boyhood of Algernon Charles Swinburne . . . with Extracts from Some of His Private Letters* (1917), and except for a few newcomers appearing now, her volume remains to this day the only source of letters from the poet to his family. Strong in mind as in body—well advanced in her eighties when she died in 1926, Mrs. Leith is said to have bathed in the Arctic from the shores of Iceland at the age of seventy—she ferociously resented and resisted any effort to disturb the marmoreal image of Algernon that she wanted to bequeath to posterity. She regarded Edmund Gosse as an impertinent snooper, and what Gosse came to think of her need not be recalled.

One has to, and one does, honor familial fastidiousness in such matters, but even accepting her premises, one must question her judgment. As an editor, she was perhaps more efficient than would have been supposed. Her facts are not often wrong; her guesses, though not always correct, are comfortably dependable; her transcriptions *seem* passably accurate. She welded parts of two letters together to make one much less frequently than editors of her generation (and earlier) usually did (but see below, Letters 1077 and 1340). In general, she leaves the impression that she could have produced any kind of collection that she wished, but three words in the title of the volume reveal the self-imposed limitations that are far more serious than her shortcomings as an editor: "Extracts," "Some," and "Private." The last word means letters from Swinburne to the editor, to two of his sisters, and to his mother (though not to his favorite sister, his brother, or his father). As for "Some," we are told nothing about the size of the collection from which the choice was made (the number must have been considerable), and the "Extracts" certifies her attitude. She calls attention to some internal deletions.

It is only natural to ask what sort of image she bequeaths. Nowhere in 250 pages of family letters can one discover how Swinburne addressed his mother and father or his sisters. They called him "Hadji" and somehow the portrait of him takes on color and warmth when he says "Pino" to his father, "Mimmy," when alluding to his mother, and "Ally," "Abba," and "Wibbie" for Alice, Isabel, and Charlotte. It would help to know what he called his other sister and his brother, and it seems to me charming to learn—what one cannot see in Mrs. Leith's letters—that he signs himself "A. C. Swinburne," in a letter to his father in 1854 and in a letter to his sister in 1908. The letters must have had God's plenty of the wonderful kind of trivia that justifies itself, something that occurs all too infrequently in Swinburne's other letters, and by allowing us only little shavings and chips, instead of whole letters, Mrs. Leith did her cousin a grave disservice.

In the next year (1918) Watts-Dunton's quondam secretary, Thomas Hake, together with Arthur Compton-Rickett, edited *The Letters of Algernon Charles Swinburne, with Some Personal Recollections,* which prints portions (sometimes fragments) of about sixty-five letters, as a corrective to the bias against Watts-Dunton that, in company with many others, they disliked in Edmund Gosse's biography of Swinburne, published in 1917. As a piece of propaganda, the book has merit. The title, however, is a misnomer, for as an edition of letters the book cannot be taken seriously. Indeed, one can scarcely imagine any *editorial* sin, capital or venial, short of actual dishonesty, of which they are innocent. A perfunctory collation of a few of the transcriptions in these volumes with the same letters as printed by them will reveal the deficiencies. In one instance (page 115) a whole page from a published essay is presented, complete with "complimentary close," signature, and postscript in the guise of a personal letter.

The only previous work that could properly be referred to as an edition was *The Letters of Algernon Charles Swinburne,* prepared in two volumes in 1918 by Gosse and Wise. This collection, 325 letters in all, was reprinted in 1927 as Volume *18* of the Bonchurch Edition of *The Complete Works of Algernon Charles Swinburne,* with thirty-three additions, bringing the total to 358. It remains the only known text of a few of Swinburne's letters, notably those addressed to J. H. Ingram.

Edmund Gosse in 1918, without making immodest claims for the collection of letters edited by himself and Wise, believed that those

325 letters were, and would "probably remain, a very considerable portion of Swinburne's Correspondence." Yet the present edition more than quintuples the size of that work. Many of Swinburne's letters, especially his early ones, as Gosse pointed out, have been destroyed, and indeed it seems almost a miracle that *any* could have survived from his youth and found their way to market. Moreover, like Wordsworth, who (as he told De Quincey) found painful the very "act of holding a pen," Swinburne described the "mere physical act of writing" as "a positive and often a painful effort." " 'Oh, Clara, if you would but teach dear Algernon how to type, how delightful *that* would be,' " exclaimed his sister Isabel, according to Clara Watts-Dunton (*The Home Life of Swinburne*, 1922, p. 220). "The incongruity of such an idea," she continued, "had the effect of making Walter and me almost double up with laughter." But though Swinburne disliked writing letters, and though there is no way of accurately reckoning how many he turned out, he assuredly produced a vastly greater number than are brought together in these pages. The total number printed here represents, for instance, substantially less than *one letter every ten days* during an entire half-century, the whole of his legal manhood.

Forty years ago Gosse was compelled to report that he was "aware of the existence of more than one group of letters, an inspection of which is still denied the general public." Times have changed. The "general public" is perhaps less easily rebuffed than in the past. Swinburne's previous editors, one of them his cousin, were all closely associated with him for an appreciable period of time. With Gosse, an intimate companion for several years, his friendship spanned three decades. Thomas Hake, having become Watts-Dunton's secretary in 1897, was in Swinburne's company for more than ten years. All three were hamstrung by various kinds of scruple which have long since lost their relevance; but the present editor, whose sole scruple, in this connection, has been scholarly integrity, is not aware of the existence of any *group* of letters omitted from these volumes. Certainly, most if not all those to which Gosse referred, the letters to Howell, Powell, and Lord Houghton, have been included.

Before moving on, it may be useful to consider briefly some letters that are purely hypothetical, and of these Swinburne's to his family are probably our greatest loss. His youthful letters are very appealing from all points of view, and those addressed to Mary Gordon (Mrs. Leith), as the few surviving fragments prove, so unself-conscious, so boyish, so enthusiastic, so topical, would be a treasure trove. Inquiry has revealed, however, that all the family letters upon which Mrs.

Leith's selection was based were burned some time after her death, according to her expressed wish. The loss is therefore irretrievable, and the disservice done Swinburne by a well-intentioned blunderer irreparable.

It has been said that letters from the poet to Mathilde Blind are extant. Edmund Gosse, hot on the scent of a report that Swinburne had been suitor to this bluestocking poetess, traced and read them, and let it be known that rumor exaggerated. On the basis of the scant and chill allusions to Mathilde Blind that survive, no one could possibly credit such a rumor, even though the letters have not again been traced. The strongest bond between the two was doubtless their devotion to the poetry and memory of Shelley.

No letters from Swinburne to Mazzini have yet appeared, despite the extensive searches that have been conducted. Convinced that such letters existed (at least, that they had been written), Gosse believed, or professed to believe, that Swinburne "poured out to Mazzini, as to a father confessor, the very innermost convictions of his soul." Actually, one could almost affirm that he never wrote a considerable number to Mazzini, about whom, as the size of his collected works will testify, we know a staggering amount, for though Mazzini frequently refers to "the Poet," inquiring about his health, his whereabouts, his activities, these very allusions reveal that poet and patriot seldom corresponded. And whether they corresponded or not, the "innermost convictions" of Swinburne's soul, as far as Mazzini was concerned, were "poured out" in his poetry, not in his letters. A glance at Swinburne's formal, awestruck epistles to Victor Hugo will reveal how he comported himself in writing to venerable objects of his admiration. Regret may therefore be left to those who would find pleasure or edification in reading the letters of Official Poet in self-abasement before Official Patriot.

Far more desirable would be the letters he must have written in the late fifties and sixties to intimate friends of his own age. Any record of his thoughts and actions during this difficult period would be worth a good deal, and the letters (for instance) to Edward Jones and William Morris would be a pure joy. In 1860 Swinburne at the age of twenty-three, Morris only three years older, Jones four—a trio still disporting with the slangy abandon of their undergraduate days, all passionately devoted to literature and art, each vying with the others in adoration of Gabriel Rossetti—could have created a memorable correspondence. No doubt, even in the agonies and exultations of youth, they wrote back and forth infrequently enough, and probably they took no pains to save each other's letters. In all conscience, it would unsettle one's image of young Morris to picture him as a letter-saver. Jones, it has been said, at a much later date burned Swinburne's letters to himself.

Ubi sunt cannot be uttered without calling up other names and the specters of other correspondences. With Ford Madox Brown, for one, Swinburne was intimate over a long period of years. He refers to Brown often in these volumes, always affectionately, and whatever correspondence they had in the sixties must have been as relaxed as their friendship, though Brown was senior by more than fifteen years and such a difference would have made itself felt. Richard Burton, to name another friend, the celebrated, swashbuckling explorer, scholar, translator, picker-up of learning's crumbs, whom Swinburne first met in 1861, would have been, and probably was, a notable correspondent, but only a couple of letters and a note have survived. With George Augustus Sala, the journalist and man-about-town whom he so much admired, Swinburne may not have corresponded at all, though their acquaintance spanned several decades and for several years they seem to have met frequently.

Simeon Solomon is another matter. More than a quarter of a century before Solomon's death in 1905, Swinburne was sickened to learn that the young artist, "now a thing unmentionable alike by men and women," was peddling letters written to him by the poet—letters, Swinburne confessed, "which must doubtless contain much foolish burlesque and now regrettable nonsense." It seems most unlikely that such letters have been destroyed, even if, in some manner, they finally found their way back to their author, and they may be expected to come to light one day.

Two other names can bring to an end this roster of might-have-been. One of Swinburne's dearest friends was John Nichol. They had been correspondents for nearly four decades, from 1857 to 1894, when Nichol died. A fair number of letters has been available, in one form or another, but the total represents an average of only about one letter a year, clearly a very small proportion of the whole. Many, of course, were lost. Others were burned by Nichol's daughter (see below, Letter 7), but of these, or of some of them, copies had been made beforehand by Gosse. For the rest, it is hard to escape the double suspicion that Nichol himself made away with them and that he thought he had compelling reasons for doing so.

The history of Swinburne's letters sometimes seems like a series of holocausts, though in one case at least there was smoke but no fire (or, to take another point of view, fire but no smoke). Not even a note has survived from what must have been a fairly extensive corre-

spondence between Swinburne and Benjamin Jowett, the Master of
Balliol, and for once the explanation is simple and straightforward.
Jowett's will directed that *all* the letters written to him be burned
upon his death. His motives certainly had nothing in common with
those of Mrs. Jack, the daughter of John Nichol, or of Burne-Jones (if
the report is accurate); it was rather the same jealousy of privacy that
prompted Mrs. Leith to a similar action. Both Swinburne's cousin
and his mentor were extremely ill-advised, for clearly the letters that
were destroyed contained some of his best efforts. No one, and least
of all Swinburne, would have cared, or dared, to write many second-
rate letters to Jowett.

Many of the letters here collected have had a curious history. Some
were used as blackmail, or something close to it, on at least three occasions during Swinburne's lifetime; some, apparently, were the cause
of an action that, though not quite treachery, was worse than a breach
of faith in the best friend he ever had. In at least two instances some
few that were printed had to be withheld from distribution or circulation. Some were in their own day both the despair and delight
of his friends. Some of the best letters that he, or anyone else, ever
wrote have lain for years in the British Museum, or in T. J. Wise's
Ashley Library, without ever having been published in their entirety,
though scholars, one after another, have combed them through, and
extracts or fragments have long adorned the biographies and critical
studies. Some have appeared in small privately printed editions, badly
transcribed, misdated, innocent of editorial apparatus, selected on no
basis but convenience or even whim, arranged in a hit-or-miss fashion,
peddled at scandalous prices. On the other hand, one group has never
been printed at all or, for that matter, even *seen,* since the indefatigable
Gosse used them, except by one writer to whom Swinburne was only a
peripheral interest. A number of the letters in print, or partially in
print, would be considered surpassingly dull reading (whatever their
other merits) by any candid man; for some others the standard descriptive tag has for years been "unpublished and unpublishable."

The letters assembled here range in date from 1854, when Swinburne was seventeen, to 1909, the year of his death. Many of them
are, of course, perfunctory and merely occasional, as was inevitable in
a day before the telephone had become an indispensable adjunct to
daily life. As a letter-writer, he is not to be compared with the great
masters in English—Dorothy Osborne, Cowper, Gray, Byron, Keats,
FitzGerald, Hopkins, Melville, James, and perhaps a few others, all superior in their various ways. But in his best letters (and they are numer-

ous) Swinburne is a rare force, and his very best specimens are surpassed only by the very best in the language. These letters are not essays. Swinburne always wrote *to* someone, and he could never have said, as Cowper did, "You must understand this to be a soliloquy. I wrote my thoughts without recollection that I was writing a letter, and to you." Nor was he altered by the composition of letters, as he was by the creative act, and he could not have written, as Melville wrote to Hawthorne, "The very fingers that now guide the pen are not precisely the same that just took it up and put it on the paper." He neither wore his one mask, like James, nor changed pose for pose, like Byron, nor, like Keats, exposed the "whole of the frontage shaven sheer." He was himself and true to himself. No man, perhaps, has ever told the whole truth in his letters, and Swinburne, though often indiscreet, seldom wrote letters with clinical candor or with artless abandon. Rather, he put himself into his poetry to a degree that is only now coming to be recognized, and this poetry, as all good poetry must be, is self-contained and self-justifying. But for a view of the whole man nothing could better complement his *œuvre* than his collected letters.

Perhaps the most inexplicable deficiency up to now has been the unavailability of Swinburne's communications to newspapers and magazines. In 1912 Gosse and Wise assembled a group of thirty *Letters to the Press*—a privately printed edition of thirty-two copies, according to the colophon—and a few other such letters were used from time to time to pad other privately printed pamphlets. But Swinburne wrote nearly five dozen letters-to-the-editor, and not only have they all never been collected in one book but many have never been reprinted in any form, several have not been included in the standard bibliographies, and at least two have remained totally unrecorded. Yet of the value of these letters there can be no question, and their part in rounding out the portrait of the artist is indispensable. Humor and logic were not Swinburne's strong points—he would have anathematized anyone who said this—and the heavy-handedness of the former is as amusing as the shiftiness of the latter, though if, as Chesterton once remarked, skill in argument consists in the ability to hide and seek simultaneously, Swinburne must be considered a superb polemicist. He was the last man in the world to admit to an error, even when faced with irrefutable, factual proof (see, for instance, the series sent to the *Spectator* in April 1884), and his slipperiness, here and elsewhere, is a delight to behold. Like Saki's Francesca, he prided himself on being able to see things from other people's points of view, which meant, as it meant for Francesca, that he could see his own point of

view "from various aspects." When he chose, he spoke with an over-
bearance hardly paralleled outside Lucretius. His vituperation and
abuse are deplored by many who remain undisturbed by far more
heinous sins in the controversialists of the seventeenth and early eighteenth centuries, but Swinburne saw himself in the main stream of a
tradition that he revered, and, political issues aside, there is much to
be said for a poet who in the 1880's could visualize himself as a
latter-day Milton demolishing, in the name of *res publica,* a Salmasius
reincarnated as Gladstone, the People's William. Alexander Pope
(with whom he had so much in common) provides a more precise
analogy than Milton, however, and one can almost imagine Swinburne
administering an emetic to Furnivall (that intruder, as he saw it, into
the "serene Republick" of letters), as Pope administered one to Curll.

One of the largest surviving groups of letters was sent by the poet to
his long-suffering publisher, Andrew Chatto, and these letters, however unyieldingly occasional and business-like, show an aspect of
Swinburne that we could scarcely unearth elsewhere. They cover a
period of thirty years. That Swinburne could have remained so icy
and so distant for so long staggers the imagination, but Chatto's patience, though it must have been a tired mare, continued to plod. It
was a descendant of Hotspur, an Ashburnham, a Swinburne of Swinburne Castle, a Jacobite gentleman condescending to a menial, giving
notice that if the publisher did not change his printer (for example)
the poet would change his publisher. Even a note thanking Chatto for
window seats provided for friends to watch the Jubilee procession
reads like a communication from the lord of the manor to a vassal
who has been privileged to render a service, and only on the rarest occasions, and then with an exquisite sense of nuance, does Swinburne
unbend from "Dear Sir" to "Dear Mr. Chatto." But Chatto stroked
him down and coddled him, sent him books and magazines, turned
away his wrath with soft answers time after time, even when, as the
annotations will sometimes show, Swinburne was unjust or unreasonable. The letters remain, therefore, not only as a chronicle of a poet's
querulousness and an index to much of his reading, as a partial
record of his finances, of his difficulties with proofs, of his deficiencies
as a proofreader, but also as a portrait of a shrewd and imperturbable
publisher who transformed a business of slightly tarnished reputation
into one of the most respected publishing houses in England.

William Michael Rossetti, with whom Swinburne corresponded for
nearly half a century, trails only Chatto and Watts-Dunton in the total
number of letters received and collected in these volumes. He was a
man with every virtue in the world but genius. "I always had a passion

for intellect, and my wish was that my husband should be distinguished for intellect, and my children too," his mother once remarked. "I have had my wish, and now I wish there were a little less intellect in the family so as to allow for a little more common sense." She could not have had her son William in mind when she said this, for it was always William to whom others (including Swinburne) turned when they needed the counsel of sobriety and steadiness, of moderation and levelheadedness, rather than brilliance, audacity, unconventionality. Temperamentally opposed, the two men made common cause in their agnosticism, their republicanism, their devotion to art, though the record shows a surprising frequency of disagreement on specific issues, and the numerous (and remarkable) letters in these volumes trace the course of their friendship, which seems never to have varied in either tempo or temperature, as accurately as a whole book might do.

Nearly a hundred letters are addressed to George Powell, of whom very little is known beyond what can be inferred from Swinburne's letters. A well-to-do Welshman, Etonian, Oxonian, perfect Wagnerite (but even he could not really make Swinburne musical), a rebellious only son, he was by no means the best possible influence on Swinburne during the sixties and seventies, and it is fair to surmise that if Powell's premature death had not terminated the friendship, Watts would have intervened, tactfully, firmly, finally. He lived in Nant-Eos, a handsome Georgian mansion, pleasantly situated a few miles from Aberystwyth. Not an altogether appealing figure, he accumulated a reputation of which the odor lingers in this small community seventy-five years after his death. He and Swinburne, according to a brief and discreet account by H. M. Vaughan in *The South Wales Squires* (1926), "especially loved to haunt a certain low-class inn in Aberystwyth, kept by a disreputable old woman whose Rabelaisian talk owned a special attraction for Swinburne." The latter knew that Powell was preserving his letters. What remains is therefore a good deal more guarded and decorous than might otherwise have been the case. Whether Powell actually destroyed some of the correspondence cannot be ascertained, but in the light of our knowledge of the man himself, meager though it is, such discretion is not quite credible, and it would not be surprising if other letters, rather less continent than these, were one day found in the gloomy recesses or drafty corridors of Nant-Eos.

Of Swinburne's letters to Simeon Solomon something has already been said. Lacking them, we have to be content with ten replies, published now for the first time, and their value—indeed, their unique value—as documents is very high. Why they were preserved remains a mystery. Swinburne's own letters, though they may have been bawdy and even obscene, would have overflowed with *espièglerie,* would have sparkled with authentic wit, with the perfection of an unexpected antic rime, with the precision and irreverence of his mimicry. We have his own word for it (see below, Letter 974) that they contained "much foolish burlesque and now regrettable nonsense" and "silly chaff indulged in long ago." One stronger than Swinburne would have found it difficult not to exert himself for an audience as worshipful as Solomon, and whatever repellent qualities the letters might have had would doubtless have been more than redeemed by the good-humored ribaldry. Unlike the Simeon Solomon seen here, Swinburne never whined, was never commonplace, but this friendship, it must be admitted, was not to his credit either in a general sense or (to cite a specific instance) as the direct cause of Solomon's change from the "happy innocent condition" before he "knew a certain poet" (see below, Letter 310A).

The notorious letters to Charles Augustus Howell, only a dozen and a half in number, have aroused more comment than all the rest of Swinburne's letters together. Possibly, they have even helped to keep alive the reputation of the poet during the last three decades. In 1885 they came into the hands of George Redway, a bookseller and publisher, who made them over to Watts, acting as Swinburne's emissary, in exchange for the copyright of the poem "A Word for the Navy" (see below, Letter 1348). Having redeemed the letters, Watts, according to the received account, tossed them into the fire. But Vulcan's fire was helpless where Vesta's had failed, as Gosse might have put it, and the letters survived, or so it appears, neither charred nor purified, and are now for the first time printed without deletions. At least four explanations are plausible. For one thing, the surviving letters to Howell may not, after all, be the manuscripts redeemed by Watts— certainty is not possible. Or, for another, Watts may have cast *some* of the letters into the fire, retaining only the less flamboyant specimens. Or, in the third place, for the sake of the dramatic effect (or for other reasons) he may have thrown all the letters into the fire*place* or heater, only to rescue them later. (In any case, it seems to have occurred to nobody to doubt the existence of a fire on July 1, 1886, the day of the covenant, when the temperature in London ranged from 68° to 73° F.) Or, finally, the story, for whatever reason, may simply be inaccurate. Far more interesting are the questions—alas, unanswerable—why, if these are the same letters, were they *not* destroyed? and by whom were they preserved, Watts or Swinburne himself?

The critic who would undertake to interpret Swinburne, the poet or the poetry, in terms of "symbolic action" would find plenty of grist for his mill merely in the external history of the letters, especially in these few to Howell. They have been said to contain "the customary puerile indecencies," to be "filthy," "shocking," "indiscreet, sometimes obscene," "indecent," "distressing," "repellent and silly." They have been referred to, over and over again, as "unpublished and unpublishable." They used to be, and no doubt still are, withheld from public inspection, shrouded in heavy paper and secured against clandestine violation by heavy cord knotted and fixed with sealing wax bearing the impress of an official stamp, deposited in a locked cabinet in the private office, and behind the desk, of the Keeper of Manuscripts in the British Museum. The parcel could be breached only by the Keeper himself in the presence of witnesses, who were obliged to affix their signatures, with the date, to the paper wrapping; another ritual, of course, celebrated their safe return. The present editor was granted the privilege of observing these mummeries, an experience that he shares with few men of our time, only after weeks of delicate maneuvering and negotiation. Several years later, a request to see the manuscripts once more, because of certain doubtful readings and illegible passages, was peremptorily refused. The editor was told that his earlier view of the letters would have to suffice, since the Keeper of Manuscripts could not "be breaking the seal every two or three years." Yet another request, put two years later still, had more felicitous results, a new Keeper having succeeded the proud and prejudiced former guardian, and the editor, therefore, is now able to guarantee the accuracy of these transcriptions.

A short series of letters addressed to the painter-poet William Bell Scott, sixteen in all, written between 1859 and 1882 and unknown until they were sold at auction a few years ago, may be considered one of the happiest (in two senses of the word) findings in these volumes, though this claim rests only upon the quality of three or four of the very earliest and two or three of the very latest in date. Scott's friendship with Swinburne might have warmed to intimacy with Lady Trevelyan, to whom so many admirers have rendered homage, as intermediary, but her premature death apparently removed the requisite binding force. Scott himself seems by no means the most attractive of men, having harbored in the company of his betters a conviction, more or less well concealed, of his own superiority that appears nowadays simply ludicrous, a pettiness of disposition that was first unmasked in his *Autobiographical Notes,* posthumously published in 1892. His hand, however, had more finesse than his intellect, and Swinburne's jibe (provoked by certain remarks in the memoir) that Scott was "born for a sign-painter in Cambo" is a cruel exaggeration.

Along with Swinburne's letters to Scott, therefore, ought to be read not only his "Memorial Verses" but also his essay "The New Terror," as well as the magnificent, and deplorable, letter to the *Academy* in December 1892.

Time has been unkinder to Watts-Dunton, to whom more than 250 of the letters in this collection are addressed, than to most of his peers. In his heyday he had to be reckoned with, but he has long since paid the price of being a reviewer rather than a critic, and today, neatly labeled novelist, poet, author of an article on poetry in the *Encyclopaedia Britannica,* coiner of the phrase "the renascence of wonder," confidant of poets, he is hardly known outside the English departments of universities. No one has even bothered to separate this "hero of friendship," as Gabriel Rossetti called him, the friend of Tennyson, Morris, Borrow, Meredith, Henley, from the dingy old nursemaid who, irresistibly, excites the satirist in every man. He has been ridiculed as a sort of Bartolo sheltering Rosina from insistent Almavivas or despised as a puritanical censor requiring an incorrigible charge to submit every lucubration to his monitory blue pencil. There is a core of truth in these two indictments (oral tradition adds a third, for which there is said to be documentary support); yet truth would be served at least as well if he were viewed not as a Bartolo but a factotum, not as a censor but an astute adviser from the real world who passionately wanted his friend to assume in the domain of contemporary letters the rank that genius put within reach. The dim portrait that emerges through his letters from Swinburne is far from an accurate or complete image. Behind the fussy dreariness there was some force, now hardly visible, that impressed itself on his contemporaries, and we need some emblem of its existence—something to show that this soft-spoken, disciplined man was actually susceptible to some degree of the passion that attracted him so strongly and strangely in his beloved gypsy lore, something to indicate that the solicitor who in his will directed his trustees "to cause my jugular vein to be incised by some medical man" actually had blood in that vein.

It seems clear, at any rate during the first half of their association, that Watts saw his friend as steadily and as whole as the most disinterested outsider, and in all justice it ought to be remembered that— whatever else—he saved Swinburne's life. The poet's mother had her reasons for saying in October 1880, little more than a year after her son's reformation, "It is the greatest possible comfort to me to have seen my very dear Son so well and happy. The contrast that it was to what I used to see him was something quite beyond words." That her maternal solicitude continued, and that there was ample reason for it, is obvious in her letters to Watts that have been printed here. "I have been wishing to ask him to come to see us, but I know that this is not safe without your care," she wrote in 1881. "I should be grateful to you for a word in answer to this if he is unable to write himself." In November 1882, three and a half years after the "rescue," the entire family worried about the advisability of his undertaking a three-hour railway journey unaccompanied, Lady Jane reconciling herself to necessity on the ground that he was not obliged to change carriages. One idea seems to have lurked forever in her mind, and though expressing herself with an almost otherworldly delicacy, she did not flinch. "I hope it is only his being very busy that has prevented his writing," she observes, uneasily, as late as August 1889, and even in July 1892, when her son was fifty-five years old and had been watched and warded by Watts for thirteen years, the question whether Swinburne could be trusted to travel ninety minutes alone was a matter for anxious conspiracy.

Watts may well have applauded each of Swinburne's productions, one after another, as the crowning jewel of them all, but his position was difficult, and, given the circumstances, no one not absolutely devoid of human understanding could have acted otherwise. "I really believe," wrote Swinburne, on a visit to his mother in 1882 (see below, Letter 1181), "the stimulus of your criticism has come to be . . . 'generally necessary to salvation' if not to creation in my case." "If I can in any way hint at the necessity for care not to *over do*," Lady Jane responded in May 1881 to Watts' appeal, "I will not fail to do so, but it is not easy—he feels so sure of my sympathy with him in the love for children that I should be sorry to check his openness with me on the subject and he is so kind in sending me copies of what he writes that I would seem unkind to do so." Like Watts, she deplored his " 'not knowing when to stop,' " as she confessed in a postscript to the same letter, and there is no reason to suspect that either of them subsequently became less perceptive or more competent to deal with a headstrong poet who, like any other artist, needed the affectionate and sympathetic appreciation of his friends far more than he needed their critical insights. Many of them, as Gosse has reported and as these letters reveal, over and over again, were occupied with the problem of what to do *"with* and *for* Algernon," but only Matthew Arnold, who was not even a friend in a personal, intimate sense, tendered him, perfectly phrased, the one formula that could have given all the guidance and protection that the others wanted for him: "Die Hauptsache ist dass man lerne sich selbst zu beherrschen." Watts, like Lady Jane, did what he had to do and wished himself capable of doing what needed to be done. Neither one of them, nor any other mortal power, was likely to have been capable of achieving more with such an extraordinary being.

Of Swinburne's letters to the dearest of all his friends, only a baker's dozen have come to light. But what letters they are! And what a pair they were—Swinburne and Gabriel Rossetti. Friendship, as Bacon (echoing Cicero) observed, "redoubleth joys, and cutteth griefs in half," it "opens the understanding." Cicero himself defined it as "an accord in all things, human and divine, conjoined with mutual goodwill and affection," adding that "with the exception of wisdom, no better thing has been given to man by the immortal gods." Here is such a friendship. Here, for once, Swinburne formed a close attachment with a man who was worthy of him—intellectually, artistically, emotionally. For once he expressed himself without restraint, with an abandon possible only where sympathy is perfect, modulating without self-consciousness from outrageous ribaldry to subtle practical criticism and ardent praise. For once he was able to talk about poetry, at length and in detail, with a great master-spirit, around whom, as someone wrote, he and the others stood like a guard of honor.

The course of this friendship, which is matched in English literary history only by the intimacy between Wordsworth and Coleridge, is too familiar to be traced here, and the dozen letters mirror a pitifully inadequate image. Eleven of them, touched with the "passion of wonder" and glowing with animal heat, enthusiasm, affection, hope, admiration, show Swinburne, over a period of three months, counseling a nervous, self-doubting Rossetti intimidated by the business of preparing for publication the poems so recently recovered from his wife's grave. They are the best possible introduction to Swinburne's spirit-stirring act of hero-worship, his essay "The Poems of Dante Gabriel Rossetti," which saluted the volume on its appearance and in which Swinburne adhered to his "devout intention," as he said, "to cut it fat"—without saying "a bloody word which is not the blasted fact." For generosity of mind in "the noble pleasure of praising" Swinburne has no peer, and in these letters, as in the essay, his praise, for once, seems just, having nothing in common with the absurd dithyrambs of a later period. If these few letters are typical, one can only regard it as a disaster that no more have been found, for the friendship soon foundered ignobly, and though to this day the cause is not *known,* a plausible explanation is, for the first time, I believe, now offered (see below, Letter 421).

The last correspondence that seems to demand special comment is a group of fifty-seven letters and notes addressed to Richard Monckton

Milnes (Lord Houghton), published here in their entirety for the first time. (Gosse and Wise printed in all only twenty-six—largely excerpts.) For sheer ebullience it would be hard to find anywhere the equal of about a dozen of these effusions confected for the man whom Swinburne used to refer to as Baron Tattle of Scandal and whom Carlyle, alluding to the antic impulses that made him draw together as house guests such disparates as Swinburne and the Archbishop of York or Mazzini and Cardinal Wiseman, dubbed the "President of the Amalgamation of Heaven and Hell Society." Before James Pope-Hennessy, his latest biographer, set the record straight, Milnes' relations with Swinburne had been misunderstood and misrepresented. He had a library of erotica that has seldom been surpassed (the field is of course specialized, statistics are incomplete), and it requires no vivid imagination to see young Algernon stepping for the first time across the threshold of this arcanum and looking with a wild surmise. In these decades the "unaffected and unashamed ecstacies of adoration," as Swinburne referred to his adolescent religious fervor, were yielded up by a postulant prostrate at the feet of a very different deity—the "Divine" Marquis de Sade. Lafourcade and Praz between them have struck off a stereotype of Milnes that will probably endure forever, despite the knowledgeable corrections of Pope-Hennessy, who was, after all, the first man after Gosse to consult at first hand the evidence in the letters of these volumes. Praz, in a beautiful metaphor that bespeaks a sense of humor as well as a potent imagination, pictured Milnes as a perverted Virgil guiding Young Innocence "through the Inferno of a library," and Lafourcade showed him gleefully pushing and encouraging Swinburne "dans certaines directions, à le confirmer dans certains des penchants les plus inquiétants de sa nature, en un mot à le corrompre intellectuellement." As a result, Milnes has become an almost allegorical figure, a toad insinuating unwonted fancies into the ear of the young poet, a presence risen beside the waters who had trafficked for strange webs with Eastern merchants and whose eyelids were a little weary.

The glozing tempter may have tuned his proem, but not quite in this way. This bluff, hearty franklin had the curiosity, and possibly the amorality, of a child, but he was in no sense insidious or subtle or (not to mince words) intelligent enough, as his latest biographer has taken pains to point out, to play such a role. Certainly, it was Monckton Milnes who first put into Swinburne's hands the works of the Marquis de Sade, but far from contriving the conjunction for the sake of an impious laboratory experiment, Milnes appears to have resisted Swinburne's importunities for nearly a year before capitulating, in

August 1862. He lent Sade with misgivings, anxious about the impact of mind upon mind. Swinburne, consequently, let his enthusiasm overflow into a long, brilliant letter which may have lulled his elder but which, despite its frivolous tone, reveals to any modern what depths had been plumbed in the springs of his being. For though Swinburne laughed in August, the Marquis had his laugh too, as no reader of these letters will fail to recognize. "They who are so fond of handling the leaves," as Sir Anthony said to Mrs. Malaprop, "will long for the fruit at last," and it is not the least of the revelations in these volumes that Swinburne bears a measure of the responsibility for the disintegration of a friend brought on in part by such a diet.

Several other features of this edition of letters call for passing comment. The early part of Swinburne's life—up to 1865, say—is still badly illuminated (nobody yet knows, to cite only one instance, precisely why he was withdrawn from Eton), and any light, from whatever direction, that can be thrown on it seems very desirable indeed. The editor has been extremely fortunate in being able to draw on two new sources of information for part of this critical, obscure period.

Ethel C. Hatch, daughter of Swinburne's college friend Edwin Hatch, to whom four letters in these volumes are addressed, has most kindly copied from her father's diary all the entries pertinent to Swinburne and consented to their publication. Accordingly, whenever possible they have been subjoined, even at the cost of some straining, as footnotes to certain of the letters. And sketchy though they are, the remarks have great charm and interest, especially since they pertain to Swinburne at this period of which so little is known.

Equally interesting are extracts from a group of letters addressed to Lady Trevelyan (and Sir Walter), mostly by William Bell Scott, among the Trevelyan papers at Wallington. Scott seems to have had a propensity for making trouble, and he had no scruples about repeating gossip, but he was a close if superficial observer of Swinburne in the early 1860's. Most of what he passed on to the Trevelyans, unlike Hatch's boyish and naïve platitudes, is quite devoid of charm. One might even detect a slight aftertaste of malice, but where else could we read that Swinburne's "peculiarities of speech and action . . . frightened his friends, and quite as much as his poems themselves brought down upon his book so much criticism" (see below, Letter 166)? Believing that these random comments are self-justifying, I have found a place for them among the letters, whether immediately relevant to the subject at hand or not.

In the interests of fair play as well as for the sake of new information, a few letters or extracts have been included addressed to Swinburne from his publisher. Beginning with *Bothwell* in 1874, Swinburne published nearly three dozen volumes, before his death, with Chatto and Windus. This house has most generously given me access to official letter-books dating as far back as 1868, five years before Andrew Chatto bought the business upon the death of John Camden Hotten, who himself, after supplanting Moxon in 1866 as the publisher of *Poems and Ballads,* had issued several things for Swinburne, including the memorable *William Blake.* The involutions and convolutions of Swinburne's dealings with Hotten are by no means traceable even yet, and it is doubtful if any affair in which two of the principals were as slippery and unscrupulous as Charles Augustus Howell and Hotten himself could ever be really disentangled. But a few pretty definite impressions emerge from these letters—for instance, of Swinburne's irresponsibility (see below, Letter 265). The copy of Hotten's financial reckoning with the poet in January 1869 is extremely valuable, and the last entry, "private a/c," should not be overlooked. The inference is inescapable that Hotten, before he died in 1873, was virtually blackmailing Swinburne. And we now know how such a stratagem would have been possible, for it is obvious (see below, Letter 462) that Swinburne co-operated (*collaborated* might be a more precise word) with Hotten in the issue of certain books from which both publisher and poet seem to have derived both satisfaction and income— *Flagellation* and *Romance of the Rod* are the two named by Swinburne. With Hotten in possession of these telltale documents, no wonder Swinburne walked so cautiously in trying to change publishers, even offering to continue the undercover assistance. No wonder Hotten's sinister allusions to a written agreement, which never appeared and which could not possibly have been produced, since it did not exist, were so annoying to the poet. No wonder Swinburne was at first so distrustful of Hotten's successor, Andrew Chatto.

This subject leads directly and naturally to the notorious essay on Swinburne by Sir Edmund Gosse, written in 1917, after the appearance of his biography of Swinburne and now (with the kind permission of Dr. Philip Gosse) printed for the first time, as an appendix to these letters. In 1917 this essay on drunkenness and flagellation and Gosse's introductory notes might have been sensational, but by now their force is spent. For the fact is, despite all the huggermugger with which this essay has been surrounded and all the hullabaloo with which it has been heralded—questions in the House of Commons put to the Secretary to the Treasury by a Member representing the Society of Authors, acrimonious correspondence in the daily papers, ardent discussion in the weeklies—it contains very little that could not be (perhaps indeed that was not) inferred from these letters. Anecdote excepted, it tells little that has not been printed over and over again. For roughly a decade and a half Swinburne was a chronic alcoholic. He was also a masochist. (Whether he was overtly homosexual, as a persistent oral tradition maintains, I do not know.) Gosse's essay is as remarkable for what it omits as for what it includes, and it would be difficult not to agree that he was warranted both in excluding what he knew (or conjectured) about these matters from his *Life* of Swinburne in 1917 and in assembling them in this form for posterity. After all, as he said, "Swinburne was a generous friend and a very fine gentleman," and Gosse respected him on both counts. "How delicate, decent is English Biography, bless its mealy mouth!" wrote Carlyle, in a review of Lockhart's life of Scott. "A Damocles' sword of *Respectability* hangs for ever over the poor English Life-writer . . . and reduces him to the verge of paralysis." Gosse, however, was not merely hampered by personal loyalty and paralyzed by a Damoclean sword, he was pursued by the Eumenides. But Isabel Swinburne died in 1915, Mrs. Leith in 1926. Watts-Dunton died in 1914, Gosse himself in 1928, and Swinburne has been dead for half a century. Yesterday's scandal has long since lost its power to shock, and to Pindar's dictum that "not every truth . . . is the better for showing its face undisguised; and full oft is silence the wisest thing for a man to heed" the most cogent retort is: "Omne ignotum pro magnifico est."

Editorial Principles

In transcribing and annotating these letters I have always tried to make readability my first concern, preferring it, in a few instances, even to consistency. Accordingly, apart from certain deviations duly noted, I have observed the following editorial principles:

1. When the source of my text is a published letter, I have reproduced the *body* of the letter faithfully. Thus all ellipses in my texts, for example, except a few in square brackets, are reproduced from my sources. In the *notes* ellipses are my own, made in the interest of compactness.

2. In all other cases I have usually expanded abbreviations, except for certain congealed forms that seem less obtrusive than whole words —for example: Esq.; St. (for Saint); Mr., Mrs., Dr. (and so on); N.W., S.W. (and the other London postal directions); e.g.; MS; Co.; p. (for page); v. (for verse); D.V. (for *Deo volente*); do. (for ditto). I have not altered the names of people, but I have expanded shortened names of magazines and other publications, ampersands, and most numbers (ex-

cept for dates in which the month is included, sums of money, and a few others), and I have lowered superior letters.

3. In all letters, no matter what the source of my text, I have normalized the date, address, and closing, adding square brackets only when an essential part of the date is an editorial conjecture.

4. Occasionally, I have retained within angled brackets canceled readings that seem worth while.

5. In identifying Swinburne's works I have nearly always noted when and where they were first published, in what volume they were first collected, and where they may now be found in the Bonchurch Edition, published by William Heinemann, Ltd., in twenty volumes, 1925–27 (Volume *18* is the collection of letters, Volume *19* Gosse's biography of Swinburne, Volume *20* Wise's bibliography). In the case of previously published letters, I have likewise noted where and when they first appeared and whether they are included in the Bonchurch Edition. In the headnotes an asterisk following such a reference to Volume *18* shows that the letter in question appeared also in the earlier Gosse-Wise compilation (1918).

6. When not specified, the place of publication is understood to be London.

7. Swinburne occasionally used the French spelling "correspondance." I have let it stand, along with a few other idiosyncratic spellings, exactly as he wrote it.

8. I have tried to identify all quotations, but unlike Swinburne I have not read everything ever written in several languages and I am not blessed with total recall.

9. I hope it is supererogatory for me to affirm that no expurgations have been made. Swinburne habitually (and mercifully) wrote a certain class of words, French as well as English, in the traditional manner —the initial letter followed by a dash. I have usually, and perhaps overscrupulously, substituted spaced hyphens (one for each omitted letter) for the dashes.

1. TO CAPTAIN CHARLES HENRY SWINBURNE [1]

MS: Yale.

Lower Easton, April 2, 1854 [2]

My darling Pino

I wish you a great many very happy returns of your birthday. I hope you and dearest Mimmie and all are quite well. I had a pleasant little talk the other day with Mr. Woodford [3] about the holidays, and he advises that I should go home on Easter Monday, the seventeenth of this month, and return the thirteenth of May, which will be a nice little holiday.

I suppose you had Holy Communion to-day as well as we here. I thought this morning of that, and how nice it was to be all communicating together on your birthday. I can go out again now, my cold being quite gone. I don't mind the cod's liver oil much, it seems such odd stuff to be taking! oil out of the liver of a cod! I get to Church again, which I am very glad of. I mean never if I can to neglect going, as I fear I sometimes did before, when perhaps I might have gone, but was not obliged: now I have been so long without it, with my colds. I hope all yours at home are quite well, and dearest Mimmie quite strong again. Will you please thank her for her letter, (I suppose the Post has been at its old tricks again, as I have got only one) and tell her that I heard that sermon she admired so much, and thought it very fine: a notorious fact which Mr. Woodford himself denies, and says it is not at all fine. I wonder what he does think fine: and he takes a very short time to write all those sermons. It is now very fine weather here, what is it like at home? it is now quite hot and like summer here. I hope I shall see you soon (in a fortnight) instead of writing, and that will be nice. It does seem to me an immense time since I saw you all.

1. (1797–1877), father of the poet; promoted admiral and retired with half pay in 1857.

2. 1854 may have been added by another hand. A manuscript in the Library of Congress (I know of no way to certify its authenticity) may be Swinburne's earliest surviving letter. Dated "Decr. 5th 1848" from Capheaton and said to be addressed to Ulrica Fenwick, it reads: "Dear Ulrica / I send you one of those book-marks which you wanted; I bought it at the Pantheon and I hope you will like it. We arrived here safe last evening, after having staid a day in London and York each; the Cathedral of the latter was very beautiful. / Yours very truly / Algernon C. Swinburne."

3. His tutor, James Russell Woodford (1820–85), consecrated Bishop of Ely in 1873.

With best love to all, and especially to you, with birthday wishes. I remain dearest Pino

Ever your affectionate son,
A. C. Swinburne

2. TO LADY JANE HENRIETTA SWINBURNE [1]

Text: Leith, pp. 39-43.

Cologne, July 18, 1855

We have come thus far on our way safe and well, though Uncle Tom [2] seems rather tired. Last night we slept at Liège, and the night before at Calais. Lord Sandwich [3] accompanied us from London to Aix-la-Chapelle, and was very good-natured; he walked with me over Liège and showed me the old Bishop's Palace, with its great cloisters. I liked the old city very much; it is so beautifully placid, down among the hills in a valley, and the country about it is most beautiful; very like Mounces [4] on a larger scale, and a little less wild, but that was atoned for by other kinds of beauty: it struck me more than any other part of the country we have yet gone through. All the hills are covered with woods, but here and there they open into smooth green lawns, and break into ravines where the streams are exactly like those of Mounces, and the water just the moss-water colour. One place was *so* like the Tyne just below Keeldar, the railway turned suddenly and curved round along the side of a steep hill, so that we could see some time before where the turn was; and the sun was out brightly although we left Liège in pouring rain and mist. The whole way from Liège hither was so perfectly lovely that I grudged the speed of the railway by which half the beauty was lost.

It was very funny landing at Calais and seeing the difference of appearance and hearing nothing but French: the hotels at each of our former resting-places were much better than this one, and Cologne

1. (1809-96), mother of the poet, fourth daughter of the 3d Earl of Ashburnham.

2. Major-General the Hon. Thomas Ashburnham, C.B. (1807-72), third surviving son of the 3d Earl of Ashburnham. Leith and (following her) Lafourcade, *La Jeunesse, 1,* 108, demoted "Uncle Tom" to a colonelcy, overlooking that he had been promoted general thirteen months earlier.

3. The 7th Earl of Sandwich (1811-84).

4. "His grandfather's shooting property in Northumberland—evidently very high praise, and the comparison occurs not seldom in describing scenery" (Leith).

2

is *awfully* dirty! The trains are very puzzling, and at Malines we waited an hour and a quarter.

Now I have got the coast clear for the Cathedral here, and really now I am come to it I don't know what to say. Such things are not to be *jabbered* of. The magnificence bewildered me on entering, the large arches and beautiful windows and the enormous size of the whole building; it was worth coming from anywhere to see. Uncle Tom was so good as to come with me to the Cathedral as the guide spoke only German, tho' I don't think he wanted to come: and waited while I saw the relics and crosses, etc., in the Sacristy, and the Shrine of the Three Kings, which on ordinary days like this costs 6 francs to see, which I willingly paid out of my own money and cheap for such beautiful sights.

The crosses of gold and jewels were most beautiful, but the old Priest who showed them said they were very heavy, and shook his head and smiled at the enormous one of silver which the Bishop carries in Processions. How any one can, I wonder; it is much higher than a man, and the biggest of them all. The tomb of St. Engelbrecht in the Sacristy is one of the most beautiful things I saw there, all the carved work and images silvergilt. But the shrine was best of all. The Priest removed a part at the head, and showed me the 3 skulls crowned and the names written in rubies. The bare dark skulls looked strange, but not, I thought, ugly or out of place in the diadems of gold and pearls. Every pillar of the shrine is of a different mosaic pattern. Down the sides are the Apostles and Prophets; at the foot the Passion in separate groups. The expression of the faces of each figure (one of Our Saviour particularly) looked wonderfully true on so small a scale. The 4 pearls at the top, and some other of the jewels about it were enormous; I never saw such a size. This is the best description I can give of the Shrine; there are, I am afraid, many other things well worth seeing that I had not time for. I grudge especially the view of the whole Cathedral from above, and a closer view of some of the east windows, the choir and the old frescoes. But I trust some day that we may all come here and see everything!

From the Cathedral the guide and I went to the Church of S. Ursula, and I saw the skulls and bones. One, they call it S. Margaret's, has all the teeth and is *too* horrid. The carved work of the Golden Chamber (where all the bones of the 11000 virgins are) was made by the Huns, the Priest said, and is very beautiful. There were all sorts of relics. Some sounded very funny; there was a thumb of S. Maternus and a tooth of S. Appollina. The old Priest was very nice, I think you would have liked him; he was so gentle and reverent that I took a great fancy to him, he showed me all the work and all sorts of things in different parts; and he said I could see S. Ursula's tomb if I waited till the service was over, which I did, and I felt quite miserable, it was such a wretched feeling that while they all were praying, old men and tiny children kneeling together, I was not one of them, I was shut out as it were. I could have sat down and cried, I was so unhappy. How I do trust that some day all will be able to worship together and no divisions and jealousies 'keep us any longer asunder'!

When the service was over I got over these feelings in examining the tomb, which was very beautiful, and seeing the rest of the Church in which was nothing but the bones, which one sees through holes in the walls, with lattices all along the sides of the Chancel.

I wanted very much to see S. George's church which is said to be so beautiful, but had no time.

I walked quickly from S. Ursula's church to the Hotel, which is a long way and the streets anything but clean. . . .[5] I have got a bottle of eau-de-Cologne at the great huge shop here, Farina's. Certainly, as the 'Handbook' notices, Cologne wants all its eau-de-Cologne to counteract certain other perfumes which its streets emit; and I cannot say that I think it would be at all a nice city but for this *eau* and the Cathedral. The guide asseverates that it once contained as many churches as there are days in the year: now there are only 25, I believe.

3. TO LADY JANE HENRIETTA SWINBURNE

Text: Leith, pp. 43-45.

Wiesbaden, July 17 [*for* 23][1] 1855

We arrived here safe on Saturday. . . . We had fine weather for our journey, and the Rhine is very beautiful and I think I should have enjoyed it much but for seeing it in a muddle of smoking and jabbering fellow-travellers, and missing half what was worth seeing on board of a nasty crowded steamer. I wish we could all go and see it comfortably together and stop and see whenever we liked; for I could not, though I tried hard, take any pleasure in steaming through fine scenery post-haste and missing half. It was very pro-

5. The ellipsis is Leith's.

1. Internal evidence shows that the correct date is almost certainly the 23d.

4

voking but I don't think I want any more felicity-hunting; and I can't say either that I like the prospect of a month here, tho' the gardens and lake are very pretty. . . . I have just had my first German lesson and like the man very much, and he says he is very satisfied with my attention, etc. . . .

E[dith] [2] will be happy to hear that we are domiciled with a Crimean soldier, Captain Jolliffe [3] I believe his name is, who was at Alma and Balaclava. Also she will be glad to hear that he employs himself on a crusade against rabbits, and has a dog which kills them to admiration.

We have got a capital courier, and the night we slept at Coblenz he and I had a walk over the hills after sunset, and managed a good night view of the Rhine and Moselle near their junction, and the surrounding country. Certainly the river is beautiful, and some of the castles very grand among their steep rocks, and the woods and vineyards close down to the great broad stream, only the steamers were so dirty and smoky.

4. TO LADY JANE HENRIETTA SWINBURNE

Text: Leith, pp. 45–46.

Wiesbaden, July 28, 1855

Last Tuesday was the duke's [1] birthday and there was an inspection of the soldiers and great rejoicings and salutes for his coming only he did not come at all; and the ways were hung with garlands and the lake was illuminated with coloured lamps hung all the way round which looked very pretty, by night.

And we have been to see the chapel built by the late Emperor of Russia for the burial of the Duchess [2] or somebody who married the Duke of Bavaria. It is very beautiful, the Altar is marble, the rood-screen painted in water-colours (I think) with figures of the Apostles, and her monument is very fine; and they give one list slippers to put on for fear of scratching the marble. Outside it is all carved on the portals, and has huge gilt doors. And we drove through the woods

2. His second sister (see below, Letter 43).

3. Hedworth Hylton Jolliffe (1829–99), later 2d Baron Hylton.

1. Adolphe, Duke of Nassau, born July 24, 1817.

2. Elizabeth Michailowna, who died in 1845; the chapel was erected in 1855.

to the Duke's hunting-place and went all over it, and there was a splendid view; and we walked to Saurenberg (?) [3] to see a very old ruin, the oldest castle built in the country A.D. 1234 (I believe it was) and the old man who showed it had fought with Napoleon in the Peninsula and against him at Waterloo. I gathered some flowers off the walls, which I send for the others if they care. It is a fine view, rather Mounces-like country, beyond; and a rather pretty walk by a stream all the way; it is 3 miles off.

5. TO LADY JANE HENRIETTA SWINBURNE

Text: Leith, pp. 46–48.

Wiesbaden, August 4, 1855

He [1] and I walked yesterday to the most lovely place on earth—a sort of mixture of the prettiest parts of Mounces and Capheaton,[2] the cave of the Robber Lutweis. I longed for you all to be there, especially E[dith], for it was admirably robberish; the old brigand lived there about the middle of the last century. He had good taste, certainly. The way thither is first up a steep hill, dotted with woods, by the most dark and wild of rambling paths to the Lockene, a sort of round building on columns whence you see the most of the Rhine and Moselle, and the further country. Then you strike right off thro' the forest by a most lovely path, and go up and down for a long way till you come to a sort of bank or wall of rocks, up which you get (for there are not bare rocks, except here and there on the top, the sides slope down, and so are very accessible) then on both sides the ground sinks and gives you the loveliest wood-scenery view that ever was seen: then you descend by another steep winding path and find a road, a stream with natural stepping-stones, which you cross— reaching a steep bank on the other side, and there is a most beautiful view of rocks which contain *his* cave, looking most inaccessible; just almost a single narrow and long platform, which might easily be defended by robbers against any amount of soldiery; it is very steep, and the cave and rocks so hidden by an outer wall of trees

3. *Sic.* But Leith's misreading makes the party walk about forty miles, and Lafourcade, *La Jeunesse, 1,* 109, by substituting Sauerburg, only halves the distance. Swinburne actually went to Sonnenberg, which is, as he says, about "3 miles off" from the hunting lodge of the Grand Duke of Luxembourg.

1. Identified by Leith as "His uncle."

2. The Swinburne family seat, near Newcastle.

whose branches protect it, that one might pass it often and never discover the soldiers *lurking* behind; in front you descend by a steep track, paved with red slugs (the only drawback to these woods) to a long meadow stretching far away between the woods which rise steeply on both sides. Through this meadow runs the stream which supplies the robbers in their high rock, towering above, with the best of pure spring water. I always drink some when I pass, it only begins a little higher up, and there are forests of wild raspberries and red-berried elders, with which latter Uncle T. fell in love, the colour is so beautiful at a little distance, and we are bringing home some seeds. We thought it would look lovely about East Dene. This meadow continues for a long way, then the woods . . . and for miles and miles you see nothing but this endless forest, high up two rocks and mountains, and, perched between the eminences, the Duke's hunting seat looks down on us far away. It was a bright but cool day, and *too* delightful! We went home by another way which took us into an opening above a steep wooded and winding valley, giving a beautiful view of Mayence and the neighbouring country. All the forest is intersected by the most exquisite paths, winding up and down, and is full of so many beautiful places that the attempt to describe them would be endless; judge of the rest by what you have heard, imperfect and faint as my description is. In the evening I went out again with Mr. C——— and had another long wood ramble; we saw among other things, the Weeping Oak; it hangs droopingly like a willow, and bears no fruit; the only one in Germany, and all the visitors come to see it.

6. TO LADY JANE HENRIETTA SWINBURNE

Text: Leith, pp. 49–51.

Wiesbaden, August 12, 1855

To-morrow early we start to sleep, I believe, at Wurtzburg and next day at Nuremberg, where we stay 3 or 4 days. It is pleasant to move again and see more places, but for some reasons I am sorry to leave Wiesbaden, especially the Forest. . . . I went to Mayence yesterday with Uncle T.'s servant, and saw the Cathedral; a fine one, but not to be seen after Cologne. There are some fine monuments,— one that of S. Boniface, erect, of red-sandstones, which interested me, as I look upon him rather as *ours,* being the patron of Bonchurch. Another of an old Crusader (very famous for its beauty) had the loveliest face you can think of, a smiling still expression, and the figure so perfect that it might move and not surprise one. The Cathedral has been terribly battered and smashed about by repeated bombardments, and little of the old part is left; but what there is they say is older almost than any other. Also, which is very rare, it has a high Altar and Choir at each end, that in the west (with splendid carvings and windows) is used on Sundays, the E. one on weekdays only. The cloisters are beautiful, and the Chapterhouse with the old Archbishops' tombs; one, Bp. Adalbert I., was seized and imprisoned by the Emperor: whereon his loving subjects of Mayence rose and seized the Emperor and held *him* prisoner till they got back their Bishop safe and sound; and he granted the citizens great privileges, to reward their loyalty. It was an enormously rich diocese and the Bps. were very powerful I believe. In the cloisters is the original monument of the Minstrel Frauenlob (Praise-women) so named for his courtesy; all is battered away but the head, which I thought beautiful. The Bishop's arms are emblazoned above in the roof. I then went up the tower to the belfry; saw the city and view of the country, with the junction of the Rhine and Maine below; and then up a ladder above the belfry into the highest point, a round gallery within the upper dome, with open-work sides, to the horror and alarm of the showman, who assured me that people hardly ever went up; but of course this determined me to go, and I did, whereof I am rather conceited, especially as the great clock struck four, making a most awful noise just as I was halfway up the ladder, and made the whole concern shake and rattle. The view was very fine.

7. TO JOHN NICHOL [1]

Text: *Early Letters.*

Balliol College, February 11 [1857]

My dear Nichol

I am sorry to hear that we are not to have you back this term, which I had rather counted upon. Our society does, however, manage to keep

1. (1833–94), professor of English language and literature at Glasgow University (where his father was for many years Regius professor of astronomy) from 1862 to 1889. Through his father, Nichol knew both Kossuth and Mazzini fairly well, and it is obvious that this *cachet* was in itself sufficient to attract Swinburne. As a teacher, Nichol was much loved by his students, and many Glaswegians even today recall him with affection. At the time of his death in 1894 he was Swinburne's oldest friend, but, curiously, he seems to have been at no time a real intimate. A cautious and rather self-conscious bawdry often appears in their letters, and there seems to be a good deal more than meets the eye (see *A Swinburne Library*, collected and printed by T. J. Wise, London, 1925, p. 174), but Swinburne's tone in addressing Nichol never once warms to the degree of abandon and familiarity that can be felt

above water, as yet, but how long it will go on without you, I don't know.[2]

Your quotation shows me what you have been reading; I hope you had as much pleasure from it as I had. To me it seems that *Aurora Leigh* is her great work, and that we have had very few such poems for a long time. I never suspected the authoress of much dramatic power; every character down to the slightest (for instance, the painter Carrington and the Howes) are so original and natural, so distinct and clearly defined, that it rivals the male Browning's character-drawing. And the three women, Aurora, Marian, and Lady Waldemar, seem to me so perfect in idea and execution, that I hardly yet know which to prefer.

Having thus inflicted my raptures upon you (which is taking an advantage, as one cannot be interrupted in a letter) I must ask you to 'row' Dicey when you next write for his heterodoxy in the Browning question. My diatribes make not the slightest impression on him and I lament to say he goes about retailing "unwisdom" from the *Saturday Review*.

Apropos of *Aurora*—some wretched man having counted (so at least he declares) the number of lines in the poem, and making it out three times as long as the *Odyssey!!* [3] Human wickedness has no limits.

---

in the letters to Gabriel Rossetti, Powell, Howell, and possibly several others. Only a few of Swinburne's letters to Nichol survive in manuscript. T. J. Wise in 1917 privately printed nine, presumably from transcripts made by Gosse, who had seen the originals, but Nichol's daughter "insisted upon the deletion of so many passages that, had these been removed, the letters would have been so completely emasculated that they would have served no useful purpose" (Bonchurch, *20*, 389). The daughter, Mrs. Jack, recently deceased, told the present editor in 1951 that she herself had burned the letters in question.

2. Old Mortality, an undergraduate society formed, in Nov. 1856, according to the immemorial pattern, was so named because of the frail health of all of its founding fathers—John Nichol; A. V. Dicey (1835–1922), who distinguished himself as professor of English Law; G. B. Hill (1835–1903), the noted editor; G. R. Luke (born 1836), a man of great promise who drowned in the Isis in Mar. 1862; A. S. Grenfell (1837–87), who became chaplain at the London Hospital; and Swinburne himself. The society was fairly luminous for nearly a decade. Its name had better suited the magazine, *Undergraduate Papers* (edited by Nichol), which expired with the third number. Nichol, who had conceived the idea of the society, was almost at once forced by illness to withdraw from Oxford till May 2.

3. The notice of Mrs. Browning's *Aurora Leigh* in the *Saturday Review* (Dec. 27, 1856), is ascribed by Merle Bevington to G. S. Venables: M. M. Bevington, *The Saturday Review, 1855–1868* (New York, 1941), p. 215. A fourth edition of Mrs. Browning's *Poems*, three volumes in 1856, included "Casa Guidi Windows" and three other new poems. The sentence ending here must have begun with the words "My diatribes."

Have you seen the additional poems in the last edition of Mrs. Browning? Some, I think, are very beautiful. I have scandalised Grenfell, I am afraid, by asserting that she is the greatest woman that ever lived, except Sappho and Deborah! I know no fourth poetess like them, certainly.

Your opinion of Dobell's *England in Time of War*,[4] expressed to me last term, induced me to read it again, thinking I must have judged too hastily; but really, except the half-dozen poems you mentioned then, I don't think there is much in the book. These, indeed, have exquisite passages, as musical and gorgeous in *words* as he ever was, but on the whole I think he does himself immense injustice.

I hope you will admire my powers of endurance when you hear that in the Christmas vacation I read *The Prelude* through from one end to the other. I can only say I should be sorry to do it again, fine as many passages are. I suppose you have heard, eminent among the "poems and rumours of poems," [5] the news of Tennyson's coming work? Of course you have also heard those who have seen the MS. aver that it is his finest work? My informant gave me a sketch of the subject, having heard Tennyson read it aloud. But all this I daresay you have heard, and all about the two ladies and the thunderstorm, which is to be so splendid.[6]

Have you seen Kingsley's *Two Years Ago*? I admire it almost as much as *Westward Ho!* [7] if not quite: it shows at least no falling off in power, tho' I think he is rather hard on that unlucky poet.

I have no more time to write, so, hoping that you will return next term quite recovered.

Laetus intersis 'divique populo.' [8]

I remain, yours sincerely,
A. C. Swinburne

4. Sydney Dobell (1824–74), poet, critic, and friend of the Nichol family. The verses appeared in 1856.

5. See Matthew 24:6.

6. *Enid and Nimuë: the True and the False,* printed as a trial book in 1857 and published in 1859 as "Geraint and Enid" and "Vivien," ultimately settled down (in 1888) as three idylls—"The Marriage of Geraint," "Geraint and Enid," and "Merlin and Vivien."

7. Charles Kingsley's *Two Years Ago* was published in 1857, *Westward Ho!* in 1855.

8. *Diuque laetus intersis populo Quirini:* "And long mayest thou be pleased to dwell amid Quirinus' folk" (i.e. among the Roman people), Horace, *Odes*, 1. 2. 45–46,

7A. TO JOHN NICHOL

MS: Yale.

Capheaton, August 12 [1857]

Dear Nichol

I have just received your letter with its heterogeneous directions. I will meet you on Saturday at Edinburgh by the train arriving 11.6 A.M. so that we shall have half the day clear. I shall enjoy this arrangement particularly, as I have always wished to see Edinburgh in despite of Tennyson's calumnious account. The whole plan seems to me perfect and is very much heightened by the chance of the introductions you mention.[1]

I am sorry my hieroglyphics puzzled you so hopelessly, but I admire greatly your escape from the difficulty as the letter came here straight —I presume by an effort of clairvoyance on the part of the postmaster at Newcastle.

I will bring such fragments of MS as are yet more than imaginary, but though they are slight enough I have sketched out the plan.[2]

---

tr. C. E. Bennett in Loeb Classical Library. G. B. Hill's impressions of Swinburne at this date earn a place in the story. On May 19, 1856, four months after Swinburne's arrival at Oxford, he wrote: "Last night I dined at the Observatory, and met a Balliol friend of mine—Swinburne—with his father, Captain Swinburne. There were two other gentlemen there besides our host, Mr. Johnson the astronomer, and as all of them but young Swinburne and myself had been great travellers the conversation was most interesting." On Mar. 4, 1857, Hill wrote: "Yesterday I was in Swinburne's rooms. I wish you knew the little fellow: he is the most enthusiastic fellow I ever met, and one of the cleverest. He wanted to read me some poems he had written and have my opinion. They are really very good, and he read them with such an earnestness, so truly feeling everything he had written, that I for the first time in my life enjoyed hearing the poetry of an amateur. He was very much pleased at the honest praise I could bestow on them." And on Mar. 18 he noted that he was reading *Aurora Leigh*, "which Swinburne lent me." On May 24 he wrote again: "Swinburne has just left me. All day I have been very much engaged breakfasting, lunching, dining out, and having Swinburne to tea. . . . Yesterday there was a Cantab present [at Old Mortality] and Swinburne and some others gave him such an extraordinary description of my love of boxing . . . that I had to make an indignant protest" (*Letters of George Birkbeck Hill*, ed. Lucy Crump, 1906, pp. 57, 66–67, 71).

1. On Sep. 3 Nichol wrote to William Jack (William Knight, *Memoir of John Nichol*, Glasgow, 1896, pp. 155–56): "Swinburne has been with me for a fortnight or so, and we have just returned from a trip to Skye . . . . Swinburne had gone on before by the main road to secure beds, but how to find the inn was the mystery. . . . We got in, however, and found Swinburne waiting for us. . . . Swinburne says we ran a Muck once or twice, and were like to have made a Mull of the affair, but on the whole it was a Rum go!"

2. Possibly the poem "The Temple of Janus," of which Lafourcade (*La Jeunesse*, 2, 209–17) printed some extracts.

11

Béranger's death [3] will be a good hook for bringing him in, and I shall offer Lamartine [4] on the shrines of the other two as a victim devoted Dîs Manibus.[5] Conceive his having set up as a rival to Victor Hugo or Béranger! like preferring le Petit to Napoleon the first.

I remain

Yours sincerely,

A. C. Swinburne

P.S. I hope you have taken up with Hawthorne [6]—he is a splendid subject (I have just read Twice-told Tales and they even beat my expectations) and a clear field.

8. TO JOHN NICHOL

Text: *Early Letters.*

Royal Pier Hotel, Ryde, Isle of Wight,
December 13, 1857

My dear Nichol

I have good news for you about the Magazine. Our incompetent friend Mansell has not sold more, he says, than eighty copies; and the advertising has been very much neglected. Besides, Luke tells me that he is very careless about concealing our names; and upon the whole I think that he will do all to ruin the paper that 'the divine right of stupidity' can. There seems to be an idea afloat that a preponderance of the 'waifs of verse' is too likely to detain [sic]; Luke and Dicey both think (and I incline to agree with them) that the publication of *Yseult* is likely rather to injure it than otherwise.[1]

Considering our position, I think it is better not to hazard too much in the poetical way of business; and in reperusing my cantos

3. Pierre Jean de Béranger, the poet (born 1780), died July 16, 1857.

4. Alphonse de Lamartine (1790–1869), poet, historian, statesman.

5. "To the gods of the dead"—the phrase is familiar on Roman tombstones and in Latin poetry.

6. 1804–64. *Twice-Told Tales,* first collected in 1837, appeared enlarged in 1842.

1. *Undergraduate Papers,* of which the initial number appeared on Dec. 1, was printed and published by Mansell, an Oxford bookseller. To the magazine Swinburne contributed four, or possibly five, "crudities," as he later and properly called them, including the first canto of "Queen Yseult" in the December number. The six complete cantos (Bonchurch, *1,* 9–62) were first printed (privately) in 1918. G. B. Hill wrote on Nov. 10, 1857, that "Swinburne is writing a ballad on Queen Yseult from the *Morte d'Arthur.* I heard part of it this evening. He is already a true poet, I say it without exaggeration" (*Letters of George Birkbeck Hill,* p. 74).

12

I think they are too imperfect, feeble and unfinished to publish for a year or two. A thorough rewriting would be good for some of them, to prevent a monotony of tone which prevails as they now stand. Therefore, pray do not think it necessary (tho' I believe you would not) to make any difficulty about dropping me for the present. Canto I. stands well enough as a separate ballad, which the others would not do. I read it one evening to Morris and the others, and they seemed to agree with me. (I need not say that I have kept your name quiet in all companies.) They all, however, praise the poem far more than I (seriously speaking) believe it deserves. Morris says it is much better than his own poem, which opinion I took the liberty to tell him was absurd. He will not publish till spring. He, Rossetti, Pollen, and perhaps Hughes and Stanhope, will be at Oxford next term; Jones and Prinsep hope to have done after Christmas.[2]

Morris's account of Browning is one of the most amusing things I ever heard; he is especially fond, it appears, of introducing Aytoun[3] into conversation and dissecting him with an operator's delight, which must be grand to see. Have you seen *Tamerton Church Tower?* It is the companion to *The Angel in the House,* and a favourite with these men, who are not wholly contented with *The A. in the H.,* much on the same grounds as yourself.[4]

I believe I am violating no confidence in making you a copy from memory of one of Morris's ballads,[5] as it will soon be published, and he makes no secret of any of his poems. I thought you might like to see it, and I can vouch for the accuracy of my copy.

By the way, I mean to commence legal proceedings against Mansell for non-payment of my just dues, being the sum of £2, sterling. Dicey is in the same state, or worse, for that estimable but unwary

2. William Morris, J. H. Pollen (see below, Letter 12). Arthur Hughes (1830–1913), Roddam Spencer Stanhope (1829–1908), Edward Jones (later Burne-Jones), and Valentine Cameron Prinsep (1838–1904) were the disciples—aspirant painters and Pre-Raphaelites—drafted by Dante Gabriel Rossetti (1828–82), to decorate the walls of the Union Society Debating Hall. Begun late in the summer of 1857, this work was never entirely completed and has hardly endured, since enthusiastic good intentions were no substitute for persistence and technical competence. Rossetti, who had left Oxford in mid-November, did not return, and without his commanding personality the platoon, like the murals, disintegrated inchmeal. Morris' *The Defence of Guenevere* was published in the spring of 1858.

3. W. E. Aytoun (1813–65), Scots poet, parodist of the "Spasmodics."

4. Coventry Patmore's *Tamerton Church Tower* was first published in 1853, and the first two parts of *The Angel in the House* followed in 1854 and 1856.

5. Probably "The Haystack in the Floods."

young man actually purchased a guinea Atlas of ancient geography with the expected reversion of his article, and if he does not get it he will be knocked off his moral and intellectual legs.

With best remembrances to your father, as well as to Mrs. and Miss Nichol,[6] I remain,

Yours very sincerely,

A. C. Swinburne

My direction, if you ever write, will be for all this vacation, 'East Dene, Bonchurch, Isle of Wight.'

9. TO EDWIN HATCH [1]

MS: Ethel C. Hatch.

East Dene,

January [*sic for* December] 28 [1857]

My dear Hatch

I am glad you can come on Saturday, as it was the day we thought of expecting you; so before answering your profound remarks on

6. John Pringle Nichol (1804–59), professor of astronomy in the University of Glasgow, Nichol's stepmother, and his sister Agnes.

1. Edwin Hatch (1835–89) was educated at King Edward's School, Birmingham (which Burne-Jones also attended), and, from 1853 to 1857, at Pembroke College, Oxford, where he became one of the "little Birmingham colony" of which Lady Burne-Jones writes. He was ordained in 1858, and after seven years' quasi-rustication in Canada he returned to Oxford in 1867 as vice-principal of Saint Mary Hall. Hatch was a scholarly theologian whose Broad Church opinions (and hopes), akin to those of his friend Jowett, prickled the suspicions, on one hand, of those who liked the Church of England as it was, and, on the other, of those who liked it as it had been. Birkbeck Hill pettishly described him in 1855 as "a pompous empty-headed fellow who has an inordinate opinion of himself, which no one in the least shares"; but the second and fourth, at least, of the imputations were assuredly wide of the mark. Hatch's diary, with parts of which his daughter has generously acquainted me, shows that the stay at East Dene began Jan. 2, 1858, and ended twelve days later. Clearly, Swinburne did not share Birkbeck Hill's dudgeon, and the visit appears to have been a continuous *conversazione:* "Readings and glorious sympathy" . . . "Talked and walked . . . through a glorious afternoon" . . . "glorious night together in the hotel: read and talked together and poured soul into soul" . . . "glorious talk on the water as the sun set." On the twelfth they "Called on Tennyson . . . : first in morning when we talked not much, he being busy with his poem. Then at dinner with him and Mrs. Tennyson: stayed till long after midnight in his glorious little room, but what he said is to be remembered not here but in my soul for ever."

Tennyson wrote to Dr. R. J. Mann that "young Swinburne called here the other day with a college friend of his, and we asked him to dinner, and I thought him a

Logic I will enter into business details, which otherwise I shall certainly forget. The ticket you take at Waterloo Station had better be to Ryde, as that will save you some expense and a great deal of trouble in paying omnibus steamer etc. etc. I never take a ticket to Portsmouth if I can help it. Your best train will be the 11 A.M. express, which is due at Portsmouth to meet the 2.30 steamer. This will take you across and you will meet the 3.30 coach to Ventnor, at Ryde. If you came later you would miss the coach and have to post over which would be thrice as expensive and unutterably dull. If you determine on this plan, perhaps you will send me a word to say so, as I will engage you a place in the coach the day before; otherwise there is always the chance of its being full when you arrive. The said coach will bring you to your destination if you tell the driver to stop here, and we shall be ready to meet you. Now I hope you admire my business capacity; but unluckily I have just got directions from my father, or in all human likelihood I should have misled you in some marvellous manner.

I am very glad you are of the same mind as myself on the 'pleasure' question; and I quite hope you will enjoy the different sort I can offer you, as much as I shall your visit. At least we have the all-consoling sea.

Ever yours sincerely,
A. C. Swinburne

10. TO EDWIN HATCH

Text: Bonchurch, *18*, 1–4*.

Oxford, February 17 [1858]

My dear Hatch

I commiserate you sincerely; but I have two things to comfort you with:—(1) Morris's book is really out. Reading it, I would fain be worthy to sit down at his feet; but I have a painful recollection [1] of *Aurora Leigh:*

> Almost all the birds
> Will sing at dawn; and yet we do not take
> The chattering swallow for the holy lark!

very modest and intelligent young fellow. Moreover I read him what you vindicated [i.e. *Maud*], but what I particularly admired in him was that he did not press upon me any verses of his own" (*Alfred Lord Tennyson, A Memoir*, ed. Hallam Tennyson, 2 vols. New York and London, 1898, *1*, 425).

1. Inaccurate as well as painful. The passage is from Book I.

Such, however, is the invincible absurdity of all poets, that he ventured to prefer *Rosamond* to *Peter Harpdon* [2] in a repeatedly rebuked and resolutely argued statement. It appears to me simple mania; but certainly I am glad of his words, for *Rosamond* is about my favourite poem, and is now verging on a satisfactory completion. The first scene as rewritten is an acknowledged improvement. But after all—!

(2) I have a message to you from Edith,[3] which I enclose in her own words. Of course if you like I will write for your book, and she can get another copy; you must not let her interfere between you and what you value. She would be in a great state of mind at the idea.

Now (to have done with the practical at once) could you tell me if about Easter I could find a day's lodging near you if I came up? I should love to see all you speak of, and also to talk with you sooner than otherwise. This is a vague vision, and certainly *cool* on my part to give you the trouble; but we might make something of it.

In redemption of my words, I enclose two of my latest grinds, regardless of postage. Lose not the priceless uniques lest the world demand the account thereof at your hands. *The Golden House* is of course *Rudel in Paradise*. The other I can only describe as a dramatico-lyrico-phantas-magorico-spasmodic sermon on the grievous sin of flirtation.[4] It was written off one evening and has never been corrected. Verdicts differ concerning it. Morris attacks it as weak and spasmodic. Nichol (in whose opinion I often trust) thinks it rather a good dramatic story than otherwise. It is of course meant for a picture of exceptional weakness; inaction of the man, impulsive irresolution of the woman; mutual ignorance of each other and themselves, with an extra dash of sensuous impulse; finally, with no ostensible cause, rupture and spiflication. Pray abuse it if you feel inclined; I am not (as you know) over-delicate and timid concerning my scribbles, and I have no tenderness for this; and if it is not what it ought to be, it is a decided failure. But I suspect I must be *Eglamor* to Morris as *Sordello*.

I long to be with you by firelight between the sunset and the sea to have talk of *Sordello;* it is one of my canonical scriptures. Does

2. Swinburne's *Rosamond* appeared in 1860; Morris' "Sir Peter Harpdon's End" was in *The Defence of Guenevere*.

3. Swinburne's favorite sister.

4. "Rudel in Paradise" was printed by T. J. Wise in *A Swinburne Library*, pp. 245–46. Lafourcade, *La Jeunesse*, 2, 65, identifies the sermon on flirtation as "Letters," an unpublished poem of which a manuscript is now in the Rutgers University Library.

he sleep and forget? I think yes. Did the first time Palma's mouth trembled to touch his in the golden rose-lands of Paradise, a sudden power of angelic action come over him? I suspect, not utterly companionless. Sometimes one knows—not now: but I suppose he slept years off before she kissed him. In Heaven she grew too tired and thin to sing well, and her face grew whiter than its aureole with pain and want of him. And if, like the other Saint, she wept, the tears fell upon his shut lids and fretted the eyes apart as they trickled. Who knows these matters? Only we keep the honey-stain of hair.

I write more folly to you than I dare to read over, because I think you wise. So take my stupidity as a compliment. If you like, and if it prospers, I will send you specimens of a new poem on Tristram which I am about.[5] I envy you your work of corrupting the young idea with Shelley. I hope you will also introduce Morris—the first edition *must* pay well. If you like or care to amuse yourself therewith, my poems are at your service. I don't care about privacy. I shudder at the idea of a young man in the sixth form being tainted by such readings as Shelley, Morris, and the unworthiest of their admirers. I should like to review myself and say 'that I have an abortive covetousness of imitation in which an exaggeration of my models—*i.e.* blasphemy and sensuality—is happily neutralised by my own imbecility.' I flatter myself the last sentence was worthy of the *Saturday Review*. I also envy your musical and architectural work. Upon the whole, if your pupils in poetry and profanity are conversible, I think that one might be worse off than you. I am sure, but for Morris, I should be.

One evening—when the *Union* was just finished—Jones and I had a great talk. Stanhope and Swan [6] attacked, and we defended, our idea of Heaven, viz. a rose-garden full of stunners.[7] Atrocities of an appalling nature were uttered on the other side. We became so fierce that two respectable members of the University—entering to see the pictures—stood mute and looked at us. We spoke just then of kisses

5. Perhaps "Joyeuse Garde" (Bonchurch, *1*, 104–6).

6. Swan seems to have existed and probably had a first name, though all the chroniclers have carelessly dropped it somewhere. (Perhaps he is the Francis Henry Swan who, aged 18, matriculated at Oxford in 1843, but whose name appears no more.) According to J. W. Mackail (*The Life of William Morris*, new ed., 2 vols. 1901, *1*, 127), he was "a friend of Rossetti's and a man of some amount of genius which verged on eccentricity" who "had taken a considerable part in executing the decorations on the Union roof."

7. Gabriel Rossetti's much-admired word for beautiful women.

in Paradise, and expounded our ideas on the celestial development of that necessity of life; and after listening five minutes to our language, they literally fled from the room! Conceive our mutual ecstasy of delight.

All my people desire to be remembered to you. I had a long letter from Edith the other day: I know you will be glad to hear this, as I am to think of Morris's having that wonderful and most perfect stunner of his to—look at or speak to.[8] The idea of his marrying her is insane. To kiss her feet is the utmost man should dream of doing.

Mind you send for his book at once; read it, and repent your former heresies, or I will review it somewhere and say that he is to Tennyson what Tennyson is to Dobell or Dobell to Tupper.[9]

Believe me,

Ever yours truly,
A. C. Swinburne

P.S. Morris sends his love to you and hopes you are getting settled. *The Albigenses* [10] are not yet organised; I must read more, and then dash at it in wrath.

11. TO EDWIN HATCH

MS: University of Texas.

Oxford, March 2 [1858]

My dear Hatch

In beginning my letter to you, I hear a voice that says 'Make lime of his bones': but I resist the gentle intimation and merely ask what the and cetera you mean by never answering me all this time? [1] If the priceless freight has miscarried, I shall do something spasmodic. Write—I suppose you have time: and then I will write you a longer letter and send you a better poem than the one enclosed.

Ever yours truly,
A. C. Swinburne

8. Morris married Jane Burden Apr. 26, 1859.

9. Martin Tupper (1810–89), poetaster.

10. According to Gosse (Bonchurch, *19*, 54), Swinburne "planned an epic poem" on this subject.

1. See above, Letter 10.

12. TO EDWIN HATCH

MS: Robert H. Taylor. Published: Bonchurch, *18*, 5–6*.

Oxford, April 26 [1858]

My dear Hatch

I am very sorry to have missed seeing you, before you left us for the improving recreation of canes and chemistry, Gregorians and castigations; I trust you will some day have had enough, and set up the staff of your tent even among Philistines to whom the penetralia of *Chambers' Magazine* are unknown land.[1] Have you seen Montégut's article on Kingsley in the Revue des Deux Mondes?[2] get it up when you have time, it is well worth while.

Item, a review of Guenevere in the Tablet—I believe by Pollen: certainly the best as well as most favourable review Morris has had.[3] That party has given us no signs of life as yet: in vain has the 'Oxford County Chronicle' been crammed with such notices as the following:

'If W.M. will return to his disconsolate friends, all shall be forgiven. One word would relieve them from the most agonizing anxiety—why is it withheld? '

'If the Gentleman who left a MS. (apparently in verse) in George St. will communicate with his bereaved and despairing Publishers, he will hear of something to his advantage. Otherwise the MS. will be sold (to pay expenses) as waste paper, together with the stock in hand of a late volume of Poems which fell stillborn from the press.'

1. Hatch may be the anonymous author of "Shelley and His Writings," *Chambers's Journal* (Mar. 6, 1858), pp. 148–51. At this time he was teaching and preaching in East London. His diary shows that he arrived in Oxford Apr. 17, "Called on Swinburne, talked in his window seat in the sunset, and then went to Morris." Next day he "Breakfasted with Swinburne—then Morris came—read together." On Apr. 20: "Poor Swinburne fearfully depressed, seemingly knowing little of trouble, even the slight one of having to read what is disagreeable—pleasant talk with him down the High at night." He "Had Swinburne to breakfast" next morning and "did not see him again." On Apr. 22 Hatch "Left for Cambridge—read Hegel all the way and enjoyed it."

2. Emile Montégut reviewed *Two Years Ago* in the *Revue des deux mondes* (Apr. 1, 1858), pp. 595–617.

3. Swinburne's ascription is not confirmed by Anne Pollen's *John Hungerford Pollen, 1820–1902* (1912), though Pollen *was* on the staff of the *Tablet*. He had painted the ceiling of the Merton College Chapel, was professor of fine art in the University of Dublin, and, despite his graver years and manner, he enlisted under Rossetti as one of the youthful decorators of the Oxford Union Society Debating Hall. In later years he was recognized as a connoisseur and amateur of the applied arts, and was the author of several books.

Even this latter—a touching effusion of the creative fancy and talented pen 'which now traces these imperfect records with a faltering hand'—has failed to move him. The town crier is to proclaim our loss to-morrow. 'Lost, stolen, or strayed, an eminent artist and promising littérateur. (The description of his person is omitted for obvious reasons.) Had on when he was last seen the clothes of another gentleman, much worn, of which he had possessed himself in a fit of moral—and physical—abstraction. Linen (questionable) marked W.M. Swears awfully, and walks with a rolling gait, as if partially intoxicated.'

Enough of so painful a subject. I hope you are not breaking your brains upon Sordello: read the other poets now alive (whom it would be invidious to particularize too minutely) and you will outgrow your absurd veneration for 'an author of some talent, but more extravagance'—vide Saturday Review, Art. 'Men and Women.' [4]

I shall be busy till Whitsuntide, so this elegant epistle is my last for some time.

Receive the assurance of my respectful consideration, and believe me

Ever yours sincerely,
A. C. Swinburne

13. TO JOHN NICHOL

Text: *Early Letters.*

[Late August 1858]

My dear Nichol
. . . And now, I want very much to know if you can tell me anything about Landor which alters the case as represented by the papers.[1]

---

4. The *Saturday Review* (Nov. 24, 1855), pp. 69–70, pulverized Browning's *Men and Women*. Paternity is attributed (reluctantly) to Browning's friend Sir Joseph Arnould by Bevington in his book entitled *The Saturday Review*, pp. 332–33.

1. In June 1857, Walter Savage Landor (1775–1864), suspecting (with reason) an old friend of several degrees of turpitude, issued a pamphlet, *Walter Savage Landor and the Honourable Mrs. Yescombe,* accusing her of misappropriation of funds. Warned of legal proceedings, Landor retaliated with another pamphlet, *Mr. Landor Threatened,* which brought down a libel suit on his head. John Forster achieved a truce by persuading him to initial a written apology and promise to sin no more, but the proud and irascible old man pampered his grudge, and in 1857 published *Dry Sticks, Fagoted* (dated 1858) which hummed with high-voltage libels thinly insulated. The law moved in, and Landor out—to Italy, where he spent the rest of his life. On Aug. 23, 1858, the court at Bristol awarded the Yescombes £750 damages for three libels and £250 for "breach of agreement." The London papers

I need not say how painful it was to me to read it with their comments. We all owe too much to the grand old man, to be willing to accept their verdict as final. Entire excuse I suppose we are not to look for, but partial reason, partial apology there must surely be. We all have an interest at stake in such a man's character. Pray do not think me the less in earnest about this matter for the absurdities in the rest of this letter. I did not like to open it with the present subject. I shall wait for your answer eagerly, knowing the opportunities of information which you possess in advantage of me. At present I am inclined to regard it as a *judgment* for his attacks on the Emperor Napoleon, and his praise of the bastard Buonaparte.

Also please tell me, when you have leisure to write me a short line, when we return to the City of the Dons, as just now I am bewildered by doubts on that important subject.

With my best remembrances to Dr. Nichol, to Mrs. and Miss Nichol, and to Mr. Crosbie [2] (if you see him), I remain,

Yours most sincerely,
A. C. Swinburne

Excuse (if it does not give you too much trouble to decipher) this truly damnable scrawl.

14. TO EDWIN HATCH

MS: Robert H. Taylor.

Capheaton, September 15 [1858]

My dear Hatch

I am very glad of your letter which I answer at once: I understand your point of view better, and you are not far wrong: I must, it seems, beware of Topsification,[1] as I don't want to have 'a hysterical shadow

---

blazoned the news next day, and on the 25th *The Times* editorialized: "A fouler libel than the one brought home to him was never written by man. . . . How ineffable is the disgrace to a man of Mr. Landor's ability and reputation at the close of a long life . . . ! A slanderer, and the slanderer of a lady—a writer of anonymous letters, and these letters reeking with the foulest odours of the dirtiest stews—a violator of his pledged word—who is it to whom these words must now be applied? —'Who would not weep if Atticus were he?' "—The best accounts of the tempest, *not* from the point of view of *The Times,* are in Malcolm Elwin's *Savage Landor* (1941) and R. H. Super's "Extraordinary Action for Libel—Yescombe *v.* Landor," *PMLA, 61* (1941), 736–55.

2. Probably Henry William Crosskey, D.D. (1826–93), Unitarian minister, geologist, politician.

1. Of becoming like Topsy—i.e. William Morris.

squeaking in' a (not surplice but) surcoat; item, imitation is not a good thing: but I am considerably fond of that party, and your reference to him threw me into a state of bitter wrath: I accepted any attack on me (and did not question your right to make it) but not a reflection on that individual:—and I must be selfish enough to ask you to tell me about my Sonnet,—*is* it cribbed? I daresay it is—but you are not to bring *that* charge against a *frate* and not be called to account. I am like Sheridan's dramatist 'Plagiary: [2] My dear Sir, upon my honour I'm *only* afraid it's too original for the depraved taste of the public.'—Sincerely, I don't at all suspect you of a desire to attack me; but the second letter made me very uncomfortable, to say the least.

Many thanks for your news—I *must* manage to see Rossetti's picture somehow. And now, to console my own vanity, I must tell you a piece of success on my part: I wrote a ballad lately, which was accepted here—in the native land of ballads—as a genuine Border specimen, and of the earliest mediaeval build! [3] The very people I learnt the old ones from when I was a kid of diminutive proportions were wholly taken in—one party was elated at such a discovery, but only wondered where it had lain all these years to escape his discovery!! I leave you to imagine my rampant conceit. It is a story of the most immoral nature—turning (of course) upon the physical condition of the (truly) abandoned stunner therein depicted. Hence it is in broad Northumbrian.

Our people send you regards etc. I am glad you begin to read V. Hugo aright. My sisters are already among his faithful worshippers— Edith above all. Get her to speak of him some day, and see the effect of my training. Cérige—(Book V. of 'Contemplations') [4] is our great favorite here. Love to people, and tell Topsy I am growing—I may say fast, so I shall keep my promise and look over his head—I really am—après!

Yours affectionately,
A. C. Swinburne

Item—my handwriting (as you see) improves rapidly—this will give you a faint idea of my present appearance—ἀκερσεκόμης [5]

2. Sir Fretful Plagiary in *The Critic*.

3. Perhaps an allusion to "Burd Margaret" (Bonchurch, *3*, 352–57), of which a holograph early version with many revisions is in the Rutgers University Library.

4. Published in 1856.

5. Liddell and Scott's *Greek-English Lexicon:* " 'With unshorn hair,' i.e. ever young (for Greek youths wore long hair till they reached manhood)"—said of Phoebus in the Homeric "Hymn to Apollo."

Shew nobody this work of art—
Burn the letter—if you disobey I'll quarrel with you for life.

15. TO WILLIAM BELL SCOTT [1]

MS: Yale.

Capheaton, Saturday, August 20[?] [1859]

My dear Mr. Scott

Lady Trevelyan [2] shewed me the invitation you made me some days back. If Tuesday would do for you I would come in by the mail-cart which comes by us about 8 P.M. If that time will not do perhaps you will tell me—as any day is the same to me: only on Friday I am promised to Wallington. I want of all things to see [the] Brabazon.[3] I only know it by references. This is shamefully short notice to ask to be taken on, but you must excuse a party who has been prostrate through catching awful colds etc. with reading French romances on the wet grass about Wallington.[4]—item, who makes this portentous

1. (1811–90), poet and painter, like D. G. Rossetti (though his inferior in both arts), whom he had known since 1847 or 1848. Scott taught in a government school in Newcastle from 1843 to 1864, and when the Trevelyans, urged on by Ruskin, roofed in the courtyard at Wallington in 1855, it was Scott who painted for the new hall a series of pictures illustrating the history of Northumberland.

2. (1816–66), born Pauline Jermyn. She married Sir Walter Calverley Trevelyan (1797–1879), 6th baronet, in 1835. Wallington, the Trevelyan home, is only a few miles from Capheaton.

3. A picture by Hercules Brabazon (1821–1906), a water-colorist.

4. Scott, in a letter not dated but clearly composed during or just after this visit, wrote to Lady Trevelyan: "Is not young Swinburne a regular trump? Sara Gamp, Pre-Raphaelite hair and also this poetry took me rather by surprise. I rather think he *is* a poet, not merely by instinct of imitation associating with Morris and others. He read to me the ballad of a lady turned into a dragon ['The Worm of Spindle-stonheugh,' Bonchurch, *3*, 358–66], and his tragedy [either *The Queen-Mother*, Bonchurch, *7*, 1–200 or *Rosamond*, Bonchurch, *7*, 201–57] so far as it is gone. His ballad really is a ballad, not a fantastic mystical modern invention, and his play characters talk like reasonable or rather unreasonable people."

In another letter, dated "Wednesday morning" (perhaps Aug. 31, 1859) he wrote:

Capheaton
Saturday
Aug. 26.

My dear Mr. Scott

Lady Trevelyan showed
me the invitation you made me some
days back – If Tuesday would do for you
I would come in by the mail-cart
which comes by us about 8 p.m. If that

[thirteen lines omitted]

just five minutes to post-time. I dare
say there is as little grammar as good writing
here yes truly
Algernon C. Swinburne

Extracts from letter 15

scrawl, being just five minutes to post-time. I dare say there is as little grammar as good writing.

Ever yours truly,
Algernon C. Swinburne

16. EDWARD BURNE JONES TO SWINBURNE

MS: British Museum.

24 Russell Place, Fitzroy Square, W.
[August 25, 1859] [1]

Dear little Carrots

. . . When are you coming back? by this day month I shall be on my way to Florence I believe with Val [Prinsep] and Charley Faulkner [2] and if you don't come to town before then it will be next term before I see you, but I am sure to be in Oxford one or more Sundays in the term. The Revd. Hatch goes to Canada this month as Dean, professor and I don't know what else with an enormous income, and an influence, which, as he truly observes, is of more weight than any amount of riches.—When you hear of me next I shall have turned humbug by profession—it pays my dear fellow—our friend has got the right end of philosophy—certainly damnation is a drawback, but what would you? everything [*word illegible*] and isn't £600 a year cheaply got at a year's outlay in cant and humbug. I feel a respect for him but look upon him as damned. —it's the way of my friends. . . .

Toujours very affectionately,
Ned Jones

"I enjoyed him here very much, and heard all his poetry. But at present there seem only two people in the world to him, Topsy [William Morris] and Rossetti, and only those books or things they admire or appropriate will he entertain. The only exception to this is unhappily French literature. I imagine it will be very difficult to find a means of changing this before its natural term expires according to the laws of poetical enthusiasm at twenty-two." (Both letters are in the Trevelyan Papers at Wallington.)

1. The date is taken from the postmark on the envelope, which is addressed to Swinburne at Capheaton. This transcript omits a full page at the beginning of the letter, and a few words at the end, the omitted passages being concerned with technical details of pictures and mixing paint.

2. C. J. Faulkner (1834–92) was one of the Birmingham colony at Oxford (where he became a dean of degrees and mathematical lecturer) and later a member of the firm of Morris, Marshall, Faulkner, and Co.

17. TO JOHN NICHOL

MS: National Library of Scotland.

East Dene, September 24 [1859]

Dear Nichol

You will not mind my writing you a word to express my sorrow. That it is deep and real you will not doubt. I do not think that among those who had known as much of your father's kindness as was shown to me there can be any who had more reverence and affection for him than I had.[1] I will not trouble you with anything further to read: you know how thoroughly I wish I could write or do anything that might be to you of the least use or comfort. If it is unpleasant to you to receive this, you will forgive me the useless writing of it.

Affectionately yours,
Algernon C. Swinburne

18. TO LADY JANE HENRIETTA SWINBURNE

Text: Leith, pp. 51–52.

Union, November [1859]

I hope, although I have had no news of it, that you are safely settled at Pau: I hope when you have time, to get a line from one of you. I have myself been rather busy since I last heard from A. and E.[1] at Tours, in working (unhappily too late) for my first examination in Classics—which turns out a failure. I *had* hoped to get it done, and have my way clear to work for honours in the spring. As it is, I shall have them both on my hands at once, and I need not add, feel ashamed of myself. In my history work it will I hope make no difference; and at all events I have it only to think of just now; and shall be able to go at it in peace. Being here, I can ask the 'historical' authorities how to set at it, with a special view to their requirements.

There is no other Oxford news that I know of, of equal importance with *my* work, prospects, etc., except the presence of a Gracious Prince of Wales and the rapturous excitement of a favoured city. He comes here to hear the speeches and throws the President of the Union into a feeble but happy ecstasy; filling also the local papers with

1. J. P. Nichol died Sep. 19.

1. Two of his sisters—Edith and either Alice or Isabel (Abba).

26

marvellous rumours of his dress, dinner, manners, suite and behaviour. . . .[2]

19. TO WILLIAM BELL SCOTT

MS: Yale.

Navestock Parsonage, Pierceford, Essex,
December 16, 1859

My dear Scott

You may suppose that your letter of the sixth was some time in finding me here, where I am staying for some weeks to read law and history for my degree, which comes on in the spring. I have got nothing ready for publication yet, and when I have I see no chance of getting funds to defray the cost—much less of discovering a judicious publisher to take the risk. Sech is life! I had a jolly fortnight in London,—left the Hogarth very flourishing,—and saw D.G.R.'s new poems and pictures. I daresay you have heard of his head in oils of a stunner with flowers in her hair, and marigolds behind it?[1] She is more stunning than can be decently expressed. I read my 'Rosamond' to the party in question and he was pleased to approve of it much more than it deserves.[2] I have put in an addition to it in the comic line—viz. a kid—which I want to shew you as I am rather proud of him. It wanted some *chaff* in it. Besides this, and some more of that interminable 'Catherine' I have written a new ballad so indecent that it beats all the rest and is nearly up to Blake's Klopstock.[3] N.B. I have

2. The Prince of Wales had entered residence at Oxford in the middle of October. On Nov. 9, according to the *Oxford Chronicle and Berks and Bucks Gazette*, town and gown celebrated his eighteenth birthday. Dinner was given to hordes (2,000 to 3,000) of school children, and £500 went for fireworks in the Merton Fields. "Three splendid balloons, appropriately designated 'Victoria,' 'Prince Albert,' and 'The Prince of Wales,' ascended during the evening, rose slowly into the heavens, dropping brilliant stars of variegated colours. . . . The concluding piece . . . seems to have elicited universal satisfaction. In the centre was the inscription—'Long live the Prince!' surrounded with circles of variegated fires, and a large figure of His Royal Highness."

1. "Bocca Baciata," a portrait of Fanny Cornforth.

2. *Rosamond* and the "interminable Catherine," as he calls *The Queen-Mother*, were published in one volume late in 1860. The comic afterthought was "Arthur, a boy of the choir."

3. The ballad is unidentified. Swinburne would have read Blake's "Klopstock" ("When Klopstock England defied") in the Blake manuscript owned by Gabriel Rossetti.

got *Blake's Dante*—seven plates—stunners. Also his Job. I shall bring them north next year. I wish to goodness I was going up this winter but I shan't be let, with that blessed Oxford ahead.

Have you seen Victor Hugo's Légende des Siècles? [4] It's the grandest book that has been published there or here for years. The mediaeval poems in it—for instance 'Ratbert'—simply whip creation into mush and molasses.

Item—I have got the immortal Whitman's Leaves of Grass and there are jolly good things in it, I allow. Do lend yours to Lady Trevelyan. Also entreat her to abstain from Hugo's 'Ratbert' till I come and read it to her.

Are you doing nothing yourself in the poetical way? I wish you would carry out your project on Savonarola. Don't you think a good dramatic subject would be Mary Stuart's amour with Chatelet? [5] one might end with cutting off his head on the stage. I want to find facts about it: do you know of any?

As for the 'Justinian' tapestry at Joyous Gard I have never found out any thing about it, and so can't write to our ex-host. But there *is* some French romance. By the way I have got such a beautiful new old one—'Floire and Blanceflour.' [6]

Have you begun Balzac yet? I found Gabriel Rossetti in the thick of him and appreciating him very justly.[7] You would rejoice in the Etudes Philosophiques which I have just purchased.

I have made a little acquaintance with Martineau (R.B. the painter),[8] do you know him, he seems very nice.

4. A series of poems first issued in 1859, enlarged in 1867, and enlarged again (finally) in 1883. Swinburne praised it publicly in the *Fortnightly Review*, Oct. 1883. His notice (Bonchurch, *13*, 112–50) said that "History will forget the name of Bonaparte before humanity forgets the name of Ratbert."

5. A *lapsus calami*. *Chastelard* (Bonchurch, *8*, 1–133) was published in 1865.

6. A copy of this twelfth-century French romance (*Floire et Blanceflor*, ed. E. du Meril, Paris, 1856) was in Sotheby's sale of the Swinburne library in 1916.

7. G. P. Boyce, the painter, recorded in his diary on Oct. 15, 1859, that he "Went to see Fanny Cornforth, and took her some apples and walnuts. She told me Rossetti had had a call from Annie Miller, who had left a card. He is in the habit, she says, of sitting in a large chair o'nights reading Balzac's novels" (*Extracts from Boyce's Diaries: 1851–1875*, The Old Water-Colour Society's Nineteenth Annual Volume, ed. Randall Davies, 1941, p. 34).
Balzac's *Comédie humaine* is divided into three parts—"Études de mœurs," "Études philosophiques," and "Études analytiques."

8. Robert Braithwaite Martineau (1826–69), a painter with slight Pre-Raphaelite affinities, had worked with Holman Hunt and was a friend of the Rossetti brothers.

You must have had a splendid autumn of it with all your visitors. As for me on leaving you I had a very good night journey and turned up in London in good time next day. Will you write to me again when you have time? it is a true work of mercy, shut out as I suddenly am from society except that of a very passable parson I admit (For he worships Sidonia).[9] To be sure I am within running distance of London. Still it is a great and rare pleasure to hear a human voice in writing. Give Lady Trevelyan my filial respects and tell her I have been living in a raging vortex of Popery but remain free as the winkle of my country in his shelly lair, or the still mite in his home of cheese.[10] Did you know that old Meinhold died a Papist? It is very sad. Nevertheless I shall see the hoary hell-beast called Pius IX. hanged by the neck. What do you think of my knave Beauharnais? [11] D.G.R. and Ned Jones have entered [the] rifle-corps.[12] Isn't that a lark? Excuse this long scrawl. With best remembrances to Mrs. Scott I am

Yours most truly,

A. C. Swinburne

9. The "passable parson" was William Stubbs, vicar of Navestock (see below, Letter 20). J. W. Meinhold (1797–1851) was a German theologian and writer whose *Sidonia von Bork, die Klosterhexe,* translated by Lady Wilde as *Sidonia the Sorceress,* was a book for which Gabriel Rossetti had (in his brother's phrase) a "positive passion." According to J. Saxon Mills, *Sir Edward Cook* (1921), p. 282 n., Swinburne told E. T. Cook in 1901 that it was a "real work of genius, but very horrible, the most horrible in literature."

10. Dickens' *Martin Chuzzlewit,* chap. 21. "Sech is life," the second sentence in this letter, is Gampese (*Martin Chuzzlewit,* chap. 29).

11. Napoleon III, son of Louis Bonaparte and Hortense de Beauharnais. In referring to him as "Beauharnais" or the "Creole" (see below, Letter 25) Swinburne, like his other denigrators (especially Hugo), questioned his paternity, implying that though he was certainly a Beauharnais (and Hortense had Creole blood), his claim to the awful name of Bonaparte was less sure. The libel was not without foundation, and among the several nominees gossip gave the best credentials to the Dutch Admiral Verhuel.

12. Great Britain was panicky with fear of a French invasion. Tennyson's "The War" ("Riflemen, Form!"), printed in *The Times* (May 9, 1859), was considered a "trumpet call," and volunteer corps, of which the Artists' Rifle Corps was easily the jauntiest, were formed everywhere. Scott, in the manuscript notes for his memoir (owned by Mrs. Gilbert Troxell, who has kindly allowed me to extract passages), wrote: "If D.G.R. ever joined the rifle-corps, he must have speedily dropt his weapon. E.B.J. made a pretty good soldier, but I feel certain Gabriel never fired a shot or attempted doing so."

20. TO LADY JANE HENRIETTA SWINBURNE

Text: Leith, pp. 52-53.

Navestock,

Ash Wednesday [February 22] 1860

It is a pity that all the law they make us learn is mediaeval and obsolete or I might cut out L[ongbourne] [1] and *do* the family on my own hook. By the by, if you want to get a better account of the whole question of history at Oxford, I recommend you to get an article by a great friend of Mr. Stubbs published in No. 1 of 'Bentley's Quarterly Review,' March/59.[2] I have just read it and I think it would interest you if you care to know about my reading and chances.

You may have seen in the *Guardian* that there is a prize at Oxford of £50 (I think) for a poem on the subject of Sir John Franklin and

1. Charles Rankin Vickerman Longbourne, of Longbourne and Stevens, Lincoln's Inn Fields, was the Swinburne family solicitor.
Late in 1859 occurred one of the first of the decisions to do something *"with and for* Algernon." He was sent from Oxford to study with William Stubbs (1825–1901), the learned vicar of Navestock, who became Regius Professor of Modern History at Oxford in 1866, Bishop of Chester in 1884, and Bishop of Oxford in 1889, and whose reputation today rests rather upon his constitutional history than upon his episcopizing. At Navestock the vicar "occasionally took pupils," wrote W. H. Hutton (*Letters of William Stubbs,* 1904, p. 50). "The most distinguished of these was Mr. Algernon Swinburne. He came at the end of 1859, to read Modern History especially. . . . He was a pupil of Mr. Jowett—'who is not the tutor I had selected for him, and hoped he would have been with,' wrote his father, Admiral Swinburne—and who described him as 'in some respects the most singular young man I have ever known,' and was apparently much distressed in the presence of genius to which he was unaccustomed. 'He has extraordinary powers of imitation in writing,' he [i.e. Jowett] declared, 'and he composes (as I am told) Latin mediaeval hymns, French vaudevilles, as well as endless English poems, with the greatest facility.' Mr. Jowett deplored the influence of the Pre-Raphaelite artists, and considered that no good—scholastically—could come of him 'unless he can be hindered from writing poetry.'
"After other observations which sufficiently displayed his want of sympathy, Mr. Jowett concluded with the following 'sentiment'—
'I incline to believe that the greatest power that older persons have over the young is sympathy with them, especially as they grow up towards manhood. If we don't allow for the strange varieties of character, and often for their extreme, almost unintelligible unlikeness to ourselves, we lose influence over them, and they become alienated from fancying that they are not understood.' "

2. The anonymous article, "Historical Study at Oxford," seems to be by E. A. Freeman (1823–92), the indefatigable historian, though this ascription is not supported by W. R. W. Stephens, his biographer and bibliographer.

the late discoveries.[3] I have written for it and shown it to Mr. Stubbs, who advises it to be sent in, and declares it *ought* to have the prize. I wish it may, but very greatly doubt. (Don't suppose I gave it too much time: it didn't take two mornings' work.) As there must be two copies (for there is a law against sending in such things in one's hand-writing lest the examiners should know whose the poem is before the prize is awarded), I will send you mine as soon as the other copy is made, if you would like to see it. If I could get money to publish any others, or some of them, which have been very successful in MS. lately, I should do myself the honour of reading you such select passages as not being too mediaeval or Shakespearian are not disqualified from family entertainment. I shall be anxious to see how you like the one mentioned above.

21. TO WILLIAM BELL SCOTT

MS: Yale.

Navestock Parsonage, Romford, Essex,
February 25, 1860

Dear Scott [1]

I send you the Livre Mystique in the sincere hope that a gracious Providence may enable you to make head or tail of it. It is my belief

3. The "Supplement" to the *Guardian* (Feb. 8, 1860), p. 4, announced a prize of £50 "to be awarded to the writer of the best English poem on 'The Life, the Character and the Death of the heroic seaman, Sir John Franklin, with special reference to the time, place, and discovery of his death.'" Thanks to Lafourcade, we now know that Swinburne's poem "The Death of Sir John Franklin" (Bonchurch, *1*, 1–8) came off second best in *this* competition, not, as Gosse had thought, in the Newdigate competition on the same subject in 1858.

Sir John Franklin (1786–1847) set out with the *Erebus* and *Terror* in May 1845, amid great fanfare, to find the Northwest Passage. After a few months the expedition, which had been provisioned for three years, was heard from no more, and in 1848 a series of expeditions of search and (it was hoped) succor was begun on an unexampled scale. It soon became clear that the explorers had perished, and the accretion of evidence continued to swell until, in 1857, Lady Franklin personally commissioned a search party to find out the whole truth. Early in 1859 the actual remains of her husband's expedition were found.

1. Swinburne had visited the Scotts on his way south. On Jan. 3, 1860, Scott wrote to Lady Trevelyan: "Who do you think has just come in? Algernon on his way home, prepared to read Hugo to you till you confess him the greatest genius that ever lived, or at least since Shakespeare" (Trevelyan Papers, Wallington). During this visit Scott began the portrait of Swinburne that he completed in October.

it is the latter, and the Seraphic individual a lusus naturae, hermaphrodite, quasi-eunuch, or—something. You know I cling to physical interpretations. I am bound to add I have never got through it. 'Madame Bovary' which I am reading is far more in my line—I regard it as one of the most perfect and complete books I know.[2] Pray get and read it—it is in the shilling Lévy series.

I have just finished dressing up 'Catherine' with a view to publication either in the spring or autumn.[3] Keep this a dead secret, please, as I want no responsible ears to hear it—not even at Wallington. I am in dealings with Pickering, who is willing to do it. If I must pay I must, but I shall beat him down to the lowest charge in a way worthy of Sir Barnes Newcome. If Catherine were not quite a failure I might bring out a collected volume upon its heels next year. It would be such a comfort to get the stage clear for new works, and all the old either published or burnt. Had I but the dross of Mammon the British public should hear and tremble. Accept meantime two out of a set of poems addressed 'To J. M. Ludlow, Reviewer': my knave, who slavers Tennyson and spits up at Hugo.[4]

2. Balzac's *Seraphita, Les Proscrits,* and *Louis Lambert* were published in 1835 in two volumes called *Le Livre mystique.* Flaubert's *Madame Bovary* appeared in 1857.

3. That is, *The Queen-Mother,* which, with *Rosamond,* was issued in Dec. 1860, by B. M. Pickering (1836–78), and then, under circumstances still obscure, was at once withdrawn and reissued by Moxon. The "collected volume" did not appear till 1866, a fact that tells enough about the success of "Catherine." Sir Barnes Newcome is a contemptible snob, mean in mind and pocketbook, in Thackeray's novel *The Newcomes.*

4. John Malcolm Forbes Ludlow (1821–1911), the social reformer and writer, spent his youth and, as Swinburne thought, drove a hard bargain with his education in France. A trip to Martinique taught him to abhor slavery, and he was also much concerned with reform in India. He later became one of the initiators of the Christian Socialist movement, and, along with F. D. Maurice, Charles Kingsley, and others, helped to found the Working Men's College. The "slaver" and "spit" that drove Swinburne to verse were Ludlow's two reviews in *Macmillan's Magazine* in Nov. 1859—"Moral Aspects of Mr. Tennyson's 'Idylls of the King'" (pp. 63–72) and "Victor Hugo's 'Legend of the Ages'" (pp. 131–41), which weighed the two poets in the scales of orthodoxy. Tennyson emerged as a "Christian poet" and Hugo as "un grand poète manqué." This set of poems is preserved in the Brotherton Collection, Leeds University, and the remaining four are printed here by the kind permission of the Librarian.

(1)   Of Ludlow

Hast thou seen, O J. M. Ludlow,
Thames, when ebb tide leaves the mud low;

1.

Because you eat the dung of Tennyson,
Are we to call that dung roast venison!

2.

Ludlow—who writes by some such fate as mocks
An eunuch with hereditary pox,
Whose style of internecine English-French,
Like burnt-out tallow, sputters into stench—
Crawls here and sucks and nibbles. Give him food:
Give him your dung: he does not want your blood.

These are the milder specimens. The others may rather be conceived
than described. They are in bold allegory.

With best remembrances

Ever yours most truly,
Algernon C. Swinburne

P.S. I had a very good voyage south, and saw Ned Jones in my passage through London. We were delayed a day off Shields and could
not get over the harbour-bar, which was our only mishap.[5]

Then the stink begins to be;
But the stink that is in thee
The strong stink of thy strange itch
Shall in time outstink Fleet Ditch:
Shall outstink the patient gods,
Space, and time's large periods.

(3)   To the same

You would touch *him!* Oh! would you, sir!
O stupid beast, yes, stupider
Than an owl's emptied [?] eye-socket!
Because the Devil calls you pet?
Spell that in French and find your name.
An ass's hoof has sense and shame
And is a capable live thing
Compared to you, you cess-dropping.
The rope's end laid about your shoulder
Shall hug your throat ere two months older.

(4) A toad spat as the sun went down his road:
'So! I have spat the sun out,' said the toad.

(6) Shakespeare's a fool and Hugo's a quack;
Ropes are not ropes, nor Ludlow's back a back.

5. Scott's manuscript notes for his memoir (owned by Mrs. Gilbert Troxell) comment here: "This voyage between the Tyne and Thames was his choice instead
of the railway, the sea being to him a nursing mother. During his stay in the north

P.P.S. Apropos, it may be worth mention that Jones is, and has put me, on the scent of the origin of that infernal lie about Rossetti which I told you had put me out so awfully to hear of. No fellow who ever had spoken to DGR would have believed it a minute— unless below the kickings of a Christian; but it is as well to know that every link of the chain of lies is severally damned by its own contradictions, and proved rather more than hopelessly impossible. I am ashamed, even for the sake of giving you the pleasure of knowing what we know, to have written so much on such a skunk of a subject.[6]

Now let it go to hell and take its forger and its hawkers with it. Amen and Amen.

22. TO LADY JANE HENRIETTA SWINBURNE

Text: Leith, pp. 53–54.

Navestock, March 11, 1860

. . . As soon as I can get my verses [1] copied you shall have them— with much gratitude for your generous offer. But I have thought— or rather Mr. Stubbs started the shining idea—that if I send you one copy some of the others might copy it out for me—which would make all safe: and as June the 1st is the day for sending it, it would give plenty of time.

I have the honour to announce that the one really awful piece of work before me is now behind me. I have completed my analysis of Blackstone's law.[2] All that remains is by comparison to the hard parts of that work as pleasant reading as Dumas. . . . As to my Ox-

---

he and Commander Jermin set out with me to visit Grace Darling's lighthouse and the scene of her heroical exploit previous to my painting it for Wallington Hall. It was a rough day, I was, as usual, very ill, while he and of course the sailor were enjoying the tossing of the waves. When the time came for his Oxford examination we heard nothing of it. His family for some reason had set their hearts on his making a college success. His preoccupation with other matters, his own poetry particularly, as his letters indicate, may account for their disappointment. <When his Atalanta appeared, with the excellent Greek in front of it, it is said some of the dons swore the lines were not his.>"

6. "I now entirely forget," Scott scribbled in a footnote to this discreet passage, "what supposed libellous report this alludes to." But see below, Letter 93.

1. "The Death of Sir John Franklin" (see above, Letter 20).

2. Swinburne's notes on parts of Blackstone's *Commentaries* survive in a private collection.

ford sojourn, I can tell you now. About a week after Easter I go up.[3] If all is well I shall have to stay the whole term. For the little examination is at the beginning and the great one at the end. . . .

23. TO LADY JANE HENRIETTA SWINBURNE

Text: Leith, pp. 54–55.

Navestock, April 15, 1860

I am so busy just now and in so many ways that you must make excuses for my letters if they are short and few. This week probably I return to Oxford: when there I will tell you how to direct to me.

I think, thanks mainly to Mr. Stubbs' help and trouble, I may expect to return with a good piece of the work done for good. As I told you before, the hardest technical work and such as would be difficult to do alone is gone through. An American book on International Laws [1] is my chief enemy just now, but I hope to settle him in a few days.

. . . When I have done with routine work I think of taking *periods* to read in contemporary books if I can keep up my present leaning towards history. I got out (the last time I was at Wallington) all sorts of things about Mary Stuart of the most exciting kind, down to an inventory of her gowns, which gave me great satisfaction, as they were very nice colours, and showed she had an eye for painting.[2] I am in the meantime taking in (at Oxford) either Charlemagne or St. Louis—possibly both. That is the sort of history I like—live biographical chronicle not dead constitutional records like the respected Hallam's,[3] over whom Mr. Stubbs and I (neither without execrations) have been breaking our teeth more or less for months. . . .

3. Easter fell on Apr. 8.

1. Henry Wheaton, *History of the Law of Nations* (New York, 1845).

2. *Lettres, instructions et mémoires de Marie Stuart, reine d'Écosse; publiés sur les originaux et les manuscrits du State Paper Office de Londres et des principales archives et bibliothèques de l'Europe, et accompagnés d'un résumé chronologique par le Prince Alexandre Labanoff* (7 vols. London, 1844). An "Inventaire de la garde-robe et autres effets de Marie Stuart et listes de ses serviteurs" is included in the last volume.

3. *The Constitutional History of England from the Accession of Henry VII to the Death of George II* (first published in 1827) by Henry Hallam (1777–1859). Stubbs objected to Hallam's secular bias.

24. TO LADY JANE HENRIETTA SWINBURNE

Text: Leith, pp. 55–57.

Oxford, June 5, 1860

I got your letter yesterday and was very glad to hear of you safe in London after all the rain, wind and snow. I am glad, too, that now you are in England I can write to you myself word of what I would not have told you while at a distance. About the beginning of last week I had a bad fall from a horse in leaping a gate. It was in the end lucky that I alighted full on my chin and the lower part of my face—but as some teeth were splintered, the jaw sprained and the lips cut up it was not pleasant. For a week nearly I have been kept in bed and fed on liquids, and still I can eat nothing but crumb of bread and such like. But I am up to-day and able to write, and quite well otherwise (*jaws* excepted) only of course not very strong. The Dr. *did* last week prohibit ideas of trying to bring my ill-fated work through to some end or other (certainly the Fates *are* against my reading for honours in history), but I must stay a day or two longer to try. If I really *cannot* do enough to get fairly through and take a decent place in the list—then of course I shall not try but come up to you in London this week. If not (that is if I do go in) I shall be 10 days or a fortnight longer . . . Mrs. Johnson [1] has been most kind—calling constantly to ask after and sit with me during the past week: I persuaded her not to send word of my accident through—until I could write myself to tell you there was no danger or serious hurt. (I hope even the cut and sprain will be well when I see you.) I thought it was not news to meet and worry you at second-hand on a first arrival. . . . [2]

Please tell me how long you stay in London and what is your next move. If I don't try (as everybody advises me not *to*) I shall be able to travel this week.

With best love to all

I am ever your affectionate son,
A. C. Swinburne

1. Doubtless the widow of Manuel John Johnson (1805–59), Radcliffe Observer, who, according to Gosse, had been a friend to Swinburne.

2. The remainder of this letter is based on the facsimile in Leith, facing page 150, and seems to belong here.

25. TO JOHN NICHOL

Text: *Early Letters.*

East Dene, Bonchurch, Isle of Wight,
September 18 [1860]

My dear Nichol

I send this to the above direction in pure despair, as you vouchsafe me not a line where to direct you in Edinburgh. Perhaps some familiar demon of that hell to which you remain half-linked may know your direction and forward it. A misplaced but conscientious zeal for my rashly given promise impels me to this act. I am leaving for Mentone in a fortnight for the winter. (Now had you and I learnt the use of rifles, we might go together and be of some use at Rome or Venice.)

I want to know where your copy of an immortal work [1] now well-nigh out of diabolic hands is to be delivered. Write me word, when you *do* get it, what extent of badness you think it reaches—what exact medium point between Martin Tupper and Stanyan Bigg.[2] My Barabbas is Pickering (give me credit for the *Byronic* appellative) [3] a reasonable and friendly Jew thus far. I wish you could have looked me up in London, where I fell under medical hands. I am very well now.

What do you think of Italian matters? Item—of to-day's new failure with regard to the . . . Creole? [4] Why could not he shoot straight, and rid the world of the—Decency forbids me to pursue the subject.

As for Naples, is it sweet? Is there anything like it in history? Why the King of Naples is not hanged by this time I can't think.[5]

Yours most sincerely,
A. C. Swinburne

1. *The Queen-Mother and Rosamond.*

2. John Stanyan Bigg (1828–65), whose poetry is associated with the "Spasmodic School."

3. For the quip, attributed to Byron, that "Barabbas was a publisher" see Samuel Smiles' *A Publisher and His Friends, Memoir and Correspondence of the Late John Murray* (2 vols. London and New York, 1891), *1,* 336.

4. Napoleon III (see above, Letter 19), at whom a would-be assassin fired a pistol in Toulon on Sep. 13.

5. Francis II had abandoned Naples to Garibaldi, who entered the city on Sep. 7.

26. TO PAULINE, LADY TREVELYAN

MS: Trevelyan Papers, Wallington. Published: Bonchurch, *18*, 8–11*.

(Maison Laurenti) Mentone,
January 19 [1861]

My dear Lady Trevelyan
    (Which a nice place it is to date from) [1]
Many thanks for your letter, which a comfortable letter it was, but
creates violent wishes to get back to England. For of *all the* beasts
of countries I ever see, I reckon this about caps them. I also strongly
notion that there ain't a hole in St. Giles' which isn't a paradise to
this. How any professing Christian as has been in France and England can look at it, passes me. It is more like the landscape in
Browning's Childe Roland than anything I ever heerd tell on. A
calcined, scalped, rasped, scraped, flayed, broiled, powdered, leprous,
blotched, mangy, grimy, parboiled country, *without* trees, water,
grass, fields—*with* blank, beastly, senseless olives and orange-trees like
a mad cabbage gone indigestible; it is infinitely liker hell than
earth, and one looks for tails among the people. And such females
with hunched bodies and crooked necks carrying tons on their
heads and looking like death taken seasick. Arrrrrr. Grrrrr.
    Wal, I feel kind of better after that. But the aggravation of hav-
ing people about one who undertake to admire these big stone-
heaps of hills and hideous split-jawed gorges! I must say (in
Carlylese) that 'the (scenery) is of the sort which must be called, *not*
in the way of profane swearing, but of grave, earnest and sorrowing
indignation, the d----- sort.' (I would rather die than write it at
length.)
    I am very glad you like my book; if it will do anything like sell I
shall publish my shorter poems soon: they are quite ready. I have
done a lot of work since I saw you—Rossetti says some of my best
pieces: one on St. Dorothy and Theophilus (I wanted to try my
heathen hands at a Christian subject, you comprehend, and give a pat
to the Papist interest); also a long one out of Boccaccio,[2] that was
begun ages ago and let drop. Item—many songs and ballads. I am
trying to write prose, which is very hard, but I want to make a few

1. The style is Mrs. Gamp's, in *Martin Chuzzlewit*.

2. "St. Dorothy" and "The Two Dreams" (Bonchurch, 2, 1–29) were first published in *PB1*. An early version of the latter, "The White Hind," exists in manuscript; a few lines are printed in *A Swinburne Library*, p. 8.

stories each about three or six pages long.[3] Likewise a big one about my blessedest pet which her initials is Lucrezia Estense Borgia. Which soon I hope to see her hair as is kep at Milan in spirits in a bottle.[4]

Which puts me in mind of a favour I want to ask of you. In the beginning (probably) of February I am going to Venice and through all the chief towns I can, and perhaps to Florence *if* I could find out whether Mr. Browning is there.[5] Now there is nobody within reach who knows as much of art as a decently educated cockroach; and I want you to have the extreme goodness to tell me what to go to and how to see Venice—buildings especially as well as pictures—before it gets bombarded—out of the British tourist's fashion. If you are not awfully busy would you write me a letter which I could get say by the week after next? considering I have read no books and am not content with the British Murray.

I wish I *had* anything to do besides my proper work if I can't live by it. Which it's very well to pitch into a party like brother Stockdolloger,[6] but what *is* one to do? I can't go to the bar: much good I should do if I did. You know there is really no profession one can take up with and go on working. Item—poetry is quite work enough for any one man. Item—who is there that is anything *besides* a poet at this day except Hugo? And though his politics is excellent and his opinions is sound, he does much better when he sticks to his work and makes Ratbert and Ruy Blas. *I* don't want to sit in rooms and write, gracious knows. Do you think a small thing in the stump-orator [7] line would do? or a Grace-Walker? [6] Seriously, what is there

3. "Dead Love" (Bonchurch, *17*, 11–16) first appeared in Oct. 1862, in *Once A Week*. The pamphlet-issue dated 1864 is, according to John Carter and Graham Pollard (*An Enquiry, into the Nature of Certain Nineteenth Century Pamphlets*, London and New York, 1934, pp. 269–71) a piracy; and, according to T. J. Wise (Bonchurch, *20*, 24–28) the piracy itself was pirated in 1904 or earlier. "The Portrait," "The Chronicle of Queen Fredegond," and "The Marriage of Monna Lisa" (Bonchurch, *17*, 3–8, 19–57, 61–64) were all privately printed in 1909. Swinburne projected a *Triameron*, modeled on Boccaccio, in which the first three of these pieces, and doubtless the fourth as well, were to be included.

4. Another Gampism (*Martin Chuzzlewit*, chap. 52). *The Chronicle of Tebaldeo Tebaldei* was edited by Randolph Hughes in 1942, Golden Cockerel Press. The Borgian hair was to be seen in the Ambrosian Library (see below, Letter 52).

5. But, as Gosse points out, he was in Rome, not in Florence.

6. See below, Letter 39.

7. That is, political, as in Carlyle's essay "Stump-Orator" in *Latter-Day Pamphlets*.

you would have one take to? It's a very good lecture, but it's not practical. Nor yet it ain't fair. It's bage.[8]

Have you heard the report that old Landor is going to republish *all* his suppressed libels in verse and prose, and more new ones? Isn't he a marvel of heaven's making? I suppose a British public will bust at once if it's nipped and frizzled and churned up to an eternal smash any more: which by the by America seems to be at this writing.

I am in love with Paris—you know I never saw it before. What a stunner above stunners that Giorgione party with the music in the grass and the water-drawer is—that Gabriel made such a sonnet on.[9] Then that Stephen preaching of Carpaccio! I never heard a word of it; but it seems to me lovely, with wonders of faces. Item the Velasquez. Item things in general. Item the little Uccello up at the top of the gallery.[10]

My parents should no doubt send all proper messages, but are probably in bed and (let us hope) enjoying a deep repose. For the hour is midnight. On this account I will now conclude with my duty and respects to Sir Walter; and am

Yours most sincerely and with a filial heart,

Al. C. Swinburne

I wish to goodness you would send me out some eligible companions. I shall have to go alone to Turin. For the English here are mainly false friends. Don't you think we shall yet live to see the last Austrian emperor hung? Is Garibaldi the greatest man since Adam, or is he not?

8. Gampese for *base*.

9. The remainder of the manuscript at Wallington is in the hand of Sir George Otto Trevelyan.

10. The pictures are Giorgione's "Le Concert champêtre" (Rossetti's sonnet "For a Venetian Pastoral," written in 1849, was first published in *Poems,* 1870), Carpaccio's "Preaching of St. Stephen," and (probably) Velasquez's "Philip IV of Spain." The Uccello is evidently a misidentification. According to John Pope-Hennessy (*The Complete Works of Paolo Uccello,* 1950), the Louvre has two Uccellos, part of "The Rout of San Romano" (180–316 cm.) and "Founders of Florentine Art" (42–210 cm.), neither of which can properly be called "little." Nor was there in the Louvre in 1861 a picture then but not now ascribed to Uccello.

27. TO WILLIAM BELL SCOTT

MS: Yale.

Maison Laurenti, Mentone,
[Late] January [1861]

My dear Scott

I have just got your letter which has made I may say a green and gushing spot in the dullest of lives. I am very glad you approve the Queen Mother on revision. (What did Rossetti say of it to you? [1] You say you heard from him about it.) I quite give in about the style: the amount of fine talk is awful and quite wrong. I think of going over it and crossing out what I find faulty, but am afraid to begin. The two scenes I prefer myself are Act Four, Scene two, and Act Five, Scene three: and the best part I *fear* concerns the luckless M. de Soubise. On the whole I like Rosamond better than the five-acter. But I rejoice that you approve of Denise. My father's criticism is that it is altogether far worse than useless—most pernicious. I quote literally. Need I add that I have grave doubts as to the authenticity of the fifth commandment in that superannuated series of Jewish axioms vulgarly known as the Decalogue?

For my work here I have done three prose stories of a mediaeval kind, about as long and as moral as those of Boccaccio's. Item—compiled a chronicle of the life of Queen Fredegond—seven chapters. Item—about three-fourths of Chastelard in the rough. Item—furnished and corrected all loose (in either sense) poems lying by me. Item—nearly completed my French novel [2] by way of relaxation—

1. Rossetti was pretty tepid. "Have you seen a new vol.," he wrote (George Birkbeck Hill, *Letters of Dante Gabriel Rossetti to William Allingham, 1854–1870*, 1897, p. 238) on Nov. 1, 1860, "—however I'm not quite sure the copies are all out yet,—viz., 2 plays by Algernon Swinburne and did you meet him in London? He is very Topsaic, with a decided dash of *Death's Jest Book*, if you have read that improving book. But there's no mistake about some of his *poems*—much more, indeed, than these published plays." On Nov. 22 Rossetti admitted (p. 243) that "I haven't yet read the first play [*The Queen-Mother*], and may get found out. He read it me in MS." And on Nov. 29 he added (p. 249): "As for Swinburne's Plays, I don't think they will be to your liking. For my own part, I think he is much better suited to ballad-writing and such like, but there are real beauties in the plays too."

2. *La Fille du policeman* (which is still unpublished) was a great success with Swinburne's friends. Meredith, for one, wrote in 1861 (William M. Meredith, *Letters of George Meredith, collected and edited by his son*, 2 vols. 1912, *1*, 55): "Swinburne read me the other day his French novel . . . , the funniest rampingest satire on French novelists dealing with English themes that you can imagine. One chapter, 'Ce que peut se passer dans un Cab-Safety,' where Lord Whitestick, Bishop of Londres, ravishes the heroine, is quite marvelous. But he is not subtle; and I don't see any

41

don't talk of French horrors till you have read the hideous disclosures of English society contained therein! Rape, perjury, murder, opium, suicide, treason, Jesuitry, are the mildest ingredients. The atrocious conduct public and private of Prince Albert is branded with deserved and scathing indignation. As for the clergy—Should it come forth and be read, I would follow it up by a tale which I have vaguely conceived already.[3] A twin sister of Queen Victoria, kidnapped on her birth by consent of the late Sir R. Peel and Lord Chancellor Eldon for political reasons—to remove a rival candidate for the throne—grows up a common prostitute—is discovered in The Haymarket by the *Lor Maire* on a profligate excursion—informed of her origin claims her rights—is confronted with queen—queen swoons—the proofs of her birth bought and destroyed—the Abp of Canterbury solemnly perjures himself to the effect that she is an impostor—finally consumed by an ill-requited attachment to Lord John Russell, the heroine charcoals herself to death. There! At this rate I shall have a series of historical romances of the Victorian period rivalling Dumas. By the by do you know old Dumas is going —to China! I have a stunning photograph of him.

This country is more like hell than you can imagine—calcined, burnt, jaw-broken hills—dolorous gorges, hideous stone terraces—

---

internal centre from which springs anything that he does. He will make a great name, but whether he is to distinguish himself solidly as an Artist, I would not willingly prognosticate."

3. Parts at least of the manuscript of *La Sœur de la reine*, which is also unpublished, survive in a private collection. W. H. Mallock (*Memoirs of Life and Literature*, 1920, pp. 56–57) says that he once heard Swinburne regale an audience with an historical drama—"a sort of parody of what Victor Hugo might have written had he dramatized English events at the opening of the reign of Victoria." In this redaction "Miss Kitty," daughter of Lord John Russell out of Victoria, grows up a common prostitute but later has respectability of a sort thrust upon her (though she remains a "public scandal"). "With regard to her other so-called depravities," Mallock wrote, "nobody entertains a doubt, but one princely admirer, of broader mind than the rest, declares that in spite of these she is really the embodiment of everything that is divine in woman. 'She may,' he says, 'have done everything which might have made a Messalina blush, but whenever she looked at the sky, she murmured *God,* and whenever she looked at a flower she murmured *mother.*' "

John Bailey (Sarah Bailey, ed., *John Bailey, 1864–1931, Letters and Diaries*, 1935, p. 175) records an anecdote, which *may* belong here, "about Queen Victoria's confessing in French . . . to the Duchess of Kent her unfortunate lapse from virtue. Ce n'était pas un prince; ce n'était pas un milord, ni même *Sir R. Peel.* C'était un misérable du peuple, en nomme *Wordsworth,* qui m'a récité des vers de son *Excursion* d'une sensualité si chaleureuse qu'ils m'ont ébranlée—et je suis tombée."

beastly olives and orange trees and not a decent bit of wood in the country. As for grass—it ought to sell £10 a blade. Certainly the devil bespat it (perhaps worse) when it was made. If all Italy is like this north frontier, let us stick to France and England. I quite believe these two and Belgium the only beautiful and habitable countries. How lovely the Amians[?] land is between all those rivers. —I am going to Venice soon—perhaps in such carnival time as they will have. If you know will you tell me how to see it best? I am horribly ignorant and want to do as well as I can by myself. There is no one here but fools and parsons,—not to use the figure called tautology. I wish to God[?] and Garibaldi (tautology) that you could come with me or send some companionable fellow instead of you. This is a good time for going—you will not be eaten alive by mosquitos and Englishmen —the Venetians are selling all they can—pictures and all for pence, we are told. Then after spring it will all be on fire you know.

I send you my finished song for the revolution [4] of which you heard the first part, I think the last time we were together. I hope you will like it—I think it about my best lyrical piece of work. Please tell me soon about Venice after you get this—and if you do, tell me too what you have been working at, I want to know. With best remembrances to Mrs. Scott

I am ever your affectionate,
A. C. Swinburne

P.S. As for your criticism of that divine book of Balzac's—rot! [5] Madame Marneffe was the greatest of her sex and an honour to humanity.

4. "A Song in Time of Revolution, 1860" (Bonchurch, *1*, 270–73), published in the *Spectator* (June 28, 1862), and reprinted in *PB1*.

5. *La Cousine Bette* (1846).

28. TO RICHARD MONCKTON MILNES

MS: The Marchioness of Crewe. Five words quoted by Pope-Hennessy, p. 128.

16 Grafton Street, Fitzroy Square,
May 4 [1861]

My dear Sir [1]

I have only just received your note [2] and am afraid it may be too late for you to get this answer in time—but I shall be happy to come to-morrow [3]—and am

Yours truly,
A. C. Swinburne

---

1. This letter signals the first meeting, surely preordained, of Swinburne and Milnes (1809–85; created Baron Houghton, 1863), though how they became known to each other is still undetermined. Gosse (Bonchurch, *19*, 27) thought a Signora Fronduti may have introduced them, but suggested also (p. 71) Lady Trevelyan as a possibility. Lafourcade, *La Jeunesse, 1,* 76, citing *Some Reminiscences of William Michael Rossetti* (2 vols. New York, 1906), *1,* 225, reminds us that both were members of the Hogarth Club. Pope-Hennessy, p. 127, shrewdly nominates J. B. Payne (see below, Letter 71) of Edward Moxon and Co., the publisher of Milnes' *The Poetical Works of John Keats* and of Swinburne's *The Queen-Mother and Rosamond.*

2. G. P. Boyce recorded in his diary on this date: "Called on Jones. Swinburne there. Walked back with him as far as Piccadilly. . . . With Rossetti and Swinburne to Gilchrist's, 6 Cheyne Row. Madox Brown looked in also. Spent a most interesting evening looking over some books of Blake's showing marked originality and marvellous imagination."

3. The friendship with Milnes prospered, as anyone well acquainted with both men could have foreseen, for each found in the other something he required and sought. Swinburne needed above all things the deference yielded to genius instead of the tolerant admiration lavished upon precocity. As for Milnes, opportunity lay in his way and, as always, he found it. A month later, on June 5, Swinburne, along with Coventry Patmore, Aubrey de Vere, and (this was another fateful first meeting) Richard Burton and others, breakfasted at Milnes' London house in Upper Brook Street. Swinburne also passed about a fortnight at Fryston, Milnes' Yorkshire home, where he again met Burton, in the middle of August. See below, Letter 29. These details are from Pope-Hennessy.

29. TO RICHARD MONCKTON MILNES

MS: The Marchioness of Crewe. Published: Bonchurch, *18*, 6–8*.

16 Grafton Street, Fitzroy Square,
October 15, 1860 [*for* 1861]

My dear Mr. Milnes

I send you to-morrow as you wished my article on Wells' 'Joseph,' [1] which has been some time doing but I wanted to make it as satisfactory as I could without transcribing half the book. It is still finer I think than it seemed in my recollection of it after a first reading; and I should be very glad if I had anything to do with helping it to a little of the credit it must get in the end.

I have consulted with Rossetti about the choice of extracts and he thinks mine as adequate by way of specimen as one can have in the space of a magazine article. I hope you will enjoy them; but the book ought to be gone through to see how good and sustained it is. I know of nothing like its entire failure in all the chronicle of obscurities; how on earth a copy could now be got, I can't think. I was driven to the dolorous expedient of hunting up the British Museum copy (entered in the wildest way in that slough of a catalogue) to collate with a MS. copy sent to Rossetti by the author, whom report makes out to be still alive in Brittany and a scandal to creation by his conduct—a rumour I have abstained from hinting at—with a few alterations in it, sometimes much for the better, but chiefly in very small things.

I ought to have thanked you before both for my parcel which came on safely to me at the Trevelyan's and for the invitation you sent me from Lady de Grey; [2] I had a nice week with them.

Since I came back to London about a fortnight since, I have done some more work to 'Chastelard' and rubbed up one or two other

1. Charles Jeremiah Wells (1800–79) was the author of the prose *Stories after Nature* (1822) and the verse-drama *Joseph and His Brethren* (1824), but his toehold on fame is supported by three poets rather than by his own writings. Keats addressed a sonnet to him, but, unable to forgive Wells' prankish spoofery victimizing Tom Keats, came later to speak of him in scalding language. Gabriel Rossetti, whose interest in Wells dated from about 1846, at one time planned a new edition of *Joseph,* and he unquestionably grafted his enthusiasm onto his young disciple, whose essay Milnes tried unsuccessfully to place in *Fraser's Magazine* (see below, Letter 716). Swinburne's "An Unknown Poet" was ultimately dusted off and revised for the *Fortnightly Review* (Feb. 1875), and in the next year it appeared, slightly altered, as the "Introduction" to a new edition of the poem. Milnes, as a Keatsian of the first order, would of course have shared Swinburne's interest in Wells.

2. The Countess (later Marchioness) of Ripon, a maternal cousin.

things; my friend George Meredith has asked me to send some to 'Once a Week' [3] which valuable publication he props up occasionally with fragments of his own. Rossetti has just done a drawing of a female model and myself embracing—I need not say in the most fervent and abandoned style—meant for a frontispiece to his Italian translations.[4] Two mornings of incessant labour on all hands completed the design; and the result will I suppose be, as everybody who knows me already salutes the likeness with a yell of recognition,—that when the book comes out I shall have no refuge but the grave.

I don't know if this will find you at Fryston but as I promised 'Joseph' I send him at all hazards: and if my letter plagues you you have your own kindness to thank.

I would also have kept another promise and sent you my Delatouche, but until I know it will go straight to your hands I dare not trust La Reine d'Espagne [5] out of my sight. Reserving always your corresponding promise, which I do not forget, that I am yet to live and look upon the mystic pages of the martyred marquis de Sade; [6] ever since which, the vision of that illustrious and ill-requited benefactor of humanity has hovered by night before my eyes, and I run great risk of going as mad as Janin's [7] friend, but with curiosity alone.

I hope my notice of Joseph will answer; I wanted to stick in a fresh pile of extracts but no doubt it must be full long as it is. With best remembrances to Mrs. Milnes

I remain yours most sincerely,
A. C. Swinburne

3. He sent "The Fratricide," which appeared in Feb. 1862, reprinted as "The Bloody Son" (Bonchurch, 2, 45–48) in *PB1*, and the story "Dead Love," which appeared in Oct.

4. *The Early Italian Poets* (1861), revised as *Dante and His Circle* (1874). The frontispiece, which was not published, is reproduced (for example) in Edmund William Gosse, *The Life of Algernon Charles Swinburne* (1917) and in H. C. Marillier, *Dante Gabriel Rossetti, An Illustrated Memorial* (1899).

5. A comedy (1831) by Henri de Latouche.

6. See below, Letter 34. "Charenton," a highly imaginative versified portrait of Sade, written long before Swinburne had read any of the works and first printed by Pope-Hennessy (pp. 257–59), is dated "Dimanche, 27 octobre, 1861."

7. See below, Letter 34.

30. TO ADMIRAL CHARLES HENRY SWINBURNE

MS: Yale.

16 Grafton Street, December 12 [1861]

My dear Pino

I send you a copy of 'Captain Ward'[1] which I have taken down from one in the British Museum, where there are seven or eight different copies. I suspect none of them are quite right as to the date of the capting's[2] achievements. The 'king' ought probably to be 'queen' as our friend lived in the time of Queen Elizabeth (I believe) and the reference to Essex must be meant for *her* Essex: but all the copies seem to have the word 'King.' There is another ballad in the book I took this one out of—'Early Naval Ballads'—called 'The Song of Dansekar the Dutchman'—which gives an account of the Captain's confederate, and is not nearly so favourable to 'proud Ward' as our present poet is; for after saying

> 'All the world about have heard
> Of Dansekar and English Ward
> And of their proud adventures every day'

it goes on to abuse them roundly for cruelty and apostasy, as thus:

> 'But their cursed villainies
> And their bloody piracies
> Are chiefly bent against our Christian friends;
> Some Christians so delight in evils
> That they become the sons of devils
> And for the same have many shameful ends.'

I am afraid 'brave Ward' was at last taken under the Turkish flag and hanged for a series of piracies and murders. A play in f[ive][3] acts was written not long after on his life and adventures. The Rainbow ballad seems to me the best I ever read of its kind, and full of life and spirit. 'Dansekar' as you will see by the extracts is curious but very stupid and heavy.

I have copied another little song from the same collection which I thought might amuse you by its excessive oddity. There are some other sea ballads given at length in the book which I have only heard

1. See Nos. 287–88, Francis James Child, ed., *The English and Scottish Popular Ballads*, 5 vols. Boston and New York, 1883–98.

2. See *Martin Chuzzlewit*, chap. 33.

3. The paper is torn here.

scraps of till now; two, for instance, on Admiral Benbow's death which are very good: and one as old as the reign of Henry VI. about the excessive sea-sickness of the pilgrims going to St. James' shrine at Compostella which is very funny and gives a poor idea of the ship-building:

> The captain called a carpenter
> To make the cabins here and there
> With many a *feeble cell!*

I hope the two ballads enclosed will amuse you, and also that you are well enough not to want their help in amusing: Aunt Ju and Aunt Bowden [4] give poor accounts of you, but I hope by this time you are better again. I am very well but have had a pain in my back rather badly for a day or two, either by a strain or rheumatic; I suppose from catching cold; but it is nearly well now.

I was at Oxford lately and saw Mrs. Johnson [5] and her children, all well and pretty comfortable in their new house. I have got my books sent up here, where they are lumbering me frightfully but at least they are no longer eating their heads off.

Best love to all, and I hope that all are getting on well. I was at Grosvenor Place yesterday but all the news from thence you will have heard I suppose already.

Hoping the Capting may give satisfaction I remain

Ever your affectionate son,
A. C. Swinburne

P.S. I hope we shall have 'gallant Rainbows' presently who will have better luck than the one which Captain Ward defeated for it looks as if we should want them. You must imagine the excitement everywhere in town just now about the war with Northern America. People seem to meet it very well I think, there is only one view of the matter taken, and a very good one.[6]

4. Two of Admiral Swinburne's three sisters—Julia (1796–1893), who died un-married, and Elizabeth, who married John William Bowden in 1828, was widowed in 1844, and died in 1896.

5. See above, Letter 24.

6. A report on Swinburne in Dec. 1861, by a humorless eyewitness from Philistia makes an effective counterpoint here. William Hardman, who saw him at Rossetti's, wrote (S. M. Ellis, *A Mid-Victorian Pepys*, 1923, pp. 78–79): "Swinburne is a strange fellow, young, beardless, with a shock head of red hair; his parents were of two na-tions, the father Welsh, the mother French, and this mixture of blood has pro-duced a singular result. Swinburne is strongly sensual; although almost a boy, he upholds the Marquis de Sade as the acme and apostle of perfection, without (as

31. TO RICHARD MONCKTON MILNES

MS: The Marchioness of Crewe.

16 Grafton Street,
Tuesday [? March 11, 1862][1]

My dear Mr. Milnes

If I may have first fault this time you may put me in the bill next time. I wish I could say it was another boy but I can't under the circumstances. As it is I know I am too lucky if I escape without doing homage to the block, and can only rely on your good nature, not to be 'complained of.'

Seriously I am, and was then, very sorry to have missed my time on Wednesday and much more so to have kept you waiting. It was a scandalous piece of oversight and idleness unworthy even of the fourth form: and I confess to deserving what I trust to escape. It is a very lower-boy excuse, but true, to plead the stupidity of influenza—I have really had a rather bad spell of it these last few days. I shall be ashamed to look you in the face on Thursday. I have written to Meredith to come not forgetting (for a wonder) the direction.

Also, stung by remorse for putting off what I always meant to do daily, I have called on Lady de Grey and found her in yesterday—it was a very pleasant visit, to me at least.

Your affectionate,
A. C. Swinburne

32. TO LADY JANE HENRIETTA SWINBURNE

Text: Leith, pp. 102–3.

4 [sic] Grafton Street, March 13 [1862]

I am sure you will understand how that which has happened since I last wrote to you has upset my plans and how my time has been taken

---

he says) having read a word of his works. Now the Marquis de Sade was a most filthy, horrible, and disgusting rascal, a disgrace to humanity—he wrote the most abominable bawdry books that ever were written. No one is fonder of good sound bawdry than I (or you), yet the Marquis completely bowls me over. I tried once to read him, but very soon stuck fast. S - - - - y mixed with murder and hideous cruelty are the prevailing features of his writings. The assembled company evidently received Swinburne's tirades with ill-concealed disgust, but they behaved to him like to a spoiled child. He has a curious kind of nervous twitching, resembling or approaching St. Vitus' Dance."

1. The date is conjectured without confidence.

up. Till last week when I was laid up with a bad turn of influenza I have been almost always with Rossetti. For the last few days I have been with a friend in the country and am nearly quite right again.

I would rather not write yet about what has happened [1]—I suppose none of the papers gave a full report, so that you do not know that I was almost the last person who saw her (except her husband and a servant) and had to give evidence at the inquest. Happily there was no difficulty in proving that illness had quite deranged her mind, so that the worst chance of all was escaped. . . . I am only glad to have been able to keep him company and be of a little use during these weeks.

Rossetti and I are going to live together as soon as we move—of course he could not stay in the old house, and asked me to come with him. Luckily I had put off deciding on a lodging as it would have been a great plague to change again. In the autumn we get into a house at Chelsea—in Cheyne Walk, facing the trees and river—with an old garden. The house is taken (like every other nice one) for the Exhibition season, so we must make shift somewhere till then. . . .[2]

1. The suicide of Lizzie Siddal Rossetti. On Feb. 10 Swinburne, Gabriel Rossetti, and his wife Lizzie had dined together in a public restaurant. Swinburne, after an early dinner, went his way, and Rossetti, after escorting Lizzie home and leaving her to go to bed, went out again. When he returned at eleven-thirty, he found her dying of an overdose of laudanum. The coroner's verdict on the twelfth was that her death was accidental. Swinburne's innocent remark that "the worst chance of all was escaped," plus some less innocent gossip of later years, seemed to hint that Rossetti might have been charged with manslaughter (or even murder), and the ghost of that conjecture haunted literary history until finally laid in 1949 by Helen Rossetti Angeli (*Dante Gabriel Rossetti: His Friends and Enemies*, pp. 195–204), who established that Lizzie's death was self-inflicted: she left a suicide note. But the "worst chance of all," official discovery, "was escaped."

2. After Lizzie's death Rossetti took a studio at 77 Newman Street (probably) early in April. Dissatisfied, he ultimately made it over to Swinburne, who, as Boyce (p. 42) notes, celebrated with a housewarming on July 11. Rossetti moved on Oct. 24 into Tudor House, 16 Cheyne Walk, where, in accordance with his antic design for living, rooms were designated for Meredith, Swinburne, and William Rossetti. That Meredith spent very little time there, however, is certain, and the duration of Swinburne's stay, which was irregular (in all senses), seems to have been much exaggerated.

33. TO THE EDITOR OF THE *SPECTATOR*

Text: *Spectator* (June 7, 1862), pp. 632–33.

Sir

I cannot resist asking the favour of admission for my protest against the article on Mr. Meredith's last volume of poems [1] in the *Spectator* of May 24th. That I personally have for the writings, whether verse or prose, of Mr. Meredith a most sincere and deep admiration is no doubt a matter of infinitely small moment. I wish only, in default of a better, to appeal seriously on general grounds against this sort of criticism as applied to one of the leaders of English literature. To any fair attack Mr. Meredith's books of course lie as much open as another man's; indeed, standing where he does, the very eminence of his post makes him perhaps more liable than a man of less well-earned fame to the periodical slings and arrows [2] of publicity. Against such criticism no one would have a right to appeal, whether for his own work or for another's. But the writer of the article in question blinks at stating the fact that he is dealing with no unfledged pretender. Any work of a man who has won his spurs, and fought his way to a foremost place among the men of his time, must claim at least a grave consideration and respect. It would hardly be less absurd, in remarking on a poem by Mr. Meredith, to omit all reference to his previous work, and treat the present book as if its author had never tried his hand at such writing before, than to criticize the *Légende des Siècles,* or (coming to a nearer instance) the *Idylls of the King,* without taking into account the relative position of the great English or the greater French poet. On such a tone of criticism as this any one who may chance to see or hear of it has a right to comment.

But even if the case were different, and the author were now at his starting-point, such a review of such a book is surely out of date. Praise or blame should be thoughtful, serious, careful, when applied to a work of such subtle strength, such depth of delicate power, such passionate and various beauty, as the leading poem of Mr. Meredith's volume: in some points, as it seems to me (and in this opinion I know that I have weightier judgments than my own to back me) a poem above the aim and beyond the reach of any but its author. Mr. Meredith is one of the three or four poets now alive whose work, perfect or imperfect, is always as noble in design as it is often faultless in result. The present critic falls foul of him for dealing with 'a deep and painful subject on which he has no conviction to express.' There

1. *Modern Love, and Poems of the English Roadside, with Poems and Ballads.*

2. *Hamlet,* III. i. 58.

are pulpits enough for all preachers in prose; the business of verse-writing is hardly to express convictions; and if some poetry, not without merit of its kind, has at times dealt in dogmatic morality, it is all the worse and all the weaker for that. As to subject, it is too much to expect that all schools of poetry are to be for ever subordinate to the one just now so much in request with us, whose scope of sight is bounded by the nursery walls; that all Muses are to bow down before her who babbles, with lips yet warm from their pristine pap, after the dangling delights of a child's coral; and jingles with flaccid fingers one knows not whether a jester's or a baby's bells. We have not too many writers capable of duly handling a subject worth the serious interest of men. As to execution, take almost any sonnet at random out of the series, and let any man qualified to judge for himself of metre, choice of expression, and splendid language, decide on its claims. And, after all, the test will be unfair, except as regards metrical or pictorial merit; every section of this great progressive poem being connected with the other by links of the finest and most studied workmanship. Take, for example, that noble sonnet, beginning

'We saw the swallows gathering in the skies,'

a more perfect piece of writing no man alive has ever turned out; witness these three lines, the grandest perhaps of the book:

'And in the largeness of the evening earth,
Our spirit grew as we walked side by side;
The hour became her husband, and my bride;'

but in transcription it must lose the colour and effect given it by its place in the series; the grave and tender beauty, which makes it at once a bridge and a resting-place between the admirable poems of passion it falls among. As specimens of pure power, and depth of imagination at once intricate and vigorous, take the two sonnets on a false passing reunion of wife and husband; the sonnet on the rose; that other beginning:

'I am not of those miserable males
Who sniff at vice, and daring not to snap,
Do therefore hope for heaven.'

And, again, that earlier one:

'All other joys of life he strove to warm.'

Of the shorter poems which give character to the book I have not space to speak here; and as the critic has omitted noticing the most valuable and important (such as the 'Beggar's Soliloquy,' and the 'Old Chartist,' equal to Béranger for completeness of effect and exquisite justice of style, but noticeable for a thorough dramatic insight, which Béranger missed through his personal passions and partialities), there is no present need to go into the matter. I ask you to admit this protest simply out of justice to the book in hand, believing as I do that it expresses the deliberate unbiassed opinion of a sufficient number of readers to warrant the insertion of it, and leaving to your consideration rather their claims to a fair hearing than those of the book's author to a revised judgment. A poet of Mr. Meredith's rank can no more be profited by the advocacy of his admirers than injured by the rash or partial attack of his critics.

A. C. Swinburne

34. TO RICHARD MONCKTON MILNES

MS: The Marchioness of Crewe. A few lines quoted by Gosse, in Bonchurch, *19*, 89; extracts published by Pope-Hennessy, pp. 148–50.

77 Newman Street, August 18 [1862]

My dear Mr. Milnes

Many thanks for your note and for my papers which came to hand together. I am glad you are getting better,[1] and even your unprovoked anathema on the inoffensive hand that writes this shall not prevent me from regretting the infirmity of yours. That is apostolic, you will admit. But, as I really do not see why you are to wish me disabled from writing (which I should be sorry for just now, as I want to finish some old work, begin some new work, and make a little practical headway in the meantime) I shall take a cruel revenge by writing you a letter of shameless extent. I have heaps of things I want to inflict the hearing of on you. So if you are not in a condition to be chattered at you had better burn this.

1⁰ You retain my Charenton[2] and desire me to clear my head of the subject. I am in a very fair way to do so; for I have just read 'Justine ou les Malheurs de la Vertu.'[3] As you seemed anxious to

1. In the summer of 1862 "Milnes suffered from a severe illness, which at one time caused serious anxiety to his family and friends" (T. Wemyss Reid, *The Life, Letters, and Friendships of Richard Monckton Milnes, First Lord Houghton*, 2 vols. 1890, 2, 81).

2. See above, Letter 29.

3. Sade's novel exists in three redactions. The first version, *Les Infortunes de la vertu,* of which the manuscript, acquired by the Bibliothèque Nationale, was

know its effect on me I mean to give you a candid record, avoiding paradox or affectation. I would give anything to have, by way of study, six or seven other opinions as genuine and frank as mine shall be.

At first, I quite expected to add another to the gifted author's list of victims; I really thought I must have died or split open or choked with laughing. I never laughed so much in my life: I couldn't have stopped to save the said life. I went from text to illustrations and back again, till I literally doubled up and fell down with laughter—I regret to add that all the friends to whom I have lent or shown the book were affected in just the same way. One scene between M. de Verneuil and Mme. d'Esterval I never thought to survive. I read it out and the auditors rolled and roared. Then Rossetti read out the dissection of the interesting Rosalie and her infant, and the rest of that refreshing episode: and I wonder to this minute that we did not raise the whole house by our screams of laughter.[4]

But on reflection I found the impression left on me to be precisely the same as that of Landor's heroine on her first view of the sea. 'Is this the mighty Satyr? *is this all?*' [5] I did think—I did hope that this one illusion might have turned out a reality. Weep with me over a shattered idol! The style of Micawber is inadequate to express my feelings.

Of course the book must be taken on its own grounds; well, assuming every postulate imaginable, I lament to say it appears to me a most outrageous *fiasco*. I looked for some sharp and subtle analysis of lust —some keen dissection of pain and pleasure—'quelques taillades dans les chairs vives de la sensation': at least such an exquisite relish of the things anatomized as without explanation would suffice for a stimulant and be comprehensible at once even if unfit for sympathy. But in Justine there seems to me throughout to be one radical mistake rotting and undermining the whole structure of the book. De Sade is like a Hindoo mythologist; he takes *bulk* and *number* for greatness. As if a crime of great extent was necessarily a great crime; as if a

---

described by Guillaume Apollinaire in 1909, was first published in 1930, with an introduction by Maurice Heine. The second, *Justine ou les Malheurs de la vertu,* was published in 1791. In 1797 Sade rejuvenated, as Maurice Heine put it, the earlier work, making it preposterously ruttish and scatological, as *La Nouvelle Justine ou les Malheurs de la vertu.* Swinburne read the 1797 version. (These facts are drawn from Maurice Heine, *Le Marquis de Sade,* ed. Gilbert Lely, Paris, 1950.)

4. Boyce recorded on Aug. 16: "Joined Rossetti at Swinburne's rooms, where they were looking over *Justine,* by the Marquis de Sade, recent acquisition of the latter."

5. *Gebir,* Bk. V, 130.

number of pleasures piled one on another made up the value of a single great and perfect sensation of pleasure. You tear out wombs, smash in heads, and discharge into the orifice. Après? You scourge and abuse your mother and make dogs tear off her breasts, etc. Après? Suppose you take your grandmother next time and try wild cats by way of a change? I for one turn upon M. le marquis like Falstaff on his drawer. You rogue, there's lime in *this* sack too; there's nothing but roguery in villainous man.[6] Shew me the point, the pleasure of all this, as a man of genius ought to do in a few touches; *that* will be worth something as a study. Dumas says of you, my poor friend, 'Le marquis de Sade, voluptueux étrange! poursuit l'idéal de l'esprit infini dans la torture de la matière bornée.' A splendid character, which might do for Nero, perhaps for Gilles de Retz;[7] but for you? Take the simplest little example of your way of work. You have, say, a flogging to describe. You go in for *quantity* in a way quite regardless of expense. You lay on some hundreds of cuts, behind and before; you assert that they drew blood; probably they did; that the recipient wept and writhed; which is not unlikely; that the inflictor enjoyed himself and was much excited in his *physique;* which is most probable of all. Well? You have asserted a great deal; prove it now; bring it face to face with us; let the sense of it bite and tickle and sting your reader. Assertion is easy work. Shew us how and why these things are as they are. I on my part assert that you never do this once. 'Tu radotes, tu rabâches, tu baisses, tes coups ratent; tu n'es qu'un ganache; c'était bien la peine de se faire enfoncer à Charenton!' I agree, regretfully, with our common friend M. F. Cossu[8] in those sentiments. Why, there is more and better sensual physiology in that little 'Manon-la-Foutteuse' than in all your great lumbering Justine. *There* one finds some relish in the style, and catches it of the writer. I boast not of myself; but I do say that a schoolboy, set to write on his own stock of experience, and having a real gust and appetite for the subject in him, may make and has made more of a sharp short school flogging of two or three dozen cuts than you of your enormous interminable inflictions; more of the simple common birch rod and daily whipping-block than you of your loaded iron whips and elaborately ingenious racks and horses. Will you reply that your critic cannot yet judge of you, being too young, too green, and physically fresh to

6. *I Henry IV*, II. iv. 137.

7. Or Gilles de *Rais* (1404–40), distinguished, on one hand, as the faithful companion of Joan of Arc and, on the other, as the prototype of Bluebeard.

8. See below, Letter 43.

fathom the mystic Apocalypse of Priapus? You shall not get off on that score, M. le marquis; not if I know it. Had you given me all these strange dishes of yours served up in the right sauce, I should at once have recognized the value of them: I might have felt doubt, disgust, aversion for this dish or that, (*notamment,* for the process of tearing one's mother to rags or beating to death a little girl in the agonies of a head broken open; also, with your leave, for those rank and rancid preparations which served as *entremets* at the great dinners and suppers of Gomorrah) but I should have appreciated, admired, tried on the whole to understand and enjoy your work as great in its own way. But as it is, your book misses aim; with half your materials another man would have built a better palace of sin—a fairer house to sweep and garnish for the advent of the seven devils. You have gathered up and arranged in rows all manner of abominations and your work is *fade* after all—flat, flaccid, impotent, misshapen, hung awry. It might be bound up with Télémaque or Paul et Virginie.[9] You are but a poor old Arnolphe after all;

Une autre chose avec deux mots en ferait plus que vous.[10]

As to your horrors—ask people what they remember, as little children, to have said, heard of, thought of, dreamed of, done or been tempted to do. Nothing in your books but will find its counterpart or type. (I remember when I was seven a most innocent little girl of six telling me of a bad dream that made her unhappy; in that dream there was the whole practical philosophy of Justine embodied; God impotent or indignant, virtue trodden under and defiled by vice, and finally the very same climax you make so much of—*the curse of Rabshakeh.*[11] Allons donc!) You call a taste for eating and making others eat foul substances, the supreme excess of libidinous and voluptuous wickedness. Priapus have mercy on you! Why not say the same of a distaste for honey and taste for mushrooms? 'Eat, yea eat abundantly,' if you like; make others eat if you can and care; take your fill and hold your tongue. As to your story and the framework of your theories—you *must* know that Justine is a juggler's show, an ingenious acrobatic performance, and no more. Very ingenious and inventive; many of the tricks and postures (Rodin's for example, Gernande's, or Cardoville's) [12] most creditable to a phallic juggler; but who on earth

9. The well-known novels by Fénelon and Bernardin de Saint-Pierre.

10. In Molière's *L'École des femmes* (V. iv. 1606) Agnès says to Arnolphe, "Horace avec deux mots en ferait plus que vous."

11. See II Kings 18:27. For "eat abundantly," below, see Song of Solomon 5:1.

12. All three are characters in *Justine.*

is to make more than its worth of the very best conjuror's exhibition!

Tenez, my friend, Arch-Professor of the Ithyphallic Science as you are, will you hear the truth once for all? You take yourself for a great pagan physiologist and philosopher—you are a Christian ascetic bent on earning the salvation of the soul through the mortification of the flesh. You are one of the family of St. Simeon Stylites. You are a hermit of the Thebaid turned inside out. You, a Roman of the later empire? Nero knows nothing of you; Heliogabalus turns his back on you; Caracalla sniffs contemptuously at the sight of you; Cotytto veils her face and the Baptae shrug their shoulders; Venus Cloacina dips down into her gutter, and Priapus turns to a mere fig tree stump. Paganism washes its hands of you. You belong to Christian Egypt; you smell of Nitria; you have walked straight out of some Nile monastery; you are twin brother to St. Maccarius; you are St. Anthony and his pig rolled into one. It matters little that you have forgotten your own genealogy, or that you operate rather on the flesh of others than your own. Your one knack is to take common things, usual affections, natural pleasures and make them walk on their heads; by the simple process of *reversing,* any one may write as good a Justine as yours. If you were once cured of that trick of standing on your head for ten volumes through, and your energies turned back into the old channel they ran in some centuries since, you would revert to the chain and the top of a pillar and ascetic worship. That is about your mark, I reckon. We took you for a sort of burlesque Prometheus; you are only a very serious Simeon Stylites—in an inverted posture. You worship the phallus as those first ascetics worshipped the cross; you seek your heaven by the very same road as they sought theirs. That is all.

I drop my apostrophe to M. de Sade, having relieved my mind for good and all of its final judgment on a matter of some curiosity and interest to me. I should like to know (if you forgive me for writing such a farrago on the chance of its finding you désœuvré for half an hour) whether you agree or not. I have said just what I think in the first words that came uppermost. I am very glad *not* to have waited (as you advised) some 29 years on the chance of being alive then to read Justine. You see that whether it drives curates and curates' pupils to madness and death or not (Janin says it does—and Janin has the lips that cannot lie) [13] it has done decidedly little damage to my brain or nerves; (unless you think the incoherence of my critical remarks a proof of incipient mania). If you keep *Charenton* 'as a physiological

13. Jules Gabriel Janin (1804–74), journalist, drama critic, and historian of the theater, whose pious article on Sade appeared in the *Revue de Paris, 11* (1834), 321–60.

extravaganza,' perhaps you will keep this prose rhapsody with it by way of comment and remark, giving as it does a sincere and deliberate opinion of the life's labours of Stylites de Sade. Seriously, is he not exactly a typical monk? not voluptuous, not sensual, hardly cruel in the proper sense of the word, but alternately bestial and spiritual, and often both at once? the aspiration, and laborious service of his 'ideal,' being as great and deep as the appetite it works through. Sancta Donatiane, ora pro nobis!

2⁰ Have you seen the latest edition of Walt Whitman's *Leaves of Grass?* for there is one new poem in it—'A Voice from the Sea' [14]— about two birds on the sea-beach, which I really think the most lovely and wonderful thing I have read for years and years. I could rhapsodize about it for ten more pages, there is such beautiful skill and subtle power in every word of it; but I spare you; if you have got thus far you must feel like Justine at the last revolution of the wheel-machine in volume four. But, whatever you do look at that bird's song.

By the by, if you can without inconvenience find the last leaf of my article on 'Cossu' (a half-sheet) which is wanting, I should be glad of it, as I forget how the burlesque ended. Item—if you have done with them, don't you think I had better have my 'puerilia' back? Consider my feelings if they ever slipped into wrong hands and the writing was recognized—c'est ça qui serait une bonne farce.

Have you seen the rest of my review of Hugo? [15] I shall remind you some day of your promised letter of introduction.

You know how glad I shall be to revisit Fryston, full or empty of visitors; in effect I should prefer the time and circumstances that let me see most of you.

One thing I forgot about that eternal phallus-worshipper—why did you never tell me what a good lyrical poet the man was? There is a song in the eighth part of 'Aline et Valcour' [16] which seems to me about the most exquisite piece of simple finished language and musical effect in all 18th century French literature. Rossetti and Meredith (to whom I shewed it at once, disguising at first the author's name to

14. "A Word from the Sea" in the third edition (dated 1860–61) later became "Out of the Cradle Endlessly Rocking."

15. His review of *Les Misérables* (Bonchurch, *13*, 151–79) appeared in the *Spectator* in 1862 in four parts: Apr. 12; June 21; July 26; and Aug. 16. It was crowned by a general article (Bonchurch, *13*, 180–88) on Oct. 25.

16. His translation of this poem (Bonchurch, *1*, 245) was printed in *PB1* as "Song before Death" with only a hint of its origin.

elude prejudice) fully agreed with me. It is something like Blake's poetry in England at the same date—both of them sweet and perfect, and unlike any contemporary work—mediaeval rather in grace and quietness of beauty.

I hope you are improving; and that Mrs. Milnes and the children are all well. With best remembrances

Your affectionate,
A. C. Swinburne

35. TO WILLIAM MICHAEL ROSSETTI [1]

MS: Rutgers. Published: Bonchurch, *18*, 12–14.

77 Newman Street, Monday [October 6, 1862]

Dear Rossetti

I am ashamed of not having answered your first note at once, but I wanted to take counsel with Gabriel on the Blake business [2] and he promised to give you my message the same day, as he was to have seen you then. It seems he never did give it, but the result we both at once came to was that, as the weather stands by this time, it would be at least useless to attempt patching or padding the book, even if one's patchwork were to come under no further supervision from a chaste publisher. The thing is done now, or rather left undone, and a quite extraneous tail or fin stitched on to the trunk of the book by way of appendage would only make the whole bulk of it more incoherent and unshapely. To give a decent revision of the leading prophetic books, it would first of all be necessary to entirely melt down and recast the chapters printed. To leave these as they are and then stick on a supplement at the end would be absurd, even if the addition

1. (1829–1919), who remained Swinburne's close friend longer than any other person—not solely through longevity. He was never the easy-going intimate of Swinburne that his brother was for a time, and (if the observation may be ventured without disparagement of this wholly admirable man), he seems to have been incapable of such abandon. William Rossetti's rectitude and self-sufficiency appear even now to have been almost otherworldly, and, in truth, though he was the most selfless of men, one can scarcely imagine him as the intimate friend of anyone. See "ALS: Swinburne to William Michael Rossetti," *Journal of the Rutgers University Library,* *14* (Dec. 1950), 1–8.

2. Alexander Gilchrist, a friend of the brothers Rossetti, died on Nov. 30, 1861, leaving unfinished a two-volume *Life of Blake,* of which parts were already in type. Mrs. Gilchrist did what she could, but most of the piecing out of the manuscript, and nearly all of the second volume, was done by the Rossettis, who solicited Swinburne for an account of the *Prophetic Books.* The work was published by Macmillan in 1863.

could be made (which even as to *manner* I don't think it could) to look as if it fitted on. Much more I think might have been done at starting without any handling of the hot cinder or treading on the quagmire which a virtuous editor seems so abjectly afraid of. As it is, it seems to me the best thing for the book and for those interested in it is to leave it alone, for fear of bursting the old bottles [3]—a Scotch publisher would no doubt receive a reference to the sacred text as unanswerable. I should have been delighted to help in the work originally, and coming in as a free auxiliary to the best of my means of work; but I see no good possible to do at this point, even if one disliked less the notion of doing service for Blake under the eye of such a taskmaster [4] as the chaste Macmillan. [5]

What I now do want to do, and mean to set about this year if I can, is the making of a distinct small commentary of a running kind, but as full and satisfactory as it could well be made, on Blake's work. [6] This would not in the least jar with the Life, from which as we see anything like a comprehensive critical 'exposition' or summary has been excluded—was probably, as Gabriel told me, never designed. In this way one might work honestly and at ease, not pushed upon or jabbered at by Scotch tongue virtues and 'the harlot Modesty.' Not that one need be over-explanatory of Blake's extreme crotchets or in the least prurient, but just fair and careful and rational, going as much to the heart of the matter handled as possible. Such a piece of work tolerably well done or loyally tried at might be of some standing value in the long run, if we could pull well together for the haven, say, of Enitharmon. I have spoken to Gabriel about the way and means, and we want you in the council. May I come to you or could you come here at any time to talk it over?

Yours sincerely,

A. C. Swinburne

3. Mark 2:22 or Luke 5:37.

4. Milton's "How soon hath time," l. 14.

5. Alexander Macmillan (1818–96), the publisher. "It might be well perhaps to mention to Mr. Swinburne, if he is so kind as to do what was proposed," Mrs. Gilchrist had written to William Rossetti on Oct. 3 (Herbert H. Gilchrist, ed., *Anne Gilchrist, Her Life and Writings*, 1887, p. 128), "that it would be perfectly useless to attempt to handle this side of Blake's writings—that Mr. Macmillan is far more inexorable against any shade of heterodoxy in morals than in religion—and that in fact, poor 'flustered propriety' would have to be most tenderly and indulgently dealt with."

6. The "small commentary" grew, with the accretions of five years, into a book of more than three hundred pages (Bonchurch, *16*, 49–350), issued in Dec. 1867 (but dated 1868). See below, Letter 53.

36. TO WILLIAM MICHAEL ROSSETTI

MS: Rutgers.

18 Grosvenor Place, S.W., November 3 [1862]

Dear Rossetti

Your Blake MS.[1] was left for packing among my books and is at Chelsea, no doubt in some box. I fear I shall not be able to see the books unpacked myself before leaving town; but of course it is there and procurable when you please. I am only sorry it should happen to be there when you want it. Of course all my boxes of books are at your service or Gabriel's whenever you like to forage; indeed I should be thankful to know they were of use, and not rusting under wood and paper. I ought to excuse myself for not reserving it at hand in case of need; but I could not well have superintended the packing myself, and understanding Green's[2] men were thoroughly trustworthy I thought it best to make them forward everything together to Chelsea, as we were all so soon bound for that haven of refuge. Especially as I understood there was no present or probable want of the Blake. Otherwise of course I must have kept it out for you.

I have written to Milnes to let me hear from him at my present direction. He was to let me know when he came to town, as we meant to go northward together, before the end of this week. I suppose the hoary villain is still speechifying among the clods, and blandly deprecating intervention or Southern sympathies. Last year I know he disgraced himself by colloguing with Northern envoys, and went into mourning after the auspicious day of Bull's Run.[3] As soon as ever I do see or hear from him I will tackle him about Blake.[4] Or if you like I will anticipate time[5] by writing at once; but I suspect if he is out of town the treasures are inaccessible till his return. I know he

1. The now famous "Rossetti Manuscript," which had fallen into Gabriel's hands for ten shillings in 1847.

2. Possibly Samuel Green, the carrier in New Compton Street, Soho.

3. Charles Francis Adams, United States Minister to England, was visiting Milnes at Fryston in Nov. 1861, when the British ship *Trent* was held up by a U.S. warship and dispossessed of Mason and Slidell, Confederate emissaries. Milnes, writes Pope-Hennessy, p. 165, "was one of very few men in the House of Commons, still more of the landed gentry, to support the North, which he did so loudly and warmly that for the first time in his life he found himself a public hero."

4. William Rossetti's share of the Gilchrist *Blake* was a *catalogue raisonné* of the designs, for which he had to take account of Milnes' excellent collection: "Could you give me any inkling of how it is to be managed?" he wrote to Swinburne on Nov. 2 (Houghton Papers).

5. *Troilus and Cressida*, IV. v. 2.

has the sense to manage all that himself and leave nothing to servants.

The only other quarter I have ever heard of Blakes through, is Kerslake [6] the bookseller, of Bristol—No. 1 Park Street: as I daresay you know. I think if he knew of any fresh ones I should have heard from him as I used to deal largely with him; but if untried he might be worth trying.

I am very much disappointed at hearing you do not mean to review Blake in Fraser.[7] Is it impossible to reconsider? for no one else I suppose could do it nearly as well, and it will be a great loss to the book, and still more (in consequence) to the general fame of Blake. I cannot see how your share of the work should interfere with your liberty of remark or with your claim to a general hearing on broad grounds. One has no business of course to comment on your decision, but I do think it very regrettable.

Yours most sincerely,
A. C. Swinburne

37. TO RICHARD MONCKTON MILNES

MS: The Marchioness of Crewe.

18 Grosvenor Place, November 13 [1862]

My dear Mr. Milnes

I have written word to Rossetti of the hour at which you can receive us. As to the Museum, it has not a tithe of what you have in the way of Blakes; and we know of no other accessible place that has.

After a promise of seeing desirable things, I engage to 'conform' to any 'custom' or even 'faith' as Shelley would add, and to be such an incredibly good boy that the great M. Rodin himself,[1] model institu- teur de jeunesse as he was, could have found no available excuse for correction.

Your affectionate,
Redgie [2]

6. Thomas Kerslake (1812–91).

7. "I have given up the idea of writing about the book in Fraser, after discussing with Froude the possible awkwardness of doing so in connexion with my suggestions for the book itself, proofs etc.," Rossetti had written.

1. In *Justine* the "maître de la pension de Saint-Marcel"—but the pension was run for uncanonical purposes.

2. "Reginald" is Swinburne's name for himself not only in the autobiographical novel *A Year's Letters* (see below, Letter 106) but also in several other pieces.

38. TO WILLIAM MICHAEL ROSSETTI

MS: Rutgers.

Fryston, Tuesday [November 25, 1862]

Dear Rossetti

Milnes asks me to write for him, being busy, to know if you can come on *Monday* next, which will be he thinks the most convenient day? [1] though any day that week would do for him. Only it must be before the eighth when he is off. Have just been assisting him to decipher a *priceless* autograph letter of the Marquis de Sade * announcing (in the most incredible spelling) 'des comedys (sic) trés dangereux (sic) aux mœurs.' Further on the Arch-Unmentionable spells 'crains' *crin!* Conceive the compositor's work in correcting Justine. Love to Gabriel, and if you see Ned [2] to him.

Yours,

A. C. Swinburne

* The handwriting I flatter myself with thinking not unlike that of *this note.*

39. TO PAULINE, LADY TREVELYAN

MS: Trevelyan Papers, Wallington. Published: Bonchurch, *18*, 14–15*.

Fryston Hall, Ferrybridge, Yorkshire,
December 2 [1862]

(Anniversary of the Treason of L. Buonaparte.) [1]

My dear Lady Trevelyan

I am leaving here next Monday [2] and want to know if you could have me then, as you was so kynd as ax. I believe Gabriel Rossetti

---

1. William Rossetti saw not only the Blake designs but also the famous house party described in *The Education of Henry Adams*, during which William Stirling, who, like Adams, was dumbfounded by "the wild Walpurgis-night of Swinburne's talk," summed Swinburne up as "a cross between the devil and the Duke of Argyll!" Swinburne stayed at Fryston about a month, leaving on Dec. 13. (See Pope-Hennessy, pp. 133–42.)

2. Edward Burne Jones.

1. The *coup d'état* of Dec. 2, 1851.

2. He actually left, however, not "next Monday" (Dec. 8), but, as Mrs. Milnes recorded in her diary (Pope-Hennessy, p. 14), on Saturday, Dec. 13.

is or will be at Scotus's,[3] so that haven is presumably barred. William Rossetti is here, and desires to be remembered and cetrer [4] to you. I have Quaggified an eminent Saturday Reviewer who before had seen no merit in the great Sala, but is now effectually converted to the Grace-Walking religion, which hitherto he allays licked.[5] I have to run down into Sussex this week to attend my grandmother's funeral: [6] but am coming back here for a day or two at the end of the week to meet other eminent men. So this is my direction till Monday. Please let me know if I am to turn up.

With my respectful duty to all friends, notamment to Sir Walter and to Miss Lofft.[7] I remain,

Ever yours sincerely,
A. C. Swinburne

3. Rossetti was at William Bell Scott's in Newcastle in order to paint an oil portrait of his patron and Scott's friend, Mrs. T. H. Leathart.

4. See *Nicholas Nickleby*, chap. 15, *Bleak House*, chap. 59.

5. Swinburne's liking for George Augustus Sala (1828–96), the fecund and popular journalist, man about town, and *bon vivant*, began early and lasted late. Lord Ronald Gower recalled that at lunch one day in 1879 Swinburne "spoke with high regard of G. A. Sala's talents as a writer," Lord Ronald Gower, *My Reminiscences* (2 vols. 1883), 2, 289–90; and Clara Watts-Dunton, who didn't bustle into the picture until years later, says that for "Sala's work he always professed a tremendous admiration," Clara Watts-Dunton, *The Home Life of Swinburne* (1922), p. 130.

Here the allusion is to "Colonel Quagg's Conversion," a story in *Household Words, 10* (1855), 459–65. The tale concerns the Grace-Walking Brethren, a religious sect in Massachusetts, terrorized by Colonel Quagg, a blacksmith who mercilessly flogged, with an oiled leather strap, any Grace-Walker passing his smithy, which lay on the only road between Punkington and Rapparoarer. Naturally, the Brethren having no taste for martyrdom, religion lanquished in Rapparoarer until, finally, Brother Zephaniah Stockdolloger volunteered to brave the bully. Sure enough, Colonel Quagg waylaid him—and found himself thrashed into near insensibility by Brother Stockdolloger, who, it seems, had been before *his* conversion a prizefighter. The Colonel "is now, as Elder Quagg, a shining and a burning light among the Grace-Walking Brethren." (See also Letter 26, above.)

6. The Countess of Ashburnham died Nov. 26, 1862.

7. Laura Capell Lofft, daughter of Capell Lofft, the "classical scholar, poet, and miscellaneous writer" (*DNB*), ridiculed by Byron in "English Bards and Scotch Reviewers." Pauline, Lady Trevelyan, died in May 1866, and fourteen months later Sir Walter married Miss Lofft, who died Apr. 2, 1879, ten days after her husband's death.

40. TO PAULINE, LADY TREVELYAN

MS: Trevelyan Papers, Wallington. Published: Bonchurch, *18*, 15–16*.

Turf Hotel, Newcastle,
Monday [December 15, 1862]

My dear Lady Trevelyan

I hope you are prepared for one thing, the natural consequence of your unnatural conduct, viz., to come and bail me out when the hired minions of oppressive law have haled me to a loathsome dungeon for inability to pay a fortnight's unlooked for hotel expenses. Nothing on earth is likelier, and all because I relied with filial shortsightedness on that fallacious letter of invitation which carried me off from Frys-ton. If I had but heard in time, I should have run down to London, and come up later. As it is I see Destitution and Despair ahead of me, and have begun an epitaph in the Micawber style for my future grave in the precincts of my native County's jail.

If by any wild chance—say by offering the head waiter a post-obit, or a foreclosure, or a mortgage, or a bill payable at three months, or a Federal bond, or an African loan, or a voucher, or something equally practicable—I can stave off the period of my incarceration so as to get to Wallington on Wednesday, I shall take the train that leaves Morpeth at 2.15 and gets to Scotus's Gap[1] at 2.50. But I cannot disguise from myself, and will not from you, that this contingency is most remote. It is far more probable that posterity will appear, a weeping pilgrim, in the prison-yard of this city, to drop the tear of indignant sympathy on a humble stone affording scanty and dishonourable refuge

To
The
Nameless
Dust
of
A.C.S.[2]

1. That is, Scott's Gap, identified by Gosse as "the station which serves Wallington."

2. See Micawber's letters in *David Copperfield*, chaps. 28, 36.

41. TO RICHARD MONCKTON MILNES

MS: The Marchioness of Crewe.

Wallington, Newcastle-on-Tyne,
December 27 [1862]

Salus in X Priapo et Ecclesiâ
Sub invocatione Beatissimi Donatiani de Sade [1]

Mon cher Rodin [2]

As we are not in school hours you will perhaps accept excuses for my not writing before. Having had absolutely nothing else to do, of course I have never found time to do this. If Joseph [3] comes to this address he will be all right. I advise you not to build upon the chance of such a very contingent reversion as that of the book will be if it hangs on the chance of my hanging myself. *That* cord will hardly bear the strain. Neither should I rely on the points of likeness between my character and that of M. Roland [4] for the likelihood of finding (as you suggest) a Justine capable of cutting me and her own chance of escape down together. Pour le faire [5] de Thémis, je m'en f - - —iche pas mal. If it *does* fall on me, and if it will not be cheating the venerable Calcraft [6] of his perquisites, I will assuredly leave you the Joseph.

Il est dommage que ce cher et digne marquis n'ait pas imaginé des supplices de mer. J'ai vu la semaine passée un effet admirable de bourrasque sur les grèves de la côte du nord. En contemplant les grandes lames blanches et roussâtres de cette mer houleuse, et les rochers crenelés qui soufflaient l'écume par mille bouches et mille

1. "Salvation in Christ Priapus and His Church by the intercession of the Most Blessed Donatien de Sade."

2. See above, Letter 37.

3. An allusion to *Madame Putiphar* (1839), a novel by Petrus Borel d'Hauterive (1809–59), who called himself the "Lycanthrope." See also Letter 500, below.

4. Whose life Justine saved. He turned out to be a sadistic counterfeiter who brutalized her in the wonted ways. His *cachet* was his pleasure in *coupe-corde*, a game in which the victim was suspended by the neck and cut down (if possible) just before death, and he explored the ultimate ecstasy when, at his behest, Justine suspended him and released him just before asphyxiation.

5. That is, *fer?*

6. See below, Letter 84.

narines de pierre, j'ai trouvé des supplices à faire bander un cadavre.[7]

It is very jolly here at this time of year, but I might have preferred that forgotten sherry of yours to the hearing of declamations and expositions against it. Only one thing could have been sweeter than a clandestine sip of it under dread of discovery by one's host—the same furtive process under terror of flagellation by one's schoolmaster. By the by for heaven's sake send me your chapter of schoolmaster's autobiography. What is the good man's honoured *name* to be? Mine is getting done and you shall have it in return as we covenanted. It will be very pretty I expect—two victims each, you will please remember. Mine are brothers. I want to see your style of flagellant fiction infinitely. I read in a public library some days since an incredibly base and absurd story against the use of birch on boys.[8] Worse than novels against the connexion of husband and wife! flying in the *face* (?) of all established and divine institutions which enable society to sit firm and keep things as one may say on a just and solid bottom! C'est infâme. On devrait tenailler la langue à ces b - - igres-là. 'Détestons ces horreurs' as M. de Bressac said to the too indocile Justine.[9]

Ever your affectionate,

Frank Fane [10]

I hope Florey [11] has not forgotten her conditional engagement to me in ten years' time *if* I am rich enough to give her a trousseau of rubies. I told Lady Trevelyan of the affecting ceremony and she expressed herself 'only too thankful to hear I had a chance of being saved by a virtuous attachment.'

7. In *Lesbia Brandon* (p. 15) Swinburne wrote of Herbert Seyton: "In thunder that drowned his voice, wind that blew over his balance, and snowstorms of the flying or falling foam that blinded his eyes and salted his face, the boy took his pleasure to the full; this travail and triumph of the married wind and sea filled him with a furious luxury of the senses that kindled all his nerves and exalted all his life."

8. See below, Letter 43.

9. But the Comte de Bressac was speaking of Christian doctrine.

10. The name of an imaginary schoolboy. Swinburne's unpublished flagellation-poem of 98 lines entitled "Frank Fane" survives in a private collection. Reggie Fane and Freddy Fane, brothers, are the names of two characters in the two-part, 94-stanza poem "Reginald's Flogging," which appeared in *The Whippingham Papers* (1888). One of their schoolfellows is named Algernon.

11. Milnes' daughter Florence, whose seventh-birthday party Swinburne had attended on Dec. 8.

42. TO RICHARD MONCKTON MILNES

MS: The Marchioness of Crewe. One sentence quoted by Gosse, Bonchurch, *19*, 84–85.

Wallington, January 2 [1863]

Cher M. Rodin

Recevez tous mes remercimens. Je viens de revoir Joseph. Cet indigne faquin est parvenu sans malheur jusqu'à son maitre. J'ai relu la scène Putiphariane. On aurait dû faire circuler cet abominable scélérat avec un godmiché chauffé à blanc.

Vous ne me parlez pas de mes supplices de mer. J'ose cependant me flatter que vous ne dédaignez pas cette idée-là. Mais, en vérité, vous êtes un homme infâââme. Croyez-vous par hasard que l'on se met en dépense d'esprit pour n'obtenir qu'un méchant bout de lettre et des excuses au lieu d'un joli petit brin de roman scholastique bien épicé, bien réchauffé, tout confit en voluptés âcres, où l'on puisse sentir des mesures aigües d'une douleur exquise et délicieuse, entendre le rifflement sonore des cinglons, les cris de la chair lacérée, les hurlemens de l'esprit en délire? Voilà ce que je veux, moi. Voilà, j'ose le croire, ce que je vous ai fait voir dans mes vieilles poésies de quinze ans. Sans cela, je vous l'affirme, vous ne tirerez plus rien de moi. Allons —à l'ouvrage. Vous en avez bien le temps—car vous êtes occupé, vous —du moins vous le dites. Il n'y a que les oisifs qui n'ont jamais le temps de faire leur devoir—ou leurs pensums. Et alors, verges d'aller leur train. Ne le sais-je pas bien, moi qui vous écris? Pourrais-je me tromper à cet égard?

La Providence est absolument sans pudeur. Ce bon M. de Sade lui a fait beaucoup trop d'honneur en l'appelant 'fantôme abominable, b----- de b----s.' Si cet homme sublime avait eu raison, mes deux cousins seraient à cet instant deux 'masses informes de chair calcinée par le feu du ciel' et je ne serais plus cadet de famille. Et cependant, voyez ce qui m'arrive. L'aîné de ces deux atroces coquins vient de prendre femme,[1] voulant sans doute faire souche d'imbéciles. Je voudrais leur envoyer pour tout cadeau un *condom* frotté d'un poison subtil, qui pourrait me défaire et du fouteur et de la fouteuse en les faisant périr par des tourmens épouvantables. (Voilà encore un supplice oublié; je commence à trouver de Sade un homme assez mesquin.) N'est-ce pas qu'on ferait avec cela un charmant bout de *roman intime?* Je m'en souviendrai en écrivant 'Justin ou les Nouveaux Malheurs de

---

1. Sir John Swinburne (1831–1914), 7th baronet, married Emily Elizabeth Broadhead on Jan. 1, 1863, and at that time only he and his younger brother stood between Swinburne and the title.

la Vertu.' Du reste, ne vous auriez plus de me donner ce nom-là: c'est le nom de mon héros vertueux. Appelez-moi du nom de mon jeune camarade de fouet, dont j'ai chanté les supplices d'une voix sympathique. Ce ne sont pas des garçons rangés, des écoliers modèles, que ces bons sujets-là.

Je viens de recevoir une lettre charmante de Victor Hugo qui veut bien m'adresser des remercimens au sujet de mes articles sur *Les Misérables*.[2] Vous croyez bien que j'en ai encore la tête toute échauffée. Si j'eusse su qu'il devait les lire, j'aurais craint de lui avoir déplu en m'attaquant aux philanthrope; j'ai aussi un peu nargué en passant la vertue publique, et la démocratie vertueuse. Il me parait cependant plus que satisfait. C'est sans doute un plaisir innocent, mais c'en est toutefois un assez grand, que d'avoir su plaire (style Linder)[?] au maître qu'on a toujours vénéré. Vous savez que je crois encore un peu à cet homme-là. A Eton, il y a huit ans, je m'enivrais de ses drames. Cette croyance m'est resté. Serait-ce donc vrai que les plaisirs innocens valent bien aussi quelque chose? Hélas! si je leur adressais cette demande, Mme. de Longueville me tournerait le dos—M. de Sade me cracherait au visage. Je vais consulter là-dessus mon directeur, le révérend père Severino.[3]

En attendant, souvenez-vous, je vous en prie, de vos obligations—et aussi un peu parfois de

Votre élève très respectueux,
F.F.

Reginald Lunsgard [4] et Algernon Swinburne vous envoient aussi l'assurance de leurs sentimens les plus distingués. Ces garçons vous prient de croire qu'ils n'oublieront jamais la vigueur aimable de vos corrections, ni la fraîcheur souple et cruelle des verges que votre main paternelle savait si bien choisir pour les écorcher. Nous porterons toujours de vos marques, ô cher maître! et nous vous ferons toujours

2. Hugo's note, from Hauteville House on Dec. 26, read: "J'ai connu, seulement à mon retour en cette Ile, vos deux excellents articles sur les *Misérables*. Je suis heureux que ce livre ait appelé l'attention d'un esprit tel que le vôtre, et que vous soyez, vous aussi, sollicité par les questions sociales; preoccupation suprême de notre siècle. Je vous félicite de votre talent, Monsieur. . . ." Swinburne forthwith asked leave to dedicate *Chastelard* (not published till nearly three years later) to Hugo, who on Jan. 8 replied briefly: "J'accepte votre dédicace et je vous remercie avec effusion. Je serai heureux de voir mon nom sur une œuvre qui portera le vôtre" (*Revue bleue, 74,* Mar. 7, 1936, 151).

3. Severino and the révérend père Clément are monks in the monastery of Sainte Marie-des-Bois in Sade's *Justine*.

4. See above, Letter 37.

voir par une reconnaissance obséquieuse que la mort seule saura dissoudre cette amitié scellée par les supplices et tracée dans le sang.

A Monsieur Monsieur Rodin
Inspecteur des Ecoles
de S.M.I.

S'adresser chez le R. P. Clément
Ste-Marie-des-Bois
près Grenoble
France.

43. TO RICHARD MONCKTON MILNES

MS: The Marchioness of Crewe.

Fontmel Lodge, Bournemouth, Poole,
January 21 [1863]

My dear M. Rodin

Having had to come down hither in something of a hurry owing to sickness in the family,[1] I have unluckily left the MSS. of our incipient fictitious-biography in Grosvenor Place. Can I write to a maiden aunt[2] rising seventy—'Be kind enough to look over a large portfolio in my bedroom containing autograph studies and sketches in verse and prose, all totally unfit for publication, ranging in date from 1854 to 1862, and forward the more offensive specimens to M. Rodin, I. D. E. D. S. M. I., near Grenoble?' After the infamous 'Broad-bottom coalition'[3] of a kinsman whom I (to put it mildly) spit at—infinitely worse than the ancient political one—il parait qu'elle est maigre comme un pieu, cette fille, et il doit la foutre sous les aisselles —can I, after this, throw away any decent chance of standing well with other members (il n'y a pas ici l'ombre d'un équivoque) of the family? There however the deposit lies, ready against my return to London, when it shall be finished and forwarded. Meantime pray let me have yours at once, and I will begin afresh. Also the head master will have a good excuse for future severities of delicate discipline, now that I am behindhand with my work. Any scrap will be a charity in this dolorous place and time. I think the prison pamphlet an exquisite suggestion. Could it be carried out we ought to *enfoncer* Carlyle and his

1. Swinburne's sister Edith, who died Sep. 25, 1863.

2. Julia Swinburne.

3. See above, Letter 42.

Model Prisons.[4] The Anti-Birch or Anti-Paedo-Pygo-Mastigias [5] (there's an Aristophanic compound I hope—as thus—αντιπαιδοπυγομαστιγίας a fellow ought really to be let off his next swishing for that neat piece of scholarship) effusion I spoke of was disinterred from a dead and rotten magazine called the Metropolitan, which I found in the Newcastle Literary and Philosophical Institute. I always look out any Rodinesque article in old reviews, where they often swarm. This present story, Richard Biddulph [6] I think by the name of it, or something of the sort, was apparently the abortion of a Jerrold [7] drunk on chicory at a breakfast given by the supporters of a Society for the propagation of spiritual providence [?] and moral masturbation by rule-of-love. The style of the whole book is the most marvellous, incredible specimen of penny-novelist's English ever emitted into light by the postern door. It ends I recollect with a boy, grown up to manhood, tearing out the pedagogue's 'living heart with his naked fingers.' Voilà. It might have been written by that philanthropist who killed a namesake of mine (Christian name) two years ago or so with sticks and ropes, *not* on the flesh.[8] Imbecile! Not thus, O Justine—far otherwise, O Rosalie [9]—were you martyrized by the great and good Rodin.

There, I consider that digressive apostrophe worthy of Bulwer.[10]

4. One of the *Latter-Day Pamphlets* (Mar. 1850).

5. Anti-child-buttocks-whipping.

6. "Richard Biddulph; or, The Life and Adventures of a School-boy" appeared serially in the *Metropolitan Magazine* from Oct. 1844 to Dec. 1845.

7. Douglas William Jerrold (1803–57), playwright, journalist, novelist.

8. In Apr. 1860, according to the *Annual Register*, Reginald C. Cancellor, a half-witted lad of 15 in a "private school of the highest class at Eastbourne," run by a Mr. Hopley, was found dead in bed. "Mysterious stories of midnight shrieks and blood-stained instruments of punishment began to be whispered about. . . . Then came the real investigation. The gloves and the stockings were stripped off, and the legs and the arms of the corpse were found to be coated with extravasated blood, 'the cellular membranes under the skin of the thighs were reduced to a perfect jelly; in fact, all torn to pieces and lacerated by the blows that had been inflicted.' There were two holes in the right leg about the size of a sixpence, and an inch deep, which appeared to have been made by jabbing a thick stick into the flesh. The appearance was that of a human creature who had been mangled by an infuriated and merciless assailant. All these appearances coincided but too faithfully with what was now learnt of the conduct of the schoolmaster." (In July Hopley was tried, found guilty, and sentenced to four years' penal servitude.)

9. See above, Letter 34.

10. See below, Letter 98.

Apropos des verges, have you read Salammbô? [11] I have just written Lady Trevelyan a brilliant account of it. The tortures, battles, massacres, and Moloch-sacrifices are stunning (I suppose I may use schoolboyish terms in addressing my scholastic lord and teacher, M. Rodin?). I want to review it somewhere; do you know of any place one could get for it? I don't want to send any more to the Spectator; I don't approve of their behaviour (e.g. never sending one one's own articles, and taking back books sent for review—notamment four volumes of Les Misérables) and their principles offend my moral sense.[12] I wish I could find some paper or review where I could write at my own times and in my own way occasional studies on matters of art and literature of which I could speak confidently. I think I could do at odd times a set of papers on French writers now to the fore, that might be worth the writing and reading. Flaubert for instance has never had a sane or decent reviewer in English. Sanity and decency being the two main props of my critical faculty, I could just supply the want. Seriously I wish such a turn of work could get done.

Revenons à nos verges. I look eagerly and with prospective excitement for Frank's revelations. If I can't match them it must be my tutor's fault. I could put in delicious and pungent details from memories not much more than seven years old yet. (Less by a year or two now I think of it. Signed—Reginald) Voyons! Meantime with love to Frank and all friends I am

Your affectionate pupil,
Redgie

I quite forgot the anagram you spoke of last time.[13] The words are

11. Published in 1862.

12. Or, more accurately, his principles offended the moral sense of R. H. Hutton (1826–97), editor of the *Spectator*, whom he nearly succeeded in cozening with the articles "Félicien Cossu" and "Les Abimes. Par Ernest Clouet," which, purporting to be reviews of two specimens of current French literature, were really wicked Algernonic hoaxes. The latter was actually set up in galleys before Hutton, who apparently intuited without realizing the facts, disburdened himself of it. "The subject seems to me to deserve no more criticism than a Holywell Street publication," he wrote on Dec. 16, 1862 (*A Swinburne Library*, p. 225), "nor could I speak of it in the *Spectator* without more real disgust than your article inspires. There is a tone of raillery about it which I think one should hardly use to pure obscenity."

13. The anagram remained with Lord Houghton's papers:

> Often at school my luck I cursed,
> For I was daily in the First:
> From nine years old to seventeen
> I knew the second well, I ween.

72

Bill and *Weal*. 'I was daily in the First' when sent up to be swished: the second explains itself. The one I may say *entails* the other. I want now to know if you have guessed the component words right.

44. TO RICHARD MONCKTON MILNES

MS: The Marchioness of Crewe.

Fontmel Lodge, February 3 [1863]

My dear Mr. Milnes

Aussi c'est sa faute à ce vieux monstre de Rodin. I *thought* something was wrong with poor old Redgie that day—never saw him look so blue since we were up to the same tutor. I implored him to let me look at the ominous little packet he had received.[1] —No; he would not.—Was it a communication from Mme. de Lorsange [2] (with whom he was flirting in a most shameless way last year)?—No. —An offer of some post fit for young men unattached, under the department of M. de Noirceuil, minister of the interior? —No. —A plenary absolution *pros*pective and *retro*spective of all his sins, under the hand and seal of M. l'abbé Chabert? —Alas, by no means. —A sermon on the errors of youth and vanity of human enjoyments, from the Most Reverend superior of Ste. Marie des Bois? [3] —Nor that.

I was at my wit's end, and could not think what was come to the poor unfortunate boy. Next day, for the sake of school friendship, and being uneasy about him in case any cruel game had been played with his nerves or brain which are as susceptible as a girl's—the only other instance I ever knew of such acute sensibilities was in the case of our late fair friend, the lamented Mlle. Justine N.—I went up to his room. (He had not appeared that day.) On getting no answer to my knocks and calls, I had the door forced. The wretched victim of M. Rodin's literary propensity was crouching down on the floor,

1. Undoubtedly the "schoolmaster's autobiography" referred to in Letters 42 and 43, above.

2. La Comtesse de Lorsange, sister of Justine, whose life is retailed—rather, wholesaled—in *Juliette, ou les prospérités du vice*. Noirceuil and the Abbé Chabert appear in the same work, as do Olympe, Princesse de Borghèse, the Cardinal de Bernis, and Madame de Clairwil, who are all referred to later. The entire second paragraph is a parody and elaboration of part of a pious article on Sade by Jules Janin (see above, Letter 34), who describes, in maudlin fashion, how one evening's exposure to a work by Sade had shocked his friend Julien into a state of driveling idiocy. The doctor's name was suggested by "Imbert," a character in *Justine*.

3. Dom Severino in *Justine*.

clutching the seat of his breeches, sobbing, with eyes of green circled with scarlet, and starting out of his head, blue-black in the face, foaming at the mouth, his teeth alternately grinding and chattering, his limbs sprawling, speechless, nerveless, idiotic. Medical assistance was called in, in the person of a Neapolitan refugee doctor strenuously recommended by Mme. la princesse Olympe de Borghèse and H. E. Cardinal de Bernis. This gentleman had during the late régime been employed under the superintendant of the Neapolitan Lunatic Hospital—a post which he had to leave for other than political reasons: though I believe he now lays it entirely on Garibaldi. Attended by a large and handsome Newfoundland dog (an animal which you know my finer feline instincts abhor), the doctor, who perfectly remembered meeting while in his old office Mesdames de Lorsange and de Clairwil on their travels, and gave unequivocal indications of interest, and even excitement on learning that his present patient was acquainted with one at least of the two ladies so hospitably entertained by his superior and himself, at once proceeded to the sick chamber. He allowed no witness and required no assistant; the operation he said might be long, must be painful, could not be certain. Though why he should want a scalpel, a bistouri, a thing like a garden idol or simulacrum, and a set of materials for cautery, to operate upon a fellow suffering from temporary aberration of mind produced by a sudden shock, I could not then and cannot now conceive. For nearly an hour the agonized watchers heard at intervals shrieks and moans issuing from the room, accompanied now and then by loud and furious barks. At the end of that time Dr. Imberti reappeared. All that man could do, he assured us, had been done. There was no hope. Exhausted by emotion, and refusing to accept any fee, he left us drowned in tears. The dog, I noticed, went off with his tail between his legs, looking ashamed, as well he might after an intrusion into the private chamber of a patient which no attachment could justify. However I do believe his master had done his best. The poor fellow is now in an asylum near Southampton: and I trust M. Rodin is now satisfied.

Need I add, that, like J. Janin in a similar case, I purloined and perused the fatal MS? M. Rodin is decidedly a man of exquisite and original powers of mind. It is interesting to compare his manner and method with those of our old tutor—poor Redgie's and mine. They wear their rue with a difference.[4] E.g. I am surprised that a man of refinement, whom I had taken to be an educational aristocrat of the purest water—and blood, should have mixed the bitter-sweet fountain of Heliconian brine, the pure salt Hippocrene of boys' tears and

4. *Hamlet*, IV. v. 183.

birchen pickle, with the obscene puddle of corduroy bourgeoisie. Is a 'greasy grasp' to pollute by its distracting and nauseous contact the skin of a boy's hands while the skin of his bottom is reddening with the voluptuous blush of a most delicate agony? Is a butcher's blood to tingle, a tailor's flesh to wince, from the discipline of nobles, the correction of a prince? The spontaneous Muse rebukes so foul a fancy. Did not that blood of the Plantagenets which (and no thanks to the Heralds' College) we both share, burn in your cheeks as in mine (upper cheeks or under I say not) at the degrading thought? F——— de Jacques Bonhomme! Not at least the same block, the same birch. No mean beasts of ushers. No canes. No fustian men. Nothing greasy. Nor do I approve of restoratives and housekeepers. Still less of the rod of thorny roses—except as a metaphor. (Vide Marino's Adone, first woodcut of the small edition.) [5] Nothing that bruises. Nothing that merely lacerates. Black and blue is hideous. *Mere* scratches and scars and gashes are stupid. *Sting* your victim well at each cut. Make fair red weals on him, tingling ridges of throbbing purple and darkening crimson. You will hurt more pungently if less roughly and savagely. No brutality. 'Il faut humer avec une volupté lente, soigneuse, concentrée, les délices de la douleur infligée ou partagée, le plaisir aigu du supplice prolongé par des raffinements délicats, dont un butor ivre ou furieux n'a jamais conçu la moindre idée.' Ah, my Titan! Enceladus-Priapus, begotten on the foam of the everlasting deep by the severed genitals of Time (see Grote)! [6] And did it not take centuries of the noblest descent to produce you in earthly likeness, a Messiah of the West, perfect, without flaw, wonderful, terrible, with no alloy of human weakness? And were you not passed, O our master and chiefest among the prophets, from the Herod Louis to the Pilate Buonaparte, from the Golgotha of Vincennes to the Calvary of Charenton? [7] Caiaphas-Talleyrand, Iscariot-Barras,

5. G. B. Marino, *L'Adone, poema heroico,* published in four volumes in Amsterdam in 1678. Stanza 17 of Canto I describes the picture:

> Con flagello di rose insieme attorte,
> Ch'avea groppi de spine, ella il percosse,
> E de' bei membri, onde si dolce forte,
> Fè le vivaci porpore più rosse.

6. In the first chapter of Grote's *History of Greece*: "Presently night arrived, and Uranos descended to the embraces of Gaea: Kronos then emerged from his concealment, cut off the genitals of his father, and cast the bleeding member behind him far away into the sea."

7. Sade was imprisoned by Louis XVI in Vincennes and by Napoleon in Charenton.

Couthon the scribe and Robespierre the Pharisee,[8] 'were these men on thy side'? Were not thy worse persecutors plebeians, bourgeois usurpers, cotton-velvet nobles, and governors made of shoddy? Was not thy little flock gathered out of the vieille noblesse—those that sat under the shadow of thy branches? And shall *we* have 'town-boys' and 'ushers' and the 'greasy-fisted' in 'faithful fustian' to minister even in the outer court of the Gentiles, even at the gentle altar of St. Scholastica, and the Lady-Chapels of Venus Flagellatrix or Minerva Betuligera? Ἀφροδίτη Μαστιγόφορος ἤ Ἀθήνη Ῥαβδοῦχος [9]

À Priape ne plaise!

45. TO RICHARD MONCKTON MILNES

MS: The Marchioness of Crewe.

[*ca.* February 10, 1863]

A [1] thousand thanks for the Punch: I had not seen the advertisement.[2] Do for heaven's sake find out the man; you must be able, knowing half the world. Quel délicieux coquin que cet homme-là! Aura-t-il du plaisir ce s - - - - b - - - - -! Can't we answer it privately, and desire him to address Mme. de Clairwil, Poste Restante, Bournemouth, Care of M. le chevalier de Sade? A widower? *Can* it be M. de Gernande [3] himself? Ah heaven, to run back but four years! would you believe that at that time I did quite well (that is, I was a *credible* being—I don't say *attractive!*) in female attire, and should have been invaluable on a pinch of theatrical necessities? It is a lamentable truth that Lady Trevelyan had then a dark project of passing me off upon Madame Sand as the typical *miss anglaise émancipée* and holding the most ultra views; we made up no end of history about it, and infinite ad-

8. The Comte Paul-François de Barras, a member of the Directoire, is said to have been libeled by Sade in *Zoloë et ses deux acolytes* (1800), under the name of Vicomte de Sabar (C. R. Dawes, *The Marquis de Sade*, 1927, p. 71). Georges Couthon, who was nearly as red-handed as Robespierre, was guillotined along with him in 1794.

9. That is, "Scourge-bearing Aphrodite or Minerva bearing a rod."

1. The beginning of the letter is missing.

2. Quoted in *Punch* (Jan. 31, 1863), p. 67, from the Liverpool *Daily Post*: "Wanted, a Young Lady, about 20, as Housekeeper to a Widower, and to take charge of three boys, the eldest ten years old. Must be of good appearance and address; accomplishments not essential. Salary £25. Address, stating age, and if willing to give corporal punishment, A. Z., Post Office, Chester."

3. In *Justine*.

ventures for the British Mademoiselle de Maupin. I saw the likeness then done the other day at Wallington, and howled over it. Such is life.[4] Now, alas! had I that chance left which my majority bereft me of, quelle chance! The wildest flattery of friendship could not now aver that even shaving and rouge would make a presentable girl of me. ὀτοτοτότοι [5] What a life lost! what a subject for romance! I once played Mrs. Skewton to admiration: [6] but what was that to this! or even the jeune fille émancipée! Ah, what prospects on all sides, but chiefly backwards! I know he will get a fool, or a 'fesseuse[?] sans pudeur' who won't work delicately and effectively. At least let us find out more about it; we may perhaps come to know him and take part in the scenes that *must* ensue; at all events we could send him the assurance of our most distinguished sympathies. It's near where you have been staying—in Cheshire—you *must* find out.

J'allais oublier deux supplices. I am amazed at the erratic—shall I say the obtuse?—imagination which could suggest Latona as the third word of my Bill-Weal acrostic.[7] (I want to know your solutions of the others left with you.) The other words are right; that word is Laura. See the Biogr[aphie] Univ[erselle] 'Laure, née de Noves, amie de Pétrarque, épousa Hugues de Sade' who begat Pierre de Sade who begat Louis de Sade who begat Jacques de Sade (Admiral) who begat Jean de Sade (Grand Constable) who begat Olivier de Sade who begat Bertrand de Sade who begat François de Sade who begat Claude-Marie-Xavier de Sade who begat Donatien-Alphonse-François, marquis de Sade, who begat Justine and Juliette! My memory overleaps some scores of obscurer names; but I hope you *now* see the point of the admirable couplet put into the mouth of the chaste heroine of Vaucluse.

Make all manner of excuses from me to Rodin. He must understand that my feelings were too much shattered by the hideous catastrophe to let him know sooner the deplorable result of his missive. I fear it will only give him pleasure. Man is a fallen animal. For my part I thirst for more. If I might add one criticism I should say no one birching was sufficiently circumstantial. Redgie and I used to suffer more than that in the simple orthodox way at the hands of the tutor [8] I

4. Gampese (*Martin Chuzzlewit,* chap. 29).

5. "Ah! woe!"

6. "I remember one occasion on which he made us all into a kind of *tableau* out of 'Dombey and Son'—himself taking the part of Mrs. Skewton in her Bath chair!" (Leith, p. 8).

7. See above, Letter 43.

8. Probably James Leigh Joynes (1824–1908) of Eton.

have told you of. His great idea (I believe *really* he had some idea of the sort) was *to inflict no pain elsewhere while the swishing proceeded.* I should have been thankful (barring the *insult* which we should have resented) for the *diversion* of a box on the ear sometimes, such as Rodin's superincumbent John 'bestowed.' I have known him (I am really speaking now in my own person) prepare the flogging-room (*not* with *corduroy* or *onion* but) with burnt scents; or choose a *sweet* place out of doors with smell of firwood. *This* I call real delicate torment. Please tell me what you think. Once, before giving me a swishing that I had the marks of for more than a month (so fellows declared that I went to swim with), he let me saturate my face with eau-de-Cologne. I conjecture now, on looking back to that 'rosy hour' with eyes 'purged by the euphrasy and rue'[9] of the Marquis de Sade and his philosophy, that, counting on the pungency of the perfume and its power over the nerves, he meant to stimulate and excite the senses by that preliminary pleasure so as to inflict the acuter pain afterwards on their awakened and intensified susceptibility. If he did, I am still gratified to reflect that I beat him; the poor dear old beggar overreached himself, for the pleasure of smell is so excessive and intense with me that even if the smart of birching had been unmixed pain, I could have borne it all the better for that previous indulgence. Perhaps he had no such idea, and I, grown over-wise through perusal of Justine and Juliette, now do him more than justice; but he was a stunning tutor; his one other pet subject was *metre,* and I firmly believe that my ear for verses made me rather a favourite. I can boast that of all the swishings I ever had up to seventeen and over, I never had one for a false quantity in my life. (Can you say the same? I should imagine you *metrical* as a boy.) One comfort is, I made it up in arithmetic, so my tutor never wanted reasons for making rhymes between his birch and my body.

You must excuse my scribbling at this rate when I once begin, for the sake of that autobiographical fact about perfume and pain, which you can now vouch for as the experience of a real live boy. I always wanted to know if other fellows shared the feeling. Conceive trying it in a grove of budding birch-trees scented all over with the green spring. Ah-h-h!

I remain

Yours affectionately,
A. C. Swinburne

9. *Paradise Lost,* Bk. XI. 414.

46. TO RICHARD MONCKTON MILNES

MS: The Marchioness of Crewe.

Belmont, Bournemouth, 12 février [1863]

Monsieur

Au sein d'une détresse profonde et, j'ose le dire, peu méritée par des vertus, j'invoque votre bonté sympathique. Il y a six mois, monsieur, six petits mois bien longs et bien malheureux pour moi, j'étais fille du président de la cour d'assises de Dijon. Protégés par Mgr. l'archevêque de Grenoble,[1] nos jours s'écoulaient dans un calme heureux au milieu de tous les vices et de toutes les horreurs. Vous savez sans doute—qui ne le sait pas maintenant, grâce aux soins estimables d'un homme illustre?—quelles furent nos habitudes et nos façons de vivre. Eh bien! monsieur, tout s'est écroulé dans un jour.

Après la séance délicieuse et si bien décrite par le philosophe justement célèbre dont je viens de parler, dans laquelle nous avons supplicié à plusieurs retours la nommée Justine, vous vous souvenez, je l'espère qu'on a remporté de chez nous cette indigne créature, déjà, il est vrai, mise en pièces, mais ayant toujours un souffle de vie à ses lèvres mutilées. Dieu m'est témoin que ce n'était pas ma faute à moi: j'ose invoquer aussi le témoignage bien plus respectable du marquis de Sade. Ce grand écrivain vous fera voir que mon amie Nicette et moi nous avons conjuré nos pères de nous accorder la permission d'achever sur-le-champ cette fille abominable. Malheureusement on n'a pas voulu nous écouter; cette éxécrable créature n'a pas versé toutes les larmes et tout le sang de sons corps odieux; le crime est resté à moitié consommé. Admirez, Monsieur, les voies de la Providence, qui a voulu aussitôt nous punir de cette vertu bien involontaire. L'infâme geôlier par les soins duquel cette prude maudite s'est évadé de son cachot—pour périr, à ce qu'on nous dit, par un coup de foudre quelques jours plus tard—mais quel supplice pitoyable, mon cher monsieur! et comme on voit bien que ce Dieu-là n'a pas d'imagination!—ce vilain homme, après avoir examiné les plaies qui sillonnaient le corps affreux de son abominable protégée, a osé venir déposer contre mon père et les siens en pleine cour. On a suborné un des jeunes gens qui nous avaient servi de

---

1. In *Justine,* though only a bishop. This entire letter purports to be a reply to the advertisement discussed in the preceding letter. Zulma de Cardoville, Nicette, and Brumeton appear in the concluding chapter of *Justine,* and the letter picks up Zulma where the novel left her. Jérôme, Gernande, Esterval, and Verneuil, who are referred to later on, are prominent characters in earlier chapters.

plastron pendant cette scène délicieuse; nous avons dû fuir. Je ne sais ce que sont devenus les autres; moi, je suis parvenue en Angleterre et maintenant je vis ici caché chez un ami auquel M. de Sade a bien voulu m'expédier des lettres de recommandation. Cet ami m'a fait voir, Monsieur, un extrait de feuilleton que vous lui aviez envoyé. Il s'agit, à ce qu'il parait, de retrouver une femme jeune, belle, érotique, cruelle, avec des goûts prononcés pour le supplice des jeunes garçons. On remettrait entre les mains de cette femme trois enfants de ce sexe. Pour le physique, Monsieur, vous retrouverez, en relisant le 20me chapitre de *Justine* (ah, fille éxécrable! je m'interromps encore pour cracher sur ton nom maudit!) vous y retrouverez, dis-je, mon portrait tracé par les pinceaux énergiques d'un grand maître. J'ose croire que le temps n'a point encore terni l'éclat quelconque de mes faibles attraits. Pour le moral, je puis l'affirmer, M. de Sade est resté au-dessous de la vérité simple et nue en me peignant comme la plus insatiable, la plus impitoyable, la plus endurcie, la plus corrompue de toutes les femmes. J'ai maintenant vingt-deux ans et trois mois, je n'ai de ma vie connu un seul sentiment de pitié; ainsi, je dois l'avouer, je me trouve de toutes les façons bien propre à servir aux plaisirs de votre ami et au développement physique et moral de ses enfants, que je brûle déjà de supplicier.

Veuillez donc faire parvenir l'annonce de mon nom et de mes qualités à cet homme aimable. Le digne père Jérôme, le vénérable comte de Gernande, la célèbre baronne d'Esterval, son ami M. le vicomte de Verneuil, ont daigné me prêter leur appui dans cette occasion: et ce sera, monsieur, pour une âme comme la vôtre, un souvenir bien consolant que celui d'avoir tendu une main compatissante à une jeune fille dans le besoin, tout en satisfaisant aux devoirs inaltérables d'une philosophie éclairée dont vous savez si bien apprécier les réclamations.

Vous demandez à mon jeune ami son avis sur l'extrait de journal que nous vous renvoyons. Il me prie de vous répondre qu'il y a là-dessous une odeur assez prononcée de nègre; qu'il n'aime pas les noirs; et qu'il se défie de l'esprit militaire. Les négresses, dit-il, sont des guenons; les soldats sont des bélîtres. Tout cela n'est vraiment bon que pour ce vieux cuistre de Rodin, qui a des idées dignes de New-York, et qui n'est après tout qu'un Américain manqué, ne comprenant rien aux gentillesses sanguinaires, aux gracieusetés cruelles, du vrai sectateur de Priape. Je vous avoue que je partage en ceci les idées de mon ami.

Pardonnez si je vous écris par sa main; mais je ne puis que dicter: je ne saurais tenir une plume. Je me suis donnée hier une entorse assez grave au poignet droit, en fouettant à l'outrance un enfant de treize ans, beau comme le jour, qui s'était rendu coupable d'un acte odieux de bienfaisance. Ce petit malheureux se nomme Arthur; il est frère cadet du jeune Frank Fane que vous avez autrefois connu. Il nous donnait des espérances délicieuses; cet enfant avait les germes de tous les vices concevables; aussi figurez-vous l'étonnement, la douleur, l'indignation de mon ami, quand il a rencontré sur une place publique ce jeune scélérat qui faisait l'aumône à un vieillard en haillons! Quelle horreur! monsieur, partagez nos sentiments. Vivement ému par ce trait de perversité, il a sauté au collet du petit coquin en s'écriant 'Ah, tu veux soulager les souffrances, toi? on t'en donnera, des souffrances!' et il l'a entraîné chez moi. Le méchant garçon sanglotait, hurlait, demandait grâce, se jetait à nos genoux. Ah! monsieur, que n'étiez-vous là! Comme il pleurait délicieusement! comme il avait peur! comme il maudissait de tout son cœur la vertu! Cependant nous apprêtons le chevalet, les cravaches, et des verges —oh! mais des verges impayables; nous avions dépouillé tout un canton de bouleaux. Je me charge des fesses; je ne veux m'occuper que de cette partie délicate; je livre à mon ami tout le reste du corps. Je me précipite sur le bel Arthur, je lui donne des soufflets, je lui arrache les cheveux d'or soyeux, je l'accable de reproches et d'outrages. Mon ami et moi nous le déshabillons; ce nouveau frère, qui remplace dans mon cœur le charmant Brumeton, lui lâche à travers les épaules une pluie furieuse de cinglons avec une jolie petite cravache; bientôt tout ce dos blanc, charnu, potelé, délicieux, est couvert de traces et de sillons sanglants. Moi, je le contenais de mes bras et de mes genoux. Dieu! comme il bondissait! comme il se tordait! comme il nous suppliait de l'épargner! Ah! monsieur, qui l'eût épargné? il aurait fallu être un rocher pour demeurer insensible à cette scène inqualifiable. Quels cris! quelles chairs! Enfin mon digne ami me cède la place. Figurez-vous ce dos nu couvert des plus belles marques rouges et pourpres depuis la nuque jusqu'au reins, et au-dessous de tout cela le lait pur et blanc, la neige chaude et frémissante, de ces fesses sans tâche! Ivre, furieuse, hors de moi, j'applique aussitôt sur cet admirable derrière deux cents coups de verges. Chaque cinglon est donné de toutes mes forces. Arthur pleure et rugit, crie et saigne de plus en plus. Enfin, en me penchant sur ses reins écorchés pour lui sangler le 2000me coup bien à travers les fesses déchirées, je sens en frappant son sang éparpillé sur ma figure et qui, littéralement, me saute aux yeux; mais je ressens aussi une douleur aigüe et qui me fait mêler aux hurlements du pauvre garçon un cri plus vif encore: je m'aperçois de cette malheureuse entorse; je crois m'être démis le poignet. Je crie, j'écume, je blasphème cette Providence abominable qui trompe encore une fois mes désirs éveillés; je demande à grand cris La Croix d'Aiguilles, invention délicieuse du génie de mon aimable père: enfin je m'appaise; je propose à mon bon ami d'exécuter sur-le-champ une idée charmante—idée, je m'en flatte au moins, pas du tout indigne de la fille du président de Cardoville; la voici. On aurait appliqué sur la fesse gauche une emplâtre de glace; on aurait piqué les chairs sanglantes à travers cette emplâtre avec une aiguille rougie au feu; ainsi on eût pu raviver, geler, et calciner à la fois les plaies de ce côté. On aurait cependant fait rôtir avec une broche la fesse droite, sans la couper; on l'aurait sauté à l'huile et au lard, et puis nous l'aurions pu manger tout vif sur le corps. Pour moi, je vous l'affirme, j'eusse pris le plus grand plaisir à manger ces fesses-là toutes crues. L'eau m'en débordait de la bouche et m'échaudait le menton (style Flaubert); j'en senti mouiller tout le bas de mes joues. —Voilà, je l'espère, une idée assez appétissante; manger tout vif un cul d'enfant cuit dans son propre sang, servi à l'huile, au lard, à la neige, et tout cela dans un même instant. Ah! monsieur, quel plaisir inexprimable que de réunir ainsi par un seul trait de génie Néron, Apicius, Orbilius, et Ivan-le-Terrible! Après cela, venez donc me parler de vos idées de jésuite, et nous reprocher, à mon ami et à moi, le culte des supplices orientaux! Je crois, oui, je le crois ferme-ment, que mon illustre ami le marquis de Sade lui-même ne répudierait point l'idée de ce supplice-là. Mais hélas! monsieur, il parait que votre malheureux pays gémit toujours sous le joug in-supportable d'un système de lois qui se mêle de réprimer les élans divins de la nature, et de protéger sous son égide méprisable cette chimère vraiment dégoûtante qu'on appelle la vertu. Mon frère me l'a dit en pleurant, votre éxécrable gouvernement, muni des pouvoirs funestes de son infâme législature, aurait pu nous en punir. Ah! monsieur, ce serait en vérité une tâche digne d'un philosophe, d'un philanthrope éclairé, d'un homme d'état sage, puissant, respectable, que d'initier des réformes au moyen desquelles on pût briser, anéantir, dissiper ces lois détestables! Les siècles à venir béniraient toujours le grand législateur qui aurait réduit en poussière des lois aussi indignes. Vous, monsieur, vous pouvez encore vous revendiquer cette gloire; vous pouvez toujours vous ceindre le front de cette auréole im-périssable. Levez-vous; éclatez; tonnez; appuyez de toute la force de votre parole la cause sainte et vénérable de vos pareils. La chambre, électrisée, vous décrétera les plus grands honneurs; ce triste pays, libre enfin des entraves abominables de la vertu, tombera à vos pieds en proférant des actions de grâces. —En attendant, j'ai dû, tout en gémissant, me soumettre à cette nécessité affreuse, ignoble, j'ai dû me contenter de faire encore refouetter le jeune Arthur par les mains de mon ami. C'était un spectacle—permettez-moi cette phrase hasardée—à faire décharger une vestale. Arthur était charmant: il a eu sous le fouet des torsions, des convulsions, des rugissements inexprimables. Jamais, non, jamais, son frère ainé n'a tant souffert sous la main de ce misérable Rodin. Enfin nous l'avons lâché; il s'en est allé noyé dans les pleurs: et je ne crois pas qu'il ira bientôt s'amuser à refaire l'aumône aux pauvres vertueux.

Cependant mon ami vous supplie de lui faire parvenir en entier la solution de l'acrostique qu'il a fait en mon honneur, et des autres que vous avez reçu de sa main. Il vous supplie aussi de lui faire parvenir des nouvelles d'un de ses amis dont je ne saurais me rappeler le nom par trop anglais. Nous allons en attendant rebassiner encore cette fois avec une infusion de vinaigre et d'eau salée les plaies du beau jeune Arthur. Idée délicieuse! je les reverrai encore, ces jolies fesses de garçon si fermes, si rondes, si bien soutenues! et en quel état! Ah! monsieur, je suffoque—je me pâme—je n'en puis plus.

Agréez cependant l'assurance de ma haute considération, et des sentiments distingués avec lesquels je suis

Monsieur,

Votre servante bien dévouée,

Zulma de Cardoville

Vous avez peut-être lu dans les journaux qu'on vient de violer 'd'une façon affreuse, avec des épisodes à faire frémir la nature' (qui par parenthèse ne frémit jamais) une jeune dame qui voyageait auprès de Lyons. C'est moi qui ai fait ce coup-là. J'ai dépucelé cette chère fille avec un godmiché, tout en m'enfuyant.

Post-scriptum

Je désire appuyer de toutes mes forces la supplique de Mlle. de Cardoville. Cette fille intéressante me parait faite exprès pour faire honneur au choix du philosophe provincial: et quand je serai de retour à Londres—ce qui sera, je l'espère, au commencement du mois prochain—j'irai moi-même soutenir sa cause auprès de vous. Pour l'entorse, franchement, je n'y crois pas beaucoup. En transcrivant cette lettre j'ai aperçu que Mlle. Zulma se branlait incessamment tout en dictant; et je lui crois encore une vigueur plus que suffisante aux deux poignets.

A.C.S.

47. ROBERT BROWNING TO RICHARD MONCKTON MILNES

Text: K. L. Knickerbocker, "Browning and Swinburne: an Episode," *Modern Language Notes, 62* (1947), 240–44.

19, Warwick Crescent,
Upper Westbourne Terrace, W.
July 7, 1863

My dear Milnes

I should like to put down in words what I said last night when considerably surprised and a little annoyed: you will see how mere talk gets turned aside from its purpose; and for reasons, I am somewhat susceptible on this point.

I know next to nothing of Swinburne, and like him much: I have received courtesy from him, and been told he feels kindly to me—I believe it, indeed. Of his works, since his first volume, I know not a line, except a poem which I looked over a long while ago at Rossetti's, and the pieces he recited the other night: I could only have an opinion, therefore, on these. I thought them moral mistakes, redeemed by much intellectual ability. They may be a sample of the forthcoming book,—or just the exceptional instances—I hope so.

When I was abruptly appealed to, some days after, for my estimate of Mr. Swinburne's powers,—I don't know what I could do but say 'that he had genius, and wrote verses in which to my mind there was no good at all.'

If I referred,—as I probably did,—to a similarity of opinion on the part of others present, it was from the reluctance I had to stand forward and throw even this cherry-stone at a young poet.

How I came by this reluctance, and keep it increasingly in spite of age ('which loses all sense of the good and the beautiful, the this and the that')—God knows! I have for thirty years my own utter unintelligibility taught with such public and private zest that I might be excused for fancying every young man's knuckles wanted 'dusting' —but I don't fancy it. Unluckily the truth is the truth, and one must speak it now and then. It was a shame in this case for Chapman to quote my blame of two or three little pieces—given on a demand for unqualified praise which was impossible—as the reason for rejecting a whole bookful of what may be real poetry, for aught I am aware: but as I am in the habit of being as truthful as I like about the quality of certain things which he patronizes, and as I never saw their titles disappear from his advertisements in consequence—I conclude that he only uses my witnessing when he wants to cover his own conviction.

> I am, my dear Milnes,
> Your[s] ever faithfully,
> Robert Browning

48. TO WILLIAM MICHAEL ROSSETTI

MS: Rutgers. Extracts in Lafourcade, *La Jeunesse*, 2, 322, 334–35.

East Dene, August 8 [1863]

Dear Rossetti

Many thanks for your note and the enclosed letters. One from Taylor [1] accompanying seemingly I can't tell what, but possibly a book he mentions of some Padre Moorchesi's [2] on the Borgias. If so could you have it sent me? also if Pope can find it my copy of Dumas' 'Les Borgia'? [3]

My other letter was from Ruskin [4] returning some MSS of mine that

1. George Warrington Taylor hardly emerges from the background. He entered Eton in 1850 and left before 1853, apparently having there some acquaintance with Swinburne. Later he did a stint in the army, and he was at some time converted to Roman Catholicism. Indigence and a love of music impelled him to be check-taker at Her Majesty's Theatre (in those days an opera house) in the Haymarket, a job that held him for two years or so till, through the good offices of Gabriel Rossetti, he became bookkeeper for the firm of Morris, Marshall, Faulkner, and Co., in which Rossetti had for a while a vested interest. Taylor brought to the company the hardheaded business brain of which it was in dire need, and was so energetic and successful that he soon became business manager. "He was a man of great ability and sweetness of character," wrote J. W. Mackail (*The Life of William Morris, 1*, 176), "incapable of taking care of his own affairs, but shrewd and careful in his management of other people's business." Lady Georgiana Burne-Jones, *Memorials of Edward Burne-Jones* (2 vols. New York and London, 1904), *1*, 291, described him as "strange, wild-looking," and William Allingham (H. Allingham and D. Radford, eds., *William Allingham, a Diary*, 1907, p. 165), calling on him in 1867, noted: "Poor Taylor—tall, with eager hatchet face—is ghastly thin but full of mental energy—vociferates, then must stop to cough." Taylor died of tuberculosis in Feb. 1870.

2. Unidentified.

3. In *Crimes célèbres,* Par MM. Alexandre Dumas, Arnould, Fournier, Fiorentino et Mallefille (8 vols. Paris, 1840–43). Pope was Rossetti's servant.

4. "The world does not want more imaginary tragedy than it possesses," Ruskin wrote, "and I think every man of intellectual power should now devote himself to overthrowing its idols and leading the way to healthy conceptions and healthy work. I should be sorry that you publish these poems, for I think they would win you a

I don't at all want unpacked: a very amiable and rather singular letter, which I fell to and answered at once and at length. I cannot understand his combining philanthropic morality with such exquisite sense of what is right and good in things far higher than any matter of right and wrong selon les reveurs. Yet I refrained from citing Justine—'La vertu, ma chère J., est une chose essentiellement stérile, impuissante, bornée, tandis que le vice fait germer et fleurir etc. etc.' appropriate as that citation, a pearl of priceless wisdom for artist or moralist, would have been; admire my chaste forbearance.

R. actually intimates that 'genius ought to devote itself' to the help of humanity and 'to overthrowing its idols,' in a word to justify the ways of Urizen to the sons of Enitharmon.[5] Quelle horreur! Yet again I abstained from replying that when a man of genius did devote himself to the benefit of humanity and the upsetting of its idols (notamment 'cette chimère méprisable qu'on appelle la Vertu, et cette chimère éxécrable qu'on appelle Dieu') and to guiding it in the pleasant paths of wisdom and Ste. Marie des Bois, humanity rewards their supreme benefactor with a madhouse or a gaol. Could he have answered that? but I keep this crushing argument in reserve.

The Blake things I wanted were these:
1. The list with dates of his books. 2. The Life which I meant to bring with me and finish reviewing while here: I suppose Pope did bring it back from Ned's all right. If I get these I can pretty well finish all my review except what refers to the yet untouched Prophecies. If attainable too I should like to consult 1) your Catalogue 2) the proofs of the Songs of Innocence and Experience 3) the prose selections. I have only the earlier and latter poems in proof sheets. I found packed up by mistake among my things the Blake MS. book and your Jones' Poets;[6] neither of which I should have taken without leave, and if you or Gabriel want them please let me know: I take good care of them meantime.

I am half living in the sea here, rough or smooth; and generally swimming riding and croquetting myself into a rampant state of muscular Christianity. I think soon of sending to press 'A Plain

---

dark reputation, and take away from your future power of teaching and delighting." (The entire letter, dated July 5, is printed in, among other places, *A Swinburne Library*, p. 261.) When and where Swinburne and Ruskin (1819–1900) first met is not known. Lafourcade (*La Jeunesse, 1*, 108) suggests Wallington in Aug. 1853.

5. See Blake's *Prophetic Books*.

6. Perhaps Benjamin Charles Jones, *One Hundred Lectures on the Ancient and Modern Dramatic Poets, the Heathen Mythology, Oratory and Elocution, Down to the Nineteenth Century*, a series begun in 1862.

Sportsman's Vindication of his Bible from the Attacks of Bishop Colenso.'[7]

En attendant with love to Gabriel and Fanny, (also to Ned if you see him) and thanks for your trouble about Blake, I am

Yours affectionately,
A. C. Swinburne

49. CHARLES BAUDELAIRE TO SWINBURNE

Text: Félix Nadar, *Charles Baudelaire* (Paris, 1911), pp. 108–11.

A Monsieur Charles A. Swinburne,
16, Cheyne Walk, Chelsea,
London.

10 octobre 1863

Monsieur,

Un de mes plus vieux amis, va à Londres, M. Nadar,[1] que vous aurez sans doute quelque plaisir à connaître. Je vous prie de vouloir bien faire pour lui tout ce que vous auriez fait sans doute pour moi, si j'étais allé m'adresser au public de votre patrie. Indications, conseils, réclames, il a besoin de beaucoup de choses.

Je sais infiniment de gré à Nadar de m'avoir demandé des lettres pour mes très rares accointances de Londres, car il m'a ainsi forcé de m'acquitter vis-à-vis de vous d'une grosse dette depuis longtemps non payée . . . je veux parler du merveilleux article (sur les *Fleurs du mal*) que vous avez produit en septembre 1862 dans le *Spectator*.

Un jour, M. R. Wagner m'a sauté au cou pour me remercier d'une brochure que j'avais faite sur *Tannhauser*, et m'a dit: '*Je n'aurais jamais cru qu'un littérateur français pût comprendre si facilement tant de choses.*' N'étant pas exclusivement patriote, j'ai pris de son compliment tout ce qu'il avait de gracieux. Permettez-moi, à mon tour, de vous dire: '*Je n'aurais jamais cru qu'un littérateur anglais pût si bien pénétrer la beauté française, les intentions françaises et la prosodie française.*' Mais après la lecture des vers imprimés dans le même numéro (August)[2] et pénétré d'un sentiment à la fois si réel

7. Late in 1862 Bishop Colenso of Natal published the first part of *The Pentateuch and the Book of Joshua Critically Examined*, a mathematical demonstration that the first six books of the Old Testament, taken literally, were a mosaic of errors.

1. Pseudonym of Félix Tournachon (1820–1910), artist and writer. Nadar confessed himself (*Charles Baudelaire*, p. 108) unable to recall why the letter had not been employed. "D'ailleurs," he added, "la chose est de peu d'intérêt."

2. (Bonchurch, *1*, 343–45), reprinted in *PB1*.

et si subtil, je n'ai pas été étonné du tout: il n'y a que les poètes pour bien comprendre les poètes.

Permettez-moi, cependant, de vous dire que vous avez poussé un peu loin ma défense. Je ne suis pas si *moraliste* que vous feignez obligeamment de le croire. Je crois simplement 'comme vous sans doute' que tout poème, tout objet d'art *bien fait* suggère naturellement et forcément une *morale*. C'est l'affaire du lecteur. J'ai même une haine très décidée contre toute *intention* morale exclusive dans un poème.

Ayez la bonté de m'envoyer ce que vous publiez: j'y prendrai un grand plaisir. J'ai plusieurs livres à publier, je vous les expédierai successivement.

Veuillez agréer, Monsieur, l'expression très vive de ma gratitude et de ma sympathie.

Charles Baudelaire

A Paris, 22, rue d'Amsterdam.
A Honfleur, rue de Neubourg.
Je suis à Paris jusqu'à la fin de ce mois et je passerai tout décembre à Bruxelles.

50. TO WILLIAM MICHAEL ROSSETTI

MS: Rutgers. Two sentences in Lafourcade, *La Jeunesse*, 2, 322.

East Dene, October 11 [1863]

Dear William

I must write you at length a word of thanks for your letter—the first I received: I have since heard from Gabriel, and answer both by this post. His letter was as kind as yours, and as pleasant to receive.[1]

I hope there is no further cause of alarm for Brown; I was very sorry to hear there had been so much. Do you know anything of a committee at Newcastle for presenting some testimonial to Scott?[2] or what sort of thing it intends to do? They have sent me their prospectus, as I suppose they have to you; and one would like to know what was in view.

When I return to Chelsea I shall enrich the house with various glories of Chinese origin, fit to make Wareham *crever* and to swamp

1. Edith Swinburne died on Sep. 25. See above, Letter 43.

2. William Bell Scott's mastership in the School of Design came to an end in 1863 or early in 1864.

Fenchurch Street for ever. Besides a huge screen [3] of which I have given Gabriel some brief account I have two painted looking glasses (flowers on the glass) and two pictures on alabaster: frames of all four delicious. Pictures represent Topsy in the pangs of labour, tarred and feathered. To the unscientific, and those later and baser 'Kings who know not' Topsy, he appears a mere bird; to the eye of Science the symbolism of the inspired artist is at once transparent.

Till I return, which will be in two or three weeks, my direction will be 'Northcourt, Shorwell, Isle of Wight.' [4] I have made great way with Blake thanks to your help. The papers sent were of great value to me; and I hope you will approve of the completed essay on the Poems and MSS. of Blake. I am curious to see the second number of the Fine Arts: I thought the list of articles fairly promising, barring one incredible announcement of a malodorous emanation from the kennel of Kingsley,[5] which seems to hold a post of some honour among the contributions.—Can you tell me if Landor's long-advertised 'Heroic Idyls etc.' are out? if so I should be much obliged if you would tell Pope to get and send me a copy: publisher is Newby! 'To such base (publishers) may we return' [6]—at ninety. With best remembrances and thanks to you and yours for the sympathy expressed in your note. Believe me always

Yours most sincerely,
A. C. Swinburne

51. TO WILLIAM MICHAEL ROSSETTI

MS: Rutgers. Extract in Lafourcade, La Jeunesse, 2, 322.

Northcourt, December 15 [1863]

My dear Rossetti

Will you see if the enclosed will do by way of cheque, and if it will, give it to Pope to take to Hoare's for me as he has done before?

3. Possibly the one alluded to by W. M. Rossetti (Some Reminiscences, 1, 283): "My brother also acquired a large and very sumptuous Chinese porcelain screen, of varied colouring, which is now a valued possession of Mr. Watts-Dunton."

4. The home of his uncle and aunt, Sir Henry and Lady Mary Gordon, the parents of Mary Charlotte Julia Gordon, who married Colonel R. W. Disney Leith in 1865.

5. The second number of the Fine Arts Quarterly Review, dated Oct. 1863, contained Charles Kingsley's article "Henrietta Browne's Picture of 'The Sisters of Charity'" (pp. 299–307).

6. Hamlet V. i. 223.

I have not a cheque-book with me but I suppose a plain word will do as well. I am ashamed you should have had the trouble of writing to remind me: [1] please convey my excuses to Gabriel also and say I hope my unpunctuality has not been very inconvenient to him. We must look up matters honestly when I come to London which will be I think in a week or two. I don't wonder you were doubtful how to direct; but the truth is having settled down here for quiet with no company but some of my nearest relations and older intimates I have shrunk from moving week after week, perhaps not wisely. But I think after being hard hit [2] one is more afraid of any change than any monotony: and so I let myself be kept beyond the date I had thought of, readily and rather thankfully: especially as one can neither do nothing, or *retremper* oneself with riding and walking, only one's choice in a place like this. I wish I could send Gabriel a photograph of it: the old gardens and hall would be in his style: and of all such houses it is about the quietest. I am very much obliged for the Blake treasures both to you and to Mrs. Gilchrist [3] and shall return the sooner for their sakes. I have done half the Life which is a new rather tough thing for me who am raw to reviewing: also some notes on the 'Gates of Paradise' which book I shall want to see again if possible to correct or complete my remarks; and as it is neither at the British Museum (is it?) or among the treasures which M. le comte de Rodin [4] has accumulated in a long and unbroken series of 'les prospérités du vice,' I can hardly make out how I am to set about it. But to a reader of the Life the matter (half-handled and half shirked as it is by Gilchrist) will seem so hopelessly and provokingly obscure that something more must be done, if (as I hope and wish) every corner of Blake's work is to be more or less reclaimed from chaos and reduced to a cosmic state for the persevering student who desires to escape from the bondage of Bowlahoola.[5]

With all messages,

Ever yours sincerely,
A. C. Swinburne

1. That he was behindhand with the rent.

2. By the death of his sister Edith. See above, Letter 50.

3. The treasures were principally the (incomplete) manuscripts of *Tiriel* and *The French Revolution* (see *Rossetti Papers*, p. 42).

4. That is, Richard Monckton Milnes.

5. In Blake's *Milton*.

52. TO ALICE SWINBURNE

Text: Leith, pp. 58–62.

Northcourt, December 31 [1863]

. . . I owe you thanks for more letters than one, which please accept in full. As to the pictures on your projected journey, I am sorry to say I know nothing of Genoa, as I was only there for a minute under violent rain; but I believe it does not shine in galleries, the effects of sea and history being its strong points. It certainly lies open beautifully to the salt lake. But at Milan you will have enough to do. 1st, the Ambrosian Library, where there is a Virgil illuminated or painted in small by Simone Menni (?)[1] for Petrarca; *also* the lock of hair and autograph letters of Madonna Lucrezia Estense Borgia: which please salute respectfully for me. 2nd (or 1st if you prefer) the *Brera*. At the end of one of the smaller rooms there is a picture for which I would give the eyes out of my head if I could see it without them: a feast in the open air, with music, men and women being played to: by Bonifazio: one of the most perfect pictures I know of any Venetian painter.[2] In one corner —that you may recognize it the sooner—there are two pages standing—a white boy tickling a black one who tries not to laugh. The Raffaelle[3] is one of those moist and sugary pictures which do not attract me; but you will have to look at it. Some Crivellis,[4] too, though unequal and not lovely, are worth looking over. Look also at some three or four small narrow pictures in the corners (unless changed) of the further large room on the left as you enter by the Luini gallery; single figures of saints standing separately in little meadows full of wild flowers, by Gentile da Fabriano;[5] very plain and *quaint,* as people call it, but with great simple beauty in them, unless my recollection flatters them: the foregrounds in flower, es-

1. The question mark probably indicates Leith's uncertainty of transcription, for Swinburne surely wrote "Memmi." The miniature is reproduced in Giovanni Galbiati's *Itinerario per il visitatore della Biblioteca Ambrosiana* (Milan, 1951), facing p. 16.

2. "The Infant Moses Presented to the Daughter of Pharaoh."

3. "Nuptials of the Virgin."

4. There are, in all, ten pictures by three Crivellis in the Brera Gallery. The most distinguished is Carlo Crivelli, with six works, of which the most famous is the altarpiece showing the Madonna and Child enthroned, with two saints on each side.

5. "The Magdalen," "St. Francis of Assisi," "St. Jerome," and "St. Dominic."

pecially. Look, too, at Gentile Bellini's 'St. Mark preaching at Alexandria.' One or two small Carpaccios [6] are worth looking up; but that great and delicious painter is only to be seen fairly in the Venice Academy; though he has one very lovely large picture at Brescia, in the same gallery with a grand portrait by Moroni. (These and Titian's St. Afra are the main things to see at Brescia if you stop at that city, which on this account it is worth while to do.) [7] I don't remind you that the supreme crown and glory of Milan is Leonardo's Last Supper, in spite of much battering of French shots and of Austrian stabling. To it of course you will be carried off at once; and you will not need to be told to look out for Luini's,[8] as you will see nothing else in the Brera to speak of till you are through no end of rooms and galleries. These are the chief things I remember on the Italian side of the frontier. If I were with you I should remember many more. If you get to Milan you ought not to be able to resist crossing the border to Verona, Padua, and Venice, taking in Vicenze. There is matter in all these names for a dozen letters. At Verona, mind you *do* San Zenone thoroughly; and as the Austrians won't give you access to the great bridge look at it from thence as you leave the church; and go into the crypts, for San Z. is great in stone and metal work. In the extreme crypt there is a Crucifixion in stone, which is exactly like an Egyptian work; just the cut of beard and turn of feature of our Egyptian relics at the Museum. I mean, of course, the human monuments, or busts, not the dog-headed gods. Examine all you can of the groups on the great metal gates, which are splendid if you make out the Old [9] Testament subjects,

6. The companion-pictures "The Dedication of the Virgin Mary in the Temple" and "The Marriage of the Virgin." The third Carpaccio in the Brera, "St. Stephen Disputing before the Synagogue," is somewhat larger than these two.

7. Scholarship, the depredations of time and men, and the acquisitive instincts of the latter have done so much in the past century to works of art in Italy that identification here is, at best, uncertain. In the Church of S. Afra in Brescia there is (or was) a "Woman Taken in Adultery" possibly done by Titian, but "The Martyrdom of St. Afra" is Veronese's and "The Baptism of St. Afra" Bassano's. The Averoldi family in Brescia owned for a while what was said to be a Carpaccio, the "Virgin between SS. Faustino and Giovita," which was sold in 1869 to a Milanese dealer who resold it to the National Gallery; but it was lost at sea on the way to London (see *The Life and Works of Vittorio Carpaccio* by Pompeo Molmenti and Gustav Ludwig, trans. by R. H. H. Cust, London, 1907, p. 196). Murray's *Handbook for Travellers in Northern Italy* (1860) lists this Carpaccio in the Galleria Averoldi and at least one portrait by Morone.

8. A total of forty-five.

9. And New, he ought to have said.

or even if you don't. Also the monuments of the Scalas, Dante's Can Grande among the lot, which are too beautiful for any other city. These must be hints enough to start with, if you want to see what I saw and remember with most liking; which I hope you will do. I write as much as possible what you can ask for, both on that account and because I have not much other material for a letter in any degree worth writing or receiving. My greatest pleasure just now is when M——— [10] practises Handel on the organ; but I can hardly *behave* for delight at some of the choruses. I care hardly more than I ever did for any minor music; but *that* is an enjoyment which wants special language to describe it, being so unlike all others. It crams and crowds me with old and new verses, half-remembered and half-made, which new ones will hardly come straight afterwards: but under their influence I have done some more of my Atalanta [11] which will be among my great doings if it keeps up with its own last scenes throughout.

I repay M——— to the best of my ability but cheaply, by blundering over Greek verbs with her. She keeps her energy fresh by her versatility. I wish you were here, and as quiet as I have happily been all this time, thanks to their kindness, instead of being pestered by strangers on a foreign coast—and that the frowzy coast of a blue pond. We saw the re-launch of a lifeboat the other day, but as the sea was smooth it was only a pretty sight, not an excitement. I walked once over to the end of the downs above Freshwater Gate: it is the finest scenery of sea-downs I ever saw, and all Mottistone and Afton Downs were new to me.

53. TO WILLIAM MICHAEL ROSSETTI

MS: Rutgers. Published: Bonchurch, *18,* 16–18.

North Court, January 31 [1864]

Dear Rossetti

I shall be in London probably by the end of the week; perhaps you will be able to let them know at Chelsea that I may be expected by Saturday or Monday at latest. I shall hope to be able to submit the Blake essay to you and talk over its chances. Being now within sight of land, I can see that it falls naturally into three main divisions 1) a revisal of the life and published designs, as distinct from any publica-

10. "The editor" (Leith)—that is, Mary Gordon, afterward Mrs. Disney Leith.

11. *Atalanta in Calydon* (Bonchurch, 7, 259–351) was published in 1865. Leith writes (p. 19) that she first heard the chorus beginning "When the hounds of spring" during this visit when she and Swinburne were riding together.

tion with a text of Blake's own; but touching upon his early poems and later controversial notes on art etc. as stages or landmarks in the narrative. 2) A review of his Poems and the illustrative work belonging to them; i.e. of the 'Songs' and the great MS. 3) The prophetic books. Of course the complete work has swollen beyond all periodical limits: of course also as I have given my best powers of work to the subject I should not like to have it hacked into or dipped about at random. But although each part is naturally full of references to the others they would separately have to be curtailed or readjusted. The first part I think would not be too big by itself for the immediate purpose; and though of course quite inadequate to express my own design and place, might thus do some service to the book. Only I should of course want to know what was to be done and to superintend the alterations; and should then wait for an occasion of publishing my completed 'Study' on Blake in a separate form. The second part is complete; the first wants only a review of the last chapter or two of Gilchrist's Life, which I have not got by me; and an additional note or two where I may work up any strays of remaining material: I want very much to see your fresh notes and am very much obliged by your permission to make use of them. The third part is of course imperfect, as I had to leave it unfinished in the summer; but a week would suffice to break the back of it. You will see that I have at least not slighted or slurred over the subject. Coming after you and Gabriel, I wanted to do something durable also for Blake, if of less direct value than your work and his; I have for once taken the same pains in arranging and designing the parts of this essay as if I had been dealing with a poem. It is about as good a memorial now as I can make it; I have worked into it with real care, and sometimes not without much labour, all the elucidations and expressions of thought or feeling on the matter that I could put into reasonable form or coherent shape. Durable or not, anything altered or displaced in it will not be in the way of improvement. My one main object has been to give the whole a certain dramatic order by taking each part from the point of view, and examining each detail in the light given by the personal character of Blake: in a way not yet attempted.—I heard the other day from Sir John Simeon [1] that Palgrave is reviewing Blake for the Quarterly,[2] he says in a spirit of intense enthusiasm. I rode across the country to Far[r]ingford the

1. (1815-70), 3d baronet, M.P. for the Isle of Wight. Tennyson called him "the Prince of courtesy" in the lyric written on his death, "In the Garden at Swainston."

2. The notice in the *Quarterly Review* (Jan. 1865), pp. 1-27, though unsigned, is presumably by Francis Turner Palgrave (1824-97), poet, critic, and nominal compiler of *The Golden Treasury*.

other day. The weather is exquisite for riding, but Mrs. Tennyson is ill now and both were invisible.

Ever your affectionate,
A.C.S.

54. TO ?

MS: Yale.

16 Cheyne Walk, S.W., February 22 [1] [1864]

Dear Sir [2]

I send you, by way of review of Mr. Gilchrist's Life of Blake, the first part of a biographical and critical essay on the works of that artist, to the construction of which I have lately given some time and care. Since it was first proposed to me to undertake this subject, I have found the matter grow under my hands imperceptibly beyond the limits I had at first thought of fixing; and having had access to some private as well as public sources which had not been fully opened up by the biographer of Blake, I have been induced to go into these at some length. Whatever of value there may be in my work as it stands will of course be impaired by dissection or division of the component parts: but in the meantime I am quite ready to separate for present purposes the introduction from the main work. If this section, containing a revisal of Blake's life and of a portion of his detached designs, and including some fresh facts which I have been permitted to make use of, should be still too long or otherwise unsuitable for the sphere of a Review as it now stands, any curtailment which might seem fit I should like to take into my own hands; for as the essay is now as careful, as exhaustive, and I believe as fair and as accurate as I can make it, I cannot, if I am to speak in public on the matter, either suppress what I do think or express what I do not. As no part has been written or worked up at random into the main body of my narrative and argument, any mere scheme of extracts will at best be imperfect, [and] it must be my business to see that it is not unfair.

I remain

Yours truly,
A. C. Swinburne

1. "19th" was written first and crossed through.

2. It is not yet possible to ascertain whom this letter is addressed to or, indeed, whether it was actually sent. In Nov. William Rossetti sounded J. A. Froude about publishing the essay in *Fraser's Magazine* (*Rossetti Papers*, pp. 63–64).

P.S. As the present article may seem inadequate by way of a review of the entire publication spoken of, it may be as well to explain that the second volume has been fully reviewed in the next division of my essay, which takes cognizance of all Blake's works now republished; the third and last sections being devoted to those books and designs which have not been included in these selections. The first volume alone is here touched upon.

55. TO LORD HOUGHTON

MS: The Marchioness of Crewe. Published: Reid, *Richard Monckton Milnes*, 2, 136–38 (incomplete); Bonchurch, *18*, 18–21*.

Albergo della Gran Bretagna,
March 31 [1864]

My dear Lord Houghton [1]

I meant to write you a word two days since and a sufficiently dolorous epistle you would have had but luckily an equivocal and occasionally beneficent Providence intervened. With much labour I hunted out the most ancient of the demigods [2] at *93 Via della Chiesa* but (although knock-down blows were not, as you anticipated, his mode of salutation) I found him, owing I suspect to the violent weather, too much weakened and confused to realize the fact of the introduction without distress. In effect he seemed so feeble and uncomfortable that I came away in a grievous state of disappointment and depression myself, fearing I was really too late. But taking heart of grace I wrote him a note of apology and explanation saying why and how I had made up my mind to call upon him after you had furnished me with an introduction: that is, expressing (as far as was expressible) my immense admiration and reverence in the plainest and sincerest way I could manage. To which missive of mine came a note of invitation which I answered by setting off again for his lodging. After losing myself for an hour in the accursed Borgo S. Frediano I found it at last, and found him as alert, brilliant and altogether delicious as I suppose others may have found him twenty years since. I cannot thank you

1. Milnes was created Baron Houghton in Aug. 1863.

2. Walter Savage Landor, who died Sep. 17, 1864, four and a half months short of his ninetieth birthday. His friendship with Milnes began in 1833. Swinburne and Milnes had been together in Paris earlier in the month, and Swinburne's recitations so excited Milnes' dying friend, Sir Charles MacCarthy, "that he had quite a bad night: he thought them wonderful and they quite haunted him" (Pope-Hennessy, p. 181).

enough for procuring me this great pleasure and exquisite satisfaction
—I am seriously more obliged for this than for anything that could
have been done for me. I have got the one thing I wanted with all my
heart. If both or either of us die to-morrow, at least to-day he has told
me that my presence here has made him happy; he said more than that
—things for which of course I take no credit to myself but which are
not the less pleasant to hear from such a man. There is no other man
living from whom I should so much have prized any expression of
acceptance or goodwill in return for my homage; for all other men as
great are so much younger that in his case one sort of reverence serves
as the lining for another. My grandfather was upon the whole mieux
conservé; but he had written no Hellenics. In answer to something
that Mr. Landor said to-day of his own age I reminded him of his
equals and precursors, Sophocles and Titian; he said he should not
live up to the age of Sophocles—not see ninety. I don't see why he
should not, if he has people about him to care for him as he should be
cared for. I should like to throw up all other things on earth and
devote myself to playing valet to him for the rest of his days. I
should black his boots if he wore any—moi. He has given me the
shock of adoration which one feels at thirteen towards great men. I
am not sure that any other emotion is so durable and persistently
delicious as that of worship, when your god is indubitable and incarnate before your eyes.[3] I told him, as we were talking of poems
and such things, that his poems had first given me inexplicable pleasure and a sort of blind relief when I was a small fellow of twelve at
Eton much beaten upon and worried some twelve years back (or
nearly) now. My first recollection of them is the Song of the Hours in
the Iphigenia.[4] Apart from their executive perfection, all those Greek
poems of his always fitted on to my own way of feeling and thought
infinitely more than even Tennyson's modern versions: and now I am
more than ever sure that the 'Hamadryad'[4] is a purer and better
piece of work, from the highest point of view that art can take, than
such magnificent hashes and stews of old and new with a sharp sauce
of personality as 'Oenone' and 'Ulysses.' Not that I am disloyal to
Tennyson, into whose church we were all in my time born and bap-
tized as far back as we can remember at all; but he is not a Greek nor

3. After the visit Landor wrote to Swinburne (facsimile in *A Swinburne Library*,
facing p. 261): "My dear friend So totally am I exhausted that I can hardly hold
my pen, to express my vexation that I shall be unable ever to converse with you
again. Eyes and intellect fail me—I can only say that I was much gratified by your
visit, which must be the last, and that I remain ever Your obliged W Landor."

4. In Landor's *Hellenics* (1847).

a heathen; and I imagine does not want to be; and I greatly fear believes it possible to be something better: an absurdity which should be left to the Brownings and other blatant creatures begotten on the slime of the modern chaos.

If I let myself loose I shall go on giving you indirect thanks for bringing me acquainted with Landor, till time and paper fail me and patience fails you. Even if I did so, I could hardly tell you what pleasure I have had to-day in a half-hour's intercourse with him: nor what delicious things he said in recognition of my half-expressed gratitude to him. It is comfortable when one does once in a way go in for a complete quiet bit of hero-worship and an honest interlude of belief to find it taken up instead of thrown away. And the chance of this I owe to you; and you must simply take my thanks for granted. It is better than a publisher to me: what more can a 'rimailleur inédit' possibly say?

I begin to remember that there are other things on earth within the sphere of correspondance; and that I ought to tell you how pleasant my one day's stay at Genoa was made by the note you gave me for Miss Wynn.[5] She and her sister not only received me in that strange land with all kindness, but also put me in the way of doing what was to be done in the way of pictures—the one good office I supremely appreciate in an unknown city. Also—I have just now come in from dining with Mr. Leader [6] and write this before going to bed. He (the last-named) is going to call for me to-morrow and show me some chapel or other full of frescoes by Gozzoli.[7] So you see if I begin to indulge in the deleterious virtue of gratitude there will be no end to my letter. Happily, when most overburdened with direct or indirect benefits, I remember the precept of a great and good man: ' "La reconnaissance, ma chère Justine, est une chimère vraiment méprisable. Toutes les formes de la vertu sont pour le véritable philosophe des exécrations dignes de la potence ou de la roue; mais celle-ci"—! Et en parlant ainsi ce libertin'—etc. etc. ad libitum.

As to the pictures here I will add but one word; Paolo Veronese's 'Martyrdom of St. *Justine*' [8] seems to me painfully and ludicrously

5. Charlotte Williams Wynn (1807–69), a cousin of Lady Houghton.

6. John Temple Leader (1810–1903) was a wealthy radical who was equally successful in politics and society, but in 1844 he abandoned both for what G. M. Young described as an "aesthetic Italian exile," living the rest of his life, after a brief stay at Cannes, in Florence, where he was noted for winter swimming and for his openhanded zeal in restoring fine old buildings.

7. The Chapel of the Medici in the Palazzo Riccardi.

8. The "Martyrdom of St. Justina" in the Uffizi.

inadequate. I blush for the artist—whom in all his other works I have hitherto had the weakness to admire. But *that* subject surely demanded far other treatment—far more robust handling. As for Titian's Venus [9]—Sappho and Anactoria in one—four lazy fingers buried dans les fleurs de son jardin—how any creature can be decently virtuous within thirty square miles of it passes my comprehension. I think with her Tannhäuser need not have been bored—even till the end of the world: [10] but who knows?

Yours affectionately,
A. C. Swinburne

56. TO JOHN NICHOL

Text: *Early Letters.*

13 Bedford Street, Bedford Square,
May 23, 1864

Dear Nichol

I have received your note just in time to answer. If I can get Dicey's present address I will arrange to come down with him—if not, I will at least try to be at Pangbourne Station in time to meet you. Few things would give me greater pleasure than to make one of our old party, and luckily the invitation has come just in time to catch me within two days of my return from Tuscany, where I have been for the last two months, till fairly beaten back by the Italian sun and starved out by the want of companionship. One thing not to be had again I have had by this excursion. I have seen and conversed with Landor, and if I may take his word for it have been fortunate enough to give him some pleasure by the dedication of the poem I am now at work on.[1]

I know that you, who were his friend and admirer before I was able to win my way to him, will appreciate my pleasure, and understand why it is natural for me to write you word of it. To see and speak with him was the one thing I most desired when I thought of starting for Florence, and as I cannot hope to enjoy this again, whereas I expect to have a first sight of the other great works of time in Florence, before the end of my time, I class this as the greatest thing achieved by me in Italy in the way of great things seen.

9. The "Venus of Urbino" in the Uffizi.

10. The allusion suggests "Laus Veneris" (Bonchurch, *1*, 146–61) in *PBI*.

1. See above, Letter 55. *Atalanta in Calydon* was dedicated to the memory of Landor, who died six months before its publication.

I wish it was for longer that you were to stay in London, but for those three days I hope to see enough of you to make up for lost time, as far as may be, and then we may manage to talk enough of these and other affairs which are better when talked over than when written down.

Ever yours sincerely,
A. C. Swinburne

57. TO JOHN NICHOL

MS: British Museum. Printed: *Early Letters*.

18 Grosvenor Place, June 19 [1864]

Dear Nichol

I write partly out of a wish to recall myself to you as an existing mortal—partly to know what you are just now doing or purposing—partly to say two things which may be worth saying or not as it happens.

I have read all Browning's new book since we parted; and while quite holding to all I said and say about his work as a poet I must also say—I have even had the candour to say to Rossetti—that I fully recognize the unique and most admirable power of 'Sludge' and 'Caliban.' I want to send you my full acknowledgment of this: because we talked enough about the matter, and because I have really derived such rare and keen pleasure, in the teeth of all personal or artistic feelings of dislike, from these two poems (if poems they are to be called) that I don't want you to suppose me insensible to their delightful qualities. I class both these above Blougram—not as intellectual exercises, but as samples of good work done. They are as good as Swift—i.e. not so good here, and better there; incomparably above Thackeray—and I think only a little below Chamfort [1] and Stendhal. This last with me is higher praise than all the rest. Not less noble is the opening of St. John—but long before the end the poem is swamped in controversial shallows, and the finer features effaced under a mask of indurate theological mud. In all the rest of the book I see much that is clever and nothing that is good—much that is ingenious and nothing that is right.[2]

1. Born Nicolas Sébastien Roch (1741–94), *moraliste*. Stendhal died in 1842.

2. Browning was much in Swinburne's thoughts in these days. William Bell Scott, after seeing him at Rossetti's, wrote to Lady Trevelyan on Feb. 24: "Algernon is not much different, only developing some singular conditions of vanity, and otherwise interlarding his discourse with ferocious invectives against Browning"

The other thing I had to say relates to a really and completely great man. I picked up a day or two since a book of Landor's printed at Oxford by Slatter [3] in 1815, of which I can find no trace elsewhere. Landor himself has doubtless forgotten its existence—and to appeal to him for news of it would be 'frivolous and vexatious.' [4] The title is 'Idyllia Nova Quinque Heroum atque Heroidum, etc.' The etc. being mainly satirical and political. It is dedicated, in an admirable 'copy' of Latin prose, to Dr. Parr [5]—of all men on earth; very reverent to him, exquisitely virulent towards others—dead and rotten enemies of the author. Altogether as beautiful a little book as I have ever seen, more delicately got up than any later edition. Most but not all of the poems have been reprinted—with very curious and interesting alterations. Now I can find nowhere any chance notice or stray reference bearing on this book—much of which though classical in form evidently deals with purely private (and presumably libellous) matters. The British Museum has no copy. No catalogue of books then printed takes any account of this one. I thought as a hereditary admirer of Landor you might (through your father's collection of books or otherwise) know something of this strange little waif of Latin verse; and if not I thought it would not be uninteresting to you to hear of its existence.

Ever yours sincerely,
A. C. Swinburne

(Trevelyan Papers, Wallington). Again, William Allingham, calling on Rossetti on June 27, wrote (*Diary*, p. 101): "Then Swinburne came in, and soon began to recite —a parody on Browning was one thing."—"Caliban upon Setebos," "Mr. Sludge, 'The Medium,' " and "A Death in the Desert" ("St. John") were in *Dramatis Personae*. "Bishop Blougram's Apology" was in *Men and Women* (1855).

3. By Slatter and Munday.

4. Perhaps Mrs. Gamp's "worritin' wexagious" (*Martin Chuzzlewit,* chap. 46).

5. Samuel Parr (1747–1825), pedagogue. He was a distinguished Latinist and a notorious Whig.

58. TO SEYMOUR KIRKUP [1]

Text: Bonchurch, *18*, 22–23*

[? July 1864] [2]

. . . names, that the *publisher* of the biography (a very contemptible cur) took fright and would not forsooth *allow* them [3] to be duly analysed. He will receive chastisement, and the subject elucidation, when my commentary appears, as they both respectively desire. Meantime I need not say how valuable any notices, or recollections, or other assistance which I might owe to your kindness would be to me. My book will at least handle the whole question of Blake's life and work with perfect fearlessness and with thorough admiration. I wish I could send you for inspection any of the engraved and coloured Books of Prophecy, but unhappily the few copies now existing fetch so many more pounds than Blake received shillings for them when alive, that only millionaires can afford to collect them, when by any rare chance they come into the market. Some of their effects in colour, notwithstanding Blake's scorn of colourists, are so exquisite and inventive that Rossetti, who in common with all great and good artists now among us admires him at his best almost beyond words, told me once that he regarded Blake as a positive discoverer of new capacities [and po]wers even in mere executive colouring.

Did you ever read his great prose-poem, *The Marriage of Heaven and Hell?* For profound humour and subtle imagination, not less than for lyrical splendour and fervour of thought, it seems to me the greatest work of its century. We all envy you the privilege of having known a man so great in so many ways.

I don't know whether Rossetti has found time to answer your letter

1. Seymour Stocker Kirkup (1788–1880), artist. He had known Blake, whom he thought "mad," and was a friend of B. R. Haydon. Many of Kirkup's letters are printed in F. W. Haydon, ed., *Benjamin Robert Haydon: Correspondence and Table-Talk,* 1876. He moved to Italy for his health in 1816, and was on the friendliest terms with Landor, the Brownings, Trelawny, and Severn. In recognition of his discovery of a portrait of Dante attributed to Giotto in the chapel of the Palazzo del Podestà (and for other services) he was created Cavaliere of the Order of S. Maurizio Lazzaro, and mistakenly inferred that this honor gave him a right to the title of "Barone," which he assumed. He was a passionate cultist in spiritualism. In 1875, at the age of 87, he married an Italian of 22. Swinburne met Kirkup in Florence in Mar. 1864.

2. Gosse and Wise conjecture for this date "Probably summer of 1864," and I can find no reason to think their guess unacceptable. They note that the "first sheet of this letter is lost."

3. Blake's *Prophetic Books* (see above, Letter 35).

forwarded through Reade [4] to me; I know that he received it with the greatest pleasure, and expressed to me his sense of your kindness. His pictures [5] of this year are magnificent; they recall the greatness, the perfect beauty and luxurious power of Titian and of Giorgione.

Excuse the length and bad penmanship of this scrawl, which I trust may not be indecipherable; and believe me, my dear Mr. Kirkup, with many thanks,

Yours most sincerely,
A. C. Swinburne

Seymour Kirkup, Esq.

59. TO JOHN NICHOL

Text: *Early Letters.*

124 Mount Street, Grosvenor Square,
[July 1864]

My dear Nichol

I send a word of thanks for your enclosure, in the midst of the horror and bustle of a first day in fresh lodgings. For eight hours on end I have been unpacking, blaspheming, arranging, losing, finding, swearing, stamping, blessing Satan and cursing. The villains who have mismanaged for me have half ruined some of my choicest books, and mislaid endless things, for which may they descend into Gehenna long before I pay their bill on earth.

I must say, however, that but for to-day's experience I might have begun to doubt my theory of the diabolic government of this worst of all possible worlds—even perhaps to believe in a beneficent super-vision which rewards virtue; for, within an hour of receiving your invaluable transcript, I went out on business—stopped, (as usual, being in a special hurry) at a bookstall, and saw, modestly retired behind more virtuous works and persons, the *Lady Sidonia von Bork,*[1] who now for the second time I beg you to accept of her person and ex-

4. Winwood Reade (1838–75), whom Swinburne had introduced to Kirkup (see *Rossetti Papers,* p. 177), nephew of Charles Reade, novelist (of a different order) himself, journalist, reformer, and controversialist, as well as a sophisticated traveler. He is remembered today primarily for *The Martyrdom of Man* (1872), an enormously popular outline of human history from an agnostic point of view. A letter from Reade to Swinburne, Dec. 2, 1866, is printed in Clara Watts-Dunton's *The Home Life of Swinburne,* p. 19.

5. For example, "Lady Lilith" and "Venus Verticordia."

1. J. W. Meinhold, *Sidonia the Sorceress.*

cuse her tattered clothes. I would not wait to dress her, lest delay so should mar the 'truly Providential' effect of the coincidence; remembering that the last wish you expressed to me when in London was to renew your interrupted cohabitation with the Lady Princess.

Otherwise I would have had her at least decently bound before offering her to any friend. But to you, I trust, her nakedness will not be so repulsive as was that of cats and dogs to Sister Dorothea.[2]

Seriously, I am glad to have fallen in with a copy—the first I have seen for sale for years—so soon after hearing of your loss. Keep this one, for the book is getting really very rare; the number printed was limited, and many copies I suspect have gone the way of all (waste) paper.

I hope you have bought and read by this time Landor's *Heroic Idyls* of last Christmas (published by J. C. Newby,[3] who of course has mangled every line). If so, I need not hope, for I am sure, that you agree with my infinite admiration of the three poems on the old age and death of Homer. I forget if you saw my Greek elegiacs addressed to him on their appearance,[4] for which I have a certain tenderness only because they seemed to please him so much.

I need not say, except for form's sake, how much Rossetti and I am obliged for your prompt kindness in making and forwarding the transcript of your extracts. Suppose all that and more to be said; and with best remembrances to Mrs. Nichol, who, I hope, is well, believe me,

Yours sincerely,

A. C. Swinburne

You don't tell me if you know anything of my priceless early Landor's *Poemata*.[5] I hope, if not this year then another, to avail myself of your invitation, but my present plans are yet in chaos.

2. Who, in *Sidonia* (Bk. III, chap. 2) "was quite shocked at the [statue of] Adam, and made a little apron to hang before him, though the abbess and the whole convent said that it was not necessary. But she told them, that unless Adam wore his apron, never would she set foot in the chapel. . . . she has been heard to wonder how the Lord God could send all the animals naked into the world; as cats, dogs, horses, and the like."

3. That is, T. C. Newby.

4. The first section of the dedicatory verses prefixed to *Atalanta in Calydon* (the other two sections were written after Landor's death).

5. See above, Letter 57.

60. TO LORD HOUGHTON

MS: The Marchioness of Crewe. Published: Bonchurch, *18*, 23–24*.

124 Mount Street, August 6 [1864]

Dear Lord Houghton

If I had not been a day or two out of town you would have got this note of thanks a day or two sooner.[1] I need not say how much I value Landor's pamphlet.[2] I only wish it could have been then, or could be now, so circulated as to be of some general and practical use. To me it is simply a pleasure to read and a confirmation of my own previous convictions.

How I am to fix my number in your capricious memory I cannot devise. Two dozen plus one hundred is a hyperbolical, a Titanic, a preterhuman and quasi-Sadique measure of *cuts* inflicted: yet this alone suggests itself to my sterile brain. Please tell me whether my twelve-and-fourteen-year-old elegiacs have given you any satisfaction. 'Full sense' was given me for the second copy (I hope you can construe that Eton phrase) and I am rather proud of it to this day.

I hope Lady Houghton is better and gains health with the summer in the country. With all remembrances

Yours affectionately,
A. C. Swinburne

61. TO MARY GORDON

Text: Leith, pp. 21–23.

[Cornwall, September 2, 1864]

I could have wished for [your][1] company yesterday night when we[2] took out horses, borrowed from a neighbouring farmer, and rode

1. According to Pope–Hennessy, p. 137, Swinburne breakfasted twice in July at Houghton's town house, and was his guest at Fryston, in Yorkshire, "from the 6th to the 22nd of August" in this year.

2. Probably *Mr. Landor's Remarks on a Suit Preferred against Him at the Summer Assizes in Taunton, 1858,* Landor's vindication (1859) of his actions in the Yescombe affair. See above, Letter 13.

1. Supplied by Leith.

2. "We" includes John William Inchbold (1830–88), the painter, one of whose pictures is named "Tintagel." Gabriel Rossetti said (*Rossetti Papers*, p. 65) that Inchbold was "less a bore than a curse," and William, who liked him, found "in him something between uneasy modesty and angular self-opinion, not promoting smoothness of intercourse." His disposition may well have been rasped by the apathy

through the dusk and the dark to the adjacent city of Boscastle. This important and flourishing seaport does not exactly boast of a highway to the sea, but it has a path cut or worn in the slope of the down, along which we let our horses (being surefooted Cornish ones who know the nature of their sea and their down . . .) feel their way till we came out one after another on a narrow standing place of rocks, breaking sharply down to the sea on both sides. This ridge of rocks shuts in the harbour, and the sea having incautiously poured in through a strait between the ridge and the cliff opposite turns twice at right-angles upon itself and makes a sort of double harbour; one parallel with the outer sea, blocked out by the rocks to which we had ridden; the other running straight up the valley to the houses of the little town as thus:

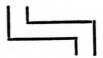

and as there is no beach or shore of any kind, you can imagine how the sea swings to and fro between the cliffs, foams and swells, beats and baffles itself against the steep faces of rock. I should guess it must be unique in England. Seen from above and on horseback it was very queer, dark grey swollen water, caught as it were in a trap, and heaving with rage against both sides at once, edged with long panting lines of incessant foam that swung and lapped along the deep steep cliffs without breaking, and had not room to roll at ease. My horse was much the pluckier, and made forward as if on a road; would, I believe, have tried to mount the rough rock-hewn steps from this natural platform to a sort of beacon at the mouth of the inlet; but seeing the difficulties of redescending (which was a delicate business as it was) I turned him round after a bit of ascent. It was not unexciting, especially by a grey and glimmering night without moon or star. Had it been on a smuggling expedition it would have been sweet indeed. Having ridden back towards the scattered lights of the town, and got on a high road again instead of a cliff path just above the sea, I tried my beast's pace at a gallop, having already tested the goodness of his head and sureness of his feet, in which he matched any possible Alpine mule. He went very well and we tore over the ground

of the public towards his work. Ruskin praised it and befriended him, traveling with him in Switzerland, and doubtless introduced him to Swinburne, whose enduring affection is shown in the poem "In Memory of John William Inchbold" (Bonchurch, 3, 235–39), published in the *Athenaeum* (Dec. 29, 1888), and reprinted in *PB3*. The poem echoes parts of this letter remarkably.

in the night at such a rate that we all but banged against late carts in the lanes, and *quite* electrified the stray population. I have bathed twice, but the sea is very treacherous and tiring; no sand, hardly any beach even at low water in the narrow bays, sudden steep banks, shelving rocks, and sea pitching violently in the entrance of the bays; so that where there are rocks to take breath at one can't make for them lest the sea should *stave* one's ribs in against the reefs; and a sea that pitches from side to side without breakers or rollers, and has no resting places except on the high and dry rocks inland, takes it out of one in swimming much more than one thinks. We are twenty-five miles from the nearest railway, and *Clatt* [3] . . . is as it were Babylon or Nineveh to *our* post town—Camelford, which is six miles inland. Nothing can be funnier than these villages except the downs and glens in which they are set. The sea-views are, of course, splendid beyond praise. On one headland (split now into two, divided by a steep isthmus of rock between two gulfs of sea, not wide enough for two to walk abreast across) is the double ruin, one half facing the other, of the old castle or palace of the kings of Cornwall. Opposite on a high down is the old church, black with rain and time and storm, black at least in the tower, and grey in the body. The outer half of the castle, on the headland beyond the isthmus is on the very edge (and partly over the edge and on the slant) of the cliff; and has indescribable views of the double bay, broken cliffs, and outer sea. Practically, the *total* want of beach at any time is a great loss.[4]

3. Identified by Leith as "our own Scotch village," that is, the village near the seat, Knockespock, Aberdeenshire, of her father, Sir Henry Percy Gordon.

4. "The same letter," adds Leith, "relates in an amusing manner how he and his companion were 'lodged and boarded in the schoolhouse,' where he once overheard a flogging going on in the schoolroom, to which his Etonian ears were specially sensitive—and sympathetic. Also he describes a local hunt in which he joined: 'how after 100,000,000 false starts the scent was lost after all, if indeed it ever existed. But we had some good gallops on our own hook, and one lark . . . which was that your cousin really lifted a gate off its hinges for a female to pass. Said female herself much of a lark, a neighbouring clergyman's wife, semi-Spanish, semi-Irish, awfully hospitable and good-natured, not to call vulgar, because *natural*; but such a comic, boisterous set of people as she was at the head of! Clergymen, agents, farmers, all much alike, and also very hospitable.'
"In a postscript to this letter—of which the latter part of the MS. is a little more wildly erratic than even his ordinary penmanship of the period—he apologises for the writing, 'as a needle and a lump of black mud are the only writing implements at hand.'"

62. DANTE GABRIEL ROSSETTI TO SWINBURNE

MS: Historical Society of Pennsylvania.

16 Cheyne Walk, Chelsea September 15, 1864

My dear Swinburne,

Mac [1] has spoken. Dont swear more than you can help. I have your M.S.S. safe again. There was a sort of talk of my looking up and putting together those against which there could be no possible objection in reason and sending them him again. He seems half inclined to the Chastelard still. But I since doubted whether such selection would meet your wishes. I mentioned the St. Dorothy as an unobjectionable poem, but Mac had some funky reminiscences of the allusions to Venus, so really it seemed a bad look out.

I hear no news in particular. Am getting on more or less with the Venus, but nothing else since finishing King René.[2] Shall have to go to Llandaff [3] in a day or so I suppose. Chapman [4] is here. Very ill but getting better I hope, and unites with me in love to you,—the which please pass on to Inchbold in my case.

Yours affectionately,
(hoping to see you soon)
D Gabriel R.

1. Alexander Macmillan, the publisher.

2. "Venus Verticordia" and "King René's Honeymoon" (Marillier, Nos. 149 and 146).

3. He had painted a triptych for Llandaff Cathedral (Marillier, No. 98).

4. George Chapman, a portrait painter so obscure that he can scarcely be identified, for William Rossetti in *Dante Gabriel Rossetti: His Family-Letters with a Memoir* (2 vols. 1895), gives the middle initial as *F* and in *Rossetti Papers* as *W*. Chapman was constantly in ill health, as Gabriel Rossetti's occasional allusions to him show, and always impecunious, and in 1866 or 1867 spent "some three or four months" with Rossetti at Cheyne Walk. As an artist-friend and a member of the Arundel Club he evidently saw a good deal of Rossetti, and seems to have been very well disposed towards Swinburne, having told William Michael (*Rossetti Papers*, p. 228) of the former's generous offer of £200 to Joseph Knight. If the George *R.* Chapman who exhibited portraits at the Royal Academy in 1863, 1870, 1873, and 1874 is the same man, it would seem that he had lived for a while in Swinburne's former quarters at 22a Dorset Street. According to William Rossetti (*Family-Letters with a Memoir, 2, 173*), Chapman died "towards 1880."

63. TO MARY GORDON

Text: Leith, pp. 24-25.

[Tintagel, Cornwall, October 2, 1864] [1]

The aforesaid [2] came to see me, who have had an adventure which might have been serious but has only resulted in laming one foot for a day or two, I hope. . . . I had to run round a point of land which the sea was rising round, *or* be cut off in a bay of which to my cost I had just found the cliffs impracticable; so without boots or stockings I just ran at it and into the water and up or down over some awfully sharp and shell-encrusted rocks which cut my feet to fragments, had twice to plunge again into the sea, which was filling all the coves and swinging and swelling heavily between the rocks; once fell flat in it, and got so thrashed and licked that I might have been ——— in ———'s clutches,[3] . . . and at last got over the last reef and down on the sand of a safe bay, a drenched rag, and with feet that just took me home (three-quarters of a mile or so and uphill mainly with stones) half in and half out of the boots which I had just saved with one hand; and then the right foot began to bleed like a pig, and I found a deep cut which was worse than any ever inflicted by a birch to the best of my belief, for it was *no end* bad yesterday, and to-day makes it hopeless to walk except on tiptoe, but as I wouldn't have it dressed or bothered I hope it will soon heal.

64. TO MARY GORDON

Text: Leith, p. 30.

[Cornwall, autumn, 1864] [1]

How satisfied I am that [your] [1] opinion of Tennyson's *last* [2] should so exactly coincide with mine. After the four great ones you mention I put the 'Valley of Cauteretz,' which I think very musical and perfect.

1. Supplied by Leith.

2. Identified by Leith as "A boy friend staying in the neighbourhood."

3. Identified by Leith as "characters in a story." As Lafourcade, *La Jeunesse*, 2, 301, pointed out, the names were certainly those of Herbert Seyton and his tutor Mr. Denham in the so-called *Lesbia Brandon*, an unfinished (and fragmentary) novel edited by Randolph Hughes and first published in 1952.

1. Supplied by Leith.

2. *Enoch Arden and Other Poems* appeared Aug. 15, 1864.

Boadicea is in Galliambics,[3] a metre in which there is only one other poem extant, the 'Atys' of Catullus; the rules are too long and too intricate to give here, even if I remembered the whole scheme, which I don't; but it is in Cookesley's Eton edition of 'Catullus' prepared for the 'young mind,' where you may safely seek it. I *tried* . . . to do my week's verses in it once, and my tutor said it was no metre at all and he wouldn't take them, because it was an impertinence to show such a set up, so it counted as if I had done nothing, and the consequences were tragic.

65. TO MARY GORDON

Text: Leith, pp. 30–31.

[Cornwall, autumn, 1864][1]

I need not say that I have *not* the pluck to try my hand again at Galliambics. . . . I should feel at every line as if I were writing down my own name in the bill: besides I might make false quantities —and *then!* . . . And *then* I showed my verses indignantly (*after* the catastrophe) to another master, and he said they were very good, and there was but one small slip in them, *hard* as the metre was; and I told my tutor with impudent triumph (knowing he had done his very worst), and he was shut up I can tell you . . . but that did not heal the cuts or close the scars which had imprinted on the mind and body of ———[2] . . . a just horror of strange metres.

66. TO MARY GORDON

Text: Leith, p. 31.

[Cornwall, autumn, 1864][1]

They[2] are generally very easy, and if you find the choruses hard you can skip or reserve them quite well. . . . the tents and stars and sea all stand out so clearly in the first few verses,[3] which are in the

3. And Tennyson (*Memoir, 1*, 436) "wished that it were musically annotated so that it might be read with proper quantity and force."

1. Supplied by Leith, who specifies that this letter is not part of the one preceding.

2. Identified by Leith as "a fictitious schoolboy character with whom he identifies himself here"—probably, that is, Herbert Seyton in *Lesbia Brandon* (see above, Letter 63).

1. Supplied by Leith.

2. Identified by Leith as "the two Iphigenias of Euripides."

3. Leith: "He specially recommends the 'Iphigenia in Aulis.'"

familiar and *fondly* remembered anapaestic metre [4]—none of your *blessed* Galliambics or such like 'impertinent eccentricities,' as they were *well* called in my case.

67. TO MARY GORDON

Text: Leith, p. 25.

[October 26, 1864] [1]

My foot is well enough now to be quite serviceable, and after full three weeks' close and often solitary confinement, I enjoy getting out among the downs and cliffs so much that I hardly know if I shall be able to tear myself away from my *last* chance of the sea this week.

68. TO EDWARD BURNE JONES

MS: Fitzwilliam Museum. Brief extract in *Memorials of Edward Burne-Jones, 1,* 282.

Wednesday [? November 1864]

My dear Ned

I write a word to say what you know, that it is not my fault. I have not called again since yesterday when I found you busy. I see just now a good deal of my mother and sisters; they have seen so much of fevers and there is still so much of delicate health in the house that they fear the chance of infection. I have been obliged on their account to promise not to run the risk, if there be any, of communicating to them a danger which I do not need to fear for myself. You may be sure I shall call and enquire whenever I can. I would rather have undertaken to keep out of their way if I could have hoped to be much with you and of any use or help to you. This of course I know that you know, and also that I hope to hear from you when I may come without fear of breaking my word.[1]

4. The meter of their *"bouts rimés* games."

1. Supplied by Leith.

1. The remainder of the letter is missing. Immediately after a holiday at Littlehampton in Sep. shared by the Morrises and Joneses, the latter's small son Philip came down with a mild attack of scarlet fever. He recovered quickly, but Georgiana Jones, his mother, was seriously infected, and gave birth prematurely (by one month) to her second son, named Christopher, "who struggled against the disease," she wrote (*Memorials of Edward Burne-Jones, 1,* 282), "through all the time that I was delirious and unable to notice him, but died just as we were hoping he would be spared for us to cherish."

69. TO EDWARD BURNE JONES

MS: Fitzwilliam Museum.

[November 1864]

My dearest Ned

I know it is not worth while but cannot help writing to say what you know, how very sorry I am and how grateful I should be for any chance of being useful. I hope the girl was right in telling me of an improvement visible. Do not trouble yourself to answer this: I send it by my servant who will bring back word. I have told him there is no answer. I hope this will not come to disturb you, and if it does you will forgive it.

Yours affectionately,
A. C. Swinburne

70. TO EDWARD BURNE JONES

MS: Fitzwilliam Museum.

Wednesday morning [November 23, 1864] [1]

My dearest Ned

You know how sorry I am, and how much more than I can say. The news has struck half my pleasure in anything away for the present. I had been quite counting on the life of your poor little child and wondering when I might see it. But since Sunday I have of course been frightened, and now the worst did not take me quite by surprise. I hope you will let me see you soon, but not that it will be of any use. When you can, please let me know. With best love to Georgie who I hope is not seriously thrown back

Your most affectionate,
A. C. Swinburne

71. TO J. B. PAYNE [1]

Text: Bonchurch, *18*, 26–27*.

36 Wilton Crescent, February 7 [1865]

My dear Sir

I must ask you to let me have back from the printers the missing

1. Date added by unknown hand.

1. James Bertrand Payen Payne (1833–98), of Edward Moxon and Co. In 1864, six years after her husband's death, Mrs. Moxon appointed Payne, then a clerk

leaves of my MS.[2] as I want to preserve it for reference. Two I think are wanting (one returned by myself) between those received Friday and the last batch; and others beginning from the second Chorus in the play.

I hope the proofs will be read more regularly and quickly as I am impatient to have the work over this week, which I really think it ought to be. I see no recent advertisement in the weekly papers. I must request that there may be enough of them inserted—as many as you think fit or useful, and as prominently. I am expecting the residue (unbound) copies of my former book,[3] which according to your suggestions I will forward to you as they come, to be readvertised with a fresh title-page.

Your very truly,
A. C. Swinburne

72. TO WILLIAM BELL SCOTT

MS: Yale.

36 Wilton Crescent, S.W., March 15 [1865]

My dear Scott

Thanks for your note and that from Lady Trevelyan.[1] I am very

employed by the firm, manager at £400, and he soon became part owner to boot, selling out in Apr. 1869, for £11,000 (see H. G. Merriam, *Edward Moxon*, New York, 1939, p. 194; see also Letter 803, below). Payne, who belonged to one of the oldest Jersey families (he was a lieutenant in the Royal Jersey Artillery, and fought for Don Carlos in Spain in 1874), was much interested in genealogy, and issued, in six parts, 1859–65, the *Armorials of Jersey* and the *Gossiping Guide to Jersey*. He also wrote monographs on the Lemprière and Millais families and a satirical play, *St. Helier the Hermit*.

2. Of *Atalanta in Calydon*, published by Moxon in March on the payment of "considerably more than £100" by Swinburne's father (see below, Letter 453).

3. *The Queen-Mother and Rosamond*. A few copies were circulated by Basil Pickering at the end of 1860, but the book was immediately transferred to Moxon. The volume remained impressively unsuccessful, and Swinburne (or his father) appears to have hoarded the "residue."

1. Lady Trevelyan wrote to Scott on Mar. 13 from Axminster (the letter is owned by Mrs. Gilbert Troxell): "Will you address the enclosed letter, as I don't know his whereabouts. What a grand poem Atalanta is! it seems to me most beautiful, and of the very highest kind of beauty. I am astonished and delighted with it— I do hope the public will appreciate it, they are stupid animals if they don't." Scott replied next day (his letter, in the Trevelyan Papers, Wallington, is dated "Tuesday"): "About Algernon's poem. I must have spoken of it long ago to you.

glad my one virtuous daughter has given satisfaction, but fear her virginity will not hold out long against the assaults of rampant critics hungry after a maidenhead. I observe also with due joy that neither of you seem to object to what the unwise Christian slaves of faith and fear characterize as blasphemous rebellion against their Supreme Being.

I am not afraid of the Festus [2] test. A year may make some difference to the readers of a Bailey or a Browning—not to mine, whose heel (whether he knows it or not) has already bruised the head [3] of the latter Philistine idol. I intend, now the main work is cleared off, that 'that twice-battered God of Palestine,' [4] Dagon-Caliban, shall 'wear my stripes impressed on him, and bear my beating to his grave.' [5]

I should like of all things to see Mr. Linton's book,[6] and should be much obliged by the copy of it. I always thought there was great merit of a weighty intellectual kind in his Plaint of Freedom,[7] though the metre is distasteful to me even in Tennyson.

Ever yours,
A. C. Swinburne

73. TO PAULINE, LADY TREVELYAN

MS: Trevelyan Papers, Wallington. Published: Bonchurch, *18*, 27–30*.

36 Wilton Crescent, S.W., March 15, 1865

My dear Lady Trevelyan

I have just got your letter which has given me the greatest pleasure

---

My opinion of it is the opinion of all here, that it is the most pure and perfect work of the kind in English, that it is a lovely and splendid work of genius. It has its peculiarities as indicating certain questionable characteristics of the author, but the paganism and the license are quite right to this classic subject, and give truth and value to every page. What its luck will be is scarcely doubtful. All the men whose opinions are worth noting, whether they have the chance of publishing these opinions or not, will now give A.S. his proper place, a high enough one. The publication will however not be very successful at first I should think."

2. A poem by Philip James Bailey (1816–1902), published in 1839, of increasing popularity and length, having been inflated by 1893, during many editions, to over 40,000 lines.

3. Genesis 3:15 or *Paradise Lost*, Bk. X. 181, 498–99.

4. Milton, "Ode on the Morning of Christ's Nativity," l. 199.

5. *Coriolanus*, V. vi. 107–8.

6. *Claribel and Other Poems* by William James Linton (1812–98), engraver, writer, republican.

7. Published in 1852, written in the *In Memoriam* stanza.

I have yet had with regard to my book. I was in hopes it would find favour with you, as I think it is the best executed and sustained of my larger poems. It was begun last autumn twelvemonth, when we were all freshly unhappy, and finished just after I got the news in September last, of Mr. Landor's death, which was a considerable trouble to me, as I had hoped against hope or reason that he who in the spring at Florence had accepted the dedication of an unfinished poem would live to receive and read it. You will recognize the allusion to his life and death at pp. 25, 26. As it is he never read anything of mine more mature than Rosamond. In spite of the funereal circumstances which I suspect have a little deepened the natural colours of Greek fatalism here and there, so as to have already incurred a charge of 'rebellious antagonism' and such like things, I never enjoyed anything more in my life than the composition of this poem, which though a work done by intervals, was very rapid and pleasant. Allowing for a few after insertions, two or three in all, from p. 66 to 83 (as far as the Chorus) was the work of two afternoons, and from p. 83 to the end was the work of two other afternoons; so you will understand that I enjoyed my work. I think it is pure Greek, and the first poem of the sort in modern times, combining lyric and dramatic work on the old principle. Shelley's Prometheus is magnificent and un-Hellenic, spoilt too, in my mind, by the infusion of philanthropic doctrinaire views and 'progress of the species'; and by what I gather from Lewes's life of Goethe the Iphigenia in Tauris must be also impregnated with modern morals and feelings. As for Professor Arnold's Merope the clothes are well enough but where has the body gone? [1] So I thought, and still think, the field was clear for me.

At the time when you were so ill I got bulletins constantly through Aunt Ju, and when things began to improve I thought of writing, but it was considered better not. I could have heard nothing more than I did, and said nothing that you did not know. At least I hope and suppose all of you know what a bad time it was for me as for the others.

I am raging in silence at the postponement from day to day of Mr. Carlyle's volumes. He ought to be in London tying firebrands to the tails of those unclean foxes called publishers and printers.[2] Meantime the world is growing lean with hunger and ravenous with expectation.

1. G. H. Lewes (1817–78), man of letters, editor of the *Fortnightly Review* 1865–66, and common-law husband of George Eliot; his *Life of Goethe* appeared in 1855. Matthew Arnold's *Merope* was published in 1858; he was Professor of Poetry at Oxford from 1857 to 1867.

2. Judges 15:4. *The History of Friedrich II of Prussia, called Frederick the Great* was issued in six volumes, 1858–65.

I finished the fourth volume last May in a huge garden at Fiesole, the nightingales and roses serving by way of salt and spice to the divine dish of battles and intrigues. I take greater delight in the hero, who was always a hero of mine and more comprehensible to my heathen mind than any Puritan, at every step the book takes. Trust in Providence somewhat spoils heroism, to me at least. The letter at the end of volume four,[3] coming where and when it does, is a sample of what I conceive and enjoy as the highest and most reasonable heroic temper. 'A God-intoxicated man' [4] of course can fight, but I prefer a man who fights sober. Whether he gets drunk on faith or on brandy, it is still 'Dutch courage,' as the sailors call it. I must say Frederick's clear, cold purity of pluck, looking neither upwards nor around for any help or comfort, seems to me a much wholesomer and more admirable state of mind than Cromwell's splendid pietism. And then who would not face all chances if he were convinced that the Gods were specially interested on his side and personally excited about his failure or success? It is the old question between Jews and Greeks, and I, who can understand Leonidas better than Joshua, must prefer Marathon to Gilgal.[5] Besides, as a chief and a private man, Frederick is to me altogether complete and satisfactory, with nothing of what seems to me the perverse Puritan Christianity on the one hand, or on the other of the knaveries and cutpurse rascalities which I suspect were familiar at times to the greater, as always to the smaller, Buonaparte. I only draw the line at his verses; and even they have almost a merit of their own by dint of their supreme demerits. As extremes meet, such portentous infamy in the metrical line becomes an inverted sign of genius. But was such a litter of doggerels whelped before by wise man or fool?

I am very glad to hear good accounts of Sir Walter and of your projects in the building way,[6] which sound alluring. I only wish you

3. Frederick's Secret Letter of Instructions to Graf Finck von Finckenstein, Jan. 10, 1757, laying out plans for use in case of defeat or of his own capture ("Should such misfortune happen me, I wish to sacrifice myself for the State . . .").

4. "Gott-trunkener Mensch," as Novalis described Spinoza—cited in Carlyle's essay "Novalis" (1829).

5. Swinburne nodded. Instead of Marathon he ought to have written Thermopylae, where, in 480 B.C., Leonidas and his troops, outnumbered more than sixty to one, held back the Persians for two days, but finally, attacked from front and rear, were overwhelmed, Leonidas being killed. Compare Joshua 10:8: "And the Lord said unto Joshua, Fear them not: for I have delivered them into thine hand; but there shall not a man of them stand before thee."

6. A "villa on the coast near Seaton, in Dorsetshire . . . ," as Sir George Otto

were in London for Madox Brown's Exhibition of pictures,[7] which is superb. I never knew till now how great and various and consistent a painter he is. If in spite of your neighbourhood to their arch enemy [8] you still retain any charity for 'the poor Fine Arts,' there is plenty to see just now of a first-rate kind: but I will not tire you any further, unless I write again.

We are all fairly well, though some of us feel this first English winter, after so many spent abroad, unpleasantly enough. I am staying just now at my father's temporary house in town, taken for the winter, and am looking out in a vague desolate way for chambers where I shall be able to shift for myself en permanence. My father as you may well have heard has completed the purchase of his place in Oxfordshire, Holm Wood. They move in, I believe, next month.

You must have seen Tennyson's book of selections,[9] and I hope agree with me that he might have made a better picking out of the lot. I say that Boadicea, as the highest if not sweetest of all the notes he ever struck, should have served as prelude to the book. The yellow-ringleted Britoness is worth many score of revered Victorias. His volume of the last summer [10] struck me as a new triumph worth any of the old; I read it with a pleasure as single and complete as I might have done at thirteen.

With best remembrances from all to yourself and Sir Walter,
Believe me ever,

Yours (in spite of ill-usage) most filially,
A. C. Swinburne

74. TO LORD HOUGHTON

MS: The Marchioness of Crewe.

16 Cheyne Walk, March 23 [1865]

Dear Lord Houghton

Many thanks for your note and enclosure. I will come with pleasure to dinner on Sunday. I can only say (to you) in answer to the unex-

---

Trevelyan wrote (Bonchurch, *19*, 295) to Gosse. "Lady Ashburton immediately bought the next plot of land, and hurriedly built a fine villa next door."

7. Brown exhibited over a hundred pictures in a gallery at 196 Piccadilly from Mar. 10 to June 10.

8. Thomas Carlyle, who, with Mrs. Carlyle, was staying in Lady Ashburton's "fine villa."

9. The *Selection* (1865), in Moxon's *Miniature Poets,* contained several new poems.

10. *Enoch Arden.*

pected charge of obscurity that I cannot see it myself or find any other critic who does. I read a good half of it one day to a circle of ladies, who are usually the first to detect and attack that fault of all others, and their verdict was that thought and style were as lucid and direct as a Times leader. I am much flattered, meantime, at the proposal, for which I presume I am indebted to you, of a review on a serious scale. I have been gathering up Burton's opinions on this and other matters. He sees nothing hard, and only doubts if pure Hellenics will thrive in this air.

I am here for the minute with Rossetti, the paternal household is on the verge of a flight to the country.

Yours affectionately,

A. C. Swinburne

P.S. Walter Landor called on me a day or two since and stayed some time. He was very full of your kindness to him and told me much family news which I daresay is none to you. I must shew you a charming letter I have received from Mr. Robert Landor,[1] and which I owe to your suggestion that I should send him my book.

74A. TO JAMES ABBOTT McNEILL WHISTLER [1]

MS: Glasgow University.

Sunday [April 2, 1865]

Cher père

I write a word to leave in case I find you gone out. Here are the verses,[2] written the first thing after breakfast and brought off at once.

1. Landor's second son, Walter Savage Landor II (1822–99), and youngest brother, Robert Eyres Landor (1781–1869).

1. (1834–1903), painter, etcher, wit, dandy, Francophile, expatriate. Swinburne did not *tutoyer* casually, and this familiar address reveals his intimacy with Whistler even more tellingly than the seven letters that have (so far) been found. Poet and painter were about equally tetchy, each had a tendency to sit attentive to his own applause, and the only surprising thing about their brilliant, public passage of arms in 1888 (Lafourcade, rising to the occasion, calls it fratricide) is that something like it did not occur sooner. "Mr. Whistler's Lecture on Art" (Bonchurch, *16*, 21–32), Swinburne's reply to the famous "Ten O'Clock" lecture (originally delivered in 1885, it was published by Chatto and Windus in the spring, 1888), appeared in the *Fortnightly Review*, June 1888. It was never reprinted by Swinburne.

2. "Before the Mirror" (Bonchurch, *1*, 260–62; first published in *PB1*), written for Whistler's picture *The Little White Girl* (now in the National Gallery, London), exhibited at the Royal Academy in 1865. Two holographs of the poem (with several interesting variant readings) are in the Library of the University of Glasgow. Neither

Sunday.

Cher père

I write a word to leave in case I find you
gone out. Here are the verses, written the first
thing after breakfast & brought off at once.
I could not do anything prettier, but if you
don't find any serviceable as an Academy-
-catalogue motto & don't care to get all this
printed under the pictures, tell me at once, that I
may try my hand afresh tomorrow again.
Gabriel praises them highly, & I think myself
the idea is pretty: I know it was entirely
& only suggested to me by the picture, for
where I found at once the metaphor & rose & the notion of sad & glad mystery in the
face languidly contemplating its own phantom
& all other things seen by their phantoms.
I wanted to work this out more fully
& clearly, & insert the reflection of the
picture & the room; but Gabriel says it is
full long for its purpose already, &
there is nothing I can supplant.

Tout à toi

ACSwinburne

Letter 74A

I could not do anything prettier, but if you don't find any serviceable as an Academy-Catalogue motto and don't care to get all this printed under the picture, tell me *at once* that I may try my hand at it to-morrow again.

Gabriel praises them highly, and I think myself the idea is pretty: I know it was entirely and only suggested to me by the picture, where I found at once the metaphor of the rose and the notion of sad and glad mystery in the face languidly contemplative of its own phantom and all other things seen by their phantoms. I wanted to work this out more fully and clearly, and insert the reflection of the picture and the room; but Gabriel says it is full long for its purpose already, and there is nothing I can supplant.

Tout à toi,

A. C. Swinburne

75. TO THOMAS PURNELL [1]

MS: Yale. Published: Bonchurch, *18, 32*.

Tuesday evening or Wednesday morning,
2 A.M. [? April 19, 1865] [2]

Dear Purnell

Sorry you should have waited in vain this evening—but you were warned. And when you know I have had to spend the time in leave-taking with a friend, starting for Africa, you will excuse

Yours ever,

A. C. Swinburne

---

has a title. The earlier manuscript, presumably the one referred to in this letter, concludes in the middle of a page with line 42 followed by this inscription: "A.C.S. to J.A.W. /April 2d /65." An additional page belonging to the same manuscript bears the final three stanzas (Pt. 3), except that the last verse of all, line 63, is on the verso. The second manuscript, obviously a fair copy, is complete. The poem is said to have been printed on gold paper and pasted to the frame of the picture; stanzas 4 and 6 were printed in the Royal Academy *Catalogue*, 1865.

1. (1834–89), journalist, drama critic, author.

2. Gosse and Wise dated this letter "1865," and identified the friend as Burton, but either they or Swinburne erred, for in 1865 Burton sailed for Brazil, Swinburne on Apr. 4 having attended a public dinner given in his honor by the Anthropological Society. On Wednesday, Apr. 12, Swinburne was present at a party given by Gabriel Rossetti at Cheyne Walk. The letter has been endorsed by some one "Easter Tuesday Winwood Reade." In 1865 Easter Tuesday fell on Apr. 18, when Reade was (apparently) in Italy, having left England exactly a month earlier. My own nomination is Sala, who *did* go to Africa in Apr. 1865.

76. TO LORD HOUGHTON

MS: The Marchioness of Crewe.

[*ca.* April 20, 1865]

Please, Sir, don't hit very hard this time—I haven't been swished yet this half, you can ask my tutor—and he says I'm not the worst boy in my division. I do think it's no end of a chouse for a fellow to be swished for his verses when he showed them up in time for school and there were no false quantities in them I'm sure. At least you might let the praeposter pick the buds off.

However, I'm not in much of a funk—a boy in my part of the school doesn't mind a swishing as much as a lower boy does. I can take a dozen cuts or so without wincing. Only let the Masters look out and not drive me to head a rebellion among the fellows of my own age, and bar them out of school.

One birch-twig I hereby pull out of the bloody bundle. As to my quantities and metre and rule of rhythm and rhyme, I defy castigation. The head master has sent me up for good on that score. Mr. Tennyson tells me in a note that he 'envies me' my gift that way. After this approval I will not submit myself to the birch on that account. The moral and religious question I give up at once. I let down my breeches, pull up my shirt, and kneel down (for the hundredth time) on the flogging block, without a word. If you apply a rod soaked in brine for that offence I confess I deserve it. I *did* shirk Chapel. I *did* take to profane swearing instead of singing in the choir. I am fully prepared for a jolly good swishing in consequence. I can't complain if you take my name out of the list for Confirmation and insert it in the flogging bill. Only don't say with my old friend of the Spectator that it isn't Greek—because it *is*. I recognize in that attack the avenging hand of outraged virtue, mindful how nearly that paper was induced, through a shameless trick (I was in the fourth form then, you know), to admit into its chaste pages a flaming eulogy of M. le marquis de Sade.[1] But the writer flogs all at random and doesn't know where to hit or how to touch up and tickle a tender part of the boy exposed for punishment.

I will tell Payne (pretty name for an usher) to send you the material of flagellation at once. It is rather hard to have to supply the twigs destined to make my own posteriors writhe and bleed, but I know it's the way of the school. I have been well flogged some four or five times already for the same fault. Tennyson and Jowett, the Athenaeum and

---

1. See above, Letter 43.

the Spectator,[2] have each had their innings. Twice I have been swished in private, and twice in public before the whole school—for 'irreverence.' My skin has the marks of the birch still on it. Pray remember this, and don't lay on too hard. My bum has been brushed often enough.

On the 23rd I will appeal in person to your levity; meantime have as much mercy as you can on the already tingling bottom of

Your affectionate though much-flogged pupil,
Frank

77. TO CHARLES AUGUSTUS HOWELL [1]

MS: British Museum. Published (with deletions): Bonchurch, *18*, 31–32*.

Ashburnham Place, Battle, Sussex,
Tuesday [May or June 1865] [2]

Infâme libertin

Write me a word according to promise—I shall be up in town in a day or two on my way *from* an uncle's [3] *to* a father's—*de famille en famille*—ô Justine! quelle horreur! and between domestic life, rural gallops with cousins, study of art and illuminated MSS. and Caxton print—and proof of a new edition of the virginal poem of Atalanta—je m'enfonce dans des systèmes qui mènent à tout—oui—chère fille—absolument à tout. I have added yet four more jets of boiling and gushing infamy to the perennial and poisonous fountain of Dolores.[4] Write—and communicate to the ink une odeur mélangée de sang et

2. *Atalanta* was reviewed in the *Athenaeum* (by Westland Marston) on Apr. 1; in the *Spectator* on Apr. 15.

1. (1840–90), a gifted, fascinating adventurer in Ruskin, Rossetti, Swinburne (and other) circles, not only witty in himself but the cause that wit was in other men. He is the subject (and in some cases the author) of many fables, and hard facts concerning him are not plentiful. The fables and facts were authoritatively dealt with by Helen Rossetti Angeli, *Pre-Raphaelite Twilight; The Story of Charles Augustus Howell* (1954).

2. "May or June" is a guess. The paper is watermarked 1864, and we know that Swinburne attended Gabriel Rossetti's party at Cheyne Walk on Apr. 15. All other evidence is inferential.

3. His mother's brother Bertram (1797–1878), 4th Earl of Ashburnham, who assembled the famous library, which included sixteen Caxtons and, among its extraordinary manuscripts, the Barrois collection, acquired in 1849.

4. (Bonchurch, *1*, 284–98), in *PB1*.

de sperme. O mon ami! abhorrons les sophismes—méprisons les banalités—vénérons le vit dressé—adorons le sang répandu.

Tout à toi,
A C S

P.S. I send you a fresh sample of Dolores. If you are amiable and write me something stimulating as the smell of firwoods,[5] you shall have the rest.

> For the Lords in whose keeping the door is
>   That opens on all who draw breath
> Gave the cypress to Love, My Dolores,
>   The myrtle to Death.
> And they laughed, changing hands in the measure,
>   And they mixed and made peace after strife;
> *Pain melted in tears, and was Pleasure;*
>   *Death tingled in blood, and was Life.*

Voilà, mes amis, une vérité que ne comprendront jamais les sots idolateurs de la vertu.

P.S. Since writing the above I have added ten [6] verses to D. —très infâmes et très bien tournés. 'Oh! monsieur—peut-on prendre du plaisir à telles horreurs?' Tu le vois, Justine, je bande—oh! putain, que tu vas souffrir'—

P.P.S. (*private*) I want you to compose for me a little dialogue (imaginary) between schoolmaster and boy—from the first summons 'Now Arthur (or Frank—or Harry) what does *this* mean, sir? Come here'—to the last *cut* and painful buttoning up—a rebuke or threat at every lash (and *plenty* of them) and a shriek of agonized appeal from the boy in reply.* I want to see how like real life you will make it. Write me this—and you shall have more of my verses—a fair bargain.

---

* Describe also the effect of each stripe on the boy's flesh—its appearance between the cuts.

5. See above, Letter 45.

6. He first wrote "18" and then changed it to "10."

78. TO LORD HOUGHTON

MS: The Marchioness of Crewe.

22a Dorset Street,
Tuesday [July 11?, 1865] [1]

Dear Lord Houghton

As my tempter and favourite audience has gone to Santos [2] I may hope to be a good boy again, after such a 'jolly good swishing' as Rodin alone can and dare administer. The Rugby purists (I am told) tax Eton generally with Maenadism during June and July, so perhaps some old school habits return upon us unawares—to be fitly expiated by old school punishment. That once I remember and admitt. The Captain was too many for me; and I may have shaken the thyrsus in your face. But after this half I mean to be no end good.

I should like to see the Post, it must be far more amusing than the Edinburgh,[3] and one prefers sound judgment to employ adulation or hollow patronage. I am only sorry to hear of your corresponding with literary blackguards, drunk or sober—equally offensive either way. From the 'able editor' [4] you mention, I have not yet recovered my stolen MS.

I wish you were in town tonight and disengaged, as Watkiss Lloyd [5] and one or two more are coming to me for a reading of Chastelard over 'aesthetic tea.' [6] You would have the chance of giving wholesome advice and due discouragement—which we know you like to do.

The book is in type all but the fifth act. I am only staying here in this heat which makes me feverish all day, to have done with the last proofs, then I return to Oxfordshire, where I hope to be soon next week. I direct this note to Fryston as I hear from Lloyd you will be there in a day or two.

I have just got the enclosed which I transmit at once. I have not

1. Lord Houghton went to Fryston (see the penultimate paragraph of this letter) after July 15 and well before July 30 (see Reid's *Richard Monckton Milnes*, 2, 142–43).

2. The Burtons left England late in May.

3. *Atalanta in Calydon* was reviewed in the *Morning Post* (July 8, 1865), p. 2, and in the *Edinburgh Review* (July 1865), pp. 202–16. The latter review, as will be seen, was by Lord Houghton.

4. Carlyle, *The French Revolution*, Bk. VI, chap. v. Swinburne's allusion is to Edward Walford (see below, Letter 420).

5. (1813–93), classical and Shakespearean scholar.

6. "Getting Under Way," *Sartor Resartus*.

seen the book since you had it, and as I borrowed it from Rossetti as a great favour I feel rather responsible for the loan. Please return it when you can, or he will tear *me* in pieces.

Yours affectionately,
A. C. Swinburne

79. TO LORD HOUGHTON

MS: The Marchioness of Crewe. Published: Bonchurch, *18*, 32–33.*

22a Dorset Street,
Friday [July 14?, 1865]

My dear Lord Houghton

I was about to write you a word of thanks for your article when I received the copy you sent me this morning. Nothing yet said or written about the book has given me nearly as much pleasure. Especially I have to thank you for the tone in which you refer to my expressed regard for Landor. As to the praise of myself, a poet more drunk with vanity than with wine could wish for no more. I only regret that in justly attacking my Antitheism you have wilfully misrepresented its source. I should have bowed to the judicial sentence if instead of 'Byron with a difference' you had said 'de Sade with a difference.' The poet, thinker, and man of the world from whom the theology of my poem is derived was a greater than Byron. *He* indeed, fatalist or not, saw to the bottom of gods and men. As to anything you have fished (how I say not) out of Mrs. Burton to the discredit of my 'temperance, soberness and chastity' as the Catechism puts it —how can she who believes in the excellence of 'Richard' fail to disbelieve in the virtues of any other man? En moi vous voyez Les Malheurs de la Vertu; en lui Les Prospérités du Vice. In effect it is not given to all his juniors to tenir tête à Burton—but I deny that his hospitality ever succeeded in upsetting me—as he himself on the morrow of a latish séance admitted with approbation, allowing that he had thought to get me off my legs, but my native virtue and circumspection were too much for him. See now the consequences—j'étais vertueux—je devais souffrir. Accomplis tes décrets, Être Suprême!

Yours affectionately,
A. C. Swinburne

80. TO LORD HOUGHTON

MS: The Marchioness of Crewe.

22a Dorset Street, W., July 27 [1865]

My dear Lord Houghton

I will come with pleasure on the fourteenth; till when I may probably be again cultivating the calmer virtues at Holm Wood.

I have seen the 'Post' review [1] by way of corrective; and am obliged to you for the loathsome but instructive spectacle of a Helot whose inebriety is more useful than any verbal or verbereal lesson that could be given to a young Spartan. Rather than only once in a year share a single vice with such a swine, I will live on tea and lemonade. I only wish the Helot had given us his views on the Greek verse of an Athenian.

Did you ever meet M. Daubignet (or -gny, I forget which but think the former) [2] who I am told is a great light at Paris for his landscapes? He is middle aged and decorated, and still very good company, which is creditable. He was being fêted here for a week or so; I met him at dinner one evening and liked him. He expressed himself much taken with my French songs,[3] which were shown him by a friend to whom I had lent them. The last (and I think best) you have not heard; I delayed the proofs of 'Chastelard' (which is now well off my hands) in order to insert it. The second edition of 'Atalanta' is to appear with 'Chastelard' in autumn. There is to be an etching of me by Whistler prefixed,[4] much to the publisher's excitement. I met at Moxon's the other day old Mr. Procter [5] and got on with him as I always do with old men—another of my Spartan virtues. He was charming et me disait des choses ravissantes—but mourned over the

1. See above, Letter 78.

2. Charles François Daubigny (1817–78), noted for his etchings as well as landscapes.

3. In *Chastelard*.

4. This plan fell through, but the etching by Whistler is well known.

5. Bryan Waller Procter (1787–1874), who wrote under the name of "Barry Cornwall." His *Charles Lamb: A Memoir* appeared in 1866. He was in his own day, which was several decades before the date of this letter, a writer of songs; and as a friend of Lamb's, a lover (and imitator) of Elizabethan drama, and an aged man he would of course have won Swinburne's admiration. His wife, Anne Skepper Procter (1799–1888), was equally an object of veneration.

hard work of seven hours a day at his 'Life of Charles Lamb,' of which project I was enchanted to hear.

Yours affectionately,
A. C. Swinburne

81. TO VICTOR HUGO

MS: British Museum. Published: *Revue bleue*, 74 (Mar. 7, 1936), 152.

22a Dorset Street, Portman Square, London, W.,
August 10, 1865

Monsieur

Vous avez peut-être oublié, parmi tout de choses plus importantes qui doivent vous occuper, que vous avez bien voulu, il y a maintenant deux ans, accepter la dédicace du livre [1] auquel je travaillais encore à ce temps-là. C'est ce livre que je vous envoie aujourd'hui.

Ce n'est qu'une œuvre de collégien que je vous dédie; mais puisque vous avez trouvé dans les articles imparfaits et tronqués que j'ai pu publier sur *Les Misérables* quelque chose qui ne vous a pas déplu, j'espère que vous recevrez avec la même bonté le livre que j'ose enfin vous offrir. Croyez au moins que si j'avais quelque chose de meilleur à vous envoyer je ne vous enverrais pas une œuvre d'adolescent. Peut-être ferai-je mieux à trente ans; mais en attendant j'ai voulu vous donner ce que j'ai de mieux.[2] Je sais au moins qu'il y a une page qui grace à vous ne périra pas; c'est celle qui porte votre nom.[3]

Recevez, Monsieur, l'assurance de ma profonde admiration et de reconnaissance éternelle.

Algernon Swinburne

1. *Chastelard,* which was not actually published till late Nov. For Hugo's acceptance of the dedication see above, Letter 42.

2. This manuscript is a first draft of the actual letter, and a canceled sentence follows here: "S'il y a dans ce livre, comme on m'a dit à Paris et à Londres, quelque chose de bon, c'est à vous que je la dois."

3. "I dedicate this play, as a partial expression of reverence and gratitude, to the chief of living poets; to the first dramatist of his age; to the greatest exile, and therefore to the greatest man of France; to Victor Hugo."

82. TO SEYMOUR KIRKUP

Text: Bonchurch, *18*, 24–26*.

22 Dorset Street, Portman Square, London, W.,
August 11 [1865] [1]

My dear Mr. Kirkup

I cannot leave town again without answering your letter. I wish you could make it convenient to pay at last a flying visit to the country which after all is originally your own. No one understands more than I do how difficult it must be to tear oneself away for a week even from the most divine land and city in the world. But if you came over for a month or so now that you can make the journey in less than a week, you would at all events meet many who would be glad of the chance of meeting you, and see where art is now among us.

I do not add that you would give great pleasure to many, and not least to me.

I forget whether I told you that your portrait of my Mother as a girl has been brought down to my Father's country-house, and hangs now in the drawing room, to the delight of us all. Before my grandmother died, it was always kept by her, and I never saw it till this year.

I was much struck by the passage in your last letter to me, where you speak of the Theory of Transmigration. Whether or not it be affirmed or denied by spirits I know that it has always appeared to me a very probable article of faith. I certainly do not remember having been another man before my birth into this present life, but I have often felt that I have been once upon a time a cat, and worried by a dog. I cannot see a cat without caressing it, or a dog, without feeling its fangs in my flanks.

I envy you your experience of snakes. I should like of all things to have them play with me and my cats. Notwithstanding I have not yet read *Melusine*.[2]

It may interest you to know that to-day, in the sale of Lord Charlemont's library by auction, there was sold a MS. of the *Roman de la Rose* with many beautiful illuminations, given by the poet

1. Gosse and Wise conjectured the date to be 1864, but the reference below to the sale of Lord Charlemont's library, which took place Aug. 11, 1865, proves them wrong.

2. A Middle English romance in which the hero, happily married to a beautiful fairy, breaks a promise and learns that his wife is a serpent from the waist down. *Melusine* was edited by Skeat for the Early English Text Society in 1866.

Baïf to Charles IX., and having also the autograph of Philippe Desportes. It has been a wonderful sale for amateurs and bibliophiles, including a book with autograph notes by Milton,[3] and many early editions of Shakespeare.

Gilchrist's *Life of Blake* is published by Macmillan, 2 vols. 8vo. I hope my treatise may appear before long, when of course I shall send it to you. What do you think of this dogma of Blake's [4] (inspired, as he asserts, not invented)? Swedenborg uttered no new truths, and did utter all the old falsehoods. Because he consulted Angels, who are ignorant about religion; instead of Devils, who hate religion and enjoy knowledge; whereas Blake piques himself on having received no information—inspiration from hell instead of heaven.

I have not yet thanked you for the present of your Arthurian notes, which to me are very valuable, and full of interest. I am glad to know that I may keep them without robbing you.

Did you ever meet with that rare book containing some of Blake's poems and headed by a frontispiece mainly designed (but not engraved) by Blake, *A Father's Memoirs of His Child*, by a D. A. Malkin? [5] Apart from the interest of its connection with Blake, it is in my opinion the most astonishing study of physiology I ever met with. This child died at six, and left stories, maps, letters, etc., full of invention and imagination, and sketches of landscape which earned (after his death) the approbation of Blake. As far as I know, the instance is unique, for it is not a sample of forcing, but of native and instinctive genius.

Believe me,

Yours very faithfully,
A. C. Swinburne

S. Kirkup, Esq.

3. *Lycophronis Alexandra.*

4. In *The Marriage of Heaven and Hell.*

5. By B. H. Malkin (1806).

83. TO JOHN RUSKIN

Text: E. T. Cook and Alexander Wedderburn, eds., *The Works of John Ruskin* (39 vols. London and New York, 1903–12), *36* (1909), xlviii–xlix.

22a Dorset Street, Portman Square,
August 11 [1865]

My dear Ruskin

I send you the song [1] you asked for, finding that I can remember it after dinner. Nevertheless it has given me far more labour to recollect and transcribe than it did originally to compose. But your selection of it as a piece of work more satisfactory than usual gave me so much pleasure that I was determined to send it when I could. Since writing the verses (which were literally improvised and taken down on paper one Sunday morning after breakfast) I have been told more than once, and especially by Gabriel Rossetti, that they were better than the subject. Three or four days ago I had the good fortune to be able to look well over the picture which alone put them into my head, and came to the conclusion which I had drawn at first, that whatever merit my song may have, it is not so complete in beauty, in tenderness and significance, in exquisite execution and delicate strength as Whistler's picture. Whistler himself was the first critic who so far overpraised my verse as to rank it above his own painting. I stood up against him for himself, and will, of course, against all others.

I am going to take Jones (unless I hear from Whistler to the contrary) on Sunday next to W.'s studio. I wish you could accompany us. Whistler (as any artist worthy of his rank must be) is of course desirous to meet you, and to let you see his immediate work. As (I think) he has never met you, you will see that his desire to have it out with you face to face must spring simply from knowledge and appreciation of your own works. If this meeting cannot be managed, I must look forward to the chance of entrapping you into my chambers on my return to London.[2] If I could get Whistler, Jones, and Howell to meet you, I think we might so far cozen the Supreme Powers as for once to realise a few not unpleasant hours.

Yours very sincerely,
A. C. Swinburne

1. See above, Letter 74A.

2. He had accepted an invitation to visit Houghton at Fryston on Aug. 14 (see above, Letter 80), but the visit was postponed.

84. TO LORD HOUGHTON

MS: The Marchioness of Crewe.

Arts Club, Hanover Square, August 25 [1865]

My dear Lord Houghton

I am kept by force in London till Tuesday.[1] There is a dinner got up chiefly on my account, to come off on Monday, where I am to meet people I don't know: and as I have promised, and can't get off without quarrelling, it appears I must stay: but I would rather be at Fryston. I will bring you Joseph [2] on the Tuesday by the noon train without fail; and am

Yours affectionately,

A. C. Swinburne

I have dreamt of nothing but Calcraft μαστιγόφορος [3] since you confided to me the great idea. Must it be but a dream? Hélas! voilà bien les Dieux.

1. Aug. 29.

2. Probably the essay on C. J. Wells' *Joseph and His Brethren* (see above, Letter 29), but possibly *Madame Putiphar* (see above, Letter 41).

3. "Scourge-bearing" (a Sophoclean epithet for Ajax). William Calcraft (1800–79) became executioner for London in 1829, and when business was not brisk, he was at liberty to work in other areas. Or, as "Annie Protheroe" in *The Bab Ballads* has it:

> "In busy times he laboured at his gentle craft all day—
> 'No doubt you mean his Cal-craft' you amusingly will say—
> But, no—he didn't operate with common bits of string,
> He was a Public Headsman, which is quite another thing."

Calcraft, who retired on a pension in 1874, had been most recently in the news as the executioner, in Glasgow on July 28, 1865, of Dr. William Pritchard, who had poisoned his wife and his mother-in-law (see August Mencken, ed., *By the Neck*, New York, 1942, pp. 127–31, and William Roughhead, *The Murderer's Companion*, New York, 1941, pp. 57–113). Pritchard's hanging, both victim and hangman being bearded, is said to have had unusual visual appeal, but Calcraft attracted notoriety of another sort a few months later during the execution of "the soldier Currie" for the murder of Major de Vere. "The Rev. J. Greener, the Presbyterian minister, arranged, it is stated, with Calcraft, that the culprit should drop at a particular sentence in his final prayer." And since these histrionics unnecessarily prolonged the suspense for a minute or two, public opinion was outraged. See the *Pall Mall Gazette* (Oct. 13, 1865), p. 9.

85. TO LORD HOUGHTON

MS: The Marchioness of Crewe. Brief extract published: Bonchurch, *18*, 33*.

Shernfold Park, Frant, Tunbridge Wells,[1]
October 13 [1865]

My dear Lord Houghton

If you are not over head and ears in social science, and out of sight or sound in the morass of philanthropy (regardless of the judgment which awaits public as well as private virtue); if you can spare a minute from the task of corrupting that exquisite animal, the adorable British working man, and making him unfit to fill with resignation the subordinate station in which an all-wise and all-good Providence has seen fit to confine him; I want you to do me a small favour in the way of instruction. What is the proper way to apply for the pensions on the Civil List designed for needy and deserving people of letters? You will at once imagine that the question has a personal interest for me as coming on all grounds under that category; but that is not at present the case. Some friends of mine want to know how to set about it and whom to address on behalf of a needy and meritorious writer of 22 years' standing.[2] I don't know, and my people don't know, and I thought as you are so general an authority on matters of literature and beneficence (subjects of which I profess to know nothing myself) I would trouble you with the question. I shall be really obliged by being told, on my friends' account, what they had better do. If you find time, please write me a word to my London address, as I shall be moving about next week. For myself, I think of addressing a memorial to [the] government which shall set forth my own claims to a pension as Defender of the Faith and moral teacher of my own generation. Mr. Maurice,[3] you may remember, considers Atalanta a complement to the hitherto imperfect Evidences of Christianity. As the second Paley, I expect at least a lay archidiaconate.

Have you read your friend and philanthropic colleague Mr. T.

1. Seat of his maternal uncle, the Hon. Percy Ashburnham (1799–1881), brother of the 4th Earl.

2. Unidentified.

3. F. D. Maurice (1805–72), moral philosopher. One of the founders of the "Apostles' Club" at Cambridge and, several decades later, of the Working Men's College. He and Swinburne had been fellow guests at Fryston in Aug. 1865.

Hughes' address on public schools? [4] it was to me (as Mr. Pecksniff says) [5] 'very soothing.'

Ever yours affectionately,
A. C. Swinburne

86. TO CHARLES AUGUSTUS HOWELL

MS: British Museum. Extract published: Bonchurch, *18,* 47*.

22a Dorset Street, W.,
Monday [? October 30, 1865]

Fripon

Tu ne mérites que la réprobation de tes confrères—mais je te pardonne. Depuis plusieurs jours, coquin, j'attends de tes nouvelles. Toi, sans doute, tu te branles voluptueusement en songeant à tes perfidies.

I want you to find out for me what (if any) day would suit Ruskin to come with yourself and Ned Jones to my rooms for an evening. He promised to come some day and I am now in town for ten days or so. There was to have been a *reading* given and he said he should like to meet you two.

Ecris-moi enfin quelque chose de piquant—viens bientôt me voir, si tu n'es pas pris à tout jamais dans les filets de la vertu—et faisons des horreurs.

Tout à toi et au Marquis,
A C S

87. TO CHARLES AUGUSTUS HOWELL

MS: British Museum.

Ste. Marie des Bois, près Grenoble, France,[1]
Wednesday, November 8 [1865]

My dear Howell

I ought to have written ages ago to thank you for the Heptameron —but I was always in hopes you would turn up according to promise.

4. Thomas Hughes (1822–96), author of *Tom Brown's School Days,* follower of F. D. Maurice. He was elected M.P. for Lambeth in 1865, and, like Houghton, attended the Social Science Congress in Sheffield in Oct.

5. In *Martin Chuzzlewit,* chap. 9.

1. More seriously, 22a Dorset Street, London.

Do come look one up whenever you can—I want awfully to see you. After you last left me, I was ineffably seedy and thought I was probably going to hell—my one hope being to meet there M. le Marquis de Sade. On Monday week I stayed in on purpose to meet you—as you left written word that you would turn up. But you didn't. La trahison, je le sais, fait bouder. Mais permettez-moi, Monsieur, de vous le dire—cela mène à tout.

Seriously (as you of course know) I am beyond words obliged to you for the gift. I value it on all accounts immensely. Cependant, please come (I am still in town for a week) and receive thanks in person. The last cartoons were not successes. De plus, I want to see my friends before going down to domestic virtue.

Ever your affectionate,
A. C. Swinburne

88. TO GEORGE POWELL [1]

MS: National Library of Wales.

22a Dorset Street, Portman Square, W.,
November 12 [1865]

Sir

I should have received and answered your letter some days earlier but for an accident which sent it after me in a wrong direction. I can now only apologize for not replying by return of post and assure you with many thanks of the great pleasure it will give me to see my name associated with your book.[2]

Believe me
Yours very sincerely,
A. C. Swinburne

1. (1842–82), Welsh squire. Besides the translations referred to below, he wrote several books of original poetry. He attended Eton and Brasenose College, Oxford (matriculated May 1861). In 1878, on the death of his father, Col. William Thomas Rowland Powell, with whom his relations were distinctly unamiable, he inherited Nant-Eos, the family seat. In 1881 he married Dinah Harris. He died Oct. 17, 1882. Three roundels in CR memorialize Powell without naming him, "A Dead Friend," "Past Days," "Autumn and Winter" (Bonchurch, 5, 13–20). The third of these concerns both Powell and Wagner, to whom Powell was so devoted and whose death followed Powell's by four months. The Brotherton Library, Leeds, has thirteen letters from Powell to Swinburne. There is a photograph of Powell (but, despite the legend, not of Swinburne) in Herbert M. Vaughan, The South Wales Squires: A Welsh Picture of Social Life (1926), facing p. 82.

2. Legends of Iceland (Second Series, 1866), translated by George E. J. Powell and Eiríkr Magnússon, was dedicated to Lord Dufferin and Swinburne.

89. TO GEORGE POWELL

MS: National Library of Wales.

22a Dorset Street, W., November 25 [1865]

My dear Sir

I ought to have written some days ago to thank you for your book,[1] but have been overworked with letters and business connected with my new book.[2] I hope you have received a copy which I told the publisher to send you in my name. Thanks also for the photograph you send me. I wish I had a better one than the villainous thing I send in exchange—which came out all spotty and blurred and wrong—but I have no decent one at hand. Pray don't believe meantime that I am so like a stage villain with erysipelas in the face. I hope we may meet if you are in town this winter, but at present shall be off into the country in ten days or so, I hope. I had the pleasure of meeting Mr. Vigfússon[3] the other day at the home of a friend to whom I have since lent your book, after reading it with great interest and enjoyment. I am impatient to see the second series on more accounts than one.

Yours very faithfully,
A. C. Swinburne

89A. WILLIAM BELL SCOTT TO LADY TREVELYAN

MS: Trevelyan Papers, Wallington.

33 Elgin Road,
Saturday morning [? November 25, 1865]

. . . I do think you could do A.S. very much benefit by seriously writing him.[1] The remark you make on his behaviour at Wallington I believe I quite understand, he suffers under a dislike to ladies of late —his knowledge of himself and of them increasing upon him. His success too is certainly not improving him, as one might easily suppose with so boundless a vanity.

His new book Chastelard[2] is just ready; it is not his publication

1. *Legends of Iceland* (First Series), translated by Powell and Magnússon, published in 1864.

2. *Chastelard.*

3. Gúdbrandr Vígfússon (1828–89), the Icelandic scholar.

1. From this letter I have excerpted the portion concerning Swinburne. See Letters 91 and 92, below.

2. Published in the latter half of Nov. 1865.

but most likely he will have copies to send, and you will perhaps see certain things there—the total severance of the passion of love from the moral delight of loving or being loved, so to speak, and the insaneness of the impulses of Chastelard—for example; which may give you a text for writing him. With all his boasting of himself and all his belongings he is very sensitive about society, and I certainly think you will do him the very kindest of actions if you can touch his sensibility on his vanity—a little sharply. Of late he has been very much excited, and certainly drinking. Gabriel and William Rossetti think he will not live if he goes on as lately without stopping. He says he is to leave town, however, for a long while, in a few days, and we hope he may quiet down. . . .

90. TO RICHARD HENRY STODDARD [1]

MS: Princeton.

22a Dorset Street, Portman Square, London (West),
November 27, 1865

My dear Sir

I thank you sincerely for your note and for the paper you sent me, which I read with interest and pleasure. That my work should find already in America such warm acceptance as Mr. W. H. Hurlbert's [2] able and friendly article has given it, cannot but be to me a far keener and fresher source of satisfaction than the hackneyed blame or shallow praise of ordinary journalism can afford. To him, as to you, I beg to send my thanks. Nothing however gives me more pleasure than the opinion expressed by you, as also by the writer of the brief remarks on 'Chastelard' in the 'Round Table,' that my last book —a work with more sides to it and with more labour in it than its predecessor—is likely to find in your country readers who after examining may accept it as worthy of their good word. I need not add how much pleasure I expect from the sight of your book of Selections [3] —nor how much I should receive from the perusal of any further notice of my poems that may appear in America. Among your writers, I perceive, blame and praise alike are thoughtful and careful—valuable therefore in either case to a writer. As a man wholly ignorant of

1. Richard Henry Stoddard (1825–1903), American poet and critic, editor of the New York *World*, 1860–70, of the New York *Mail and Express*, 1880–1903.

2. William Henry Hurlbert (1827–95), journalist, author, drama critic. The review is unidentified.

3. *The Late English Poets* (New York, 1865), an anthology.

professional business, unknown to the press and unconnected with literature, I cannot judge how it might be best to deal with foreign publishers. My own interest in the matter must I presume in any case be small in comparison to their possible profits abroad and my own at home.

Believe me, my dear Sir,

Yours sincerely,
A. C. Swinburne

R. H. Stoddard, Esq.
New York

91. TO PAULINE, LADY TREVELYAN

MS: Trevelyan Papers, Wallington.

22a Dorset Street, W., December 4 [1865]

My dear Lady Trevelyan

I know not how to thank you sufficiently for the kindness of your letter. I cannot express the horror and astonishment, the unutterable indignation and loathing, with which I have been struck on hearing that any one could be vile enough to tax me, I do not say with doing but with saying anything of the kind to which you refer. The one suggestion is not falser than the other. I am literally amazed and horrorstruck at the infamous wickedness of people who invent in malice or repeat in levity such horrors.

I cannot believe such persons can really or seriously injure those who are conscious of no wrong done to them which might explain their enmity. It is I who should feel ashamed to meet and disgraced by meeting people capable of believing me improper for them to meet. I can only imagine 1) that the very quietness of my way of living as compared with that of other men of my age exposes me, given up as I almost always am to comparative solitude, to work at my own art, and never seen in *fast* (hardly in *slow*) life—to spitefulness and vicious stupidity, 2) that as you say I must have talked very foolishly to make such infamies possible. All I can ever recollect saying which *could* be perverted was (for instance) that 'the Greeks did not seem to me worse than the moderns because of things considered innocent at one time by one country were not considered so by others.' Far more than this I have heard said by men of the world of the highest character. This sort of thing, I was told afterwards, might be thought *wild* and offensive by hearers who were bent on malignant commentary, or 4) [*sic*] I do remember saying, 'if people

137

read the classics, not to speak of the moderns very often, they must see that many qualities called virtues and vices depend on time, climate, and temperament.' The remark may have been false or foolish, but who could have imagined it (until he had proof) capable of being twisted into an avowal that I approved vice and disapproved virtue? Any one who says he has heard me speak personally, as if *I* agreed with other times or disagreed with this, lies. Even when talking thus at random, in an atmosphere of men's chaff and loose hasty words, I was always *careful* to draw the difference. And now I have really told you all. I was once told before that a friend 'had heard said' that I boasted of distributing indecent books at Oxford. I quite expect soon to learn that at school I committed murder.

Once more, I cannot think how—and I would fain try—to thank you enough for the great and undeserved kindness which impelled you to write as you did. It consoles me under the horror of knowing what unscrupulous and shameless enemies one may make without knowing or deserving it, to remember how unlike to these are others —and if the one sort are my enemies the other are my friends. If you could write me a single word to say that you believe me and are satisfied by this hurried answer, it would be a fresh and almost as great a proof of kindness. I dare not undergo the pain of reading your letter again, and will endeavour to forget the cruelty and horror of such reports in their absurdity; but your goodness to me on the occasion I never shall.

Believe me for ever

Yours most gratefully and sincerely,
A. C. Swinburne

I do not ask who spoke to you against me as having *heard* me say things I never did say. If you thought it right to tell me as a warning I know you would.

92. TO PAULINE, LADY TREVELYAN

MS: Trevelyan Papers, Wallington.

Arts Club, Hanover Square,
Tuesday, December 5 [1865]

My dear Lady Trevelyan

I wrote to you this morning in such a hurry and posted my letter within so nearly twenty minutes after receiving yours, that now towards evening I feel that I may not have sufficiently thanked you. I assure you, upon my honour, that if this could have happened without giving you pain I do believe I could hardly wish it had not. I

only wish to heaven that at any time or in any way I could—not repay, which would be impossible, but—express to you otherwise than
by inadequate words my sense of your goodness to me. Six hours ago,
I was so utterly amazed, horrified, agonized and disgusted, that I could
hardly think of anything but the subject of your letter. Now I can
hardly think of anything but your inexpressible kindness in writing.
I *cannot* thank you enough. That is nothing to say. And if I now try
to say anything more I feel I shall begin to talk more wildly than ever.
Only I do entreat you to believe in my gratitude. Nobody in my life
was ever so good to me as you have been. You must know what pain
any man would feel on hearing what you tell me—what shame
any man must feel who was conscious that, in however innocent and
ignorant a way, he had (I will not say deserved, but) exposed himself through rashness and inexperience to such suffering as I underwent in reading what you wrote. I know I have not deserved to feel
pain—and shame I do not feel, because I have not deserved it. The
pain I feel no longer—and what I do feel is a gratitude, and even a
sort of gladness that anything should have happened to make me
know so fully how great and noble, how beyond all thanks and
acknowledgement, your kindness could be. I repeat it, upon my
honour, this and this alone is what I now feel. I can think just now
of nothing else. For years I have regarded you—as I trust you know
or believe without words of mine—with a grateful affection which I
never could express. Now I can say less than ever how deep and true
is my sense of obligation to you. You were always kinder to me (when
much younger) than others—now you are kinder than I could have
dared to think of. I am amazed beyond words at people's villainy or
stupidity—but yet more at people's goodness.

I am sure I have written at random, and 'spasmodically'—but I
will not read over my note, and I cannot but send it this evening. I am
sure my first was too incoherent, and dealt too much with the matter
at hand, to be properly grateful. But I hope you knew, and do
know, with what gratitude and affection I must be

Always yours,
A. C. Swinburne

P.S. I see this is *too* chaotic—but please excuse it. I never do cry, and
never did I think much as boy or man for pain—and this morning
when I wrote I never felt less tempted—but this time I have really
felt tears coming more than once.[1]

1. Part of Lady Trevelyan's reply, dated **Dec. 6**, is in *A Swinburne Library* (p.
229): "Now do, if it is only for the sake of living down evil reports, do be wise in
which of your lyrics you publish. Do let it be a book that can be really loved and

93. TO PAULINE, LADY TREVELYAN

MS: Trevelyan Papers, Wallington. Published: Bonchurch, *18*, 35–38*.

22a Dorset Street, W., December 10, 1865

My dear Lady Trevelyan

I would have written two days since in answer to your last and most kind letter, but that I wanted to take time and reply as fully as I could. I must first, and once again, thank both yourself and Sir Walter alike for your great kindness. You will both, I hope, believe that I know how much I am indebted to the friendship and the courage which made you defend me against the villainy of fools and knaves. I wish I could better express my gratitude to him or to you. But I tried to express it in my second letter written and posted on the same day as that which you answered. I know I must have failed, but I did what I could. Since writing to you, I have been reminded of things as infamous and as ridiculous inflicted upon others as undeserving as even I am. Two years ago, for instance, I was informed (of course on the best and most direct authority) that a friend of yours as of mine had boasted aloud of murdering his own illegitimate children.[1] That they never had existed was of course nothing to the purpose. Fortunately, in this case, I was cited as a witness—and did pretty well, I believe, knock that rumour on the head. I cannot but suppose that all these agreeable traditions arise from one infamous source. When it is found out, we may hope to suppress it once for all. Meantime, upon the double suspicion, I have refused to meet in public a person whom I conceive to be possibly mixed up in the matter. At all events, I know that I have done the man no wrong—for a more venomous backbiter, I believe, never existed. The difficulty in all such cases is to come forward, collar your man morally or physically,

---

read and learned by heart, and become part and parcel of the English language, and be on every one's table without being received under protest by timid people. There are no doubt people who would be glad to be able to say that it is not fit to be read. It is not worth while for the sake of two or three poems to risk the widest circulation of the whole. You have sailed near enough to the wind in all conscience in having painted such a character for a hero as your Chastelard, slave to a passion for a woman he despises, whose love (if one can call it love) has no element of chivalry or purity in it; whose devotion to her is much as if a man should set himself to be crushed before Juggernaut, cursing him all the while for a loathsome despicable idol. I suppose people would say that Chastelard was a maniac. . . . Don't give people a handle against you now. And do mind what you say for the sake of all to whom your fame is dear, and who are looking forward to your career with hope and interest. . . ."

1. See above, Letter 21.

and say 'I am told you accuse me of having confessed to something disgraceful. Give me your reasons for this lie!' Of course no one could wish to see his name dragged into and through the dirt of such a quarrel: and therefore any gentleman is at the mercy of any blackguard—for a time.

As to my poems, my perplexity is this: that no two friends have ever given me the same advice. Now more than ever I would rather take yours than another's; but I see neither where to begin nor where to stop. I have written nothing to be ashamed or afraid of. I have been advised to suppress Atalanta, to cancel Chastelard, and so on till not a line of my work would have been left. Two days ago Ruskin called on me and stayed for a long evening,[2] during which he heard a great part of my forthcoming volume of poems, selected with a view to secure his advice as to publication and the verdict of the world of readers or critics. It was impossible to have a fairer judge. I have not known him long or intimately; and he is neither a rival nor a reviewer. I can only say that I was sincerely surprised by the enjoyment he seemed to derive from my work, and the frankness with which he accepted it. Any poem which all my friends for whose opinion I care had advised me to omit, should be omitted. But I never have written such an one. Some for example which you have told me were favourites of yours, such as the Hymn to Proserpine[3] of the 'Last Pagan'—I have been advised to omit as likely to hurt the feeling of a religious public. I cannot but see that whatever I do will be assailed and misconstrued by those who can do nothing and who detest their betters. I can only lay to heart the words of Shakespeare—even he never uttered any truer—'Be thou as pure as ice, as chaste as snow [sic], thou shalt not escape calumny.'[4] And I cannot, as Hamlet advises, betake myself 'to a nunnery.'

I believe my aunt Julia is now with my father and mother at Holm Wood, Shiplake, Henley-on-Thames, where I mean to spend this Christmas, not having seen them for some months.

Meantime you will, I am sure, be glad to hear that my luck is look-

2. "I went to see Swinburne yesterday and heard some of the wickedest and splendidest verses ever written by a human creature," Ruskin wrote to Lady Trevelyan on Dec. 8. "He drank three bottles of porter while I was there. I don't know what to do with him or for him, but he mustn't publish these things. He speaks with immense gratitude of you—please tell him he mustn't" (the rest of this letter, from the Trevelyan Papers, Wallington, is missing).

3. (Bonchurch, _1_, 200–206), published in _PB1_.

4. _Hamlet_, III. i. 140–42.

ing up in the beautiful literary world of publishers and readers. I have already the wildest offers made me for anything I will do; and expect soon to have in effect the control of a magazine which I shall be able to mould and use as I please.[5] This has always been a dream of mine; and very likely I shall come to grief, as Byron did on a similar occasion. Have you seen Moxon's series of 'poets'? There are new things (as of course you know) in the Tennyson [6] which are worth looking up—and I don't remember seeing it this year at Wallington. I am *doing* Byron [7] for the series as well as Landor: and I am to meet my partners in the serial work, Tennyson and Browning, at a publisher's feast some time this week.[8]

I am sorry you don't like Chastelard personally, as I meant him for a nice sort of fellow. I send you the proof of a review which the writer sent to me, as evidence that some people like him. I must say I thought I had made him behave in a rather chivalrous way—*notamment* in the third and fifth acts. I think it was George Meredith who once told me that, considering his conduct to the Queen, I had produced in him the most perfect *gentleman* possible.

It is rather a 'trap' to send you these proofs at the end of a long letter—but I didn't mean to entrap you into writing or returning them till you have nothing better to do; and then you know what pleasure you will have given me.[9]

Yours most sincerely,
A. C. Swinburne

5. See below, Letter 95.

6. See above, Letter 73.

7. The preface (Bonchurch, *15*, 120–39) to the *Selection* (1866) from Byron, in Moxon's *Miniature Poets,* was reprinted in *ES.*

8. See below, Letter 94.

9. William Bell Scott wrote to Lady Trevelyan Dec. 10 (Trevelyan Papers, Wallington; I extract only the portion concerning Swinburne): "What you say of A.S. is only to a certain extent gratifying. You know he has been warned in all sorts of ways by Gabriel and myself and has scouted the warnings, and now his collapse into deprecation and denial is only, I fear, through cowardice. He is a craven when it comes to the point [?]. Your threatening him with a demi monde was an admirable hit. You will have done him great good by your writing, but it will not be in Rossetti's power or mine, I fear, to suppliment [*sic*] your work. He has for weeks been talking against Rossetti in a very unhappy way after all that has passed, just because R. will not always stand him now and I fear he has parted company with me. I wanted him to give me a sitting for the poet in the little orchard picture, and wrote him to come on Thursday or Friday—on Thursday he would receive your letter, would he not?—and he has neither come nor written. However

94. TO LORD HOUGHTON

MS: The Marchioness of Crewe. Published: Bonchurch, *18*, 34*.

22a Dorset Street,
Friday evening [? December 15, 1865] [1]

My dear Lord Houghton

As I do not doubt your kind intention, I will only ask—Why? where? and how? Last time we met I had been spending the soberest of evenings here before starting to pick you up at 11 o'clock, which I understood was the order of the day. You as we returned seemed considerably infuriated with my unpunctuality—which I did not attribute to any influence of Bacchus on yourself. I am not aware of having retorted by any *discourtesy*. As the rest of the evening had been spent, after the few words of civility that passed between Mr. Tennyson and me, in discussing Blake and Flaxman in the next room with Palgrave and Lewes,[2] I am at a loss to guess what has called down such an avalanche of advice. I have probably no vocation and doubtless no ambition for the service of Bacchus: in proof of which if you like I will undertake to repeat the conversation of Wednesday evening throughout with the accuracy of a reporter, as it happens to be fixed in my memory. I don't doubt your ability to do likewise, any more than the friendliness of your feeling towards me, of which I have proofs in plenty. Otherwise I should not care to defend myself against an admonition which if not 'discourteous' is certainly not 'common.'

I remain

Yours affectionately,
A. C. Swinburne

I may be wrong in my conclusion. In the meantime the honours he is receiving from America and at home, are not reducing his egotism."

Another letter from Scott to Lady Trevelyan (dated merely "Wednesday morning" and without watermark but apparently written during this period) contains this passage: "Did you see A.S. and give him good advice? He was to come out here on Sunday evening by appointment with Simeon Solomon,—I hope he has not jumped to the belief that I was your informant—though the unhappy fact is so patent that any one might have told you."

1. This letter certainly follows Letter 93, above, written on Sunday, and, since Tennyson left London on the 18th, Wednesday the 13th is the only possible date for the *soirée*.

2. For one reflection of this conversation see below, Letter 96. The "party" was presumably given by the firm of Moxon and Co., publisher of both Swinburne and Tennyson. Palgrave had edited Wordsworth in Moxon's *Miniature Poets*.

94A. TO JAMES ABBOTT McNEILL WHISTLER

MS: Glasgow University.

Holm Wood, Shiplake, Henley on Thames,
January 3, 1866

Cher père

Je t'envoie un journal Américain [1] qu'on vient de me remettre, dans
lequel il est question non seulement de ton indigne fils mais de son
père vénéré. J'espère que du moins cela te fera rire. On doute de ton
pays—mais on se prosterne à tes genoux: c'est assez réjouissant. Il est
évident qu'on n'a reçu que des louanges à ton égard.

Mille amitiés à ton frère et à tous les nôtres.

Ton fils,
A. C. Swinburne

On vient de publier sur moi des feuilletons écrasants à Boston. À
New York on dit que je suis fou, parceque je mets V. Hugo au-dessus
des poètes Anglais. Tu vois qu'on m'égorge sur le cadavre du Maître
—comme un jeune page de mélodrame.

95. TO WILLIAM MICHAEL ROSSETTI

MS: British Museum. Extract in *The Ashley Library, A Catalogue* (11 vols.
1922–36), *9* (1927), 133.

Holm Wood, Shiplake, Henley on Thames,
January 4, 1866

Dear Rossetti

I have so much to say that I tremble to think how much of my paper
and your time will be taken up. However, 'let us be methodical, or
we are nothing.' [1] I cannot of course tell what Payne, the real man-
aging publisher, a loose-tongued and well-meaning sort of man, may
have said or hinted; and therefore I can only say what I have now to
say to you privately and in confidence. Some time since he made to me
in person almost any offers if I would engage myself in any way to
support or direct his forthcoming venture, in the not improbable event
of his original editor proving inadequate. I at once told him that I
could undertake nothing in the way of business or of regular super-
vision; that it would interfere with my work, and (still worse) with
my leisure; and that it would be unfair to him if I should even in

1. Unidentified. C. K. Hyder (*Swinburne's Literary Career and Fame*, Durham,
N.C., 1933, pp. 29–30) lists several New York and Boston reviews of this period.

1. Unidentified.

appearance accept an office of which I neither could nor would discharge the duties. But, I added, I was willing to assist thus far. I would contribute, and would do what I could to induce others to contribute whose names would do honour to the magazine; and my conditions, putting apart the money question, would be these; that I should have power to insert and to reject *any* article I chose, whether approved or not by the working editor. Payne then proposed that I, on my own terms, should do as much or as little as I pleased, he undertaking to provide a man of position and intelligence to do the daily work that Thackeray did himself for the Cornhill who would always admit and listen to me when I chose or cared to interfere. I thought this all well enough and only stipulated that my name should not appear except as a contributor; that I should be wholly unfettered, and yet free to take the reins for a minute or two in my own hands when I pleased; and that it should be understood that I had nothing to do with the management, would not look over MSS., and would not be responsible for the good or bad luck of the venture. These moderate and reasonable terms were gratefully jumped at; and as a first step in business I got Gabriel to promise he would send something of his surviving poetry, much to Payne's exultation. As soon as I saw my way I meant to apply for support to you and to Topsy. Meantime all is as yet in the clouds. This of which I have spoken passed under seal of secrecy, and I for my part can truthfully say that I have never till now given a hint of it to anyone. These are the simple facts; but though I shall never appear as an 'able editor' [2] and can always deny the opprobrious charge with a clear conscience, still it seems not unlikely that I shall when I please have something to do with the matter; and anyhow I am certain that the article of which you write would be at once and thankfully accepted.[3] (I believe the first number will appear in March at earliest. I have promised it some instalment of my notes on Florentine drawings.) [4] Both the subject of the story and the writer's position would make it a windfall for a rising magazine. I will, according as you please, either speak to Payne on the subject when we meet, or write to him at once. I need not ask you to contradict all rumours of my future editorship, which are untrue as it is and might easily become unpleasant to all parties.

Now I am going to ask your help and advice in a matter of business

2. See above, Letter 78.

3. See below, Letter 96.

4. (Bonchurch, *15*, 155–95), published in the *Fortnightly Review* (July 1868), reprinted in *ES*.

regarding only my own interest. I have made for this Miniature series of Moxon's a book of selections from Byron, with a critical essay prefixed which has cost me some time and trouble. It will appear on the first of next month; and today Payne writes to ask what he is to pay into my banker's hands on this account. What do you think I ought to say? An illustrious Scotch person by the name of Buchanan [5] has done, it seems, a like office for Keats, and received £10 in return. This sum the publisher is willing to lose, and to cancel the poor devil's work, if I will do Keats instead on those terms: and won't I? and wouldn't I gratis? This forthcoming Scotch edition of Keats, who hated the Scotch as much as I do (Scotus [6] I consider Northumbrian by adoption and Scotch no longer) has long been a thorn in my side: and apart from the delight of trampling on a Scotch Poetaster, I shall greatly enjoy bringing out a perfect edition of Keats with all his good verses and none of his bad. But all this does not help me to see what under the circumstances I ought in justice to demand for the Byron, a work less delightful and more laborious. The same question perplexes me with regard to the Blake MS. As to coercion, I should like to see my publisher wince or hesitate at any offered book of mine! snakes would wake in that case, and walk their chalks. Some. But what am I to ask for it? (i.e. for the first 1000 copies.) And had I better, do you think, insist on a certain sum to be prepaid, for each edition of each book (as I did with Chastelard; but I may not always be able to get my price on these terms, it being a speculation merely on the publisher's part); or accept what Payne proposes, two-thirds or thereabouts of the profit on every copy sold, he undertaking to publish any book of mine on these terms, and to act as my banker so far as to supply me with £50 or £100 when I please, or as he says any sum in reason as far as his means go, as long as I publish with him alone and in some degree further his undertaking in the magazine way? This latter plan I find hitherto convenient enough, and he is still some £50 in my debt. But I have so much ready, and so many projects in hand—my Poems [7] first of all, which must be got out in the spring—that these questions become serious and pressing; and I am so ignorant and inexperienced as to be thankful for hints or help.

5. Robert W. Buchanan (1841–1901), a poet and novelist remembered now only for the mud-slinging article "The Fleshly School of Poetry" in 1871 (see below, Letter 402), which he recanted long before his (and shortly after Gabriel Rossetti's) death.

6. William Bell Scott.

7. *PB1* appeared in July.

I shall be very much obliged if you will write me a word on this subject when you have leisure.

I enclose for your behoof and Gabriel's a sweet morsel of criticism. Please let him see it, and then let Moxon's people have it back as I want them to use the *last* sentence by way of advertisement. I sent Gabriel my selections from Byron to revise if he had time and would take the trouble. If he can't and you can, would you glance over them and tell me your opinion as to admitting more or less or other passages than I have marked? It ought to be at Moxon's in a day or two, or we shall be hurried and harassed towards the end of the month.

One word more about the Blake MS. As you say and as I know there are passages to be changed or cancelled which refer to Gilchrist's book. Would you mark them for me with a pencil that I may be sure of your judgment, and act accordingly?[8] it would save me more trouble than it would give you. Would not any republication of the select poems interfere, really or seemingly, with Macmillan's edition? I know it might be done legally, but I would rather leave them alone, especially as nothing could improve upon Gabriel's selection, and the essay of itself is long and complete enough. When it comes forth, I should like with your leave to inscribe it to you. This, as Gabriel knows, I have always hoped to do, but while it was in the twilight I didn't care to say anything about it. I am very sincerely glad you think so well of the book; as to my interpretations, I confess I have quite forgotten what they were, though I know the poems by heart.

Will you ask Gabriel from me if he has seen the following passage in one of the Fenian trials? 'Witness added that the prisoner assured him there were more Bs[9] than one in the next street. Just outside Dublin he was led to expect he should meet by night with no less than 8000 Bs.' Literally, that is in a paper of this morning or yesterday evening. On reading it, I exclaimed with Justine, 'Oh! monsieur— quelle dépravation!' Imagine a revolution carried through by such agents, and Irishmen too!

I have numberless more serious things to say and to ask, but must stop and get into bed.

Ever yours,
A. C. Swinburne

8. For Rossetti's reply finessing this request see T. J. Wise, *A Bibliography of the Writings in Prose and Verse of Algernon Charles Swinburne* (2 vols. 1919–20), 2, 393. (The holograph in the British Museum is dated merely Jan. 14, and Wise's "1865," which ought to have been bracketed, is incorrect.)

9. That is (in the newspaper), Brothers—of the Fenian Brotherhood.

P.S. Have you read Dasent's [10] new Icelandic book, Gisli the Outlaw? It seems to me more beautiful and delightful than I can say. The sense of fate pressing upon a hero and felt far off by him alone is as grand as in the purest Greek Poetry; and the life in all parts of the book is wonderful.

96. TO J. B. PAYNE

MS: Donald F. Hyde.

Holm Wood, January 5 [1866]

My dear Sir

Thanks for the reviews, which you shall receive again in a day or two: as also, if you please, another batch as large which has been sent me from America. I finished my preface to Byron yesterday, and send it by this post. It has cost me more time and more trouble than I meant to spare it; but I am punctilious about my work in prose, and like to have it well finished when the subject is serious. It is a thing I am glad to have done; I hope it will not look formidably long, and suppose it will make somewhat less than twenty pages of close print. You will see that it could not be further contracted, the matter in hand being so wide and diversified. As to terms, I will write about them when you have seen the selections. It is thought here that I have not made extracts enough to fill one of your volumes. If so, I would add the second act of Cain in full (these two scenes hold the kernel of the poem, and will stand, as a shorter poem in dialogue, by themselves—which no mere extract or fragment will), and Beppo, which is charming and takes little room. Then I think the volume will be full. I dare say when you get this the book will be in your hands, as I have not heard from Rossetti.

With regard to the Keats I shall enjoy doing it of all things as you propose; but in throwing overboard your Scotch Jonah,[1] you must make him understand that I have nothing to do with his part of the business. Not being by profession a man of letters, the matter is nothing to me except as a labour of love.[2] I should not edit what I did not like for any money; and of course the same amount of original work would be worth to me, if anything, somewhat more than £10. He is

10. G. W. Dasent (1817–96), scholar, student, and translator of Norse literature; knighted in 1876.

1. Buchanan (see above, Letter 95).

2. I Thessalonians 1:3.

not therefore to imagine himself aggrieved by me, because you, un-asked and without suggestion, propose to me of your own accord to edit the selections from Keats. With any previous arrangements now cancelled I naturally have no concern. I regard your proposal as a compliment and hope to shew as much. Let me know when you pro-pose to have the book out. As I know Keats by heart I could write down my proposed selections in order without reference to his works. There is only the essay to write, which will be an easier and more wholly pleasant labour than that on Byron has been.

Let me know when anything is settled further about the magazine, as a friend [3] has told me privately of something which would be I conjecture rather a godsend to it—a photograph of Roman life by a gentleman who was lately for four years the American Consul there and is now *do.* in Crete.[4] It appears he is willing to publish it now in some English periodical. I am not sure whether I could secure it for yours, but believe it might be done. It is I am told very ably written, full of interest and of facts new to us, and *not* controversial, which would of course have spoilt all: it seems already to have made a pri-vate sensation. This sort of thing can rarely be had, and is of universal interest if good.

I have had a note from a critic of long experience and high standing to whom I had caused my Essay on Blake to be sent in MS. for his opinion and revision. I have resolved to publish it soon, as he writes this: 'It is a splendid piece of the high critical order of work, and an admirable model of such prose as only the fewest are capable of even attempting. I should consider its publication as the greatest serv-ice at present possible to Blake. Among the select few, I think the essay, if published, would produce an effect only inferior to that of your poems. I take it the only possible form of publication would be that of a volume by itself.' The editor of the Fortnightly Review [5] wanted a detachment of it when I told him the whole was beyond the limits of a periodical; but I never sent or shewed it. When it is again in my hands and I have made one or two small cancels or alterations, we can discuss the matter and I can send you the MS.

Many thanks for Dasent's book, which is most beautiful and has

3. W. M. Rossetti (see above, Letter 95).

4. William James Stillman (1828–1901), consul in Rome 1862–65, in Crete 1865–68, and later known as a journalist. His wife, Marie Spartali, was one of Gabriel Rossetti's latter-day models. The "photograph" is perhaps the title-piece in Still-man's *The Old Rome and the New and Other Stories* (1898).

5. G. H. Lewes (see above, Letter 94).

given me the greatest pleasure in reading that I have had for long, and believe me my dear Sir

Very truly yours,
A. C. Swinburne

97. TO GEORGE POWELL

MS: National Library of Wales.

22a Dorset Street, W.,
Wednesday [? January 10, 1866]

My dear Sir

I regret that we should always have missed each other; but for many months I have been in town only for a few days at a time, and am now here for this week only. If it would be convenient for you to call here at any time on Friday, the only day on which I hope to have time to myself, I shall be much pleased to meet you at last. I ought of course to call on you earlier, but I hope the fact of having three books [1] on hand will excuse me and explain how I come when in town to be pre-engaged in a business way as well as in a social. I shall be curious to study your new book,[2] apart from the personal interest which your kindness has given me in it: especially as I have just read with the greatest admiration and pleasure Dr. Dasent's 'Gisli,' which has once more excited my interest in Icelandic legend.

Believe me

Yours very sincerely,
A. C. Swinburne

If you can and will come on Friday afternoon or evening, perhaps you will send me word of the hour by return of post, that I may make sure of meeting you.

1. *A Selection from the Works of Lord Byron, William Blake,* and *A Year's Letters* (*Love's Cross-Currents*).

2. *Legends of Iceland* (Second Series) (see above, Letter 88).

98. TO SIR EDWARD LYTTON-BULWER [1]

Text: *The Life of Edward Bulwer, First Lord Lytton, By His Grandson, The Earl of Lytton* (2 vols. 1913), 2, 432.

Holmwood, Shiplake, Henley-on-Thames,
January 17, 1866

Sir

I should have written before to thank you for a double kindness, had your book and letter been sooner sent on to my present address. As it is, you will no doubt understand how difficult I feel it to express my thanks for your gift, and for the letter, to me even more valuable, which accompanied it. To receive from your hands a book [2] which I had only waited to read till I should have time to enjoy it at ease as a pleasure long expected, and deferred for a little (on the principle of children and philosophers) was, I should have thought till now, gratification enough for once; but you contrived at the same time to confer a greater pleasure—the knowledge that my first work, written since mere boyhood,[3] had obtained your approval. Of the enjoyment and admiration with which I have read your book I need not say anything. Pleasure such as this you have given to too many thousands to care to receive the acknowledgment of one. Such thanks as these I have owed you, in common with all others of my age, since I first read your works as a child; the other obligation is my own, and prized accordingly as a private debt, impossible to pay, and from which I would not be relieved.

Believe me,

Yours very sincerely,
A. C. Swinburne

1. The popular novelist (1803–73) became on July 14, 1866, first Baron Lytton.

2. *The Lost Tales of Miletus* (1866).

3. Taken literally, this could only mean *Chastelard*, which, though published after, was written before *Atalanta*. But on Feb. 13 Lord Lytton wrote to his son: "Have you read Swinburne's Poems? I have only read the *Atalanta*, which I think promising and vigorous" (*The Life of Edward Bulwer*, 2, 433).

99. VICTOR HUGO TO SWINBURNE

MS: British Museum. Published: *Revue bleue*, 74 (Mar. 7, 1936), 152.

Hauteville house, 23 janvier 1866

Monsieur

Mon fils, le traducteur de Shakespeare est en ce moment près de moi. Il m'a fait une nouvelle lecture de votre pathétique drame de *Chastelard*. J'ai pu, grâce à lui, en saisir mieux toutes les beautés. Il était charmé de vous traduire après avoir traduit Shakespeare, et il sentait en vous une continuation de cette sublime poésie. Votre œuvre est au plus haut point émouvante et humaine. Elle parle à la fois au cœur et à l'âme, au cœur par la passion, à l'âme par l'idéal. Un grand succès vous est dû. Vous vous rattachez glorieusement aux grandes traditions de l'art universel, et votre talent honore la littérature contemporaine.

Vous me dédiez votre belle œuvre en termes qui me touchent profondément. Recevez mon remerciement ému et cordial.

Victor Hugo

100. TO ?

MS: Historical Society of Pennsylvania.

22a Dorset Street, W., February 1 [?1866] [1]

Dear [*word illegible*]

I was unlucky in missing you last night but it was no fault of mine. I waited till 9½ and then, hardly thinking you would come, was obliged to be off, chiefly on personal business of a 'publishing' kind and partly to see the last of Whistler as he could not come to meet us, and really was off to California. Jamieson has been here this morning, and I have explained to him and he to me how we missed each other. Believe me

Yours sincerely,
(and in haste),
A. C. Swinburne

1. It has not been possible to decipher (satisfactorily) either the date or the name of the addressee. In the photostat the year-date seems to be "92," a manifest absurdity. The Director of the Historical Society of Pennsylvania writes that in the original the date looks more like "72," which is only less acceptable than "92." The letter apparently belongs to 1866, referring to Whistler's departure for *Valparaiso*, whence he returned in Oct. The name of the addressee, a word that looks like "Penern" or "Severn," is equally baffling. Nor have I been able to identify "Jamieson" in the third sentence.

101. TO JOSEPH KNIGHT [1]

MS: Yale.

22a Dorset Street, W., February 4 [1866]

My dear Mr. Knight

I was going to call on you this afternoon, but thought at the last moment that I might find myself an intruder upon some busy time. So I write instead to ask if you will look me up as soon as you can, and tell me when. Tomorrow (Monday) I am engaged from 3 P.M. onwards. On Tuesday I have nothing to do, and if you would see me in the evening it would be not only a pleasure but a great service to me, as I am in a business dilemma from which no other friend could be so likely to release me by his advice. I have detected in my publisher a double breach of faith [2] so inexcusable that, seeing to what a disadvantage my visible inexperience has already exposed me, I wish now not to take a step further without consulting some one who can give me good counsel. I need not say how much it would oblige me.

Believe me,

Ever yours sincerely,
A. C. Swinburne

102. TO F. J. FURNIVALL [1]

MS: Yale.

22a Dorset Street, W., February 8 [1866]

Dear Sir

The book you write about [2] is now in the hands of our friend Mr.

1. Joseph Knight (1829–1907), drama critic for the *Literary Gazette,* the *Athenaeum,* the *Sunday Times,* and the *Daily Graphic.* From 1883 till his death he edited *Notes and Queries,* and he contributed more than five hundred biographies to the *DNB.* Swinburne's real fondness for Knight later is proved by the offer in 1867 (recorded in *Rossetti Papers,* p. 228) to lend him £200 at a time when he was himself impecunious. See also Letter 111, below.

2. See below, Letter 104.

1. Frederick James Furnivall (1825–1910), the indefatigable scholar who founded the Early English Text, Chaucer, Ballad, New Shakspere, Shelley, Browning, and Wyclif societies. Moreover, he was a pioneer in the Working Men's College, a grandparent of the *Oxford English Dictionary,* and, in addition, one of the most quarrelsome men in the history of letters, though in his feud with Swinburne in the seventies he found his equal.

2. Lawrens Andrewe, *The noble lyfe & natures of man, of bestes serpentys fowles & fisshes yt be most knowen,* from which extracts were printed by Furnivall in

E. B. Jones, to whom I have lent it for a few days. As far as I am concerned I need not say it is much at your service; but as the copy is imperfect at the end, and as it does not appear to be unique, I suppose a better copy would better serve the purpose of a reprint. That it is extremely rare I gather from the fact that my uncle Lord Ashburnham, who has been a book-collector for some forty years at least, had never seen or heard of it, and he had set himself to collect precisely the sort of books to which this belongs. It was printed, he tells me, in Antwerp (this he looked up in Ames and shewed me, but I have not the reference); the type is foreign, and many of the woodcuts plagiarized from Gesner's Historia Naturalis.[3] Those which are original are rude and comic in the extreme. It came into my father's hands as part of a library left to him, containing the books of Horace Walpole and his friend Mr. Bull of Ongar, a great collector in his day; and it has been clipped by the eighteenth-century binder.

If it is reprinted (and it certainly seems to me worth while to reprint) the woodcuts should be reproduced, they are three quarters of the fun.

Many thanks for the book you send me. I have not yet read it but it seems very interesting.

I may add that the grammar of the Nat. Hist. book is something amazing—the words 'he,' 'she,' and 'it' are interchanged in the same sentence with reference to the same beast, and there are two or three *words* used I never saw elsewhere, but this may be merely my ignorance.

Yours sincerely,
A. C. Swinburne

F. J. Furnivall, Esq.

The Babees Book for the Early English Text Society in 1868. As many subsequent allusions show, Swinburne was inordinately, almost childishly, proud of this book, exhibiting it, decades later, to one visitor after another. See, for example, the account of Louise Chandler Moulton's second visit in the *Pall Mall Budget* (Sep. 27, 1888), p. 11 (based on an article in the Boston *Sunday Herald*), and of Maarten Maartens' visit in 1895 (see below, Letter 1660).

3. Conrad Gesner, *Historia animalium* (Zurich, 1551).

103. TO CHARLES AUGUSTUS HOWELL

MS: British Museum.

22a Dorset Street, W., February 8, 1866

Pig!

Why do you make and break promises? Come and see me if you can. That you are alive I know from others who have met you abroad. And I have expected you (being but young and foolish) ever since we last met in Cheyne Walk. And in three or four days must be out of TOWN [1] (which I write *big* that it may be impressive). Write! and come! and if you won't, be ------ [2] (blank).

Yours affectionately (if you come),
A. C. Swinburne

And if you don't come BE D----D.
Oh! Monsieur [3]

104. TO J. B. PAYNE

MS: John S. Mayfield.

22a Dorset Street,
Saturday, February 17 [1866]

Dear Sir

In reply to your note, as it treats of two matters, I will begin by answering the passage which most concerns me personally, and that as briefly and clearly as possible.

1) Had I or another sent you the anonymous MS [1] of which you speak, for acceptance or rejection, I should have been anything but surprised if you had rejected it. On such terms I have no doubt you would last year have rejected 'Atalanta'; you did not, on the understanding that all costs would be defrayed by me. I do not in the least complain of anything you say with regard to the anonymous MS: it is at least as flattering as the book in my opinion deserves; but I have reason to complain of your saying it now that the proper time has gone by. Some months since you asked to be allowed to consider yourself the natural publisher of my future works, on terms which appeared

1. But he was in town on Feb. 16, and Boyce, dining and playing billiards at the Arts Club, reported: "Swinburne in a very excited state, using fearful language."

2. Ink is splotched here to express vehemence.

3. These two words stand alone on the facing page.

1. *Love's Cross-Currents* (see below, Letter 106).

not unreasonable. I then told you that I never meant to publish anonymous poetry; that I very probably might desire to send you, without my name and without in any way committing myself to their authorship, MSS which I should wish you to print as though they were avowedly or probably mine. To this you assented with some show of eagerness; which you now appear to have forgotten. You then received from me two MSS, at various times, which you undertook at once to publish on the terms proposed by yourself: the last sent was my essay on Blake. The first, after hearing its nature, you accepted as an anonymous work, of doubtful authorship, backed up in private by my name, and sent unread to the printer's, promising to return it in type. You now decline to fulfil that promise. You are at liberty to change your mind and refuse to fulfil an unwritten engagement. But I find with astonishment that you have done another thing which you were not at liberty to do. I hear from Mr. Winwood Reade that you have actually shewn him the anonymous MS as a work of mine, and read him extracts from it as such. He knows now, that even had you known it to be mine you could only have known it by pledging your honour to secrecy. Either then you told him as a fact what you only guessed to be true, or you were guilty of such a breach of faith as I will not dwell upon. I am willing to allow for natural forgetfulness, however dangerous in a business matter; but for this I can scarcely allow.

If you still desire to publish my Poems, ⟨my Essay on Blake,⟩ my Notes on Art or any other book signed by my name, you will let me know your terms in writing, and I will consider them fairly. But I will not run blindly into a verbal agreement, made without witnesses, and depending upon memory in which no confidence is to be placed.

As regards myself, I will add here that I see in none of the papers any of the promised advertisements of Chastelard. When the materials are ample, such neglect seems to me a disadvantage; but it is for you to decide, having bought the edition; and for myself I care nothing about puffs.

I am sorry this part of the letter has been of necessity so long. I will now only ask you to return at once the MS confided to you which you decline to publish.

2) As to Byron, I am surprised to see the Invocation omitted from Manfred. It can hardly have slipped your memory that I told you when we talked it over that this, as his finest lyric, must at all costs be retained. ⟨I also think⟩ The 'Seven Spirits' in the first act I left you free to insert or reject. In this matter my credit as editor is involved; yours

only as publisher is involved in the external beauty or ugliness of the book; but you will let me protest against the mean-looking omission of separate headings to the separate extracts. In Don Juan the effect is ridiculous. Canto 1 is huddled pitifully upon Canto 11 as if only a few lines intervened. I observe the reverse in your selections from Tennyson, where you carefully put 'From *the Princess*' before one extract, 'From the same' before the next, giving each a separate page. The effect of the contrary is most pitiful, and most confusing to the eye—meaner even than the printing of a cheap novel.

I remain

Yours truly,

A. C. Swinburne

P.S. The selection from Keats I will edit as proposed, on terms which certainly are not to my advantage, as if my work is worth a shilling it is worth over ten pounds; but I wish that the book should be decently well done, and this I believe myself competent to do.

P.P.S. With regard to my Essay on Blake, I will send the missing transcript to the printers as soon as I can lay hand on it; but if, as I fear, the copy made by me is lost or hopelessly mislaid, some one must be employed to copy out the necessary extracts in the print-room of the British Museum. I must ask you either let me have a written agreement that I am to receive two-thirds of the profits if any, you taking the risks; or else, which I should of course prefer, to let me know what sum you are prepared to pay down.

I have just noticed the omission of the 'Giaour' extract. It should come ‹I think› after 'Childe Harold.' This you promised to see to. Any consequent delay is no fault of mine.

105. TO CHARLES AUGUSTUS HOWELL

MS: British Museum.

22a Dorset Street, W., February 21 [1866]

My dear Howell

Come to me if you can on Friday or Saturday, which you please. I heard from Gabriel that you were awfully busy, so though I wanted very much to see you I quite understood that you could not come. Pray don't imagine I was really hurt by your not writing or calling. On n'a pas trop d'amis dans ce f - - - - monde, and we can't *afford* to misunderstand each other; I can't at least.

Houghton is in town and wants very much to meet you. I am sure you would like him. Let us go some day if possible.

Ever yours affectionately,

A. C. Swinburne

I have written a lot more of *your* book which I want you to see.

106. TO WILLIAM MICHAEL ROSSETTI

MS: British Museum. Extract in *The Ashley Library, A Catalogue, 9* (1927), 134; two sentences in Lafourcade, *La Jeunesse, 2,* 301.

22a Dorset Street,

Tuesday [March 20, 1866] [1]

Dear Rossetti

I think I threatened you with the infliction of my first attempt at serious prose work,[2] perpetrated in '62. If you have not time or inclination to go through with it, send it back without a thought of 'pro and con,' or (as Houghton shamelessly asserts a French friend once said to him!!) the 'before and behind' of the question. It is a guileless book, the effusion or emission of ignorant innocence; but I find that even in its MS. form it has admirers. So, unless counselled otherwise, I think of bringing it out as it stands on the first occasion: not of course with my name appended. If you really find it worth reading through, and will give me your verdict on the book as a whole, I shall of course be glad. You will see in it the full development of one or two characters hinted at or sketched retrospectively in the unfinished hybrid book [3] of which you have heard so much lately. This book stands or falls by Lady Midhurst; if she gives satisfaction, it must be all right; if not, Chaos is come again.[4] From the Galilean or gallows-worshipping point of view, I am aware she and it and I must be all together condemnable, but we do not appeal to that tribunal. Seriously, if you have time, and if you care, to read this 'étude' or 'novelette' or whatever the term for such a thing may be, I shall be grateful for your verdict, whatever form it may assume.

I have been studying with deep delight your kids' books, and am

1. The letter was marked by William Rossetti "March 21st, 1866"—the date it was received.

2. Serialized in the *Tatler* in 1877 as *A Year's Letters* and published in book form in 1905 as *Love's Cross-Currents* (Bonchurch, *17,* 65–258).

3. *Lesbia Brandon* (so called).

4. *Othello,* III. iii. 92.

more obliged for them than ever. My own humble poems 'vont bon train'; I have sent off today 56 pages of revised proofs, containing some of my best.

Your affectionate,
A. C. Swinburne

Thursday night

I find this note hasn't gone, by some blunder, so send it now, reserving on second thought the MS till I see or hear from you.

107. TO JOHN RUSKIN

Text: Bonchurch, *18,* 11–12*.

22 Dorset Street,
Wednesday [? March 21, 1866] [1]

Dear Ruskin

I am glad you like my little essay,[2] and gladder to hear that you think of coming to look me up. But I do not (honestly) understand the gist of what you say about myself. What's the matter with me that I should cause you sorrow or suggest the idea of a ruin? I don't feel at all ruinous as yet. I do feel awfully old, and well may—for in April I believe I shall be twenty-five,[3] which is 'a horror to think of.' *Mais*———! what have I done or said, to be likened to such terrific things?

You speak of not being able to hope enough for me. Don't you think we had better leave hope and faith to infants, adult or ungrown? You and I and all men will probably do and endure what we are destined for, as well as we can. I for one am quite content to know this, without any ulterior belief or conjecture. I don't want more praise and success than I deserve, more suffering and failure than I can avoid; but I take what comes as well and as quietly as I can; and this seems to me a man's real business and only duty. You compare my work to a

1. Gosse and Wise erred badly in attributing this letter to Feb. 1862. Ruskin wrote to Lady Trevelyan on Feb. 25, 1866 (Trevelyan Papers, Wallington): "I have not seen Algernon again. I was hopeless about him in his present phase, but I mean to have another try soon."

2. The preface to his *Selection from the Works of Lord Byron.* His mother acknowledged *her* copy of the essay on Mar. 21: "I do admire your preface most extremely; I don't think too much can be said of it . . ." (Lafourcade, *La Jeunesse, 1,* 236).

3. Probably a misreading of "29."

temple where the lizards have supplanted the gods; I prefer an indubitable and living lizard to a dead or doubtful god.

I recalcitrate vigorously against your opinion of 'Félise,'[4] which is rather a favourite child of mine. As to the subject, I thought it clear enough, and likely to recall to most people a similar passage of experience. A young fellow is left alone with a woman rather older, whom a year since he violently loved. Meantime he has been in town, she in the country; and in the year's lapse they have had time, he to become tired of her memory, she to fall in love with his. Surely I have expressed this plainly and 'cynically' enough! Last year I loved you, and you were puzzled, and didn't love me—quite. This year (I perceive) you love me, and I feel puzzled, and don't love you—quite. 'Sech is life,' as Mrs. Gamp says;[5] *'Deus vult;* it can't be helped.' As to the flowers and hours, they rhyme naturally, being the sweetest and most transient things that exist—when they *are* sweet. And the poem, it seems to me, is not long enough to explain what it has to say.

Yours affectionately,
A. C. Swinburne

108. TO PAULINE, LADY TREVELYAN

MS: Trevelyan Papers, Wallington. Published: Bonchurch, *18,* 39–40*.

22a Dorset Street, W. [*ca.* March 22, 1866]

My dear Lady Trevelyan

I am very glad you approve of my rough notes on Byron.[1] Of course when I wrote them I hoped you would; and the essay is honest so far as it goes, but was of course curtailed and confined in the dismallest way. I am going to 'do' Keats[2] as soon as my own book is out. I hope Sir Walter will join the Cruikshank committee.[3] I am told by a personal friend of his that the poor old great man is very *hard up,* and could not, if he died tomorrow, leave his wife enough to live upon after so long a life of such hard work. I daresay Scotus will have told you all about this much better than I can.

4. (Bonchurch, *1,* 318–27), in *PB1.*

5. *Martin Chuzzlewit,* chap. 29.

1. See above, Letter 107.

2. See above, Letter 95.

3. George Cruikshank (1792–1878), the caricaturist and illustrator. The "personal friend" is probably Charles Augustus Howell (at this time still Ruskin's seneschal), who, according to William Rossetti (*Some Reminiscences,* 2, 327), was "foremost" in getting up the subscription for Cruikshank.

I was very sorry to hear of your having been again so ill.[4] I hope and trust that you are well now. My mother has been going on in the same way, which is most improper, but is now beginning to pick up strength after a severe illness, and can at least sit up and write to me. That both my maternal relatives should be so ill at once is too much for a filial heart. Pray set a better example in future.

Ruskin and Meredith, among others, both write to me about the Byron in a most satisfactory way: but your note has given me more pleasure than theirs. As to the forthcoming magazine,[2] having declined any share in the business work for myself, I was in hopes it would have fallen into the hand of Wm. Rossetti, who would have done the necessary work better than any one I can think of. As it is, if I contribute, it will be on the old terms, that anything I sign shall go in, anything (in reason) I wish admitted or excluded shall be, and generally that when I please I may have a finger or *ten* fingers in the editorial pie. This is really all I know of the project. I met the working editor (as is to be) yesterday, and he seemed sensible and well disposed.

I hope soon to send you my own *Poems,* and am,

Yours affectionately,

A. C. Swinburne

109. TO WILLIAM MICHAEL ROSSETTI

MS: Rutgers. Extract in *Journal of the Rutgers University Library, 14* (Dec. 1950), 5.

22a Dorset Street,

Monday [March 26, 1866] [1]

My dear Rossetti

I hope you cannot doubt that I am and must be sincerely grateful for an act of such real friendship as yours. You are among the one or two friends I have from whom I cannot say that it *surprises* me. From you I should expect no less friendliness and confidence. This is the first I have heard of the matter.[2] I have certainly objurgated more

4. Sir Walter and Lady Trevelyan, together with Ruskin, left for Switzerland on Apr. 24, partly because of Lady Trevelyan's health. She died in Neuchâtel on May 13.

1. Supplied by William Rossetti.

2. Referring to imbroglios at the Arts Club, from which he was compelled to resign in 1870. See above, Letter 103.

In 1917 John Bailey reported (Sarah Bailey, ed., *John Bailey, 1864–1931, Letters and Diaries,* 1935, p. 175): "At dinner I talked to ——— about Swinburne, whom he knew; he was a little in that Arts Club set. He told me Swinburne's quarrel

than one waiter, and remember bending double one fork in an energetic mood at dinner. I had already thought of withdrawing at or before the end of my present year of subscription. As to freedom of voice or tone—I am stunned daily by more noise at that place than I ever heard (or, you may suggest, made) in my life. If I damaged a valuable article belonging to them, why did they not send in a bill? If again there is any animus against me I should prefer to withdraw. I have remained in order more frequently to meet a few intimates, who relieve if they cannot redeem the moral squalor of the place. I know but few members, and never knowingly cut or 'ignored' any.

I will be guided by your own advice in the matter; and am with many thanks

Ever yours sincerely,
A. C. Swinburne

P.S. I had forgotten my MS. Knight (under the rose) is kindly trying to get it out for me *in disguise*. When I have it to myself, and whenever you like, I shall be very much obliged if you will read and judge it.

Your affectionate,
A.C.S.

110. TO LORD HOUGHTON

MS: The Marchioness of Crewe. Published: Bonchurch, *18*, 40*.

[April 1866]

Dear Lord Houghton

I got a note yesterday about the dinner and will say my say as I can. Of course I shall blow a small trumpet before Hugo. I thought something might be said of the new *mutual* influence of contemporary

---

with the Committee was due to the fact not only that he was too constantly drunk there but that on the final occasion, being drunk and not able to find his hat, he tried others, and as each proved too small for his enormous head he threw it wrathfully on the ground and stamped on it—which naturally brought some complaints to the Committee next day. He complained that Gosse (in his life) had given nothing of Swinburne's humour, much of which indeed was not very printable, though essentially harmless enough—as his invention about Queen Victoria's confessing, in French for some reason, presumably because A. C. S. liked talking French—to the Duchess of Kent her unfortunate lapse from virtue." See above, Letter 27.

French and English literature—e.g. the French studies of Arnold and the English of Baudelaire.[1]

Yours affectionately,
A. C. Swinburne

111. TO JOSEPH KNIGHT

MS: E. B. Hall (who supplied the transcript).

22a Dorset Street, W., April 2 [? 1866]

My dear Knight

I have this instant heard that you seem to think me somehow or other aggrieved or vexed by something done or said—(God, or his brother the Devil knows what) said or done or supposed—on your part. I cannot risk this sort of misconception in the case of a friend; and, though literally rushed with immediate business, write at once to say, as I said on hearing of the matter, that no idea could be false or more unjust to me personally. Last Wednesday (I think that was the day—or Tuesday?) when you were here I was afraid to detain you—and vexed only at the idea that you might have been standing on ceremony with me as *reader* and *host*. You should not have supposed me capable of pique on such infantine grounds with any one—much less with a friend.

I shall be out of town tomorrow for about a week—but hope to see or hear from you next week. Meantime

Believe me yours most truly,
A. C. Swinburne

112. TO GEORGE POWELL

MS: National Library of Wales. Extract in Lafourcade, *La Jeunesse*, *1*, 202 n.

22a Dorset Street, April 19 [1866]

My dear Sir

I have this instant received your new volume,[1] just as I was beginning a note in answer to your letter which reached me the day before.

1. At the Royal Literary Fund Dinner on May 2 Swinburne followed Charles Kingsley in acknowledging a toast to "The Historical and Imaginative Literature of England." Extracts are printed in Gosse's *Life* (Bonchurch, *19*, 137), and by Lafourcade, *La Jeunesse*, *1*, 238.

1. See above, Letter 88.

I cannot thank you enough for the gift of 'Les Travailleurs de la Mer'; [2] but I should have done my best to thank you some time since, had I not stupidly mislaid your address. I hope you are not altogether domiciled in Paris, and that I may hope to meet you in London before this season is over.

I might offer another excuse for the tardiness and inadequacy of my thanks, namely that I am just now overwhelmed by the labour of correcting the proofs of two books [3] which are forthcoming at once. If you have never passed through the ordeal of this purgatory I hope you never may; for I know nothing more wearisome and bewildering.

Before your new volume reached me, I had met with it at the house of a friend whom if we meet this season I should like you to meet—Mr. William Morris, author of 'The Defence of Guenevere.' He is as much interested as you are, though as ignorant as I am, concerning Icelandic matters. He is in my opinion, and in that of older and wiser men, one of the best poets of the time, and a great admirer of your work and Dasent's.

The same day that your letter reached me I saw in the papers a notice of the death of a man whom I deeply admired and believed in—Charles Baudelaire.[4] As you are now in Paris you may have heard more of the matter than has appeared in the English papers. I hope to write a little notice of his death, as I did before of his work; and I want to lay hold of any facts I can. My friend M. Fantin-Latour, the artist,[5] whom you may know by name if not personally, was his friend also; but Fantin had not I think met him for some time back. It is a great loss to all men, and great to me personally, who have had the honour to be coupled with Baudelaire as a fellow labourer, and have exchanged with him messages and courtesies.

With renewed thanks, believe me

Yours most sincerely,
A. C. Swinburne

2. Victor Hugo's new novel.

3. *PB1* and *William Blake,* though the latter was not published till Dec. 1867 (dated 1868).

4. The *Pall Mall Gazette* (for example) reported on Apr. 16: "M. Charles Bandelaire [*sic*], the well-known realist French poet, author of the 'Fleurs du Mal,' has just died at Brussels." Baudelaire actually died, however, in Paris, Aug. 31, 1867.

5. Théodore Fantin-Latour (1836–1904), in whose company Swinburne and Whistler visited Manet's studio in Mar. 1863 (see below, Letter 629). In 1871 Fantin-Latour wanted to include a portrait of Swinburne in "Un Coin de table," a picture honoring Baudelaire, but Whistler was not in Paris and Fantin-Latour feared that Swinburne had become too renowned to be approached directly (see Adolphe Jullien, *Fantin-Latour, sa vie et ses amitiés,* Paris, 1909, p. 81).

113. TO CHARLES AUGUSTUS HOWELL

MS: British Museum.

April 26, 1866

Est-ce qu'on ne vient donc plus voir ses amis et frères en J.C.? Mais monsieur cela mène à tout—absolument à tout. Voilà deux foutus mois que je t'attends—et pas plus de ce bougre-là que sur ma main. Viens donc bientôt ou bien je dirai partout que tu t'abîmes dans des infamies 'que la plume même des furies ne saurait transcrire.'

A C S

114. TO GEORGE POWELL

MS: National Library of Wales.

[? June 1866]

My dear Mr. Powell

I should like of all things to come out to you some day this week, and if I can I will—anyhow I am greatly obliged by the invitation. I am quite well except for being such a dormouse as to sleep all day when I should be at work. I was out yesterday when your page called.

Yours most sincerely,
A. C. Swinburne

115. TO GEORGE POWELL

MS: National Library of Wales.

22a Dorset Street, W.,
Tuesday night [ca. June 26, 1866]

My dear Mr. Powell

So sorry to have been out just today when you called. I wanted so much to see you that I was going to write a note anyhow and explain that I could not come last week and if I had, should have been a detestable guest: having been bilious more or less for days and days. I am all right now, but if I had looked you up after my last illegible note it would have been to very little purpose. Now I must thank you— being again able to hold a pen and command a thought at the same time—for the books you left with me. 'Guy Deverell' [1] I think too hasty—too blurred and 'blottesque'—the daub of a clever painter—a 'brilliant potboiler,' if you know that slang phrase of the studios. But—! I thought I was too old to dream of books, but I have not yet ceased to dream of 'Uncle Silas.' [1] The vigour of effect is wonderful. I only wish the edges were a little smoothed off (not as to the 'criminal' or 'terrific' side of course, but) as regards the construction of incident and character. Even Uncle Silas would be more terrible and admirable if we saw him better. I don't know if I am intelligible when I say that he would be more ghastly if he were less ghostly. As it is, the splendid and shadowy figure suggests, here and there, insanity; which is not terrible in the artistic sense—only pitiable, repellent, perplexing. One other cavil; Mme. de la Rougierre (I hardly like yet to write her name!) is too ugly to be tragic. There is too much repetition of 'wet grin,' rotten teeth, bigness and baldness of head. She is grotesque. Far more terrible to a child, I fancy, would have been a lost funereal woman, as cruel, cynical, fond of hideous and deadly humour, who should have retained a hellish hint of beauty, a livid remnant of passion. At this hag, an excitable child would have felt inclined to laugh as well as tremble; it would have cried no doubt, but grinned—and then rebelled. A little more evolution of character and less repetition of effect would have made the book really great. But certainly the author may claim the praise given by Hugo to Baudelaire [2]—that of having invented 'un frisson nouveau.'

I shall write a review—which I never do in print—if I continue. Hoping soon to see or hear from you

Believe me ever

Yours most sincerely,
A. C. Swinburne

116. TO CHARLES AUGUSTUS HOWELL

MS: British Museum.

[? July 1866]

My dear Charlie

Come and see your affectionate pupil soon or what will become of my lessons? I shall never know them at this rate and shall be in rows with other idle boys. I haven't seen you for ages. Can nothing be done about the seaside? Also, can you let me have your transcript of Blake as far as it goes? We are at a standstill for want of it again.

Your affectionate,
Algernon

1. By Sheridan Le Fanu (1814–73), Irish novelist. *Guy Deverell* was published in 1865, *Uncle Silas* in 1864.

2. In a letter on Oct. 6, 1859.

117. TO GEORGE POWELL

MS: National Library of Wales.

22a Dorset Street, W.,
Sunday morning [? July 8, 1866]

My dear Mr. Powell

The first clear day I have this week—say if possible Wednesday, I will come down to you and shall be thankful both for change and company. I must see my book [1] fairly out, and blunder follows blunder with these unblessed printers, delaying me and all things. If they could be *put in the bill* each time, as their betters have been, it might do some good.

We must have time to talk over various things when we meet. Tell me if Canterbury is not the nearest station to Lee, and I will see about getting down in good time.

Ever yours sincerely,
A. C. Swinburne

118. TO GEORGE POWELL

MS: National Library of Wales.

Arts Club, Hanover Square,
Monday [? July 16, 1866]

My dear Mr. Powell

If you are not too much disgusted with my delays I mean to come down to you tomorrow by the 12.00 train. I send this note by way of herald, that my advent may not be too startling.

Yours very sincerely,
A. C. Swinburne

119. TO J. B. PAYNE

Text: Bonchurch, *18*, 41*.

[Early August 1866]

My dear Sir

I write at once to thank you for your prompt answer to my note. The man's negligence was the more vexatious to me as it made me necessarily appear neglectful of my friends, but I trust it is remedied by this time. I wrote about the advertisements in consequence of

1. *PB1*, published about July 16.

hearing so many people remark that they had seen none or few, which looked as if the book were not yet ready. In a day or two I hope to send you the missing pages of my Blake MS. Meanwhile, would it not save time if the printers were to put in type, and send me in slips, the remainder of the MS. for correction, and insert what is wanting when the book was paged? I am in a hurry to have done with it at last.

Yours very truly,

A. C. Swinburne

P.S. Excuse my scrawl, I cannot get a decent pen. I wish you could recommend me where to deal. I reopen this to add that the two copies sent to my father's at Holmwood did arrive safe: as also one sent to Mr. Powell at Lee.

120. TO GEORGE POWELL

MS: National Library of Wales.

22a Dorset Street, W., August 2 [1866]

My dear Powell

(Voilà le mot lâché—and now I defy you to revert to 'Mr.' unless you mean to shut me up) I received last night directed in your hand a box which proved to contain the most beautiful little cup of substance unknown to me, but 'chatoyant' almost with soft red colours. Thanks for such a graceful gift which is a real pleasure to the eyes, and also for your invitation to Wales, which one of these days I shall be delighted to act upon. The place sounds charming, as well as your plans; and I hope you will be able to set right or to upset all inconvenient relatives. Keep my books as long as you like, and return them when where and how you please; but don't send Alberto Mario's Red Shirt [1] with them, as I know it well; thanks all the same.

That Joshua poem in the Châtiments [2] I take to refer to the constant and for the time fruitless appeals of the weaker party of freedom against the party of force, till the day when the walls of tyranny are to fall at the mere sound of the 'clarions of thought' so often blown in vain and answered by laughter. I am very glad you enjoy that great book so thoroughly. The songs are like no other poet's.

1. Alberto Mario (1825–83), Italian revolutionary and writer. He was a disciple of Mazzini and had spent some time in England. *The Red Shirt. Episodes* was published in London in 1865.

2. In Hugo's *Les Châtiments* (1853) the first poem of Bk. VII ("Sonnez, sonnez toujours, clairons de la pensée").

I had much more to say, but am too busy today with other writing. Believe me therefore at once and with all regard

Yours very sincerely,
A. C. Swinburne

By the by we were much disappointed last week at missing you, but it was my fault, I ought to have made sure, and I suppose you never got my note to Blackheath asking you to dine with me and meet some friends this day week: but I thought it was understood when we parted that any day that week would find you disengaged, and at Blackheath. But for wanting the 'first cause' of our feast, it went off very well, and I think you would have enjoyed the company, which as well as the rest of the entertainment had been selected by me with an eye to that end. Next time you are in London we will hope for better luck.

121. TO JOSEPH KNIGHT

MS: Yale.

22a Dorset Street, W., August 3 [1866]

My dear Knight

I am vexed to hear of your buying a book of mine, which I should have sent you but that I understood from Payne he had already sent you a copy in your official capacity. I need not once more say how much obliged I am for the trouble you have taken to push forward my unmanageable offspring.[1] Is the objection moral or literary? The latter I could understand, as 'letters' look heavy to the eye of an intelligent public; but the poor book seems to me distinctly decent and moral.

I am very glad you enjoy my poems now they are at last off my hands. I have exhausted myself with a quasi-venereal enjoyment of the incomparable article in the Athenaeum today.[2] Do pray, if you can, find out the gifted author and present to him my warmest thanks for such delicious and exquisite amusement as I never ventured to anticipate. 'Absalom—Gito—filth—most disagreeable—very silly—parrot of Mr. *Browning*(!).' I succumb, and acknowledge that God can create greater fools than we can imagine. I forgive God much for the sake of such a joke. It does Him credit—even Him.

Can you come to me either to dinner at 7 or tea 8 or 9 any day this

1. See above, Letter 109.

2. See below, Letter 122.

week after Tuesday? I have not seen you for ages and it would give me great pleasure if you could—and would.

Ever yours,
A. C. Swinburne

122. TO LORD LYTTON

Text: *The Life of Edward Bulwer*, 2, 434–35. Also in Bonchurch, *18*, 41–42*.

22a Dorset Street, Portman Square, W.,
August 6 [1866]

Dear Lord Lytton

Your letter was doubly acceptable to me, coming as it did on the same day with the abusive reviews [1] of my book which appeared on Saturday. While I have the approval of those from whom alone praise can give pleasure, I can dispense with the favour of journalists. I thank you sincerely for the pleasure you have given me, and am very glad if my poems have given any to you. In any case, I with the rest of the world, must remain your debtor for much more—without prospect of payment.

Nothing would give me more pleasure than to accept your kind invitation, should it be convenient to you to receive me for a day or two in the course of the next fortnight. For some ten days or so I am hampered by engagements, difficult to break even for a day.

Believe me, with many thanks for the kindness of your letter,

Yours very truly,
A. C. Swinburne

123. TO LORD LYTTON

Text: *The Life of Edward Bulwer*, 2, 435. Also in Bonchurch, *18*, 42–43*.

22a Dorset Street, W., August 10 [1866]

Dear Lord Lytton

I will come on the 16th if that day suits you. I shall be very glad to see Mr. Forster,[1] for whose works I have always felt a great admira-

1. *PB1* was reviewed on Saturday, Aug. 4, 1866, in the *London Review* pp. 130–31; by Robert Buchanan in the *Athenaeum*, pp. 137–38; and by John Morley in the *Saturday Review*, pp. 145–47. (See C. K. Hyder, *Swinburne's Literary Career and Fame*, pp. 37–45.)

1. John Forster (1812–76), historian and biographer of Goldsmith (1848; revised 1854), Landor (1869), and Dickens (1872–74). He and Swinburne were together at Knebworth for about six days.

tion. I cannot tell you how much pleasure and encouragement your last letter gave me. You will see that it came at a time when I wanted something of the kind, when I tell you that in consequence of the abusive reviews of my book, the publisher (without consulting me, without warning, and without compensation) has actually withdrawn it from circulation.

I have no right to trouble you with my affairs, but I cannot resist the temptation to trespass so far upon your kindness as to ask what course you would recommend me to take in such a case. I am resolved to cancel nothing, and (of course) to transfer my books to any other publisher I can find. I am told by lawyers that I might claim legal redress for a distinct violation of contract on Messrs. Moxon's part, but I do not wish to drag the matter before a law court. This business, you will see, is something worse than a scolding, to which, from my Eton days upwards, I have been sufficiently accustomed.

Yours sincerely,
A. C. Swinburne

124. TO GEORGE POWELL

MS: National Library of Wales. Brief extract in Lafourcade, *La Jeunesse*, *1*, 240.

22a Dorset Street, W., August 10 [1866]

My dear Powell

I send you last week's reviews of my unhappy book, together with yours of the Morning Post.[1] This, as George Meredith said in a note to me, is decidedly 'The Era of the Tame Ox.' The hound of a publisher has actually withdrawn from circulation my volume of poems—refuses to issue any more copies 'through fear of consequences to himself.' Of course I shall take Atalanta etc. out of his villainous hands—but then, to whom (as Catullus says [2]) shall I give them? C'est embêtant. I have this minute written to Lord Lytton to get his advice. I am going to his place next week for a day or two, where I am to meet Forster the essayist who was an old friend of Landor's—a tie between us, to begin with. How do you get on with my dear old friend's book? Read the 'Pericles and Aspasia' thoroughly, and the

1. Powell's and Magnússon's *Legends of Iceland,* Second Series, was reviewed in the *Morning Post* on July 28, 1866, p. 3.

2. In the first line of Poem One.

Pentameron: [3] you will then begin to see how great a man he was. Let me hear from you soon and believe me

Yours most sincerely,

A. C. Swinburne

125. TO LORD LYTTON

Text: *The Life of Edward Bulwer*, 2, 436–37. Also in Bonchurch, *18*, 43–44*.

22a Dorset Street, W., August 13 [1866]

Dear Lord Lytton

I am much obliged by the letter of advice you wrote me, and if Lord Houghton had not gone off to Vichy, I should certainly take counsel with him. As it is, I am compelled to decide without further help. I have no relation with Messrs. Moxon except of a strictly business character, and considering that the head of their firm has broken his agreement by refusing to continue the sale of my poems, without even speaking to me on the matter, I cannot but desire, first of all, to have no further dealings with any one so untrustworthy. The book is mine. I agreed with him to issue an edition of 1000 copies, he undertaking to print, publish, and sell them, and if the edition sold off, I was to have two-thirds of the profits. He does not now deny the contract which he refuses to fulfil; he simply said to a friend who called on him as my representative [1] that, on hearing there was to be an article in *The Times* attacking my book as improper, he could not continue the sale.[2] As to the suppression of separate passages or poems, it could not be done without injuring the whole structure of the book, where every part has been as carefully considered and arranged as I could manage, and under the circumstances, it seems to

3. Landor's *Pericles and Aspasia* (1836) and *The Pentameron and Pentalogia* (1837).

1. Evidently, Gabriel Rossetti, who wrote to his brother on Sep. 27 that together with Frederick Sandys he "devoted one afternoon to what we considered a friendly duty towards Swinburne; though not certainly, as you know, because we think the genius displayed in his work benefits by its association with certain accessory tendencies." William Rossetti identifies this "friendly duty" as "calling on the publishers, and endeavouring to accommodate matters" (*Family Letters with a Memoir*, 2, 192).

2. S. M. Ellis, ed., *The Hardman Papers, A Further Selection, 1865–1868* (1930), p. 192: "It seems that Dallas was the cause of this; he had written a crushing review for *The Times*, in which both Poet and Publisher were held up to the execration of all decent people. The article was in type, when a private hint was given to Moxon, in order that he might, if so inclined, disconnect himself from the bawdry."

me that I have no choice but to break off my connection with the publisher.

I have consulted friends older than myself, and more experienced in the business ways of the world, and really it seems to me I have no alternative. Before the book was published, if my friends had given me strong and unanimous advice to withdraw or to alter any passage, I should certainly have done so—in two instances I did, rather against my own impulse, which is a fair proof that I am not too headstrong or conceited to listen to friendly counsel. But *now* to alter my course or mutilate my published work, seems to me somewhat like deserting one's colours. One may or may not repent having enlisted, but to lay down one's arms except under compulsion, remains intolerable. Even if I did not feel the matter in this way, my withdrawal would not undo what has been done, nor unsay what has been said.

> Yours truly,
> A. C. Swinburne

126. TO ALICE SWINBURNE

Text: Leith, p. 84.

22a Dorset Street, August 13 [1866]

I send you two letters from Lord Lytton about my book, which are worth many reviews. . . . The printed reviews have pitched into me so violently that the head of Moxon's firm refuses to fulfil his agreement to sell any more copies or make me any compensation. So I suppose I shall have to go elsewhere.

I am going to Lord Lytton's on Thursday (the 16th). He has written me this morning a very kind, long letter.

127. TO CHARLES AUGUSTUS HOWELL

MS: British Museum.

[August 14, 1866]

My dear Howell

Pray come tomorrow to breakfast or luncheon as soon as possible. I want to see you and am very sorry you have been so ill. I am seedy enough myself.

I got an anonymous note today threatening to 'cut off my stones' within six weeks if my poems are not withdrawn, and then brand me as a ——. I don't see the connection of ideas—but you shall see the note.

Your affectionate,
A. C. Swinburne

128. TO GEORGE POWELL

MS: National Library of Wales.

[August 15, 1866]

My dear Powell

I am sorry to hear of your accident, but hope you are all right now. Write and tell me how you get on. I am going tomorrow to Lord Lytton's on a short visit but any note directed here will reach me. I send you as a curiosity a letter I received yesterday.[1] Keep or destroy it as you please. Some advise me to apply to the police, others to take no notice—and I shall not take any, it would be useless—I hope you got the reviews.

Ever yours,
A. C. Swinburne

129. TO LORD LYTTON

Text: Bonchurch, *18*, 44–45*.

22a Dorset Street, W., August 17 [1866]

Dear Lord Lytton,

I could catch neither train nor post yesterday, being too unwell all day to arise. As I am quite well to-day, I hope this will reach you before the afternoon train, by which I propose to come down. I am very sorry to be a day late in thanking you personally for your letter and advice.[1] I am,

Yours very truly,
A. C. Swinburne

1. See above, Letter 127, and below, Letter 174.

1. Swinburne was at Knebworth from Aug. 17 to the 25th. On Aug. 20 Lord Lytton wrote to his son: "Staying here also is A. Swinburne, whose poems at this moment are rousing a storm of moral censure. I hope he may be induced not to brave and defy that storm, but to purgate his volume of certain pruriences into which it amazes me any poet could fall. If he does not, he will have an unhappy life and a sinister career. It is impossible not to feel an interest in him. He says he is 26 [*sic*]; he looks 16—a pale, sickly boy, with some nervous complaint like St. Vitus' dance. He has read more than most reading men twice his age, brooded

130. TO CHARLES AUGUSTUS HOWELL

MS: British Museum. Published (without the second postscript): Bonchurch, *18*, 45–46*.

> Knebworth, Stevenage, Herts.,
> [*ca.* August 20, 1866]

My dear Howell

You never turned up on Wednesday night and kept my unhappy old female sitting up for you till three, and on Thursday I was very seedy and awaited you in vain. O monstre! —applaudis-toi, homme infâme. Oh! monsieur—cela mène à tout.

I want you to get for me two Chastelards and a Byron, and send them here *at once* if possible. Excuse my troubling you about my own errands, but I know you won't mind, and I can't write to Moxon's. I've had a note from Hotten [1] which I must answer at once. Lord Lytton advises my reissuing the Poems at once with him and breaking off wholly with Payne, which is satisfactory. He says either Hotten should buy the surplus copies of the edition, in his own interest which would be impaired if Payne sold it as waste paper. Or—I must buy them up under a friend's name *as* waste paper, if so he designs to sell them. Or—Payne must be compelled to destroy them instead. —This is his advice as a man of business. Will you tell Hotten this and let him act on it. Please too find out what H. proposes about my Blake, which is nearly all in type. If he offers to buy it up I shall not allow Payne to publish it or anything more of mine. Please ask also about

---

and theorised over what he has read, and has an artist's critical perceptions. I think he must have read and studied and thought and felt much more than Tennyson; perhaps he has over-informed his tenement of clay. But there is plenty of stuff in him. His volume of poems is infested with sensualities, often disagreeable in themselves, as well as offensive to all pure and manly taste. But the beauty of diction and masterpiece of craft in melodies really at first so dazzled me, that I did not see the naughtiness till pointed out. He certainly ought to become a considerable poet of the artistic order, meaning by that a poet who writes with a preconceived notion of art, and not, as I fancy the highest do, with unconsciousness of the art in them, till the thing itself is written. On the other hand, he may end prematurely both in repute and in life. The first is nearly wrecked now, and the 2nd seems very shaky. He inspires one with sadness; but he is not so sad himself, and his self-esteem is solid as a rock. He reminds me a little of what Lewes was in youth, except that he has no quackery and has genius. I thought it would interest you to dot down these ideas of a man likely to come across your way, and may serve to warn you first against his mistakes, and also against much intimacy with him personally. I suspect he would be a dangerous companion to another poet. And he seems to me as wholly without the moral sense as a mind crammed full with esthetic culture can be" (*The Life of Edward Bulwer, 2,* 437–38).

1. John Camden Hotten (1832–73), the publisher.

the *remainders* and next edition of Chastelard—Atalanta—and the Q. Mother. Lytton thinks H.'s offers very fair, and advises me to arrange in the same way about the other books. So if H. likes to offer for them and arrange with Payne separately, well and good. I will reply as soon as he makes his offer. With Payne I will hold no further communication except through a third party. All this you may shew or read to Hotten if you please. Pardon for the trouble my friendship entails on you and believe me

Your affectionate,
A. C. Swinburne

I hope your cousin [2] is well, please remember me to her. It is very jolly here, people, place and weather. The furniture would at once cause Gabriel to attempt murder of the owner through envy—rich are the cabinets etc.—in every hole and corner.

(Private)

(PPS) If you *have* heard of any boy being *swished* lately in our schools, let me hear of the distressing circumstances. Ecris-moi quelque chose de piquant, by way of *salt* to all this business.

131. TO J. C. HOTTEN

MS: British Museum.

Knebworth, Stevenage, Herts.,
[ca. August 20, 1866]

Sir

Before leaving London I asked my friend Mr. Howell to let you know that I accepted the terms offered by you for my books.

Yours truly,
A. C. Swinburne

132. TO J. C. HOTTEN

Text: Facsimile and letterpress in S. C. Chew, *Swinburne* (Boston, 1929), p. 74, and facing pp. 74–75.

Knebworth, Stevenage, Herts.,
[ca. August 20, 1866]

Sir

Before leaving London I asked my friend Mr. Howell to let you know that I accepted your offer of £200 for 1000 copies of my Poems, made through Mr. Knight.

2. Kate Howell, whom he married in Sep. 1867.

My agreement with Moxon is cancelled by his own act. Having undertaken to sell the edition in hand, he now of his own act has withdrawn it and intends to sell the copies as waste paper. This in your interest as in mine must not be allowed. They must either be bought directly by you, or as waste paper by me acting through a third party. This is the advice of my friend Lord Lytton with whom I have talked over this whole affair. It should be done at once that there may be no delay in the reappearance of the book. Moxon has no further claim than on these copies, and of the profit on these his nonfulfilment of contract has robbed me. It is the same with the copies of Atalanta and The Queen Mother he has on hand, and with the proofs of my forthcoming prose work. These I am free to call in and resell, having received nothing for them and desiring no further dealings with Moxon. He has paid for 1000 copies only of Chastelard. I am willing to treat with you separately for these, and should of course be glad to see all my books issued by the same publisher. You will let me know your offers for these (at the rate of 1000 copies of each, not deducting whatever you may [pay] to Moxon for his copies) and I will at once let you hear from me in answer, as soon as I have consulted the eminent men of letters, by whose advice I have hitherto been guided.

Yours truly,
A. C. Swinburne

133. TO GEORGE POWELL

MS: National Library of Wales. Two sentences in Lafourcade, *La Jeunesse,* *1,* 240 n.

August 25 [1866]

My dear Powell

So sorry to hear you are still suffering from your accident, I hope the shoulder will be all right by the time you get this. I have asked my housekeeper about the missing papers, and she is certain that she posted them—as I am that I gave her them to post. I fear therefore they must be lost for good and all.

I have just come up from Lord Lytton's after a very pleasant week's visit. His son[1] was not there, to my regret: I believe he is now in Spain.

1. Edward Robert Bulwer Lytton (1831–91), 1st Earl of Lytton, Viceroy of India (1876–80). His verse, now long since decently buried, was for a while published under the pseudonym "Owen Meredith."

My book will be reissued in a few days—I must stay to see it out and to settle about other things of mine which I want to bring out this year. If you can receive me on (say) the third or fourth of September, I should like of all things to run down and look you up for a few days. I want a little taste of the sea more than I can say.

Write me word if this is convenient or not, and believe me

Ever yours most sincerely,
A. C. Swinburne

134. TO ALICE SWINBURNE

Text: Leith, pp. 84–85.

22a Dorset Street, August 28 [1866]

. . . I left Underworth [1] on Thursday after a very pleasant week. Lord Lytton was most kind and friendly, and we had long talks over all sorts of things and books and places. One day I got a letter from a clergyman [2] expressing admiration of my last book and indignation at the attacks made on it, and sending me a volume of his sermons in return; rather an odd tribute, but satisfactory as showing I have not really scandalized or 'horripilé' all the respectable world. We drove up to London the whole way from Knebworth (30 miles) in Ld. Lytton's private carriage, taking luncheon; it was a nice change from railways, and very queer entering London gradually in that way. As we drove in he told me a most exciting ghost story, whereat he is great. Another day we went to Verulam and St. Albans and over the ex-cathedral, which is superb.

1. Leith's misreading of "Knebworth."

2. Identified by William Rossetti as "Mr Purchase, the Brighton clergyman now [Nov. 1869] making so much noise in the way of ritualism" (*Rossetti Papers,* p. 335). Sotheby's *Catalogue of the Library of Algernon Charles Swinburne, Esq.,* June 1916, includes two works inscribed by John Purchas (1823–72) to Swinburne: *Death of Ezekiel's Wife,* inscribed "Algernon Charles Swinburne, Esq. from ye Author J. P. Augst. 17, 1866"; and "Sermon at Brighton" (1866), inscribed "A. C. Swinburne, Esqre. from the Author J. P."

135. TO J. C. HOTTEN

MS: British Museum. Printed: *A Swinburne Library*, p. 23.

[? August 30, 1866]

Dear Sir

I send the proof [1] which of course *was* here and turned up at once. I hope you will get it in time to avoid any inconvenience.

Yours truly,

A. C. Swinburne

P.S. I have only glanced at the proof—if there are any small errors left, please correct them.

136. TO CHARLES AUGUSTUS HOWELL

MS: British Museum.

[? September 1866] [1]

(Private P.S.)

Voilà mon cher. I hope that will do as M. de Gernande said when he dug his wife's eyes out.[2] There's a note for you which deserves a *lovely* sketch of switching by return of post. Send one, and make a day to call soon.

Tout à toi,

A. F. de Sade

137. TO J. C. HOTTEN

MS: Halsted VanderPoel.

[Early September 1866] [1]

Dear Sir

In compliance with your desire I am willing to write a few lines on a matter which (as it concerns myself alone) I should have been willing to leave untouched, had not others assumed the right to make it their affair as well.

1. Probably of *William Blake*.

1. The date is a guess. The paper is watermarked "SON / 5," and the ink is red.

2. *Justine*, chap. 17.

1. This incomplete letter, written in red ink on three sheets of blue foolscap paper (of which the first two are watermarked "1866"), is apparently the beginning of an early version of *Notes on Poems and Reviews* (see below, Letter 144).

The state of the case, then, is this; For a little more than a year I had employed a single publishing house as the channel for the issue of my books. Certain terms, not (I presume) unfavourable to the representatives of that firm, were agreed upon between us, under which they bound themselves to publish certain works of mine. These terms were not proposed by me. They were proffered by the other party to the agreement, who at that time expressed a fear that I might publish elsewhere and a hope that I would not. I therefore permitted him to issue the second edition (1,000 copies) of 'Atalanta in Calydon' and an edition of my 'Poems and Ballads' of the same size on the same terms. Shortly after the appearance of the latter book, which had lain long between his hands, I received from him an intimation that he would no longer issue it. After this breach of contract without warning and without apology, I at once sent word to him that I should of course withdraw from his hands all other works of mine. One edition (1,000 copies) of 'Chastelard' he had purchased from me. Neither for 'Atalanta' nor for the 'Poems' have I ever received any money; I have on the contrary paid money to him on account of the former. Supposing therefore that he had never sold one copy since either book came out, the property in them would still be mine, not his, when his bill was paid. I presume however that he has sold, say, a dozen of each. Even if he has not sold one, the fact remains that he undertook the risk and expense of each book, leaving to me two-thirds of the profit remaining from the sale when these costs had been met.

Enough now of this; I am not unwilling to have done with his affairs and him. Neither am I at all curious to inquire whether his breach of contract may have been spontaneous or suggested. I pass on to matters, however contemptible, yet for the moment of more importance than this.

As long as the attacks on my book—I have seen a few, I am told there are many—were confined within the limits of the anonymous press, I let them pass without the notice to which they appeared to aspire. Sincere or insincere, scurrilous or respectful, I let them say out their say unheeded. I have never lusted after the praise of journalists, I have never feared their abuse. *Sint ut sunt, aut non sint.*[2] But you, who are now about to reissue my book, are now involved in the matter; and you inform me that you are on this account distinctly threatened with prosecution by persons responsible for the menace, having names of their own and faces not muffled under masks. In recognition of your honourable dealing with me in this

2. "Let them be as they are, or not at all"—words attributed sometimes to P. Ricci, General of the Jesuits, and sometimes to Pope Clement XIII.

matter, I am bound by my own sense of right to accede to your wish that on your account if not on mine I should make some reply to the charges brought against me—as far as I understand them. The work is not fruitful of pleasure, of honour, or of profit; but like other such tasks it may be none the less useful and necessary.

Certain of my poems, it appears, have been

138. TO GEORGE POWELL

MS: National Library of Wales.

22a Dorset Street, W., September 2 [1866]

My dear Powell

I must after all put you off for ten days or so, as I must on leaving town go to see my mother who has been ill and stay a week or so. After that I hope to come on to Wales, if it is not too late for you.

Ever yours sincerely,
A. C. Swinburne

139. TO J. C. HOTTEN

MS: Huntington Library.

22a Dorset Street, W.,
Tuesday, September 4, 1866

Sir

I accept the terms offered by you for my books now in type—viz. £200 in ready money for 1000 copies of my 'Poems and Ballads'—9d. per copy for the second edition (1000 copies) of 'Atalanta in Calydon' —1 sh. per copy for 1000 copies of 'Chastelard'—2 sh. per copy for the remaining copies of 'The Queen-Mother' first edition etc.: and one fourth of the published price of 1000 copies of my forthcoming book on the 'Life and Works of Blake.'

Yours truly,
A. C. Swinburne

140. JOHN RUSKIN TO SWINBURNE

Text: *A Swinburne Library*, p. 263.

Denmark Hill, September 9, 1866

My dear Swinburne

I did not like to thank you for the Poems before I had read them, and their power is so great, and their influence so depressing, that I can read but very little at a time. I have been ill, besides, and unable to read anything.

It is of no use to tell you what you, like all good artists, know perfectly well of your work; and from my own manner of later work you know also very well that I can understand yours, and think of it as I ought, which is all that needs to be said between us, it seems to me, as to the art of the book.

For the matter of it—I consent to much—I regret much—I blame, or reject nothing. I should as soon think of finding fault with you as with a thundercloud or a nightshade blossom. All I can say of you, or them—is that God made you, and that you are very wonderful and beautiful. To me it may be dreadful or deadly—it may be in a deeper sense, or in certain relations, helpful and medicinal. There is assuredly something wrong with you—awful in proportion to the great power it affects, and renders (nationally) at present useless. So it was with Turner,[1] so with Byron. It seems to be the peculiar judgment-curse of modern days that all their greatest men shall be plague-struck. But the truth and majesty which is in their greatest, causes the plague which is underneath, in the hearts of meaner people, smooth outwardly, to be in them visible outside while there is purity within. The rest are like graves which appear not—and you are rose graftings set in dung.

I'm glad to have the book at any rate. I cannot help you, nor understand you, or I would come to see you. But I shall always rejoice in hearing that you are at work, and shall hope some day to see a change in the method and spirit of what you do.

Ever affectionately yours,
J. Ruskin

1. J. M. W. Turner (1775–1851), the landscape painter.

141. JOHN RUSKIN TO EDWARD COLERIDGE [1]

MS: Rutgers. Extract in *Journal of the Rutgers University Library, 12* (Dec. 1948), 8–9.

Denmark Hill, S., September 12, 1866

My dear Mr. Coleridge

I am glad you wrote to me about Swinburne: and glad that you think I may do him good. But he is so boundlessly beyond me in all power and knowledge that the only good I *can* do him is to soothe him by giving him a more faithful—though not a less sorrowful, admiration than others do.

I went abroad this year with two old friends—Sir Walter and Lady Trevelyan of Wallington in Northumberland. Lady Trevelyan died at Neuchatel on the 13th May; and I sate all that Sunday by her deathbed; she talking a little now and then, though the rattle in the throat had come on early in the day. She was an entirely pure and noble woman, and had nothing to think of that day but other people's interests. About one oclock—nine hours before her death, she asked me very anxiously what I thought of Swinburne—and what he was likely to do and to be. (She had been very kind to him in trying to lead him to better thoughts). And I answered—that she need not be in pain about him—the abuse she heard of him was dreadful—but not—in the deep sense, *moral* evil at all, but mentally-physical and ungovernable by his will,—and that finally, God never made such good fruit of human work, to grow on an evil tree. So she was content: and that was the last thing she said—except to her husband—and a little word or two to me—to make me understand how they both cared for me.

I tell you this because I doubt not his mother and sisters will be thankful to know it. The *one* thing that those who love him have to do for him is to soothe him and trust in him;—his whole being is crude and mis-create at present—the divinity in the heat of it sputtering in the wet clay—yet unconquered.

But *his* clay is porcelain—jasper—I am bitterly anxious about him, not for the tone of his life—but for its endurance. I am afraid only of his dying. It is the judgment upon this modern race of ours easily

1. The Rev. Edward Coleridge (1800–83), nephew of S. T. Coleridge. He was vicar of Mapledurham, and a fellow of Eton College. His first wife was the daughter of John Keate, headmaster of Eton. Swinburne's library included a copy of Scott's *Lady of the Lake* inscribed: "Algernon Charles Swinburne, Eton, Dec. 5, 1853, with the kind love and good wishes of his friend Edward Coleridge" (Lot 691 in Sotheby's *Catalogue,* June 1916, of the sale of Swinburne's library).

traceable to the punishable causes that their greatest men shall have flawed or cancerous spots in them—and that most of them shall die early—Burns—Keats—Byron—(and Shelley would not have lived.)—Turner dying in many senses early enough—though the half of him lived on decaying slowly—Beranger, Victor Hugo—have longer life—not less corrupt. There are conceptions of *purity* in Swinburne—(Atalanta, and the opening speech of Althea to wit) beyond anything that so strong a man ever wrote—as far as I remember—(for Wordsworth's purity is half weakness) what you tell me of his family accounts for this.

As for criticising the poems—that is a wholly unnecessary piece of business—and would only irritate him. I don't see anything to criticise in Atalanta—and if there be—he will find it out himself—he will not listen to me or anyone; and *ought* not, except to know what we enjoy and what we don't. (I've got the original MS of the Hymn to Proserpine, and wouldn't part with it for much more than leaf gold. Say to his people that there are many who much more want praying for than he. We all want it alike I fancy—but he's worth a good many sparrows and won't be lost sight of.

Ever truly yours,
J. Ruskin

142. ADMIRAL CHARLES HENRY SWINBURNE TO JOHN RUSKIN

MS: Rutgers.

Holm Wood, Henley on Thames,
September 17, 1866

Dear Sir

It is not with any desire to draw you into correspondence or to burthen you with the trouble of answering me that I write. But I cannot bear to remain silent after reading the letter you have written to Mr. Coleridge about my Son. It is so kind, so beautiful, so soothing, and expresses so truly the thoughts and feelings that his Mother and I have long had about him that I am sure you will allow us to express our gratitude to you. It is a great comfort to us to know that he has a friend who understands him so well and can sympathize with him. We all care for sympathy, but he is so far beyond us that it is not easy in his case to give it, at least with reference to his writings: and they contain passages that give us great pain and sorrow, and check the longing desire to be pleased. But we see him changing, and I have a strong trust that if it please God to spare his life he will leave those blemishes behind and do good in his day.

In early life he was very reverent, and intensely admired all things great and beautiful, his Mother carefully sowed good seed in the promising ground, surely it shall bear fruit! such Friendship as yours must hasten its coming.

Begging you to pardon this intrusion and to accept our thanks
I am dear Sir

Gratefully yours,
C H S

143. JOHN RUSKIN TO ADMIRAL CHARLES HENRY SWINBURNE

MS: Rutgers.

Denmark Hill, S., September 18, 1866

My dear Sir

Indeed I am made happy by your letter—both in knowing that I have been able to be of some comfort to you—and in knowing that Algernon *has* such a father, who will still love him and trust in him whatever the world says.

And I am sure he, having this support—and this charge also—of his father['s] love—another honour of his house—that all will yet be well. Even now—you ought not—none of us ought—to be pained grievously by anything in these poems. The common world cannot distinguish between Correggio's Antiope, and a Parisian street lithograph, and mistakes—(Carlyle said this long ago)—'the ill-cut serpent of Eternity for a common poisonous reptile.' The real guilt is on the part of those who have degraded themselves to this error. There is hardly a piece of music written now in Europe—hardly a spectacle on any European stage—which is not more or less guilty and vile in a sense in which no thought of your son's ever could be—and it is the people who indulge in this continued viciousness who will most attack his work. The more I read it—the nobler I think it is. It *is* diseased—no question—but—as the blight is most [?] on the moss-rose—and does not touch—however terrible—the inner nature of the flower.

There are sick men—and whole men; and there are Bad men, and Good. We must not confuse any of these characters with each other.

I hope to see your son soon—I have been ill and sad myself—and had no life or help to give him—or I should have done so before now.

Ever sincerely yours,

J. Ruskin

Cannot you enjoy (for one out of many instances of noblest work in these poems) the three last stanzas of the ode to Victor Hugo without any bye-fear or pain?

144. TO WILLIAM MICHAEL ROSSETTI

MS: British Museum. Extract in *The Ashley Library, A Catalogue, 9* (1927), 134.

Holmwood, Henley on Thames,
[September 28, 1866] [1]

Dear Rossetti

Please send me the Examiner and Athenaeum.[2] I have seen neither and can't get them. You don't give the dates so I ask you to take this trouble, as I am wild to see them. My vindication [3] is finished, revised, and in Hotten's hands for immediate issue. Can you suggest a satisfactory title for it? I am at my wits' end. Pray help if you can. I have proved Dolores to be little less than a second Sermon on the Mount, and Anactoria than an archdeacon's charge. I am delighted to hear of a critic who takes the same view. As to the Asinaeum, it is my wash (or rather p - - -) pot; over the 'Saturday' have I cast out my shoe.[4]

Our dear Barone [5] wrote to me before about his Menander rifaci-

1. Supplied by W. M. Rossetti.

2. On Sep. 22, 1866, the *Examiner* (pp. 597–99) printed a favorable review (unsigned, but by Henry Morley) of *Chastelard* and *PB1*. The *Athenaeum* on the same day commented (p. 371): "Mr. Swinburne, it is said, is preparing a reply to those critics who have marked and reproved the faults in his *Poems and Ballads,* for which work a new publisher has not yet been found. If Mr. Swinburne's reply be in good metrical form, void of the offences, the general censure of which elicits the forthcoming answer, the public may be congratulated; and in the result, we hope, the poet too. It may win back for him the public esteem which he so lightly forfeited, for the time. It is for him now to win or to lose the future."

3. *Notes on Poems and Reviews* (Bonchurch, *16*, 351–73).

4. Psalms 60:8 and 108:9. In Bulwer's novel *Paul Clifford* (1830) Peter MacGrawler edited a periodical called the *Asinaeum*.

5. Seymour Kirkup.

mento, which I should like to see. Tell him when you write that I am waiting to send him book and pamphlet together. As to your prospects of the North American Review [6] I think they are more than dubious now I have read the article on Atalanta and Chastelard in MM. Lowell and Norton's pages.[7] It is the most abject sample of insolent incompetence and pretentious idiocy I ever saw—not even amusing, like the 'groans of the Britons.' [8] I hope your work will not be wasted; anyhow I shall feel the same interest in and gratitude for it, but what to suggest I don't know. That pellet of decomposed dung technically known as Payne actually stands out for half the American profits of the book he has tried to ruin, and may keep them; but I do think the dog ought to be exposed.

As to your screed of friendly counsel concerning Bacchus—oh! monsieur! vous me dites là des choses—qui mènent a tout. I own the soft impeachment [9]—now and then—notamment when we met last. It's the fault of good conversation—never so good as tête à tête of a night—and that means—Bacchus. I will never trespass on your hospitality again, however, nor, certainly, 'ask for' any (like Oliver Twist) [10] after such a warning. Du reste, permit me to recall to your mind the words of wisdom uttered after dinner and before torture by M. le comte de Gernande: 'L'ivresse, mes amis, est un vice vraiment délicieux et dont le véritable philosophe ne saurait se passer. Apprends, Justine, que tous les vices s'entrelacent et que celui-ci conduit à tous les autres; c'est pourquoi le vrai sage est toujours prêt à s'y vautrer.'

'Oh monsieur! ce raisonnement est vraiment affreux.'

'Affreux, soit,' lui répond ce libertin, en dechirant de ses ongles crochues [sic] le con délicat de notre orpheline. 'Vois donc, putain, je rebande, grâce au vin. Allons, bougresse—implore ton foutu Dieu—tu vas souffrir énormément.' [11]

There is a sermon in return for your admonition—may both be alike blest to us, and bear fruit unto damnation!

6. See below, Letter 149.

7. Charles Eliot Norton (1827–1908) and James Russell Lowell (1818–91) were temporary co-editors of the *North American Review*, which in Apr. 1866 included the review by the latter referred to here.

8. From a letter sent to Rome in 446 by the Britons, according to Gildas.

9. Sheridan, *The Rivals*, V. iii.

10. In the opening chapter.

11. A Swinburnian improvisation on Gernande's theme (*Justine*, chap. 15): "C'est que rien n'est délicieux comme de se gorger de mets succulents . . . ."

'Mais raisonnons,' as the Most Rev. Father Severino observes. 'Il faut un peu de vertu dans ce bas monde.' I am going to send you a bit of hymn as well as a bit of sermon. Seriously it struck me as so very beautiful that being entirely new to me (in this form) I thought it might be to you. It is an old English Catholic hymn on Paradise; [12] unequal, but splendid at its best. I found it in a book of Dr. Neale's belonging to my sisters, I daresay yours know it.

> Our sweet is mixed with bitter gall,
>   Our pleasure is but pain;
> Our joys scarce last the looking on,
>   Our sorrows aye remain; (1)
> But those they live in such delight
>   Such pleasure, and such play, (2)
> That unto them a thousand years
>   Seem but as yesterday.

Isn't that (1) like Shelley's 'We look before and after' and 'our sincerest laughter with some pain is fraught'? And isn't the last bit (2) magnificent in sound and effect?

> Thy gardens and thy gallant walks
>   Continually are green;
> There grow such sweet and pleasant flowers
>   As nowhere else are seen
> There trees for evermore bear fruit
>   And evermore do spring;
> There evermore the angels sit
>   And evermore do sing.

This bit reminded me of 'The Blessed Damozel,' as the other of 'The Skylark.' If you think I overrate it, you will remember my natural bias towards the Christian religion, and excuse the prepossessions of a believer. Seriously, as verse, isn't it splendid in structure and musical repetition?

I hope I have not bored you with this most heterogeneous amalgam of the Marquis and the Galilean, with neither of whom, I know, you sympathize as much as I do. I shall be infinitely obliged if you can send me the newspapers by return of post: and am

Ever your affectionate,
A. C. Swinburne

12. From "Jerusalem, My Happy Home" in *Hymns, Chiefly Mediaeval, on the Joys and Glories of Paradise,* translated or edited by John M. Neale (1818–66), published in 1865. (I have seen only the second edition, 1866, from the text of which Swinburne's verses differ slightly.) See also Leith, pp. 32–34.

145. TO ?

MS: British Museum. Printed: *A Swinburne Library,* p. 196.

[? October 1866] [1]

On the occasion when I was foolish enough to repeat to you Palgrave's talk, it is possible (though I hope it is not the case) that in the heat of the moment I may have unintentionally so perverted or misquoted his words as to leave upon your mind the unwarrantable impression that while extolling the sincerity of another man's work he taxed your own with insincerity or with anything worse than misdirection: a verdict which of course I consider absurd but which I cannot see that any man has a right to consider personally offensive. If however I was indeed so unguarded in my report of a matter which I fully admit I should have done better not to mention to you at all, I owe to him and in a less degree to you the reparation I now make by saying so: but in effect I remember nothing of the kind. At a later date when I gave you offence by behaving as under the circumstances was required by the common civilities of gentlemen to a man who had always behaved to me with great courtesy—and who had at the worst given you no greater ground of offence than half the reviewers of my poems (whom I have no objection to meet on decently civil terms) have given me—I was compelled to be more openly courteous and friendly than I might otherwise have felt to be absolutely necessary, in order as far as possible to efface or atone for the effect of what appeared to me (to say the least) ill-judged and uncalled-for incivility on your part. Had I not tried to do so, I should have seemed to approve it. You may remember that I was not alone in the view I took of the course of conduct most proper for all our sakes.

I have no more to say; I have said thus much once for all, not without weighing my words carefully. I returned yesterday to town and am off again in two days. Finding your letter on my table I thought it best to reply at once, as we may not have occasion to meet between Tuesday and Friday. You must not suppose that I ever did or do now wish to dictate to you. We shall both of course do in this and all other matters as we please and as we think right; and this being the case, there can be no need to recur to the subject of this note.

I send by book post, with all apologies, the book of yours which,

1. The fact that the paper is watermarked "1865" and that this letter seems to be related to Letter 146, below, helps to justify the date conjectured, which is otherwise a pure guess. I have no idea whom the letter is addressed to, but Wise's nomination of John Churton Collins is highhanded nonsense. Lord Houghton or Gabriel Rossetti would be a much more acceptable conjecture.

partly it seems through my carelessness, was rebound by mistake; [2] and remain

Ever yours,
A. C. Swinburne

146. TO WILLIAM MICHAEL ROSSETTI

MS: Rutgers.

Holmwood, Henley on Thames,
Wednesday [October 3, 1866]

Dear Rossetti

I return you the papers with many thanks, and forward the North American Review [1] which Hotten was some time in sending me—so perhaps he has not yet got hold of another. It is much at your service, and of no farther use to me. The Examiner [1] article (not I should guess by Forster but *might* be) was of some interest to me, and must I suppose muzzle or gag the hounds who want to bite as well as bark—prosecute as well as revile. Nevertheless my pamphlet may not be useless or superfluous. I am reading the volume of Froude's [2] quoted by the reviewer; have you yet embarked on it? We sent for it hither on the day it appeared.

Pray assure Palgrave, in case the matter should ever turn up between you by any chance (of letter or otherwise), that I never for one moment dreamt of anything unfriendly on his part; that I never till now heard of such an idea existing anywhere in the region of possibilities; and that I am most sincerely obliged, though not surprised, by his intended good offices towards my book. I have never either met with or heard of anything but goodwill and courtesy on his part. It was I think Gabriel who first told me of his defence of my poems from the attacks current—having himself heard of it on all hands. From him and Sandys I certainly derived an impression that Woolner had all but indirectly suggested or approved the conduct of Payne—who certainly lied to that effect, as he now gives himself once more the customary lie to the contrary effect: but I never gave much (or any) heed to the news, rising as it did out of that bottomless and drainless cesspool of lies and counter-lies, the mouth of Mr. J. B. Payne.

2. See above, Letter 78.

1. See above, Letter 144.

2. Volumes *9* and *10* of the *History of England* were published in 1866. For Swinburne, J. A. Froude (1818–94), mostly because of his view of Mary Stuart, was a continual irritant.

Even were it not superfluous to anticipate that person's own certain course by giving him the lie, Woolner's denial would of course be conclusive against his assertion or insinuation.[3] I desired the above-named thief to send an early copy to Palgrave of my poems. As he said he did so, I presume it is safe to infer he did not, even should he now admit the latter.

Should you write again, I shall be grateful for news of Gabriel, Ned, Howell and friends generally.

Ever yours affectionately,
A. C. Swinburne

147. TO J. C. HOTTEN

MS: British Museum. Printed: *A Swinburne Library*, p. 32.

Holm Wood, Henley on Thames,
[*ca.* October 4, 1866]

Dear Sir

Let me have the proofs and MS of my pamphlet as soon as you can, as I leave in a few days for Wales. I am surprised at not hearing further about the other arrangements, as it must be a fortnight since I wrote to you.[1] The title of my pamphlet will be 'Notes on Poems and Reviews.' I see by certain printed impertinences that people have been at the trouble to forge rumours about it, which I presume cannot be helped, or I should request you to keep things quiet till the time of publication, as I do not care to see my affairs handled by absurd scribblers in the newspapers.

Yours truly,
A. C. Swinburne

3. Scott wrote (*Rossetti Papers,* p. 207) to William Rossetti on Sep. 16, 1866: "I heard that Woolner was the man to bias the publisher and carry the point, in the consideration of the withdrawal of Algernon's book; and I at once wrote Woolner, and asked him the question direct. I enclose his letter and Payne's, which you can return to me when read. You will prevent Gabriel or anyone else repeating the assertion—(observe, Woolner says directly that Payne had seen or heard nothing of him for many months)—and do justice to an old friend. The story I heard had nothing to do with Gabriel." See also *Family-Letters with a Memoir, 2,* 192.

Thomas Woolner (1825–92), sculptor and versifier, had been a Pre-Raphaelite Brother and was an intimate friend of the Trevelyans. Frederick Sandys (1829–1904) was one of the painters in Rossetti's orbit. Swinburne's "Cleopatra" (Bonchurch, *2,* 60–64) and the drawing by Sandys that inspired it appeared together in the *Cornhill Magazine* (Sep. 1866), pp. 331–33.

1. An envelope (without a letter) in the British Museum shows by the postmark that he posted a letter to Hotten on Sep. 20 from Holmwood.

148. D. G. ROSSETTI TO ALFRED TENNYSON

MS: Yale.

16 Cheyne Walk, October 6, 1866

My dear Tennyson

This letter does not come with the least intention of troubling you for an answer, which it does not need, but it is necessary I should write it.

Edward Jones told me today that when he lately saw you, you were speaking of the qualities which displease you in Swinburne's poetry, and after attributing their origin in one respect correctly, you added that you supposed they might be also owing to his intimacy with me.

As no one delights more keenly in his genius than I do, I also have a right to say that no one has more strenuously combatted its wayward exercise in certain instances, to the extent of having repeatedly begged him not to read me such portions of his writings when in M.S. I remember that in a conversation I had with you when returning from Mr. Procter's some months ago, I stated this; though not then in denial to reports of which I then knew nothing, and which seem to have more weight with you than my statement. So let me now say distinctly that any assertion to the contrary is either ignorant gossip or lying slander.

The attacks on Swinburne in the press have been for the most part coarse and stupid; and it is only to a very few, such as yourself, that I should at this moment say anything which could by any possibility be misconstrued as taking part against him. I trust to your not so construing it; but having made such efforts as I could before his book appeared, in what I thought his interest, I cannot now myself submit to misrepresentation in a quarter where I should much regret it.

I am, my dear Tennyson

Yours very truly,
D. G. Rossetti

A. Tennyson Esq.

149. TO WILLIAM MICHAEL ROSSETTI

MS: British Museum. Extracts in *The Ashley Library, A Catalogue, 9* (1927), 135–37, and in Lafourcade, *La Jeunesse, 1*, 247 n., 252, 266.

Holmwood, October 9 [1866]

Dear Rossetti

Before I got your letter this morning I was thinking of writing to

Hotten, to desire him to do what he has done unbidden.[1] I am very glad he did it, and much pleased by his way of doing it. For of course a suggestion from you is a very different thing from a suggestion from him. (I am also very glad that Gabriel and Scotus should have seen my proofs.) As to the legal part of the affair—references to prosecutors, swindlers, etc. etc.—that of course I leave entirely to my publisher. He is welcome to cancel (after notice given) anything of the sort he pleases. It was only on his account and at his desire (you might remind him) that I undertook to touch on the matter. With regard to the other details of which you speak, you will see that I have adopted almost all of your suggestions. Ephesus and Félise are the only two points on which I hold out.[2] The first 'profanity' is too minute a gnat, among my flock of camels, to be strained[3] at even by a Nazarene throat or Galilean gorge. As to the antitheism of 'Félise' I know of course that *you* know that the verses represent a mood of mind and phase of thought not unfamiliar to me; but I must nevertheless maintain that no reader (*as* a reader) has a right (whatever he may conjecture) to assert that this is *my* faith and that the faith expressed in such things as the 'Litany' or 'Carol'[4] or 'Dorothy' is not. Of course it is a more serious expression of feeling; and of course this is evident; but it is not less formally dramatic than the others; and this is the point on which it seems to me necessary to insist and fair to enlarge. Indeed I foresee I shall soon have to defend myself from the charge of being a moralist—a deist—even (chi lo sa?) a Galilean. It is really very odd that people (friendly or unfriendly) will not let one be an artist, but must needs make one out a parson or a pimp. I suppose it is part of the fetid and fecund spawn of 'the Galilean serpent.'[5] In the eyes of 'that cursed, crawling, Christian crew' one must be either St. Francis of Assisi or the Marquis de Sade. The name of the latter of these two great poets and evangelists reminds me of what I should have begun

1. William Rossetti wrote (*A Swinburne Library*, p. 264) on Oct. 7: "Hotten sent me on Friday the proof here enclosed of your pamphlet, and requested me to call upon him yesterday for some speech concerning it, which I did. After interchange of our views regarding the matter, I offered to write to you about it, which he gladly accepted. . . ."

2. The (or an) allusion to Ephesus (see I Corinthians 15:32) remained in *Notes on Poems and Reviews*, but the passage on "Félise" went.

3. Matthew 23:24.

4. "A Litany" and "A Christmas Carol" (Bonchurch, *1*, 222–26, 346–48), in *PB1*.

5. Shelley's "Ode to Liberty," l. 119.

with. I for myself would rather see your review of my work issued as a pamphlet here than submitted to transatlantic editors and sub-editors. Nor should I fear that anyone might think it was done on Hotten's account; and I don't doubt you would make it plain that it was not *merely* an act or expression of personal goodwill. The one advantage it might give to my enemies and yours and all men's (not counting as men the swine of Gadara [6]—by the by I always enjoyed that feat of the Nazarene's and thought it worthy of an elder God—but I trust you won't think that I am turning orthodox because I can appreciate a puerile spree on the part of our (very) common Redeemer)—the one danger I can foresee is that these said Gadarenes might grunt or bleat to the effect that your review or essay was simply a piece of amicable fuggery, not of cool and judicial criticism. All human or non-porcine creatures would know better; but it is not every swine's nose (worse luck) that wears a ring. But of course, whether this chance can be met with or not, I should infinitely prefer, I should regard as much the higher compliment, the appearance in London of a pamphlet of yours than the issue of an article in an American review.[7] It would be indeed—you know that I speak seriously and deliberately—in my opinion, a distinction of which I should not have dreamed, and worth in my eyes all the review articles, signed or unsigned, that ever appeared. This I am bound to say in honesty, as you ask what I think; but, as honestly, I must say that I should be sincerely sorry and vexed if any expression of my feeling were to overbalance or outweigh your own.

Apropos des [*sic*] bottes—if it were published here, would it be advisable to refer en pleines lettres to the Most Holy Saint Gilles de Rays, or the Blessed Donatien-Alphonse-François, Marquis de Sade? [8] It is sweet to me that my name should be mixed with theirs. How sweet I need not say, nor how deeply I enjoyed the allusion when I first heard it; but I doubt if it be politic. Still, far be it from me to dictate or suggest, and my personal feelings you know. 'Orate pro nobis peccatoribus' [9] I say to those twin saints.

6. Mark 5:1–16, or Luke 8:26–39.

7. Because of J. R. Lowell's censure of Swinburne in the *North American Review* (see above, Letter 144), Rossetti's essay in defense ("Swinburne's Poems and Ballads A Criticism"), which had been offered to the magazine, was instead issued as a pamphlet by Hotten in 1866 (see *Rossetti Papers*, pp. 194–99, 206).

8. Finally, the first allusion was rejected and the second hushed to "such a son of Belial and of cretinism as the producer, predestined to a madhouse and a hardly utterable name, of some 'scrofulous French novel / On grey paper with blunt type.' "

9. "Pray for us sinners" (II Thessalonians 3:1 in the Vulgate).

I must write to Hotten and ask him to send me the number of the Examiner from which your extract comes,[10] and that of the Spectator of which you tell me a metrical assault is indeed 'nuts'[11]—one must use either schoolboyish or Sadique terms on such occasions. It was cruel, unfriendly, not to buy up and send one copy at least of an effusion which I feel must be delicious. It was I think the R. Père Silvestre[12] who observed—'L'opprobre, ma chère Justine—l'infamie— a un attrait très piquant, et qui ressemble énormément au fouet. Accable-moi de sottises, d'injures, de mots affreux; tu me feras plaisir. Entasse sur ma tête toutes les horreurs imaginables; ô putain! cette infamie, ces reproches, ces horreurs ne me feront que plus sûrement bander? Hélas! il n'est que trop vrai; le vit nerveux de cette anthropophage le démontre assez; et notre orpheline, en voyant dresser son engin, fond en larmes; elle reconnait que la vertu elle-même peut devenir maquerelle, et que par ses paroles chastes et religieuses elle vient effectivement de branler moralement le plus infâme libertin du monde.' such, or nearly such, I fear and hope, will be the effect of a poetic castigation on me. Excuse my repeated citations; there are (witness my works passim) two writers whom I cannot refrain from quoting, God, and de Sade. I am aware that they are both obscene and blasphemous.

I have begun verse again after many months of enforced inaction through worry and weariness. I am writing a little song of gratulation for Venice[13] with the due reserves and anticipations; and hope to wind up the scheme of the poem by some not quite inadequate expression of reverence towards Mazzini. I have already touched on most other of the later patriots and martyrs—I am half afraid and half desirous to touch on him—i.e., to lay my lips on his feet. If I do finish this poem at all to my satisfaction, there will be a bit of enthusiasm in verse for once—rather. After all, in spite of jokes and perversities—malgré ce cher Marquis et ces foutus journaux—it is nice to have something to love and to believe in as I do in Italy. It was only Gabriel and his followers in art (l'art pour l'art) who for a time frightened me from speaking out; for ever since I was fifteen I have been equally and

10. On Oct. 6, the *Examiner* printed a letter in defense of Swinburne (by Lord Houghton, but signed "Nothing if Not Critical") to which there is probably an oblique allusion in Rossetti's essay.

11. "The Session of the Poets," by "Caliban" (a pseudonym of Robert Buchanan), in the *Spectator* (Sep. 15).

12. In *Justine*.

13. *A Song of Italy* (Bonchurch, 2, 303–29), published in 1867, reprinted in *STN*.

unalterably mad—tête montée, as my Mother says—about this article of faith; you may ask any tutor or schoolfellow. I know the result will be a poem more declamatory than imaginative; but I'd rather be an Italian stump-orator than an English prophet; and I meant to make it acceptable to you and a few others of our sort. As far as I can judge, I think it contains already some of my best verses. Only, just as one hears that intense desire has made men impotent at the right (or wrong) minute, my passionate wish to express myself in part, for a little, about this matter, has twice and thrice left me exhausted and incompetent: unable to write, or to decide if what has been written is or is not good. I never felt this about my poems on other subjects; and I'd give a year of my life to accomplish the writing of a really great song on this one. If national or translatable, so much the better; but anyhow, I feel with child (and probably abortive) till I have emitted something. I want to show you what I have done; a little encouragement would do me all the good in the world. There are, I must say, passages of triumphant vituperation as to Justice and Pius-Iscariot which I think not quite unworthy of my master Hugo in his abusive moods.

Do you happen to know Linton's address? I haven't it by me, but Scott I suppose knows. I want him to have a copy (my present, of course), through Hotten, of my poems; and it's useless writing to H. without an address given. *Item*—as I shan't be in town (I'm off to Wales next week—but this address is a safe one)—perhaps you wouldn't mind giving Hotten this list of people to whom I want my pamphlet forwarded. Yourself, Gabriel, Ned, Howell, Scott, Ruskin, Brown, Sandys, Lord Lytton, Forster (I've got his address in London, but Hotten would know), and our dear Barone [14] *with* the Poems *and* my love; also any other friend or acquaintance who would care to have a copy; but these certainly. *Item*—half a dozen or dozen, say, to me, for private distribution at once. Item, one to Palgrave, please tell Hotten, with my compliments. Excuse my giving you all the trouble, it's by way of making things swift and sure.

Can you find a better heading to my pamphlet than I have given? I must have it short and single: your first suggestion I thought rather too elaborate and *familiar,* for a title-page, though perfectly expressive of the character of the essay. Since reading the 'Examiner' I have thought of a delightful and most sufficient title for it, 'Les Malheurs de la Vertu,' but I might be accused of sacrilegious plagiarism from an elder brother. Tell Scotus that I like his impudence on the matter, and that those who *do* 'know me' know me for an example of injured innocence which it would be difficult to parallel in any martyrology

14. Seymour Kirkup.

196

from Jacobus de Voragine down to Fox.[15] N'importe; as a disciple of
the Galilean, I forgive him. It is I believe my duty. Love to him (*not*
J.C. but W.B.S.), and all friends from

Your affectionate,
A. C. Swinburne

P.S. I may just add that I don't agree about the suggestion of printing
my pamphlet as an appendix to my book. It would in my opinion be
making far too much of an ephemeral and contemptible subject. If
the poems are fit to live they must outlive the memory of this; and I
don't like such an association, even in idea. E.g., Byron's letter to the
'British Review' [16] is a charming small bit of separate fun, but he
would never have issued it as an integral part or a complement of
Don Juan.

P.P.S. I add a word or two to shew that I have read and weighed
what you say about my poems. I should not like to bracket 'Dolores'
and the two [17] following as you propose. I ought (if I did) to couple
with them in front harness the 'Triumph of Time' [18] etc., as they express that state of feeling the reaction from which is expressed in
'Dolores.' Were I to rechristen these three as trilogy, I should have to
rename many earlier poems as acts in the same play. I have got this
morning (Wednesday) your second letter and Hotten's proof. There
is, as you will see, nothing to alter in consequence, as I have done
more (though otherwise) than he suggests. Let him cut out if he pleases
the note on 'Queen Mab.' The other two points—the word 'indict,'
and the allusion to 'many' attacks—shall stand; [19] even I have seen
more of the latter than he speaks of, by far, and have not seen all, as
I know, by any means. 'Indict' (without explanation) means 'impugn.'

I am much flattered by Mill's approval, as I greatly admire his
'Liberty,' the one book I have read of his; but I should hardly have
been more surprised by hearing that Carlyle has expressed a fervent
admiration of 'Justine.'

I hope you will prevail on Scotus to reissue his poems in some form

15. Jacobus de Voragine's *Golden Legend*, a medieval compilation that was
Caxton's most popular production, and John Foxe's *The Acts and Monuments of
the Church* (1563), popularly known as "The Book of Martyrs."

16. Riposte to the heavy-handed criticism of Canto I of *Don Juan*. See Byron's
Letters and Journals, ed. R. E. Prothero (6 vols. London and New York, 1898–1901),
4, 346–47, 465–70.

17. "The Garden of Proserpine" and "Hesperia" (Bonchurch, *1*, 299–308).

18. Bonchurch, *1*, 169–81.

19. He seems, however, to have compromised on the first point and yielded on
the second.

more or less select, with excerpts from 'Hades' and the 'Year of the World,' so gathered and arranged as to be readable apart from the context as independent poems, mixed in among earlier and later lyrics. 'Death' seems to me about his noblest piece of verse, and one of the finest in the language; and the 'Sphinx' only less grand than it in form, and in conception as grand. Perhaps he might add a new poem or two—e.g., his 'Temptation of Anthony,' which is very fine in my opinion.[20]

Will you ask Hotten for me if he has the proofs and M.S. of *our* Blake, and Howell if his promised transcript is nearly done? I want to know that all my belongings are safe out of the den of thieves in Dover Street. Item—perhaps you would ask him, how about the American money [21] and the solicitor's opinion? It is one way of thanking you for the trouble you have already taken, to ask you to take more. It is at once pleasant and safe to have a friend in these matters by way of witness and adviser at once; and you know how truly I feel obliged to you.

Please look well to my 'Notes,' and decide for me. I send it back to you on purpose, and then pass it back to Hotten.

150. TO GEORGE POWELL

MS: National Library of Wales.

Holmwood, Henley on Thames,
Wednesday [October 10, 1866]

My dear Powell

Can you receive me on Saturday or Monday next, or a day or two later it may be? I shall be very glad to come and look you up. I have just touched up my last proofs for the present and hope to be at peace for a few weeks.

My mother is now well, though her last illness was serious; and on leaving you I shall probably return hither. Write me a word to say you have received this and are (or are not) ready to receive the writer, who is

Always yours most truly,
A. C. Swinburne

20. Scott's *Hades* was published in 1838, *The Year of the World* in 1846. "Death" and "To the Great Sphinx" were in his *Poems* (1854), and his *Poems, 1875*, included "Anthony."

21. See above, Letter 144. "Den of thieves" is from Matthew 21:13 (etc.).

151. TO J. C. HOTTEN

MS: British Museum. Printed: *A Swinburne Library*, p. 33.

Holmwood, October 10 [1] [1866]

Dear Sir

I have just got your note, and was (when it came) about to return the proof of my pamphlet to Mr. Rossetti. I am very glad that you sent it to him and laid the matter in full before him. I have, as you will see, at once adopted your suggestions. The reference to a threat of prosecution was made simply on your account, and in consequence of what you said to me. It was this, you will remember, that made me think of noticing the affair at all: and this is my reason for objecting to any title for my pamphlet which would make it look like an answer to the reviews, of which I should naturally have taken no notice whatever. I am, you will understand, particularly reluctant to be classed (even by the lowest scribbler in the 'Star') among the small literary fry of people who write in answer to their reviewers. Also, it is not exactly a reply to any critic or critics that I have written, but rather a casual set of notes on my poems, such as Coleridge and Byron (under other circumstances) did on theirs. I think a few extracts from the Examiner article might serve your turn in the way of reprint—but by no means the entire article as it stands. I hope you have got my Blake proofs and MS from Moxon's—I am uneasy till I hear of their being safe out of such hands. What does the lawyer say of the American profits on which I wrote my opinion to you and him?

I think still that

Notes on Poems and Reviews
by A C S

is as good a title as we can have (*without* any italics or inverted commas), being simple and unobtrusive, and free of any direct allusion which I should not like. I return the proof to Mr. Rossetti as it came through him to me. I think you may as well (if you like) cancel the note at pp. 11–12, which was inserted on account of what you told me about the menaces made to you on the ground of 'profanity' etc. But this, as well as all questions of form and size, I leave entirely in your hands. In other points the pamphlet must appear just as it stands in the revised copy which I have asked Mr. Rossetti to forward to you. He will also give you a list of the persons to whom I should like it to be at once sent in my name. I hear from him that there was some attack made on me in the 'Spectator' of September 8th or 15th *in verse*, which he thinks I ought to see. I should be much obliged if you could *at*

1. Erroneously transcribed as "18th" in *A Swinburne Library*.

once send it me, as I am out of the way of seeing past numbers of journals, in a country house some way off a town of any sort, and I shall probably be moving into Wales next week. The present address will always find me.

Yours very truly,
A. C. Swinburne

P.S. In reissuing my book, I hope you will see to the two misprints I pointed out to you—at p. 146 'Fair seasons' should be 'Four seasons' —at p. 181 *'Where* lives' ought to be 'Whose lives.' These blunders are so grave that they ought to be rectified immediately.

152. TO WILLIAM MICHAEL ROSSETTI

MS: Rutgers.

[October 13, 1866] [1]

Dear Rossetti

Thanks once more for your latest note. I think it so advisable to eschew allusions to identity of sex between lovers—which 'no English mother could explain to her younger daughters'—that not only I won't insert anything at p. 9 after the words 'one and another,' but will ask you to get the passage at p. 11—('the speaker sweats and swoons)—*Stet* so far—at sight of her *female* favourite in the *embrace* (or *arms*) of a man'—as follows: '—at sight of her favourite by the side of a man;' which is both safer and more accurate. Please tell me the spelling of infuso*ria* or *-ae* (but I *think* the *-a* is a plural?) and Loreto or *-etto* which *you* seem to have corrected.[2]

Will you forgive my disagreeing about a motto, especially from the works of an author who should long since have been relegated to the same shelf with *Justine?* I don't see that any is needed—or any of the citations in the text would have done. A *text* I really should not like to prefix unless one could attain something exquisitely vexatious to the Christiano-Britannic mind.

À propos the prose quotation (from B. Jonson) at p. 6,[3] *e*ffect should be *a*ffect. I meant to have written of these corrections to you or to Hotten last night by way of P.P.S.

H. has sent me that sublime of blackguardism from the Spectator [4]

1. Supplied by William Rossetti.

2. The four references may be found as follows: Bonchurch, *16*, 357, 358, 354, 361.

3. Bonchurch, *16*, 354.

4. See above, Letter 149.

—much, *you* will believe at least, to my amusement—and nothing to any other sensation—except a slight nausea to the address of the able editor.[5]

Ever yours,
A. C. Swinburne

I have read (did I say it before?) your sister's poem in M'Millan [6] with great admiration—by far the best bit of English terza rima I know.

153. TO GEORGE POWELL

MS: National Library of Wales.

Holmwood, Henley on Thames,
Saturday [October 13, 1866]

My dear Powell

I sent you a note on Wednesday which you could not have got when you wrote the letter I got today. I and all mine are well and I shall like of all things to run down to you. Please write again and name a *day* and *train* and *station* suitable. I am quite ready, having done with the proof of my defensive and offensive pamphlet—Laus Diabolo. I send you what I got yesterday from London. The 'last thing out in blackguardism.' [1] I hope, before you put it to its natural use, it will make you laugh for a moment at the poor hound who wrote it, as heartily as I did.

Ever yours most sincerely,
A. C. Swinburne

154. TO F. G. WAUGH [1]

MS: Harvard.

Pent, Aberystwith [*ca.* October 27, 1866]

Dear Mr. Waugh

Many thanks for your offered hospitality of which I shall avail myself as soon as may be, but I fear not over soon. I leave this pleasant

5. R. H. Hutton. For "able editor" see above, Letter 78.

6. "By the Waters of Babylon," *Macmillan's Magazine* (Oct. 1866), pp. 424–26.

1. Buchanan's "The Session of the Poets" (see above, Letter 149).

1. Francis Gledstanes Waugh (1846–1902) is about as obscure as any man can be who attended a public school (Rugby) and a university (Oxford), and became an ordained minister. Of Waugh's connection with Swinburne little is known (see

Thule of Wales in a day or two; and here you may imagine your letter was some time in reaching me, having various courses to take and discrimina rerum to pass through. Indeed I suppose the fun going on of which you speak will be past by this time, so that the direct invitation has become indirect but will be none the less remembered.

I see you have seen the last newspaper follies and 'literary' impertinences connected with my inoffensive name. There is a quiet little pamphlet of mine on the verge of birth, sarcastic and elucidative as I hope in some small degree; but the exquisite title which MM. the penny pressmen have invented I leave wholly to their use when they may want it. It is strange what small fictions people will invent. I am not given to 'parley' with the swine of journalism; but to court their displeasure and chastise (if I choose) their insolence. I call my pamphlet simply 'Notes on certain Poems and Reviews.' I am glad you have something coming out (for aught we know here of the days of the month they may be and probably are out already) in the magazines, and shall look them up. My 'Cleopatra' was done long since for the drawing's sake simply and came in just as it were at its tail.

How very noble is most of Meredith's 'Vittoria'; [2] but of late he has been falling or tripping rather here and there into his old trick of over refining. Art must dispense with hairsplitting; and he can so well afford to leave it. The vexatious and laborious error of microscopic manipulation of minutiae to such artists as Holman Hunt (There's alliteration—and I never saw it till now.) Nothing can be more truly and tragically great than the operatic scene or the 'Duel in the Pass'; indeed the whole figure of Angelo is (as the French say) 'epically' noble. Such a painter has no right to put us before or behind the scenes with riddles and contortions in place of clear narrative and large drawing.

Hoping we may meet before very long in London if not in Oxford. Believe me

Very sincerely yours,
A. C. Swinburne

---

below, Letter 470A). They probably became acquainted through Meredith (Mrs. Waugh and the second Mrs. Meredith were old friends), but possibly the intermediary was F. T. Palgrave, who was in touch with both men at this time (see *Francis Turner Palgrave: His Journals and Memories of His Life* by Gwenllian Palgrave, 1899, pp. 98–100, 252).

2. Published in 1867. The two allusions below are to chaps. 21 and 26.

155. TO GEORGE POWELL

MS: National Library of Wales.

Holmwood, Henley on Thames,
November 2 [1866]

My dear Powell

I send you a copy of my new pamphlet which I find on my return is already published. I hope you will approve of its tone and write me a word what you think of it. You will be sorry to hear that my mother is so unwell with feverish influenza that I have not yet seen her; and she is especially sorry that this illness prevents us from asking you to return my visit, which she had hoped to do at once. I trust it will not be long before she is well and you disengaged enough to accept an invitation. I add a domestic detail; could you let Stephen inquire at the Queen's whether or not I left a shirt and collar behind me, which I know was packed by him, and unpacked, but the repacking in the morning was left to the waiter while I breakfasted in a fearful hurry —thanks to the inattention on the attendant's part—and on arriving here I found none? Per contra, I believe I did the busman out of his fare—6d—which he only came for when the train was starting and I could not get at it and was taking leave of O'Halloran.[1] Will you see to the saving of my honour in this? With best regards to O'H. as to you
   Believe me

Ever yours most sincerely,
A. C. Swinburne

156. TO LORD HOUGHTON

MS: The Marchioness of Crewe. Extract in Bonchurch, *18*, 46–47*.

Holmwood, Henley on Thames,
November 2 [1866]

Dear Lord Houghton

I fear I shall not be in town next week, though, not having been there for ages, I should like; but I am here en famille for some time (gaining in health and moral tone), and besides my mother is just now far from well. I read your speech at Cambridge—better reported than in the Times,[1] which retransformed Shenstone to Shakespeare as Oxford had transformed Shelley to Shenstone. Did you see the leading ar-

---

1. See below, Letter 161.

1. Houghton's inaugural address on Oct. 30 for the new rooms of the Union Society at Cambridge was reported in *The Times* (Oct. 31), p. 10.

ticle next day intimating that Cambridge was as indifferent to me as Oxford then to Shelley? They must indeed be deep in the mist and mire of Boeotia and Philistia. At the twin-sister of owls I hardly remember a motion bearing upon art or literature.

I am glad you like my *riposte*. I thought the sharper, shorter, and singler in tone it was, the better. My motto is either to spare or strike hard. Mere titillation is lost on porcine hides.

The paper in Fraser [2] I have not seen but am expecting. I have had letters already from Ruskin and your friend Mr. Conway,[3] who recalls our meeting under the auspices of the sea-birds, and intimates that having begun fighting my battles in the New York Tribune he means to continue apropos of the 'Notes,' of which I have sent him a copy. It is a very courteous and friendly letter.

If you have read the 'Drum Taps' of his countryman the great Walt (whose friends I see have published a pamphlet in *his* defence, I daresay you agree with me that his dirge or nocturn [4] over your friend Lincoln is a superb piece of music and colour. It is infinitely impressive when read aloud.

Yours affectionately,
A. C. Swinburne

157. TO WILLIAM MICHAEL ROSSETTI

MS: Rutgers.

Holmwood, November 2 [1866]

My dear Rossetti

I am ashamed to be by this time three or four letters in your debt; but much wandering and some days of illness—a very severe bilious attack—made me long incapable of writing, often as I meant to try. I am very glad that even on the terms you mention your pamphlet is to appear in London, and am hungry to see it. Houghton in a note this morning seems to intimate that Palgrave has written in its defence and the Poems'; I have sent for Fraser. Then, Mr. M. D. Conway (do you know what his article on Whitman in the Fortnightly [1] is like?) has

2. "Mr. Swinburne and His Critics," *Fraser's Magazine* (Nov. 1866), pp. 635–48. The article (unsigned) is, on the whole, very favorable.

3. See below, Letter 160.

4. "When Lilacs Last in the Dooryard Bloom'd" in *Sequel to Drum-Taps* (1865–66).

1. *Fortnightly Review* (Oct. 15), pp. 538–48.

written very courteously, to the effect that having already 'taken up the cudgels' for me 'in the *New York Tribune*' [2] he wants to follow up this review by one of my *notes,* of which I have sent him a copy. They look very well in print. I should like much to see the article on Whitman [3] you speak of. As to Howell and the Marriage of Heaven and Hell I daresay his account is correct, barring that the imperfect transcript must be among my papers in London. I am in anguish at having just discovered *such* a motto for my Notes in Tristram Shandy [4] —'Prithee, shepherd, whose are all these jackasses? what, is there none to carry them?' speaking of critics in the original, cela va sans dire.

Is not yours from Shelley's Defence of Poetry too much as if in answer to a personal charge against me such as was made against him in his lifetime? they have imputed to me only the guilt of writing not of acting viciously. I would cancel the intermediate sentence about Homer, Tasso etc. Then the first and last sentences do admirably. Many thanks for looking up the ipsissima verba (or ipsissorum verbibus) of Frederic.

> Yours affectionately,
> A. C. Swinburne

158. TO J. C. HOTTEN

MS: Yale.

Holmwood, November 3 [1866]

Dear Sir

Can you send me the articles *from which you quote* (in the advertisements published in today's Saturday Review) [1] in the Examiner, Reader, and Scotsman? The others of today I have seen. I am glad Mr. Rossetti's book is nearly out.

> I remain
> Yours very truly,
> A. C. Swinburne

2. C. K. Hyder (*Swinburne's Literary Career and Fame,* p. 282) notes that the "New York semi-weekly *Tribune* for November 20 contains a dispatch [concerning Swinburne] from a special correspondent in London, probably Moncure D. Conway."

3. William Douglas O'Connor's pamphlet, *The Good Gray Poet: A Vindication.*

4. VI. i.

1. He ought to have written "today's *Athenaeum,*" for Hotten had no notice in the *Saturday Review* on this date.

159. TO J. C. HOTTEN

MS: John S. Mayfield.

Holmwood, Sunday [November 4, 1866]

Dear Sir

I forgot yesterday in writing to you the existence of the 'London Review.'

If that worthy journal contains any notice of my pamphlet,[1] please forward it at once.

I see you advertise my 'Blake' as forthcoming, and I wish it were out. As far as the text goes, the one thing wanting is a full transcript of 'The Marriage of Heaven and Hell' from which I quote at some length. I once transcribed Lord Houghton's copy, but my transcript was lost or stolen: and I have neither time nor patience to resume the task. Could not some trustworthy person be found to do the job? Three or four hours would suffice; and if the man were safe I think it might be managed.

Meantime, if (as I suppose) you have my proofs and MSS. I wish you would send me the last few sheets (*MS* and proof together) for correction. I think of enlarging the final paragraph, which was rather hurried through.

Yours truly,

A. C. Swinburne

P.S. Show this to Mr. W. Rossetti and to Mr. Howell who may be able to help in this matter.

P.S. There are two more misprints in my unfortunate 'Poems'—slight but ugly, which must be corrected.

1) At p. 90
for '*Nor* for their sakes'
read '*Not* for their sakes'

2) At p. 84
for φυχάριον—νεκρόν
read ψυχάριον—νεκρὸν

These I have just hit upon;[2] the others I think you have by you.

1. It did. "Mr. Swinburne's Defence," *London Review* (Nov. 3), 482–83.

2. Part of a quotation from Epictetus of which the last line but two of "Hymn to Proserpine" is an adaptation. These errors were corrected, but in later years when the type was reset new errors appeared in the same quotation.

159A. TO J. C. HOTTEN

MS: John S. Mayfield.

November 6 [1866]

Dear Sir

Thanks for the note forwarded from Mr. Forster who reminds me of my unfulfilled promise of a copy of the Poems; I have told him that neither you nor I had one till now, but that he will at once receive one from you in my name. Please send it to his London address. He is very complimentary as to the pamphlet.

I wrote to you yesterday as to Blake, and receive to-day a letter containing a fresh incident regarding him and Sir Thos. Lawrence, which is worth a place in some note.

1) I must have the final proofs and MS. which I had not received from Moxon's.

2) The transcript of 'Heaven and Hell.' Of these I spoke yesterday. As to the plates I think it might be worth while for me to come up to London for a day on purpose to see about the matter. I would arrange if convenient to meet Mr. Rossetti and Mr. Howell at your shop and thence we might go to look over the British Museum collection. One or two of the plates to his 'Jerusalem' would do well; but the field of choice is so wide that I should like to have the help and advice of friends. If we can arrange a day which will suit them I will try to be there at the right hour. I suppose you will see them before long, and be able to find out and let me hear.

When will Mr. Rossetti's book be out? I had a note to-day complaining that the writer could not get a copy of my Notes for which he had written after reading the reviews but was told it was not out. Is there any delay or error in the matter[?] of trade?

Yours truly,
A. C. Swinburne

160. TO M. D. CONWAY [1]

Text: Typescript in Rutgers Library. Extracts in Lafourcade, *La Jeunesse*, 2, 324, 353–54 (from a transcript owned by Wise).

Holmwood, Henley on Thames,
November 7, 1866

My dear Mr. Conway

I cannot wait to hear from you in answer to my last note. I have just

1. Moncure Daniel Conway (1832–1907). Reared in the disciplines of the Commonwealth of Virginia and the Methodist Church, Conway clear-sightedly turned

read your article on Walt Whitman, which you had sent me before, but which has only reached me today. One passage above all others delights me—that in which you speak of his amorous embrace of the sea in bathing. I am sure he would, and hope that you will, excuse me for not having read or enjoyed it till now; for at the time it appeared, and for a fortnight after, I was fighting the tides as a swimmer on the west coast of Wales. I knew that the man who had spoken as he has of the sea must be a fellow seabird with me; and I would give something to have a dip in the rough water with him. This at least we have in common, for after twenty minutes' profane swearing at the keepers of the shore, I did last week frighten them into giving me entrance to the sea, which they thought too fierce to be met and swum through; and the result of my swim, I am told, is that I have 'won their hearts for ever.' Since I was thirteen I have always got on with sailors and fishermen and such like men, so from what you say I judge and hope I must have some points in common with Walt Whitman.

A friend of mine, Mr. Winwood Reade, is just starting from Paris for America, with an especial hope (he tells me in a letter received this morning) to make the acquaintance and, if it may be, to earn the friendship of the said Walt Whitman. I think he deserves it, but I envy him the occasion. I always smelt the sea in that man's books, and never in any Englishman's now alive. He ought to know that there are some Englishmen of my age who truly and deeply admire and enjoy his work, and some older who applaud and understand it.

Another thing may be worth your knowing and his; that in many points both of matter and manner—gospel and style—his *Leaves of Grass* have been anticipated or rivalled by the unpublished semi-metrical 'Prophetic Books' of William Blake (which I presume you have never read?). This I have proved [2] in my forthcoming book on the suppressed works of that great artist and thinker, whose philosophy, to my mind far deeper and subtler than his rival Swedenborg's, has never yet been published because of the abject and faithless and

---

his back on both, enrolled in the Harvard Theological School, and emerged a Unitarian. In 1863 in England he earned some notoriety as an especially addlepated abolitionist, and early in 1864 accepted the pulpit of the South Place Chapel, Finsbury.

Swinburne probably came upon him at Lord Houghton's, but, Conway, being a zealous pusher of Whitman's English reputation, may have known him through William Rossetti.

2. See the conclusion to *William Blake*, Bonchurch, *16*, 342–45.

blasphemous timidity of our wretched English literary society; a drunken clerical club dominated by the spurious spawn of the press.

However, I have printed (with comments of my own) a good deal of these books. Written in the same semi-metrical verse (or prose) as the Leaves of Grass, they preach almost exactly the same gospel; and I think might interest Walt Whitman and his admirers in America, where I suppose these books of Blake's (who regarded them as the real grave work of his life) are as little known as here—less known they cannot be. In the original 'Prophecies' there are passages quite as broad (and perhaps more offensive) as any in the *Leaves of Grass*. These I have not quoted in my critical essay; but the gist of them is precisely that of Walt Whitman's book—in other words, healthy, natural, and anti-natural. But I abstain, (for once) in print, because I want to see what I hope may yet be achieved by subscription—a complete or quasi-complete edition of Blake's works; photographs thoroughly well done of his chief drawings; artistic engravings of his chief pictures or 'frescos,' to use his own term; and a full though critical edition of his writings. Then only one of the greatest of Englishmen— a poet when there was no poet—an artist when there was hardly an artist—a republican under the very shadow of the gibbet which George III (who flung Blake's drawings away when they were laid before his miserable blind eyes) had prepared for all such men—a lover of America, of freedom, and of France from the first and to the last—the one single man in London who dared go out with the red cap on his head (not through bravado, but simply as a matter of principle)—then only, I say, will this great man be understood. It seems to me that Walt Whitman belongs to the same race of men; and if so, I am certain he will understand the mystical heterodox 'prophecies' of Blake which the publishers of his biography and re- mains were afraid of, but which I intend to bring before the world.

Yours sincerely,

A. C. Swinburne

P.S. As your article of October 15th begins with the oriental refer- ences, I will ask if you know an anonymous translation of the Rubáiyát of Omar Khayyám? 'C'est là ma bible à moi'—as a French friend once said to me of a different sort of book. To me it seems to stand midway between Lucretius *De rerum Natura* and Walt Whit- man's *Leaves of Grass*—and to be very like both; which is in my mind as high praise as can be given.

November 8th. I have just got your letter in time to add a word of acknowledgment. Your apologue of the Doctor and his stethoscope is excellent, and I am glad you like my notes so well on a second reading. Much of my Blake was in type when the Poems appeared, but having lost a transcript of his first book, *The Marriage of Heaven and Hell,* I must wait till another can be made. Then Hotten would at once I suppose be able to forward proofs. As I meant to print that very heterodox prose poem almost at length (it ends with a poem of Thanksgiving for the American and French revolutions) I must delay till then. I have read the press articles on my Notes; they are indeed rich.

161. TO G. B. O'HALLORAN [1]

MS: T. E. Hanley. Published: *London Mercury, 14* (August 1926), 337.

Holmwood, Henley on Thames,
November 7 [1866]

My dear O'Halloran

I had all but sent you a copy of my 'Notes' enclosed to Powell's address, when it struck me that he might be away and your copy follow his to the confusion of us all. Write me word what you think of it, and let me see also your article. I see my lash has made the cockney pressmen wince and scream already. I hope the pamphlet will bring me what I value far more than this little triumph; approval from those friends whose verdict is valuable to me. I have had sundry letters about it this week—from Ruskin and Forster among others, strong in laudation of my clear and defiant exposition of faith.

Pardon my abuse of journalism—you know what the term implies in London as in Paris. Have you seen an American pamphlet by an Irishman (Wm. D. O'Connor) on Walt Whitman, a poet whom I introduced (in print) to Powell a short time since? The subject made it very interesting to me, as I have a great admiration for Walt Whitman and knew till now nothing of his private life and character, except that he had been dismissed from office on the same grounds which caused my book to be treacherously withdrawn for a time. It is worth your reading and *he* is well worth your study, if he has not already won it. I am sure you will thank me for an introduc-

1. Of George Butler O'Halloran almost nothing is known except that he was a friend of Powell's. According to a cutting in Powell's scrapbook, "Gleanings," in the library of University College of Wales, he gave public readings, and he composed and printed a poem (signed "Wrexham, 1st February, 1870") in memory of John Cox, bookseller, librarian, and postmaster at Aberystwyth.

tion (if you want one) to so true and great a poet, faulty and foolish as I think him now and then.

If you ever are likely to come up Londonwards, I hope we may have at least one sociable evening together and talk over this and other matters. But give me warning in case I should be as usual out of town; and believe me

Yours sincerely,
A. C. Swinburne

162. TO J. C. HOTTEN

MS: British Museum.

Holmwood,
Friday evening [November 9, 1866]

Dear Sir

You need not send any paper but the 'London'—Fraser and the rest I have. Punch I have not seen, and should like, as I always want to see attacks.[1] Moxon had the whole of Blake in second or third proofs as you will see by his accounts. The whole of Blake's 'Marriage of Heaven and Hell' must be transcribed. I will then mark the extracts. The only copy I know is Lord Houghton's. I wish you had spoken more plainly of his 'suggestion' or said nothing about it. I will say plainly that *any* suggestion made about my affairs to a third party is officious and *useless*—I take unasked advice from no one, friend or not—especially not at second hand.

Yours truly,
A. C. Swinburne

163. TO WILLIAM MICHAEL ROSSETTI

MS: Rutgers.

Holmwood, November 12 [1866]

Dear Rossetti

The 'Star' paragraph[1] which you send me is correct throughout. Conway tells me he fears there is little likelihood of my obtaining honest terms from this man Carleton,[2] under the circumstances, un-

1. "Calling a Thing by Its Right Name," *Punch* (Nov. 10), p. 189.

1. Unidentified.

2. G. W. Carleton, the New York publisher of *Laus Veneris and Other Poems and Ballads,* issued on Nov. 3. See the excerpt from his letter to Swinburne, Bonchurch, *20,* 63.

less he can make some arrangement in my name about advance sheets of the Blake. With regard to this book I wish, as Hotten may have told you, to come up and consult with you on any day you may be able to spare me a part of, that we may select at the Museum what designs we please by way of illustration: two or three I presume will suffice. I have received from Hotten the last (rough) proof of the Blake with the MS: also three corrected sheets, marked (apparently in your handwriting) with the numbers of some that seem to be wanting. Now unless I am wrong they were all revised and returned to Moxon's by me in order. Duplicates may be at my rooms, but to this I can see on coming up. I hope it will be possible to have the book out by Christmas. Please fix a day when I may come up by a morning train and call first on you at Somerset House.

Conway's short (I suspect, curtailed) notice of Whitman is very interesting and friendly—as personal in detail as the 'Good Grey Poet' which he had sent me. The latter fills me with apprehensions for the safety and prosperity of the said poet. Considering the reckless indulgence in virtue which he appears to practise, I dread that he may be doomed to afford one more example of its perils and misfortunes. 'Il a voulu faire du bien—soulager des souffrances—il doit lui être réservé quelque chose de vraiment affreux. Accomplis tes décrets, Etre Suprême.' Owing perhaps to a judicious abstinence from any such tempting of an easily tempted Providence, I have been very well since I wrote last, and unafflicted by Urizen. I have seen Fraser which is duly abject; I thought I knew the hand at first sight. Hotten refers to some abuse of me in Punch; have you seen it, and what is it like? The same H. alludes vaguely to some 'suggestion' made by Houghton to him; I have told him in terms of peremptory civility either to speak out or say nothing about hints which 'when made at second hand are equally officious and *useless.*' I wish he would send me the reviews he cites, as he promised (Scotsman, Reader, etc.); he is a 'wexagious' correspondent, as Mrs. Gamp says.[3] Above all I am athirst for your book. The price I thought sounded high for the size I expected.

Conway, Ruskin, Forster and others have written about my Notes in the strongest terms of praise. I am glad you think they have told. I saw R.B. the second in the Asinaeum;[4] he seems to have attempted a combination of Charles Reade's style with mine, to no great purpose.

Yours affectionately,
A. C. Swinburne

3. *Martin Chuzzlewit,* chap. 46.

4. Buchanan's review of *Notes on Poems and Reviews* in the *Athenaeum* (Nov. 3), pp. 564–65.

164. TO GEORGE POWELL

MS: National Library of Wales. Brief extracts in Bonchurch, *19*, 149–50, and in Lafourcade, *La Jeunesse, 1,* 241 n.

22a Dorset Street, November 21 [1866]

My dear Powell

Many thanks for your present (which is now awaiting me at Holmwood) and for your note which preceded it. My mother is well again, and all my people are coming up to town this week for ten days or so, after which they and I with them mean to return to Holmwood for the Christmas season. They join me in hoping you will be able to accept our invitation either before or after this sacred season; and you must know how glad we should all be to see you. With regard to your parent I think you are right to abjure his grounds until the day when he shall relieve them and the world of his benignant presence.

A lady at Florence has written a poem about me and my critics in which it is stated that the seven leading angels of heaven are now occupied in singing my praises before God and returning thanks to him for my existence. This is cheerful to know, and gives one heart to resist even your attack upon my late proceedings. I quite agree that usually any such notice of attacks is undesirable; but here and now it was inevitable. I must send you, if you have not seen it, my friend W. M. Rossetti's essay on my works. Remind O'Halloran (with best remembrances) that he has not yet sent his promised article. I want to shew you the report of my speech at the Literary Fund Dinner,[1] which is very queer to read, seeing what rows I have got into since. I have gone through five editions in as many days in America; a sterile success which brings much clamour and no profit with it. Excuse this egotistic scrawl and believe me always

Yours affectionately,
A. C. Swinburne

165. TO GEORGE POWELL

MS: National Library of Wales. One sentence in Bonchurch, *19*, 150.

22a Dorset Street, W., November 29, 1866

My dear Powell

I am sorry this infernal weather upsets you as it does most people. Come and see us with the New Year, which will not be welcomer. (To the average Briton I should have to add a reminder that the N.Y. was

---

1. *The Royal Literary Fund. Report of the Anniversary* (1866), p. 27. See above, Letter 110.

always a festival.) I send you by way of stimulant my copy of my notes on Byron, as you said you had not seen them. Remind O'Halloran, with best remembrances, that he promised me a reply in print to my notes on another than Byron, which I have not yet received.

I have been doing more verses on Italia [1] (excuse—I *can't* spell it Englishwise) which some people think as good at least as my best things. Of course as a fanatic I can't judge—and it looks to me simply flat and inadequate; but I think the verses are good *for me* however bad they may be for her. (I mean *it*.)

Write me word what you think of my Byron. I shall be here a week or so, but either this or the Holmwood address can never fail of me. You should come and see the pictures in London this winter—there are *some* beauties.

Always yours affectionately,
A. C. Swinburne

P.S. As to your father, forget his existence—especially during an English November. It is clear to me that Uncle Silas [2] was a comparatively desirable relative. Certainly during his too long life I think in your place I would *not* set foot in grounds which are his—until they become yours and regain their native attraction. If you could come up for (a day or two if you like) a week or so to London just now I think I might return your hospitality by finding you houseroom and attendance. Do, if you can, come for three days and run about with me to studios and places.

A. C. Swinburne

166. TO GEORGE POWELL

MS: National Library of Wales. One sentence in Lafourcade, *Biography*, p. 183.

22a Dorset Street, W., December 12 [1866]

My dear Powell

How shall I thank you enough for the inestimable autograph? [1] I should have written before but have been bedridden or helpless upwards of a week with another of those damned bilious attacks which

1. *A Song of Italy*. The manuscript, dated at the beginning "*Nov.* 14, '66," is titled "Italia" (see Bonchurch, *20*, 78).

2. See above, Letter 115.

1. Probably Sade's (see below, Letter 167). Scott wrote to Sir Walter Trevelyan on Dec. 3: "Algernon Swinburne is now in town again, and as far as I have seen has given up the peculiarities of speech and action that frightened his friends, and

prove the malevolence of the Deity, and his ability to excel in ingenious cruelty that illustrious work of his hands, the Marquis de Sade. You will see the poem of mine of which you heard part at Aberystwith in the January number of the Fortnightly Review.[2] What is the subject or purport of your new Sadique epistle?

Best regards to yourself and to O'Halloran from

My dear Powell
Yours most sincerely,
A. C. Swinburne

167. TO GEORGE POWELL

MS: National Library of Wales.

Holmwood, December 26 [1866]

My dear Powell

When your last note reached me in London I was still too ill to write without exertion, or I should have written earlier. I am all right now and live in hopes of seeing you in January, if you can manage it among your manifold engagements. I hope it will be in January as you will then meet my brother [1] whom I want you to meet because he is passionate for music and your example would not be lost on him. My art is at a discount here, but yours idolized; you could Schumannize and Wagnerize among us to some purpose. Remember that we hold you engaged. I will give you samples of the autographs you want in plenty. Meantime accept my thanks for the beautiful agates

---

quite as much as his poems themselves, brought down upon his book so much criticism. He has republished it by Hotten and some remarkably able articles in Fraser's Mag. and elsewhere have taken up his defence. William Rossetti has published a criticism as a small volume, a copy of which he tells me he has sent you. I think you will consider it well done, and without blinking the questions involved, treats Algernon in the friendliest spirit. On the whole Swinburne seems to have overcome his opponents, and all we who consider his poetic powers so highly are exceedingly desirous of seeing him recover himself, drop certain things and take his place his place [*sic*] as a poet" (Trevelyan Papers, Wallington). Boyce, on the other hand, recorded in his Diary on Dec. 14: "Dined at D.G.R.'s. Fred Burton, Sandys, Jekyll, Howell, Gagley, Jimmy Whistler and brother, Swinburne and Ormesby. Left with the 2 last. O. and I saw S. who was rather drunk, safely into a cab at Pimlico."

2. "Child's Song in Winter," reprinted as "Winter in Northumberland" (Bonchurch, *3*, 105–13) in *PB2*.

1. Edward Swinburne (1848–91).

which have lain here waiting for me, as I expected to leave London earlier: the larger is the most exquisite and 'oceanic' in colour I have seen. Mr. Magnusson left a card on me, it seems an hour or two only before I started hitherwards, when I must have been out or laid up —for indeed I got out of bed to travel. Will you tell him when occasion offers how vexed I was to miss him? De Sade's second letter is very curious. Thanks for the transcript. His spelling is invariably bad. My copy of his monstrous offspring is still in the hands of an Eton friend, who having been incessantly whipped during the rosy years of boyhood—rosy in bottom as in face—takes, I fear, a voluptuous interest in the Titanic flagellations which crown its pages. I send this to Aberystwith as I suppose they have your direction and am ever

Yours most faithfully,

A. C. Swinburne

168. TO WILLIAM MICHAEL ROSSETTI

MS: Rutgers. Brief extract in Lafourcade, *La Jeunesse*, 2, 473.

Holmwood, December 26 [1866]
+ *Postrid: Nat: Dom:* + [1]

Dear Rossetti

I am going to begin instead of leaving off colla bocca dolce.[2] My father and mother desire me to ask if you could not come down to us for a few days? it would give them such a real pleasure if you could. It's not an hour and a half from London to the house here. If you haven't time at this sacred season, what *is* the use of the Galilean festival? The longer the better, but one day would be better than nothing, if only to make friends. I would meet you at the Reading station at any time you liked; there are plenty of trains.

As to Payne I have written in full to Hotten, saying I think *he* should be the first mover.[3] Notice of course must be taken: but, as proprietor of the edition whence these copies are stolen, he, being the immediately injured and defrauded person, would reclaim his property with a better grace than I should have in coming forward to enter the lists of publicity against a knavish tradesman. They might say I had begun complaining of Moxon's hard wage, and that I

1. "The day after the birth of Our Lord."

2. "With fair words."

3. Rossetti, learning that Payne was clandestinely selling copies of *PB1*, had sent the news to Swinburne four days earlier (see *A Swinburne Library*, pp. 27–28, and *Rossetti Papers*, pp. 199–200).

should not like. Come, and let us talk over these and pleasanter matters tête à tête and at once. And if you can, please bring me from Hotten's two copies of my P. and B., I have none left; and pray remind him to see that not a copy goes forth with the 'bowers' misprint on the first page. Tell him I found one such to my horror on the railway stall at Reading.

I hope the Incorruptible came duly to hand and gave satisfaction.

I spent part of last evening in writing (part of my poem on Italy) a funeral paean in praise of Milano, Orsini (especially), and tyrannicide in general—without reference to the 'King of the Jews.' I want you to hear my additions to this poem, which is not done yet.

With renewed and earnest invitations (your coming would be a great pleasure to all, and to me, you know how great).

Ever yours,
A. C. Swinburne

169. TO R. H. STODDARD

MS: Berg Collection, New York Public Library.

Holmwood, Henley on Thames,
January 1, 1867

My dear Sir

I begin the first day of this new year by writing to thank you and excuse myself. I should have answered your last letter and Mrs. Stoddard's very kind and flattering enclosure long since, but that while in London for the last month or so I have had as little health as leisure. Now having plenty of both I can only beg you to accept this note in part discharge of my debt. I am much obliged by your able and friendly defence and much amused by the attack which evoked it. I am by this time case-hardened, and (to borrow Thackeray's favourite and effective metaphor) am mentally in the same condition as the skin of a public schoolboy after the twentieth or thirtieth application of the birch—too well used to it for any cut of a master's rod to make the tough hide wince. MM. the critics must pick out a smaller boy if they want to make him cry. Considering that about ten or eleven years since I was a public schoolboy myself, I am especially delighted with the passage which proclaims me 'no longer a young man.' Age must be rapid in America if men between twenty and thirty are counted as past youth. The singer 'Sordello' [1] (!) may

1. Swinburne had been attacked by "Sordello" in the New York *Evening Post*, and on Dec. 11 Stoddard had replied in his defense. (See C. K. Hyder, *Swinburne's Literary Career and Fame*, p. 282.)

satisfy himself on that score; for as to my years, are they not numbered in the pages of the Garter King at Arms—or (again to quote Thackeray) [2] 'the British Snob's Bible'? I have so often been regarded as a youngster and 'boyed' like Coriolanus in Antium [3] that it is a relief to find there is one person who believes in my maturity on internal evidence. I had the pleasure before leaving London to meet Mr. Lorimer Graham,[4] who did me the honour to call at my chambers. I hope on his return from Paris, whither he was then bound, to extend our acquaintance. Through his means I discovered, what ought to be made public, that Messrs. Moxon, after violating their agreement to sell my Poems (which of course they had seen both in MS and type)—after their bill of printer's charges etc. had been paid in full (N.B. I never sold them a single copy and never received from them a single penny on account)—after advertising in all the literary papers that they had withdrawn the book and had nothing to do with it—after professedly delivering over to me or my agents, on legal application and payment of their whole demand, the entire unsold edition—are now secretly selling copies withheld or rather stolen at one guinea each: books which are no more their property than the clothes I wear. After this it will hardly surprise you to hear that the same respectable publisher, under pretence of not knowing my address, refused to forward letters and parcels sent to me from America, which were transferred to the Dead Letter Office, and only reached me, in time, circuitously and accidentally. Theft and lying, in short, have throughout this matter distinguished the dealings of this most respectable firm; nor, to my knowledge, is the case a singular one. I have been asked to show it up in the newspapers; but that is not in my line. My present publisher, having bought the edition

2. *The Book of Snobs*, chaps. 3, 6.

3. *Coriolanus*, V. vi. 100 (at Corioles, however, not Antium).

4. James Lorimer Graham (1835–76), American dilettante. He spent 1862–63 in Europe, and after three years or so in New York returned to Europe in 1866. In 1869 he was appointed U.S. consul-general for Italy and became part of the colony of English-speaking expatriates in Florence, remaining there rather than following the government and his office to Rome. William Rossetti, calling him the "Yankee millionaire," first brought him and the new Moxon fray to Swinburne's attention in a letter on Dec. 22 (*A Swinburne Library*, pp. 27–28). Their friendship appears to have been fairly close. Graham's library, now in the Century Association in New York, contained five volumes inscribed by Swinburne, and after Graham's death in Florence, Apr. 30, 1876, Swinburne composed an "Epicede" (Bonchurch, *3*, 66–67) to his memory—published in the *Athenaeum* (June 10, 1876) and reprinted in *PB2*.

of me, has been directly robbed and his pocket picked of these furtive guineas; and I have told him it is for him, if he pleases, to move in the matter and call as witnesses Mr. Graham and myself, who have both volunteered our evidence in writing.

Excuse the length and egotism of this paragraph, but I thought the matter worth your knowing, that in case any one of your acquaintance should think of dealing with Moxon's you might be able on good authority to warn them of the certain, the inevitable swindle that would ensue.

It would give me the greatest pleasure could I hope to meet either Mrs. Stoddard or yourself in London or Paris. I have long dreamt of going to America, but other calls, and above all the 'strenua inertia'[5] proverbial among our kind, detain me as yet. If you know Mr. Grant White may I ask you to convey to him my best thanks for his review [6] and for the note which he sent to me with it? These were among the papers diverted from their address by the Moxons out of pure lying spite, which reached me at last together with a poem by Mr. Bayard Taylor [7] which he was good enough to send me. I want to thank all my friends at once and excuse myself for a tardiness which was no fault of mine. You may care to know that a lyric of mine is appearing (I have not seen it out yet) in the Fortnightly Review. I am now writing a hymn of triumph for Italy.

Ever yours sincerely,
A. C. Swinburne

170. TO J. C. HOTTEN

MS: Yale.

Holmwood, January 2, 1867

Dear Sir

I was somewhat surprised at receiving the enclosed instead of any answer from yourself. I must refer you to my last letter, and request that you will inform Messrs. Dalston and Son [1] that I have nothing to do with the matter in question.[2] I have set on foot no proceedings,

5. "Energetic idleness" (Horace, *Epodes* 1.6.28).

6. Richard Grant White (1821–85), whose review appeared in the *Galaxy* (Dec. 1, 1866), was a critic and a famous editor of Shakespeare.

7. See below, Letter 185.

1. J. N. Dalston and Son, solicitors in Piccadilly.

2. See above, Letter 168.

nor shall I do so. It lies between yourself and Moxon. You will of
course do as you think fit. I should advise you to secure the missing
copies, *and above all else the full proofs of Blake,* and drop the matter. As for me, I beg I may hear no more about it. My arrangement
with you is clear and satisfactory, and with Moxon's I have no more to
do.

I shall be obliged if you will send me two copies of my Poems
(corrected—I saw at Reading station a copy for sale with the hideous
misprint 'bowers' for 'hours'—*pray* let no others get abroad, as nothing could more annoy me) and one of my 'Notes.' I want to send them
to Capt. Burton [3] in Brazil. Can you give me an idea of the cost of
postage? I should be further obliged if you could get me a copy of the
Fortnightly (January) and one of Théophile Gautier's book—Les
Grotesques—one franc, Michel Lévy; a common book, but I have
mislaid my copy, and want it for immediate use.

Yours very truly,
A. C. Swinburne

J. C. Hotten, Esq.

P.S. Please send me *at once* the January number of a Cambridge
Magazine called 'the Light Blue' containing an article on my Poems.[4]

ACS

171. TO C. W. ADAMS [1]

MS: Rutgers.

Holmwood, Henley on Thames.
January 4, 1867

Private

Dear Sir

My personal experience of the courtesy, veracity, and general
trustworthiness of the firm called Moxon and Co. tallies so well with
your own that I am not surprised even at the correspondance you for-

---

3. See below, Letter 174.

4. "Mr. Swinburne and His Poetry," in the *Light Blue* (Jan. 1867), pp. 10–15, signed
"Hal, Caius Coll., C. G., Trin. Coll." The latter was Carleton Greene (1844–1924),
who later became an Anglican priest.

1. C. Warren Adams, editor of the *Church and State Review,* author of *Ronald
Vaughan* (1856), a novel, and of *Queen Jane* (1874), a verse-tragedy in five acts. (I owe
the identification to John S. Mayfield, whose collection includes a letter from Adams
to Hotten, dated Jan. 2, 1867.) Adams owned the firm of Saunders & Otley.

ward to me. I can only say that upon such evidence as they offer I would not condemn a dog, much less mistrust a man. All I remember of the matter is that Payne (I think) once mentioned to me your review as not having then received a copy, and asked for my instructions on that score. Of course I desired that a copy should be sent, and received a promise to that effect. Of course also I cannot say whether it was ever carried out, nor do I expect to receive any proof of a convincing kind. This of course was before the breach of faith which induced me at once to have all outstanding printer's bills etc. discharged, and to withdraw from the hands of that firm all books of mine—except, as I now find, the copies of a book which was not their property furtively detained and furtively disposed of.

As, in spite of advice to the contrary, I have determined to take no legal notice of this fraud, and to adhere to my resolution to hold no communication whatever with Moxon and Co., I need not say that I should not willingly be brought forward in this matter or mixed up in any way with anything that concerned them.

Sincerely regretting that the misuse of my name should have been made the means of exposing you to the impertinence habitual to such persons

I am Dear Sir
Yours faithfully,
Algernon Ch. Swinburne

C. W. Adams, Esq.

172. TO WILLIAM MICHAEL ROSSETTI

MS: Rutgers.

Holmwood, January 4 [1867]

Dear Rossetti

We shall be delighted to see you on the twelfth (U.V.)[1] and only wish you could stay a little longer if only to explore the curiosities of the library, which will I think interest you. We have been snowed up here as well as you in London, and unable to get to and fro, but the twilight and frost make fine weather of it by day, though this morning we were down to five degrees.

I hope your first volume of essays on art[2] will be duly followed up

1. Urizen volente. Rossetti went on the 12th and returned on the 14th (see *Rossetti Papers*, pp. 220–21).

2. *Fine Art, Chiefly Contemporary* (1867).

by others. Meantime I look forward to seeing this one. I daresay before the advent of *our* Blake.

I saw the Reader [3] last week; it is well that the mask of eighteen centuries should be torn from 'the triple tyrant,' [4] but I dread anti-theism being vulgarized in the hands of weaker brethren. I feel rather as Voltaire might have felt, could the author of Candide have foreseen the advent of his 'enfant terrible,' the author of Justine. (Speaking of Urizen, do you know Servetus' name for the Most Holy Trinity? *Cerberus*. No wonder Calvin burnt him.)

There is a train (only one convenient) about the time you name—3.40 from Paddington to *Shiplake,* where you will find me waiting. My mother thinks the Reading road will probably be still (as now) almost impassable or at least unsafe for the horses. Shiplake is the nearest station and the road is not so steep.

Don't trouble yourself to see Hotten. I have written all I had to say to him.

Ever yours,
A. C. Swinburne

173. TO J. C. HOTTEN

MS: Huntington Library.

January 6 [1867]

Dear Sir

You can hardly have looked at the proofs you send, or you would have seen that they are identical with those sent in the autumn, corrected, and returned. Not one misprint has been corrected, not one omission supplied, by the printers. At this rate we may go on for ever. You must get printers who know their work and attend to corrections. I have no time to waste in doing the same drudgery three or four times over. You have sent me so much waste paper: until the MS. of the part treating of the 'Heaven and Hell' is in type (slip 81) how can I point out what citations are to come in, and where. Again—have you got all the proofs (revised as they were by me) up to *p.* 97? and where are the corrected proofs from *slip* 92–107? Stereotype is right; whether Blake used the word accurately I do not know.

In the last proof I returned, full directions were given for all insertions and alterations. If you refer to it and desire the printers to abide by it there will be no more trouble as regards this part.

3. "The Church of England," *Reader* (Dec. 30, 1865), pp. 729–30 (unsigned).

4. Milton, "On the Late Massacre in Piemont," l. 12.

Have you secured the 75 copies of the Poems of which Mr. Dalston speaks? If so, as he says legal redress is unattainable (I presume you read his letter to me?), it would be waste of time to take any steps in the matter—for me at least; you of course will decide for yourself. Let me have the Cambridge Magazine as soon as you can.

Yours truly,
A. C. Swinburne

174. TO RICHARD F. BURTON [1]

Text: Bonchurch, *18*, 47–49*.

Holmwood, Henley-on-Thames,
January 11, 1867

My dear Burton

I was within an ace of losing your letter altogether, and only recovered it from the Dead Letter Office by accident—or rather by the intervention of that all-wise and beneficent Providence which regulates all sublunary things. You may know perhaps that Messrs. Moxon & Co., to whom it was addressed, tried to swamp my book by withdrawing it from circulation when the storm of warm water began to seethe and rage in the British tea-kettle, trusting that in British eyes their fraudulent breach of contract would be justified by the plea of virtuous abhorrence. Of course I withdrew all my books from their hands, and declined any further dealings with such a den of thieves. Consequently these denizens of the Cities of the Plain,[2] whose fathers somehow escaped with Lot and his respectable family, pretended ignorance of my address (which, as well as my present publishers, they knew well enough the day before), and dismissed a whole heap of letters, papers, and books sent me from America to the Dead Letter

1. Sir Richard Francis Burton (1821–90) and Swinburne first met, at one of Milnes's stag breakfasts, on June 5, 1861, and it requires no imagination at all to understand how the virile bawdry and swagger of this cultured latter-day Elizabethan must have mesmerized the young Swinburne, sixteen years his junior. Even a lesser egotist than Burton would have found Swinburne's admiring appreciation irresistible. Swinburne told Arthur Symons (*Dramatis Personae*, Indianapolis, 1923, p. 244) that they "had taken . . . a curious fancy, an absolute fascination, for each other," and Luke Ionides recalled, or so he said (*Transatlantic Review*, Mar. 1924, p. 24), having once seen Burton "walk downstairs carrying Swinburne under his arm; after putting him down on the pavement he called a hansom. Swinburne could not find the step and complained that 'hansoms were getting their steps higher and higher each year.'" (See also Pope-Hennessy, pp. 122–26, 132–34.)

2. See Genesis 19 and Matthew 21:13 (etc.).

Office. But for this you would have heard from me long ago, and received the book and pamphlet I now send you. You would have had them long before if I had had your address.

I am very glad you like my swallow song,[3] as I do your version of the Rondinella as far as given. I am still the centre of such a moral chaos that our excellent friend Houghton maintains a discreet and consistent neutrality, except that he wrote me a letter thoroughly approving and applauding the move taken; but I have not set eyes on his revered form for months. Your impending opulence, and my immediate infamy, will too evidently cut us from the shelter of his bosom. I wish you had been at hand or within reach this year, to see the missives I got from nameless quarters. One anonymous letter [4] from Dublin threatened me, if I did not suppress my book within six weeks from that date, with castration. The writer, 'when I least expected, would waylay me, slip my head in a bag, and remove the obnoxious organs; he had seen his gamekeeper do it with cats.' This is verbatim, though quoted from memory, as I bestowed the document on a friend who collects curiosities. I beg to add that my unoffending person is as yet no worse than it was. This was the greatest spree of all; but I have had letters and notices sent me (American and British) by the score, which were only less comic whether they come from friend or foe.

I hope we shall have you back before '69, not only for the cellar's sake, sublime as that 'realised ideal' is certain to be. I have in hand a scheme of mixed verse and prose—a sort of étude à la Balzac *plus* the poetry [5]—which I flatter myself will be more offensive and objectionable to Britannia than anything I have yet done. You see I have now a character to keep up, and by the grace of Cotytto I will endeavour not to come short of it—at least in my writings. Tell me, if you have time, what you think of *Dolores* and *Anactoria* [6] in full print.

I hope you will prevail on Mrs. Burton to forgive the use made in the former poem of the B.V.U.,[7] whose son I saw the other day

3. "Itylus" (Bonchurch, *1*, 187–89), in *PB1*. The "Rondinella" is unidentified.

4. See above, Letters 127 and 128.

5. *Lesbia Brandon.*

6. (Bonchurch, *1*, 190–99), in *PB1*.

7. Not clear—"Blessed Virgin Urizen" being unacceptable. Perhaps he wrote "B.V.M." Mrs. (afterwards Lady) Burton (1831–96), born Isabel Arundell, a Roman Catholic, took her religion even more seriously than she took herself.

mentioned in a tract by a Rabbinical Atheist as 'Joshua ben Joseph.'
I wish I could run over to '5 o'clock tea,' but can only send remembrances to you both, and hope you will not have forgotten me when you return to this 'plaisant pays.'

Toujours à vous,
A. C. Swinburne

175. TO CHARLES AUGUSTUS HOWELL

MS: British Museum. Published: Bonchurch, *18*, 50*.

Arts Club, Hanover Square,
January 15 [1867]

My dear Howell

Can you come with Wm. Rossetti and me to the museum tomorrow at twelve to select from Blake's work there the engravings for my book? Hotten is to meet us there. If you can't or don't care to come, look me up (giving notice) some day this week.[1]

I am up only for a few days about this Blake business, and I want to see you, it is ages since I did, and I hear you have been seedy, which is wrong, and mène à tout.

Your affectionate,
A. C. Swinburne

176. TO GEORGE POWELL

MS: National Library of Wales.

Holmwood, Saturday [?January 26, 1867]

My dear Powell

Come either Wednesday or Thursday and we shall be delighted to see you, but say which day, as you named both. Come by the 3.40 train to Shiplake in a *Henley* carriage (the others go on) and the carriage (non-railway) will be waiting for you at the station.

Ever yours,
A. C. Swinburne

1. Howell evidently defaulted, for he is not mentioned in William Rossetti's diary notice of the visit (see *Rossetti Papers*, p. 221).

177. TO GEORGE POWELL

MS: National Library of Wales.

Holmwood, January 31 [1867]

My dear Powell

Come on Monday by all means and be welcome on all hands. I was beginning to wonder whither you could have flown. Remember the 3.40 to Shiplake.

> Ever yours,
> (now in haste),
> A. C. Swinburne

178. TO GEORGE POWELL

MS: National Library of Wales.

Holmwood, Friday [February 8, 1867]

My dear Powell

Many thanks on all our parts for the music, which has given my sisters great pleasure. My mother will be much obliged if you will pay the subscription for three months in her name, that being just a guinea. She sends the enclosed prescription as promised. I hope you are all right and have had no returns of tic. Thanks for your message from Hotten. If you have occasion, will you tell him to send *last* week's Saturday Review, which has an article on G. Meredith's *Vittoria* that I want to see?

> Ever yours sincerely,
> A. C. Swinburne

179. TO J. C. HOTTEN

MS: British Museum.

Holmwood, February 18 [?1867] [1]

Dear Sir

You must really speak to the people you employ to send papers. If I cannot be supplied regularly with what I want, I had rather be told so. This is the *third* week since I left town—and now at last I receive, *not* The Saturday Review and Spectator of yesterday—but a

---

1. "The Saturday Review . . . of yesterday" suggests that Feb. 18 (which in 1867 fell on Monday) was on a Sunday, but the eligible years (1866, 1872, and 1877) in this case can all be ruled out.

set of *old* weekly papers, some three weeks old—Athenaeums (which I didn't order) and so on. Now I can be much better served if necessary at the next town. You also send me *duplicates* of Trollope's last numbers [2] which I have received already in regular order. This is a waste of time, money, and patience. Pray give them a good 'rowing' and let me know if I am to expect things *regularly* henceforward.

Yours truly,
A. C. Swinburne

180. TO WILLIAM MICHAEL ROSSETTI

MS: Rutgers. Brief extracts in Lafourcade, *La Jeunesse*, 2, 358 n., 473.

Holmwood, February 20 [1] [1867]

Dear Rossetti

I should be of course delighted to be of any use to you, but I have not a guess at Bendyshe's address (unless it be Poste Restante, Malebolge, care of Sig. Vanni Fucci [2] which might perplex the Postmaster General) nor do I know how to get it, having never had any correspondance with him. Qu. would Hotten know? I will keep your note by me in case. But anyhow you have surely more than satisfied

2. *The Last Chronicle of Barset* was issued in weekly parts from Dec. 1, 1866, to July 6, 1867 (see below, Letter 181).

1. To the unpracticed eye the zero in "20" looks like (and may be) "8," but Swinburne's "8s" are almost always distinctive and, in addition, the latter date is improbable (see below, Letter 181).

2. Dante's *Inferno*, xxiv.125. Thomas Bendyshe (1827–86), though little is known about him, holds his own in the glittering pageantry of Swinburne's friendships, even in competition with personalities as flashing as Gabriel Rossetti, Houghton, Burton, Sala, and Howell. The fourth son in an old and distinguished family, he attended Eton and King's College, Cambridge, becoming a fellow in 1848 and a senior fellow in 1868. In 1865 he was expelled from the Conservative Club for supporting J. S. Mill in the Westminster election, and in the same year purchased the *Reader*, a star-crossed weekly called by Walter Graham (*English Literary Periodicals*, New York, 1930, p. 331) "one of the finest literary journals of the nineteenth century." Vice-President of the Anthropological Society of London, he translated and edited ("from the Latin, German, and French originals") *The Anthropological Treatises of Johann Friedrich Blumenbach* (1865), and William Rossetti wrote (*Rossetti Papers*, p. 380) in 1869 that Swinburne was enthusiastic about the "*Mâhabhârata,* which he has been looking at in a French translation under the auspices of Bendyshe." He was a member of the Cannibal Club (see below, Letter 250), was aggressively atheistic, and was a notoriously strong-minded and (apparently) unpopular senior fellow of King's (see William Austen Leigh, ed., *Augustus Austen Leigh, Provost of King's College, Cambridge*, 1906, pp. 95–107, 112–13).

all demands of courtesy by writing to the address of the dear defunct journal,[3] and might at once make use of your own—I am sure I should.

I hardly like to ask you to take so much trouble—but perhaps if you or if Howell (as he has seen the things about and knows my *chaos*) could do it, it might save me a journey—as to look over the scattered proofs of the Blake in my rooms (none are locked up or put away, I know) and see if *slips* (not sheets) H,I,K, are to be found corrected—Hotten says they are missing—and whether found or not, tell him to get the book complete in sheets as soon as possible.[4] It has been *twice* revised (with additional notes) and ought to be all right if trouble and bother can make it. Perhaps you could find time to help me in looking it over. I have added from an anonymous source a note on Theism [5] which is not yet in type: I expect it will make Urizen tremble in his bottes éculées à la Robert Macaire!

I have nearly finished my Italian poem [6] with a sort of hymn from all the cities severally to Mazzini which I think you will like. I am glad to see by the papers that Scotus's Deluge sold for £125 the first day of exhibition in Edinburgh—not that it is much but I suppose the fact will please him.

I am very sorry you have had a loss in your family.[7] With best remembrances from mine and me

Ever yours,
A. C. Swinburne

181. TO J. C. HOTTEN

MS: British Museum. Printed: *The Ashley Library, A Catalogue, 6* (1925), 76.

Holmwood, February 22 [1867]

Dear Sir

I send you all the proofs I have by me revised in full, with one or two alterations and additions. The slips 82–90 I cannot correct *again*

3. The *Reader,* which expired after three and a half years of life, in July 1866.

4. On Feb. 22 William Rossetti "Called on Hotten relative to the proofs of Swinburne's *Blake,* which are in some muddle" (*Rossetti Papers,* p. 224).

5. Described (Bonchurch, *16,* 202 n.–204 n.) in *William Blake* as a "fragment or 'excursus' on a lay sermon by a modern pagan philosopher"—who was first identified as Sade by Lafourcade, *La Jeunesse, 2,* 354–56.

6. *A Song of Italy*.

7. Rossetti's aunt, Margaret Polidori, died on Feb. 8.

without either the missing revise or my own MS, neither of which is by me. The rest of the book is all right. When the missing parts are supplied I should like to see the book throughout in sheets (up to slip 80 I did see it revised, and sent it back to Moxon's—whose delays are the cause of all the trouble, combined with the want of a copy of the 'Heaven and Hell') to compare with the slips, which the printers must return to me. (You may as well keep this note for reference.) When I am in town (in ten days or so) I will look up the loose sheets of my MS. if they are not sent me by a friend. I wish to have the *latter* part of the book (as was done in the 'Life of Blake') paged on one side 'William Blake' and on the other headed with the name of the work treated of. I am glad you are getting on with the illustrative work.

Can you get me the 'Round Table' of January 5th either as a loan or a purchase, I don't care? and a later number in which it seems they announced a new poem of mine,[1] which I for one never heard of? I should like too, if accessible, to see in full the San Francisco article from which there were extracts given in 'Public Opinion.'[2]

Please send me as early copies as possible of the Cornhill, Macmillan, and Fortnightly Review for March. I suppose they will all be out on Tuesday.

N.B. Last week again I got a *second* copy of Trollope's last number of 'Barset'[3]—and as I only ordered it of you it must be some blunder of your people's. One copy came quite right on Saturday morning, as it ought and as I expect it tomorrow, and another late on Monday of the same, which is pure waste and carelessness. I have not used and don't want the duplicates; they can be sent back if you like.

Yours truly,

A. C. Swinburne

P.S. There is no need for an index, I think; there are but three divisions of the book to mark. If Mr. Howell is in town I think he will be able to procure the rest of Blake as he knows the owner, and I do not. I have no doubt he will, if you apply to him.

1. "According to the *Round Table,* Mr. Algernon Charles Swinburne has written a Hymn of Praise for Italy, which, we believe, has not yet been published" (*Public Opinion,* Feb. 9, 1867, p. 165). See below, Letter 358.

2. Not traced.

3. See above, Letter 179.

182. TO WILLIAM MICHAEL ROSSETTI

MS: Rutgers.

Holmwood, February 22 [1867]

Dear Rossetti

I have sent on (or rather am sending by this day's post) your note to Bendyshe. Hotten tells me the 'fac-similist's' work for Blake goes on well; perhaps some day in passing you would have leisure to ask for a sight of it and give sentence, for I told him I must have it resubmitted to you or Gabriel first for judgment. Many thanks about the proofs, there is a note missing which I cannot supply without either this revise or the MS. at hand—and neither are within reach. My Italian poem is completed at last, and thought well of by others than me. I hope the troubles in the South will not take a dangerous turn. I should have all hopes of a present revolution and republic if there were no chance of a second French intervention. What we want is a successful Orsini,[1] to plunge France into a Medea's caldron of life-restoring troubles and ferments.

I should be really obliged if you could without too much trouble procure and forward me the Pall Mall number of Monday last which you tell me of; also, if discoverable, that containing their review some fortnight since of Meredith's Vittoria.[2]

Ever yours,
A. C. Swinburne

183. TO GEORGE POWELL

MS: National Library of Wales.

Holmwood, February 22 [1867]

My dear Powell

My mother and sisters desire me to send you their best thanks for the music which is bearing fruit and giving pleasure on all hands—also for the receipt. Don't leave London just yet. I shall be up in a week or so and we might go about and see people. I write on the chance that you may not have left, knowing how delusive are the engagements of men and lawyers. You may congratulate me on the completion of my Italian poem, and believe me

Ever yours sincerely,
A. C. Swinburne

1. See below, Letter 194.

2. Jan. 25, 1867, pp. 10–11.

184. GEORGE MEREDITH TO SWINBURNE

Text: W. M. Meredith, ed., *Letters of George Meredith, 1,* 188–90.

Kingston Lodge, Kingston-on-Thames,
March 2, 1867

My dear Swinburne

I have waited to read the Ode,[1] and also to ship off my Arthur for Switzerland. The Ode is the most nobly sustained lyric in our language, worthy of its theme. Broader, fuller verse I do not know. I had a glance at the proofs, and my chief sentiment was envy. Now I can read without that affliction. For me there will never be time given even to try the rising to such a song. I am passionately anxious to see the 'Italy' and have a thousand spirits of fancy about it. Let me know when you return to town, and when you will come and pay us a visit. I need not say that my wife will be glad to see you. Has she not fought your battles? I was in Austria when the heat of the storm was raging. I returned from Italy in the winter after all was over. It would not have been my advice to you to notice the reviewers: but it is certainly better never to keep red-hot shot in store, and perhaps one broadside in reply does no harm. I wish rather that it had been done in verse. As for the hubbub, it will do you no harm, and you have partly deserved it; and it has done the critical world good by making men look boldly at the restrictions imposed upon art by our dominating damnable bourgeoisie.—'Vittoria' passes to the limbo where the rest of my works repose. You alone have hit on the episode of the Guidascarpi. I have not heard or seen another mention of it. I would have carried it into fulness, but the vast machinery pressed on me. My object was not to write the Epic of the Revolt—for that the time is yet too new: but to represent the revolt itself, with the passions animating both sides, the revival of the fervid Italian blood; and the character of the people: Luigi Suracco, Barto Rizzo, etc. Agostino Balderini is purposely made sententious and humorously conscious of it: Carlo Ammiani is the personification of the youth of Italy of the nobler sort. Laura Piaveni and Violetta d'Isorella are existing contrasts. —I am afraid it must be true that the style is stiff; but a less condensed would not have compassed the great amount of matter. —I see the illustrious Hutton of the 'Spectator' laughs insanely at my futile effort to produce an impression on his public. I suppose I shall have to give up and take to journalism, as I am now partly doing. —Yes! if you could get a place to say something of 'Vittoria'! Morley stated your suggestions to me, and appeared willing that it should be done in the 'Fort-

1. "On the Insurrection in Candia" (see below, Letter 185).

nightly,' if your, or some such good name fathered the article. But his opinion is that it should be a general review of me: the writer could dwell on the work pleasing him best. There is some doubt about giving a special review of a novel that has appeared in the 'Fortnightly' pages. Adieu, my friend. I beg you to write to me, as I have requested. Arthur is away, by this time in Berne. What is the address of Sandys? I do not see him at the Garrick. —I want you to bring Baudelaire when you come; and anything you may think of besides, in the way of verse. I am being carried off from the Singing. I stand on an inexorable current. I shall look forward to meeting you with great pleasure.

Your faithful and affectionate,
George Meredith

185. TO BAYARD TAYLOR [1]

MS: John S. Mayfield.

22a Dorset Street, Portman Square, W.,
March 18, 1867

My dear Taylor

I begin without ceremony to tell you that you cannot regret more than I do that our intercourse should have been this first time so brief and broken. I hope next time will atone for the shortcomings of this. To have had your intimacy was a great pleasure and interest, and it is a greater to be assured it is not to pass over, and to know the nature of your feelings towards me. There are few indeed about me whose friendship could take a form so gratifying—I would have said so flattering, but the word is hateful. I assure you that I prize the possession of your letter and the recollection of your society alike and most highly.

I wish indeed [in] this Siberia, this exile's Lapland, for my chosen Mother Italy, but I do not see my way to the time or (in fact) the funds sufficient for the full and free enjoyment of change of landmark yet. I

1. (1825–78), traveler, translator of *Faust*, poet, novelist, and dramatist. His own account of this brief acquaintance with Swinburne is fairly cold-blooded, and his letter on the subject to E. C. Stedman (see below, Letter 186) is extraordinary. On Mar. 19 Taylor wrote from Gotha, his wife's home, to J. G. Whittier: "Swinburne is a reproduction of Shelley, of imagination all compact, frail, sensitive, rebellious and with a colossal wilfulness. He is a great but utterly unbalanced poet, and, I fear, will never do justice to his own powers" (*The Unpublished Letters of Bayard Taylor in the Huntington Library*, ed. by John R. Schultz, San Marino, Calif., 1937, p. 100).

have had a letter from Mazzini [2] on my poems, especially the Cretan Ode,[3] which has given me (though not wholly worthy of it) the same delight it would have given to Shelley, had the Fates sent him such a tribute. If you do not know him, pray when at Florence accept the use of my name with my old friend and my family's, the Baron Kirkup (No. 2 Ponte Vecchio). You probably have met him at Florence—elsewhere I know you have not as he has not moved for thirty or forty years further than Pisa. His services to Dante, Giotto, and the world you must know, and may guess at his value in Florence as a guide knowing each crypt and corner. If you go there soon and see him, please give him my best regards. I hope [this] will come safe. I address *Poste Restante* as you give no address but Gotha.

Yours most faithfully,
A. C. Swinburne

186. BAYARD TAYLOR TO E. C. STEDMAN [1]

Text: *Philological Quarterly, 13* (1934), 297.

[Lausanne, April 24, 1867]

In all important respects except one I found him to be very much what I had anticipated. The exception is, instead of being a prematurely blasé young man o' the world, he is rather a wilful, perverse, unreasonable spoiled child. His nature is still that of the *young* Shelley, and my great fear is that it will never be otherwise. He needs the influence of a nature stronger than his in everything but the imaginative faculty—such a nature as Byron's was to Shelley. Again, a clear headed and hearted woman could cure him of his morbid relish for the atrocious forms of passion. He has a weak moral sense, but his offenses arise from a colossal unbalanced affectation. This, or something like it, is the disorganizing element in his nature, which quite obscures the organizing (that is artistic) sense. What I admire in him —yet admire with a feeling of pain—is the mad, unrestrained preponderance of the imagination. It is a god-like quality, but he sometimes uses it like a devil. He greatly interests my intellect, but he

2. Printed by Lafourcade, *La Jeunesse, 1,* 253–54. See below, Letter 191.

3. "On the Insurrection in Candia" (Bonchurch, *2,* 261–69) was printed in the *Fortnightly Review* (Mar. 1, 1867), pp. 284–89, and reprinted in *SBS.*

1. Edmund Clarence Stedman (1833–1908), poet, critic, essayist, Wall Street broker. John S. Mayfield has proved to me that the letter was addressed to Stedman, not, as hitherto supposed, to R. H. Stoddard, and I have adopted a dozen substantial emendations based on Mayfield's photostat of the MS.

does not touch me magnetically. He could have no power over me, but on the contrary, I felt that I should be able to influence him in a short time. I had a letter from him the other day, which shows he feels an intellectual relationship between us. Now this is not a question of relative poetic power, but of a certain diversity of qualities, and I don't mean to be egotistic in saying that I might perform somewhat of the same service for him as Byron for Shelley. I feel that (if it is not already too late) I could help him to some degree of poise, of system, of law—in short, art.

In this sense he moves my deepest sympathy, for I see now the matter that might be moulded into a splendid poet relapsing into formless conditions. It is sad, it is tragic—and if this fancy of mine be foolish, there it is nevertheless. Without this sense of giving assistance, a week alone with Swinburne would be intolerable to me, to any other human being. The preponderance of some disorganizing force in him gave me a constant keen sense of pain. I have urged him to join us in Italy next winter, but I doubt whether he will succeed in doing so. If he comes, and I find there is no hope of establishing any germ or central point of order in his nature, I shall really be forced to keep out of his way. He is now, with all his wonderful gifts the most wretched man I ever saw.

I said that he has a weak moral sense, but his English friends say that he has none at all. Here I don't agree with them, and moreover I don't think they quite understand his nature and therefore can't be of much service. One thing is certain—his aberration of ideas is horrible. He told me some things, unspeakably shocking, which he had omitted from his last volume. I very freely expressed my opinion and he took it with a gentle sort of wonder! He is sensitive, hugely ambitious and utterly self-absorbed—which things have wrought disease. If I did not think so, I should never wish to see him again.

There, that's enough on this point, I'll to bed.

187. TO KARL BLIND [1]

MS: British Museum.

22a Dorset Street, W.,
Monday [? March 25, 1867] [2]

My dear Sir

It will give me great pleasure to see you here on Wednesday. I am

1. (1826–1907), German political refugee, author, propagandist.

2. The paper is watermarked "1867."

truly glad you should regard my work as you do, and feel the honour done to it and me.

I have been ill with influenza for two days, but am better and hope to be soon well.

Yours faithfully,
A. C. Swinburne

188. TO GEORGE POWELL

MS: National Library of Wales.

Wednesday [March 27, 1867]

My dear Powell,

Many thanks for your splendid album. It is a most acceptable present. There was nothing I wanted more—and it has come oddly close on my birthday.

Ever yours,
A. C. Swinburne

189. TO GEORGE POWELL

MS: National Library of Wales.

Thursday [? March 28, 1867]

My dear Powell

I shall enjoy going with you to the concert of all things and hope we shall soon run over again to Jones's—he wants much to see more of you. I am very pleased by what you say of my last poem [1]—of course it is my favourite. You must tell me in time how and when and where we are to meet on Saturday.

I think your remarks on Justine the most sensible I ever heard. They quite give my own feelings, with which I never found any one to agree before. Usually that work is either a stimulant for an old beast or an emetic to a young man, instead of a valuable study to rational curiosity.

Excuse this scrawl, I am hurried and tired.

Ever yours,
A. C. Swinburne

1. "Ode on the Insurrection in Candia."

190. TO GEORGE POWELL

MS: National Library of Wales. Brief extract in Bonchurch, *19*, 154.

Arts Club, Hanover Square,
Sunday [March 31, 1867]

My dear Powell

I was most sorry to miss you *and* Mme. Schumann [1] yesterday, but it could not be helped. 1) Your note only came that morning 2) I did not get it till about two P.M. 3) I had (and kept) an engagement for the evening which might have been risked by my starting so late for the Crystal Palace. You will not wonder at the care I took to keep it, when I tell you that it was an engagement to meet Mazzini. I did; I unworthy spent much of last night sitting at my beloved chief's feet. He was angelically good to me. I read him my Italian poem all through and he accepted it in words I can't trust myself to try and write down.

I will be with you tomorrow at six at the St. James' Hall if well enough—but today I am rather exhausted and out of sorts. Il y a bien de quoi. There's a tradition in the Talmud that when Moses came down from Sinai he was 'drunken with the kisses of the lips of God.'

Ever most sincerely yours,
A. C. Swinburne

191. TO LADY JANE HENRIETTA SWINBURNE

Text: Leith, pp. 91–94.

Arts Club, Hanover Square,
Sunday, March 31 [1867]

I must write again to tell you what has happened to me. All last evening and late into the night I was with Mazzini.[1] They say a man's highest hopes are usually disappointed: mine were not. I had never dared to dream of such a reception as he gave me. At his desire, I read

1. Clara Wieck Schumann (1819–96), wife of the famous composer and well known in her own right as a composer and, more especially, a pianist.

1. A letter from Mazzini to Swinburne, dated Mar. 10, 1867, is printed by Lafourcade in *La Jeunesse*, *1*, 253–54, and nothing could have been more shrewdly calculated to enchant the poet. "Don't lull us to sleep with songs of egotistical love and idolatry of physical beauty: shake us, reproach, encourage, insult, brand the cowards, hail the martyrs, tell us all that we have a great Duty to fulfill, and that, before it is fulfilled, Love is an undeserved blessing, Happiness a blasphemy, belief in God a Lie. Give us a series of 'Lyrics for the Crusade.' Have not our praise, but our blessing. You *can* if you choose."

him my verses on Italy straight through; of course I felt awfully shy and nervous when I came to the part about him personally, but when I looked up at him I saw such a look on his face as set me all right again at once. If you had ever seen him, I am sure you would love him as I do. I had heard he was growing rather frail and weak with years and troubles. But he was as bright and fresh and energetic as a man could be. I am not going to try and tell you what he did me the honour to say about my poetry and the use of my devotion and belief to his cause. He says there is too much of *him* in my poem on Italy. I wanted to know how one could have done it otherwise. He has asked me to go and see him whenever I like. The minute he came into the room, which was full of people, he walked straight up to me (who was standing in my place and feeling as if I trembled all over) and said 'I know *you*,' and I did as I always thought I should and really meant not to do if I could help—went down on my knees and kissed his hand. He held mine between his for some time while I was reading, and now and then gave it a great pressure. He says he will take me to Rome when the revolution comes, and crown me with his own hands in the Capitol.[2] He is as ready to go in for a little joke such as this or bit of fun, and talk about anything that may turn up, as if he was nobody. He is a born king and chief and leader of men. You never saw such a beautiful smile as his. He is not the least bit discouraged or disheartened—and I don't know how any one could be who had ever seen his face. It is literally full of light; he has the largest and brightest dark eyes in the world. He is clearly the man to create a nation—to bid the dead bones live and rise.[3] And he is as simple and gentle and pleasant —with the most exquisite refinement of manner—as any one could be. In cast of feature he is a little like my uncle Ashburnham,[4] on a smaller scale of size, with twice the life and expression. I know, now I have seen him, what I guessed before, why, whenever he has said to any one, 'Go and be killed because I tell you,' they have gone and been killed because he told them. Who wouldn't, I should like to know? I never answered his letter, but last night I told him that on receiving it I felt there was but one person on earth to turn to and tell of this great honour and delight, and that of course was my mother. I think it pleased him. I know he was very fond of his. But though she had a greater and better son, I don't think she had one more fond of her. . . .

2. As Petrarch was crowned in 1341.

3. Ezekiel 37:3.

4. Bertram, 4th Earl of Ashburnham.

. . . Please give him [his father] [5] for Tuesday my best love and many happy returns of the day. *My* birthday I mean to consecrate by going to the Chief. I must stay up a little because of my portraits,[6] or else I should have run down already. Powell is in town, and full of Mme. Schumann's concerts. I hope to be able to go with him and hear her. He has bestowed on me a superb photographic album, which was a most acceptable present, as I wanted one to put you all into.

Ever your most affec. son.

192. TO KARL BLIND

MS: British Museum.

Arts Club, Hanover Square
[?March 31, 1867]

Dear Sir

I have no words to thank you for the great kindness you have shewn me. To be permitted to meet face to face the man who from my boyhood has been to me the incarnate figure of all that is great and good, is in itself a privilege beyond price or thanks; that it should be granted to me through and by you, enhances it.[1]

Believe me for ever

Most truly and gratefully yours,
A. C. Swinburne

Karl Blind, Esq.

5. Leith's gloss.

6. See below, Letter 198.

1. Gosse (Bonchurch, *19*, 154) credited Benjamin Jowett with a share in the backstairs strategy to bring about this tryst, but Lafourcade, hinting at political, rather than domestic, conspiratorial motives in Blind and Mazzini, is probably nearer the mark. In any case, it is clear that if Swinburne *was* ravished, never was victim less reluctant. Whoever the strategists were, the tactician was Thomas Purnell, who, learning that "A Song of Italy" was in proof-sheets, deftly dropped a word in the right place, and Swinburne was invited to read his poem to "The Chief." Purnell described the evening, briefly but in hushed accents, in *Every Saturday* (May 4, 1867), pp. 551–53. William Rossetti (*Rossetti Papers*, p. 230) reported on W. B. Scott's authority that Mazzini "walked straight up to S[winburne], who fell on his knee before him, and kissed his hand."

193. TO KARL BLIND

MS: British Museum.

22a Dorset Street, W.,
Wednesday [?April 3, 1867] [1]

My dear Sir

If I am well enough on Sunday I shall be delighted to come—but I have not been quite well ever since Saturday, and feel today too faint and unwell to face the idea of going out. In either case I am equally obliged to your friends for their kind invitation.

With kindest remembrances

Believe me ever faithfully yours,
A. C. Swinburne

194. TO ALICE SWINBURNE

Text: Leith, pp. 80–84.

April 10, 1867

Your letter, if late, was all the more welcome. . . . Please thank - - - - - [his mother] [1] very much for her letter and reassure her concerning my Chief and myself; he is not at all likely to despatch me on a deadly errand to Rome or Paris, nor have we Republicans any immediate intention of laying powder-mines under Windsor Castle. . . . She will understand (to be serious) why I cannot reply to her letter. I love her and him too much to write to the one about the other when I see it is hopeless to make the one share my love for the other. I only wish that she and you and all of us could see him. I am as sure as I am of writing to you now, that you all, or anybody who was not a blockhead or a blackguard, would throw in their lots with me. I have heard since (from an ultra-Tory) two little facts which I will put in here. In '64 there was a row about Mazzini in our beautiful Parliament,—and some nameless and unnameable creature got up and abused my chief. At the end Lord Stanley got up and simply said—'Has the honourable gentleman ever *seen* M. Mazzini?' . . . Again, when Orsini had failed in bombarding M. Louis Bonaparte, and the chief was accused of taking part in the affair (1857, if you remember) and had put forth in a letter to the *Times* his denial—saying in his great way

1. The paper is watermarked "1866." The propriety of the date that (in the absence of evidence) I have divined can be appreciated better than it can be justified.

1. Leith's substitution—Swinburne probably wrote "Mimmy."

that he never did write to papers or notice accusations, but now he would for the sake of others—the *Times* next morning opened its first leading article with a remark to the effect that the question was now set at rest, and he had nothing to do with it. 'M. Mazzini has said so; *and M. Mazzini never lied.*' [2] Those were the words. Now please remember who Ld. Stanley is, and what the *Times* is. You could not find anywhere a man or a journal more averse to Mazzini's principles. I don't know when such a tribute was paid by unfriendly hands to the greatness and goodness of any man. As for me, all I say in defence of my idolatry is this: I just ask you to meet my chief. I know you too well to doubt the result—for I believe fully in the maxim of Dr. Arnold. . . . I took courage to tell the chief that it was in our sort of people that he must look for real faith and self-devotion to a cause which could do us personally no good and no harm—*not* in the Bright [3] (Anglican-Radical) set. Don't let [my parents] have any uneasiness or vexation about me because I have at last attained the honour of meeting my chief. Even that cannot make me love him more or believe more in the Republican cause. . . .

I must stay here some time on account of my portrait,[4] which is not yet begun, but as people say I am looking quite well again I shall *sit* at once. And I think I shall stay up for the Exhibition,[5] &c., and then come down for a bit if you will have me. But I hope you will all come up for the said Exhibition, early.

Last night I had to entertain a poor boy of sixteen, son of Dr. (*not* M.D.) Westland Marston,[6] all but wholly blind, who for some

---

2. Felice Orsini (1819–58) attempted to assassinate Napoleon III Jan. 14, 1858. Six years later the matter of Mazzini's complicity in another plot against the French ruler was broached in questions leveled against James Stansfeld (see below, Letter 432), a junior Lord of the Admiralty and friend to Mazzini. The latter's denial appeared in *The Times* (Jan. 15, 1864), p. 9, and the *fourth* leading article on the same day, pp. 8–9, characterized him as a man of "perfect truthfulness." Hansard's *Parliamentary Debates* harbors no exchange involving "Lord Stanley" in this connection. See Swinburne's poem "For a Portrait of Felice Orsini" (Bonchurch, *4*, 301) in *Studies in Song* (1880).

3. John Bright (1811–89), the political reformer.

4. See below, Letter 198.

5. See below, Letter 196.

6. Philip Bourke Marston (1850–87), a minor poet, and his father, John Westland Marston (1819–90), a minor dramatist. Newton Crosland, a friend of the father, was pretty chilly towards the son, saying (*Rambles Round My Life*, 1898, p. 82) that he "was not to me an interesting young man. He was eccentric and very self-sufficient. He became an Agnostic, and seemed to me to believe in nothing particular

time has lived (his friends tell me) on the hope of seeing me (as far as he can see). I thought it so touching, remembering my own enthusiasms at that age—that I said I should be glad to have him at my rooms (with his father and a friend or two) and they chose last night. The day before a friend brought me the most frantic set of verses written by this poor blind fellow and addressed to me. I was rather worried, but I thought of his affliction and made up my mind to read the poem and make him as happy as I could. And I think for once I have succeeded in doing another a good turn, for he certainly did enjoy the occasion. I gave him chocolate bon-bons, etc., and read to the company unpublished things of mine—among others the little old Jacobite song [7] that you and A.[8] liked so much when I read it you at Holmwood. It was really very touching to see the face that could just see where I was across the table looking at me—and growing so feverishly *red* that his father went over once or twice to see if he was all right. It is not because he went in for me that I cared about it, but a thing of that sort *must* make one compassionate. . . . And he did seem to enjoy himself so much that I really felt it was worth living, to give so much pleasure to a poor boy afflicted as he is from his birth.

195. TO WILLIAM MICHAEL ROSSETTI

MS: Rutgers. Brief extract in Lafourcade, *Biography*, p. 151.

[April 29, 1867] [1]

Dear Rossetti

If you haven't seen or heard from me for such ages it is because I am still half dead with bilious influenza. It's very hard lines even for the Supreme Being as I have abstained from sitting up or drinking or any irregularity in a way worthy of a better cause and effect. I console myself with Bendyshe's hymn or 'grace before meat'—

'Damn God, from whom all evils flow'

have you heard it? it is worthy of the 'Suicide.'

---

but himself. He was buried, at his own request, in unconsecrated ground as a protest against 'ecclesiastical superstition,' and to show his disregard of revealed Religion."

7. "A Jacobite's Farewell" (Bonchurch, 3, 279), a song included in *Lesbia Brandon*, was first published in the *Magazine of Art* (Jan. 1889), and reprinted three months later in *PB3*.

8. Presumably his sister Isabel (Abba).

1. Supplied by William Rossetti.

Meantime accept anticipatory thanks for your review,[2] which I am eager to see. Some day Mazzini is coming here to meet you, Scott, Brown and Howell—and I must have Ned. I have had two long interviews lately with the Chief. He is more divine the more one sees him. We are quite on familiar terms now and what a delight this is to me I needn't tell *you*. He is very busy even for him and vexed just now about Garibaldi who *will* go off on his own hook at the wrong time. He said things to me and told me stories that honestly I can't write about. He looks very well and fresh though one finds him buried alive in papers. You won't wonder I can write of nothing else, and will excuse this sick scrawl. About the 'Men of the Time' business that you wrote about long since, the more I think of it the less I like this habit of living biographies. I could give you an especial reason—but anyhow I do object, and seriously, on principle, to the sort of thing. I should rather like to send a 'blague Sadique' by way of autobiography but it would be too dangerous even for

Your affectionate,

A. C. Swinburne

196. TO LADY JANE HENRIETTA SWINBURNE

Text: Leith, pp. 94–96.

Arts Club, Hanover Square,
May 7 [1867]

. . . As to my chief, if you are really anxious about his influence upon me, you may be quite at rest. I do not expect you to regard him with my eyes, but you must take my word for it that nothing but good can come from the great honour and delight of being admitted to see and talk with him. He is always immensely kind and good to me, but all he wants is that I should dedicate and consecrate my writing power to do good and serve others exclusively; which I can't. If I tried I should lose my faculty of verse even. When I can, I do; witness my last book, which I hope you have received at last. . . .

You must all come up for the picture exhibitions of the year, which are excellent, as if to make up for last year's failures. There is no *very* great picture in the Academy, but quite an unusual show of good

2. Evidently, Rossetti's collection of reviews called *Fine Art, Chiefly Contemporary*.

ones, in my humble opinion.[1] Tell M.[2] to go and look at a small boy by Millais,[3] whose (the child's, *not* the painter's) father I know very well; I think it will gratify her. It is seriously a lovely bit of painting, and of a really pretty child; a better picture than his more ambitious ones, which disappointed me. Old Landseer's white bulls [4] are perfectly magnificent, both beasts and painting. There are very few good landscapes, but two or three really good seascapes—one by Hook,[5] a boat rowed by boys on the edge of a full rising wave, curving into a solid mound of water before it breaks; both the faces (the elder half-laughing, the younger boy grave and girding himself up for the pull) and the water, are quite right. It made me thirsty to be in between the waves. Whistler, who doesn't like Hook's pictures as a rule, pointed it out to me as good. . . .

197. TO GEORGE POWELL

MS: National Library of Wales.

22a Dorset Street, W., May 7 [1867]

My dear Powell

Even had you been able to receive me I could not have come to you —I have been awfully seedy—'staying out' in fact—for some time back till the change of weather. Now I am in a great state of health and spirits [1] and I hope you both are. Of course I saw at once how right

1. William Rossetti, on the other hand, wrote in his diary on May 6 (*Rossetti Papers*, p. 231): "Went for a short time to the R.A.; it strikes me as a very vulgar and tawdry exhibition. Millais, I fear, going off seriously. . . ."

2. Unidentified. Mary Gordon Leith?

3. "Master Cayley," son of C. B. Cayley (1823–83), the translator of Dante, who had been engaged to Christina Rossetti, had studied Italian under her father, and was a friend of both her brothers.

4. "Wild Cattle of Chillingham," by Sir Edwin Landseer (1802–73).

5. "Mother Carey's Chickens" (the picture also shows an old man), by J. C. Hook (1819–1907).

1. "I had yesterday Swinburne!" Mazzini wrote on May 6 to Emilie Venturi (E. F. Richards, ed., *Mazzini's Letters to an English Family, 1861–1872*, London and New York, 1922, p. 164). "We spoke of Prometheus and of you: having stated in the course of conversation that you were an exceptional woman, the Poet said that it was enough to be five minutes with you to get that conviction. There! He was going somewhere in Wales: coming back, he would *certainly* go and see you! Meanwhile the 'Song' is ignored in the daily Press: *la conspiration du silence.*" For Emilie Venturi see below, Letter 308.

your doctor must be in recommending isolation. I hope the régime has been useful. Give my best remembrances to Charner [2] and best wishes for his rétablissement. Between you and the sea he ought to get on well.

I have been myself a prominent instance des *malheurs* de la *vertu,* for I never lived more carefully and chastely and soberly and never had such a bad fit of bilious influenza. 'O Justine! Éxécrons ce Dieu, cet abominable b——e de Dieu, qui laisse ainsi gémir la vertu—' etc. etc. ad libitum. I trust you continue to draw comfort and strength from that pure and profound source. Come up and see the exhibitions, they are very good. Write soon and believe me

Ever yours affectionately,
A. C. Swinburne

198. TO GEORGE FREDERICK WATTS [1]

MS: Huntington Library.

22a Dorset Street, W.,
Monday evening [?May 20, 1867]

Dear Sir

I find it will be impossible for me to call to-morrow; but if Wednesday at 11 A.M. will do, I will be with you punctually. If you cannot then give me a sitting, perhaps you will let me know tomorrow.

Yours very truly,
A. C. Swinburne

199. TO GERALD MASSEY [1]

MS: University of Texas. Published: Bonchurch, *18,* 50–51*.

22a Dorset Street, Portman Square, W.,
May 22, 1867

Sir

I must apologise for having left so long unanswered a letter which it was a pleasure to receive. I have been unwell and preoccupied of late, and I fear a very bad correspondant—and having first put apart,

2. Unidentified.

1. (1817–1904), the celebrated painter.

1. Gerald Massey (1828–1907), a poet highly praised in his day, is not likely to emerge from his present eclipse. He took on various tinges of liberalism with a small range—from Chartism to Christian Socialism, from Mazzini to Garibaldi. Moreover, he lectured in Great Britain, the United States, and Australia on spiritualism and

and then mislaid your letter, was unable to write to any purpose for want of a direction. As soon as I received it I desired my publisher to forward to you my last books, supposing that he had your address. I hope you have received them before now.

Of your work on Shakespeare's sonnets I read something when it appeared, but had not time to follow it out, though interested alike in your subject and your view of it. Hitherto I am myself unconvinced that any of the series were written in the character of another real person; they all seem to me either fanciful or personal—autobiographic or dramatic. But I hope before long to study the question started by you more fully.

I have been reading this evening your essay on Lamb in the 'Fraser' of this month. Will you excuse the protest of a younger workman in the same field as yourself against your depreciatory mention of Lamb's poetry? I remember hearing Tennyson speak of it in the same tone; but against both my seniors I maintain that there are two or three poems and many passages of serious and noble beauty besides the verses you quote on his Mother's death. I have always thought that but for his incomparable prose the world would have set twice as much store by his verse. As a fellow-student and lover of his genius and character you will understand my wish to admire him and have him admired by others on all sides: and you will see also with what interest and attention I have read your essay.

Believe me

Very truly yours,
A. C. Swinburne

Gerald Massey, Esq.

200. TO GEORGE POWELL

MS: National Library of Wales. Brief extracts in Bonchurch, *19*, 154, 157 and in Lafourcade, *Biography*, p. 194.

22a Dorset Street, W., May 22, 1867

My dear Powell

I have to begin all my letters with excuses for idleness—but if you knew! Thanks (though late) for your last note. I hope you both keep

---

mesmerism, and there is no doubt a connection between this interest and his book *Shakspeare's Sonnets Never Before Interpreted: His Private Friends Identified, Together with a Recovered Likeness of Himself* (1866), which argues that the sonnets were addressed either to the Earl of Southampton or, in the dramatic *persona* of the Earl, to Elizabeth Vernon.

well, and that you will both pull on together for years yet. If this damned climate, the antechamber of a hell of sleet (witness today— *two* violent snowstorms on the Derby day!) won't admit Charner to a winter ticket (as indeed I think we shall all have to emigrate) get him into the Riviera, que diable! it's the dullest bit of earth in Europe I should think, but you can't die there if you try, and the climate is divine for invalids though *I* who am never unwell but by my own doing for a day or two can't breathe it, it's so ultra stimulating and soothing at once to the nerves. Then in a year's time from this we might all be allowed by gods and doctors to meet in Lombardy or Tuscany, which would be celestial. Pray continue to run up hither and see the year's pictures—there are many exhibited that it would be a sin to miss. I call it a really good season, sent to atone for the last.

As you ask I must answer that I have not had the promised Icelandic dainties [1]—but don't trouble yourself or Mr. Magnusson about them. I am writing a little sort of lyric dirge for my poor Baudelaire,[2] which I think is good as far as it has got. But London and business or (worse) society are awful clogs on poetry. Also I am in the honourable agonies of portrait-sitting—to Watts. Of course it is a great honour for one to be asked to sit to him, now especially that he accepts no commissions and paints portraits only for three reasons—friendship, beauty, and celebrity; having the 'world' at his feet begging to be painted. But it takes time and trouble, and he won't let me crop my hair, whose curls the British public (unlike Titian's) reviles aloud in the streets.[3] Il faut souffrir pour être—peint: but the portrait is a superb picture already, in spite of the model, and up to the Venetian standard, by the admission of other artists—a more than fair test.

I am glad you like the délaissement [*sic*] of Louis XI. and Charles le Téméraire,[4] and hope the 'philosophy' of a later novelist supports and enlightens you. 'Car la vertu, soyons-en bien convaincus, étant la plus odieuse des chimères, doit amener les malheurs les plus effroyables—oui, coquine—inouis—ah! etc. etc. etc. I tremble when I reflect that I have sent £20 (nearly my last—the price of my Cretan ode) to the Greek Committee. 'J'ai commis une bonne action—je dois *souffrir*—Accomplis tes décrets, Etre Suprême!

(Vide *Justine* passim)

1. Perhaps *Legends of Iceland,* Second Series (1866).

2. See above, Letter 112. "Ave atque Vale" (Bonchurch, *3,* 44–51) was published in the *Fortnightly Review,* Jan. 1868, and reprinted in *PB2.*

3. Proverbs 1:20.

4. The allusion is not clear.

With best remembrances to Charner and O'Halloran
Believe me

> Ever yours affectionately,
> A. C. Swinburne

201. TO LORD HOUGHTON

MS: The Marchioness of Crewe.

22a Dorset Street, W., June 28 [1867]

Dear Lord Houghton

I will come on Tuesday with pleasure. When your two notes from Paris reached me I was busy and not well and put off answering till it was past the time; but in any case I could not have tried my hand at the Hymn, even for the joke's sake. I have been given a curious autograph letter, year 8 of the Republic, in which the Citizen Sade, ex-marquis, now *minus* the *de,* invites some friends to his house to hear the reading of a new work still in MS. Imagine a respectable evening circle convened to listen to a MS. by *that* author—and the modest deprecation with which he would unfold the papers and begin!

> Ever yours faithfully,
> A. C. Swinburne

202. TO LORD HOUGHTON

MS: The Marchioness of Crewe.

Dorset Street, July 2, 1867

Dear Lord Houghton

I am kept in bed all day with a severe bilious attack, which came on suddenly this morning. I am very sorry to say that I shall be, in consequence, unable to come to dinner with you this evening.[1]

Believe me

> Yours faithfully,
> A. C. Swinburne

1. He would, at all events, have been a startling addition to a dinner party that numbered, according to T. Wemyss Reid's guest list (*Richard Monckton Milnes, 2,* 176), "Viscount Halifax, Mr. Gladstone, Mr. R. C. Winthrop, Mr. Bright, Sir Bartle Frere, Mr. Albert Rutson, Mr. Frederic Harrison, Mr. Milnes Gaskell, M.P., Hon. Julian Fane, Sir Francis Goldschmidt, Mr. R. Monteith, M.P." At midnight on July 2 Houghton wrote an account of the evening to his wife: "A pleasant dinner is enclosed. I suppose the company thought so, as they are only just gone. Bright stayed to the last, talking very instructively of the past and future. Gladstone was

203. TO KARL BLIND

MS: British Museum.

22a Dorset Street, Portman Square, W.,
July 5 [1867]

My dear Sir

It will give me the greatest pleasure to be with you on Saturday (tomorrow) at six. I have long wished for the honour of meeting M. Louis Blanc.[1]

With kind regards to you and yours, believe me

Very sincerely yours,
A. C. Swinburne

I have received a most flattering note from Victor Hugo in answer to my verses addressed to him.

204. TO VICTOR HUGO

MS: British Museum. Published: *Revue bleue, 74* (Mar. 7, 1936), 153.

22a Dorset Street, W., July [13?, 1867] [1]

Monsieur

Depuis plus d'un an j'avais hésité—voulant et ne voulant pas envoyer les vers que je vous avais addressés [*sic*].[2] Ce n'est pas que

---

talkative and gay; Gaskell silent. Lord Halifax was roughly pleasant; Julian Fane, full of his daughter, whose health we drank; Monteith, abstracted, but not absurd; and Mr. Winthrop asked much of you. Swinburne accepted and never came, *more suo. . . .*"

1. (1811–82), radical French statesman-in-exile. Lafourcade (*La Jeunesse, 2,* 307) thought Pierre Sadier in *Lesbia Brandon* might have been drawn from Louis Blanc; Randolph Hughes in his edition of the unfinished novel (p. 367) rejects the suggestion. Swinburne's three sonnets on Blanc (Bonchurch, *6,* 25–26) were published in the *Fortnightly Review* (June 1883), and reprinted in *MHOP*. See also Letter 205, below.

1. Lafourcade (*La Jeunesse, 1,* 90 n., 239), assigns this letter to 1866, though it is surely the reply alluded to in Letter 206, below. Hugo's letter to Swinburne, also in the British Museum, is dated July 1, 1867, and postmarked July 2 from Guernsey, and the envelope is endorsed by Swinburne "July 1st, 1867 (Poems and Ballads)." Swinburne's letter to Hugo is watermarked 1866.

2. "To Victor Hugo" (Bonchurch, *1,* 274–80) in *PB1*. Hugo's acknowledgment of the volume read: "Mon honorable et cher confrère, Devant votre livre je suis Tantale. Figurez-vous ma faim et ma soif et mon supplice. Je ne sais pas l'anglais. Une gracieuse amie m'a traduit les nobles et magnifiques strophes que vous m'adressez. Vous êtes par la fierté de l'inspiration et la hauteur de la pensée, au premier rang des poètes d'Angleterre, et aucun ne vous dépasse. Je suis glorieux de votre haute et touchante sympathie et je vous envoie mon plus cordial *shake-hand*. Victor Hugo."

j'aie douté de votre bonté—mais l'offrande m'a paru trop indigne de l'autel. Et maintenant, comment saurais-je vous remercier? il faudrait recommencer et résumer tout ce que les œuvres du plus grand des poëtes de ce temps ont fait pour moi depuis mon enfance. En vérité, je ne saurais vous exprimer ma profonde reconnaissance—mais au moins je veux que vous sachiez que ce n'est point à un ingrat que vous avez adressé de si bonnes paroles. Il y avait deux hommes que j'ai espéré—tout enfant—de pouvoir un jour rencontrer—vous et Mazzini. Encore une fois je vous remercie de tout mon cœur. On userait sa vie à vous remercier. Vous avez trop fait pour nous tous. Pour vous remercier dignement—il faudrait vous égaler. Pardonnez-moi si je vous suis importun en écrivant comme je fais au courant de la plume. Et surtout, croyez à ma reconnaissance—qui devrait mieux s'exprimer.

Si j'étais vraiment le grand poëte que vous voulez bien m'appeler—et si vous saviez comment depuis ma douzième année j'ai été hanté et fasciné nuit et jour par votre poésie—alors, peut-être, je saurais mieux vous répondre. À présent je ne sais que dire car je ne saurais me figurer que des vers de ma façon aient pu vous donner du plaisir. Si cela est, ce n'est encore qu'une dette que je vous dois.

Mais, en effet, comment vous remercier? Tous les ans vous nous faites voir quelque chose de sublime. Croyez, je vous en prie, que vous avez en Angleterre parmi les hommes de mon âge toute une école 'bien pensante' et dévouée.

Je voudrais que mon livre fût digne d'être parcouru par mon cher et grand Maître auquel il doit tout ce qu'il a de bon, si toutefois il en a: mais on ne saurait donner que ce que l'on peut. Si mes vers vous ont donné un instant de plaisir, c'est assez pour moi.

Algernon Ch. Swinburne

205. TO KARL BLIND

MS: British Museum.

22a Dorset Street, W.,
Saturday evening [July 13, 1867]

My dear Sir

Most unfortunately I had this morning another bad attack such as I had at your house [1]—but even worse—a regular fainting fit—and they telegraphed for my father from his countryhouse, who wants to

---

1. "We were sitting after breakfast, when Swinburne fell down in a fit," Lord Houghton wrote to his wife on the same day (Pope-Hennessy, p. 137). "Tweed was out, but I got Dr. Williams in a few minutes & there is no immediate danger. I have telegraphed to his family, & I suppose someone will come up and look after

remove me from London tomorrow. You will believe how truly I feel this second disappointment. A thousand thanks to Miss Blind [2] for her kind present and note just received. I shall take the Poems with me out of town to read carefully at leisure. I am not now strong enough to write more. With best remembrances to you and yours.

Ever faithfully yours,
A. C. Swinburne

206. TO JOHN NICHOL

Text: *Early Letters.*

22 Dorset Street, W., Saturday [July 13?, 1867]

Dear Nichol

Next to the pleasure of meeting you again comes the pleasure of receiving your letter. I had, and have, so many things to say to you that I don't know where to begin, and must take a shot at random.

I forget if Louis Blanc is a friend of yours, or was of your father's. I met him the other day, and was much struck and delighted. You know, I suppose, that he has left England for good. I saw the very last of him, at home, later even than Mazzini, who had just left when I arrived.

I should like of all things to have next spring to spend with you in a walking tour, and, as far as I know, hope it may be feasible. In the autumn I have some thoughts of going to Munich (of all places) with an old schoolfellow and friend,[1] to see the opening of Wagner's Theatre and the performance of his as yet unknown opera which is to take four nights to represent, and embody the whole of the Nibelungen. Conceive—if you know the *Lohengrin*—what a divine delight it will be. But I presume the destinies will intervene and make it impossible.

I haven't been (as you have heard) at all well lately, and am not

---

him: he was looking wretchedly ill before. Dey is quite in his element looking after him. Jowett seemed much affected."

Thomas Woolner, who was also present, wrote to Sir Walter Trevelyan next day: "That poor little Swinburne had a dreadful fit yesterday at Lord Houghton's. From all accounts he seems to lead a sadly wild and unwholesome life. He made a great commotion, as you may imagine, at the breakfast table among the assembled guests" (Trevelyan Papers, Wallington).

2. Blind's stepdaughter, Mathilde Blind (1841–96), whose volume of verses *Poems by Claude Lake* was published in 1867.

1. George Powell.

now. The changeable weather in this malodorous town is playing the deuce with me—let alone worries, with which the gods take care to keep me supplied. I hope you and yours are free from any such inflictions.

I am truly glad you like my notes on Byron, and when we meet, we'll argue out the point you have mooted. I do seriously think his name—or birth—or whatever one must call it—was a clog to him *at starting,* and therefore more or less a lifelong evil.

I have three copies of O'Connor's pamphlet on Walt Whitman— one sent me by M. D. Conway (I forget the first source, you see!), one by my publisher, and one by the author. I like it for its very outrageousness and excess; but I don't think it is likely to make converts. About the *Drum Taps* I at once agree and disagree with you— *i.e.,* there was some half of new things in the book so beautiful and noble that I can't think of the rest or care for it. On the whole, though, I have little doubt you are right—but how perfect and how grand is that dirge for President Lincoln, 'When lilacs last in the dooryard bloomed'?

Apropos of my 'heresy,' please observe that it simply arose out of this, that I have friends who served on both sides (I mean some on the North and some on the South side—it was the unluckiest chance) and can honestly sympathise with either. There, the Republic to be preserved entire—and there, the divine right of insurrection; both are grand causes in my eyes, and I hope will always be. I was nearly going off this week on a swimming escapading tour with an aide-de-camp of General Lee's [2]—I defy you not to like him if you knew him—who was personally in all the battles of the war, I believe, and one of the nicest fellows alive, and open, as such men should be, to admiration of all fallen causes and exiled leaders. I'm not saying they're equal in worth, you know—heaven forbid! Only I must say failure is irresistibly attractive—admitting as I do the heroism of the North.

As to Maximilian, I'm sorry for him, and most because his execution [3] will vex V. Hugo and others—but I stick to what I said on first hearing the news—that it isn't a Hapsburg they've shot—it's the French Empire. Vive Juarez! [4] I did say 'Ce n'est point un homme que

2. Probably Kipling's friend (in later years) Col. Henry Wemyss Feilden (1838–1921), who served in the Confederate army with the rank of A.A.G. from 1862 to 1865.

3. He was shot on June 19.

4. Benito Juarez (1806–72), statesman and president of the Mexican Republic.

l'on vient de fusiller là—c'est le Bas-Empire!' And it is—we shall see else.

I have had such a note from Hugo [5] about my poems that I have had to put off answering him for a week. When I do, I must touch on this business. I trust you agree with me that it cannot but mean ruin to the empire of the 2 Décembre. Of course, you saw V. H.'s note to Juarez interceding for the Austrian?

As to Southey and Landor, of whom you write, I have always thought, and especially since I had the honour of intercourse with Landor, that the root of it was just personal liking and kindliness of nature. You see S. was the first and almost the only critic who ever praised L.'s verses at starting, and he always maintained this early opinion. If you remember how few comparatively even now are at all acquainted with Landor's poetry—(e.g., I was chaffed last year by the papers for talking of him as a poet at all comparable to Byron and Wordsworth) I think you will appreciate rightly his manner of speaking about his old friend. And really the last time I took up a book of Southey's (*The Curse of Kehama,* I think) it struck me that L. was right and there was really something genuine and fine in it.

I shall lay hold of Thoreau on your recommendation. What do you think of Emerson's new poems? [6] Geo. Meredith agrees with me in greatly admiring the four stanzas headed *Brahma.*

Ever yours,
A. C. Swinburne

207. ADMIRAL CHARLES HENRY SWINBURNE TO LORD HOUGHTON

MS: The Marchioness of Crewe.

Holmwood, Henley on Thames,
July 14, 1867

My Lord

I beg to thank you for your kind attention in sending me the Telegram to warn me of my Son's illness; it reached me at 4 P.M. yesterday. I went to London by the first Train and finding him at your House well enough to move I took him at once to his Chambers.

By the advice of Mr. Tweed and of Dr. Alison,[1] who met him at

5. See above, Letter 204.

6. *May-Day and Other Pieces* (1867).

1. John James Tweed, surgeon, and Somerville Scott Alison, physician, both of Park Street, Grosvenor Square.

my request, I have brought my Son home where I trust that care and more regular hours and diet will do him good.

I have to thank your Lordship also for the Letter you were good enough to leave for me on quitting London; and I gladly avail myself of this occasion to express my grateful sense of the kindness you have shewn to my Son for many years.

I have the honor to be

My Lord
truly yours,
C. H. Swinburne

208. TO J. C. HOTTEN

MS: British Museum.

Holmwood, Henley on Thames,
Wednesday [July 17?, 1867]

Dear Sir

As I shall be here probably two or three weeks, please send to this direction the Percy Ballads [1] (of course the cheapest one—£2. 2s. I think altogether) (first part of serious and first of humorous) already published. I expected to have had them last week. Also, as soon as out, Matthew Arnold's 'New Poems' now advertised.

Yours truly,
A. C. Swinburne

I particularly want these books as soon as possible.

209. TO LORD HOUGHTON

MS: The Marchioness of Crewe. Published: Bonchurch, *18*, 51–52*.

Holmwood, Henley on Thames,
Thursday, July 18 [1867]

My dear Lord Houghton

My father came up in the afternoon of Saturday and I came down hither with him on Sunday, having again seen Mr. Tweed who had a talk over me with Dr. Alison, my father's medical attendant, who has known me for years, though I have never hitherto had much occasion to trouble him professionally. They have together prescribed for me a course of diet and tonic medicine and advise country air; since my arrival I have not felt a moment's pain or sickness, and am now really quite well, though rather tired and weakened.

1. See below, Letter 213.

Nothing could be more attentive than your people were to me until I was able to move. I was quite sorry for the trouble given to you and them—and as grateful for the care and kindness. I find Mdme. Mohl [1] was good enough to call and ask after me—but I had left town. Will you thank her for me and tell her how much better I am?

Besides Alison's and Tweed's prescriptions we have a very good doctor here constantly at hand—Reading being but a short drive hence. The weather is wavering between sun and rain, but the air here suits me well. I am prescribed 'light literature'—of all things! as if I ever indulged in heavy! I am sure Alison has a vague idea of hours spent in hard study of philosophy and history—though I assure him that the most abstract authors I read are Flaubert and Trollope.

Yours affectionately,
A. C. Swinburne

210. TO CHARLES AUGUSTUS HOWELL

MS: British Museum. Published: Bonchurch, *18*, 52–53*.

Holmwood, Henley on Thames,
July 23, 1867

My dear Howell

I write as I cannot hope to see you before your marriage [1] comes off, only to say how heartily I wish you all the joy possible, and shake hands across the paper. It is for my own satisfaction; I should not like to feel excluded from among the friends who wish you joy. I would give much to have something better to send than my love and good wishes. Take them in default of the better thing, and write me a line if you have leisure. I suppose your time is now near at hand, and I am here under doctors' hands for a month more at least. I had a very bad attack a week since, beginning with a sudden and *unprovoked* fainting fit about noon. My father was telegraphed for

1. Mary Mohl (1793–1883), *née* Clarke. An Englishwoman married to Professor Julius Mohl, she lived in Paris for nearly forty years and presided over a salon in the old grand, but lighthearted, manner (Pope-Hennessy, p. 144 n.).

1. "In September, 1867, Howell married his cousin, Miss Kate Howell, a very amiable lady and a favourite with all his friends," writes Helen Rossetti Angeli (*Dante Gabriel Rossetti: His Friends and Enemies*, p. 141). "The wedding, at St. Matthew's, Brixton, was well attended. William and Christina [Rossetti] were there, and the [William] Morrises, Burne-Joneses and Madox Browns. Lucy Madox Brown acted as bridesmaid."

and I was brought down hither next day. I am all right now, only not over strong, and have to take care and submit to the care of others. I find comfort in reflecting that I am not the first or the un-luckiest of innocent sufferers. Oui—voilà bien les malheurs de la vertu. It has been worse than a week of swishings—Eton (I know) or Harrow (I should think): pity a boy equal to such Divine discipline. I hope you and yours will remain in Fate's good books. Give my love to Ned and Gabriel and all friends—and with renewed love and wishes to yourself believe me always

Your affectionate,
Algernon Ch. Swinburne

211. ADMIRAL CHARLES HENRY SWINBURNE TO LORD HOUGHTON

MS: The Marchioness of Crewe. Brief extract in Bonchurch, *19*, 157–58.

Holmwood, Henley on Thames,
July 26, 1867

Dear Lord Houghton

In reply to your Lordship's friendly enquiry I am happy to say that my Son's health appears at present to be very good. He is attended by Dr. Wells of Reading, to whose care he was handed over by Dr. Alison and Mr. Tweed, and who is quite satisfied with him.

He recovered his appetite as soon as he got home, and fell willingly into regular hours and habits, as he always does when he is with us. He is tractable and willing to do every thing that is required of him. It cannot be expected, and therefore is not insisted upon, that his mental faculties should lie fallow, but we do all we can to keep them tranquil.

We feel him to be safe while he is here; the trial and test of his firmness will come when he shall return to the temptations to which he has been hitherto exposed.

I purpose to shew him your Lordship's letter, I think it may strengthen his resolves.

I have the honor to be
My Lord
sincerely yours,
C. H. Swinburne

212. TO GEORGE POWELL

MS: National Library of Wales. One sentence in Lafourcade, *Biography*, p. 45.

Holmwood, August 3 [1867]

My dear Powell

Here is the poem you asked for. I have slipt in three new stanzas which improve it. It will appear ultimately in the Fortnightly. I would have sent it at once, but for illness idleness and business alternating. I have been *bad* with a strained knee—very bad for 48 hours, but it is nearly well. Do whatever you like with the 'Vigil,'[1] it is wholly at your service and any friend's.

It is awful to think of Collections after Election Saturday—enough to bring down fire from heaven. Is there never to be a rebellion among the fellows? is Eton to be indeed a miniature England, slave of its own languor and custom? and yet it *has* seen Shelley—and Me. Couldn't oldsters like you and myself get up a revolution—debauch with principles of licence and revolt the fifth (say) or (at worst) remove? If they bear this they may bear all. Servum pecus![2] I should like to see two things there again the river—and the block. Can you tell me any news of the latter institution or any of its present habitués among our successors? the topic is always most tenderly interesting —with an interest, I may say, based upon a common bottom of sympathy.

My mother had a glimpse of you, a day or two since in passing at Slough Station but you had fellows with you (she says) and didn't see her.

With best regards from all and thanks for calling at Hotten's believe me ever

Yours affectionately,
A. C. Swinburne

213. TO J. C. HOTTEN

MS: British Museum.

Holmwood, August 8 [1867]

Dear Sir

Will you send (*for me* and in my name) three or four copies of my

1. "A Lost Vigil," published in the *Fortnightly Review* (Dec. 1867), and reprinted, as "A Wasted Vigil" (Bonchurch, *3*, 34–36), in *PB2*.

2. "Slavish herd"—Horace, *Epistles* 1. 19. 19.

Poems to Lord Houghton? I owe him presentation copies and he has asked me for some to take abroad. He suggests that I might send a copy of my essay on Byron to Lord Broughton (Byron's friend Hobhouse,[1] as no doubt you know). Will you get one for me and send it to his address as from me? Hill Street Berkeley Square is the address but I don't know the number.

I hope you put my name down as a subscriber of £2.2s. for the Percy MS.[2] as I observe this is far the cheapest way. Do you know when the second volume will be out? I see the papers say soon. Please send me as soon as you can on Saturday evening the Saturday Review and Spectator, and so every week as long as I stay here: I am rather short of papers and if there is anything amusing in any, English or American, I should be glad if you would forward it—letting me know if you wanted it again. How does the Blake go on?

Yours truly,
A. C. Swinburne

P.S. I have heard through our neighbour Sir Robt. Phillimore,[3] who is sure to have seen it, that there has been some notice—he thought at first in the Pall Mall Gazette—of my review in the Fortnightly for July.[4] If you find any there or elsewhere please send it to me. I want also a copy of the numbers in question of the Fortnightly Review.

214. TO LORD HOUGHTON

MS: The Marchioness of Crewe. Published (with deletions): Bonchurch, *18*, 53–54*.

Holmwood, August 8 [1867]

Dear Lord Houghton

I have written to Hotten to send you the number of copies of Poems desired. Thanks again for all the trouble you took with me. I have had no return of fainting or any discomfort here beyond a strained knee. They doctor me with tonics and champagne, and I thrive so well that having no one to speak to and nothing to do beyond the family wall I shall end by writing something which will make the author 'du hideux roman de J - - - - - -' turn enviously in his grave. One always writes

1. John Cam Hobhouse (1786–1869), created Baron Broughton in 1851.

2. J. W. Hales and F. J. Furnivall, eds., *Bishop Percy's Folio Manuscript: Loose and Humorous Songs* (1867), *Ballads and Romances* (3 vols. 1867–68).

3. The Right Hon. Sir Robert Joseph Phillimore, Bart. (1810–85).

4. "Morris' 'Life and Death of Jason'" (Bonchurch, *15*, 50–61), reprinted in *ES*.

des horreurs when one is en famille. I have two innocent songs forth-coming in the Fortnightly: [1] also some prose notes.[2]

I have given my copy of the philosophic romance above named to an Eton schoolfellow [3] who has been here to see me, having taken a small house close to Eton where he has boy cousins. I rejoice to hear from that quarter rumours of wars and rebellions: and on hearing such I wrote to my friend proposing that he and I as oldsters should give hints, direct, propagate, instigate the rearing of barricades etc. next half. He has culled for me some newly-budded 'blossoms of the block,' as one may call the narratives of swished youth, which are neither fruitless nor unfragrant. 'I think' he says 'I can procure a genuine birch which has been used.'

> 'Dolce sentier—colle che mi piacesti
> Ov'ancor per usanza [Amor] mi mena!'

as sang the lover of Madame Laure de Sade.[4] The work of her great descendant (not by the side of Petrarca) is not, you see, thrown away on children of Eton. May it be truly blessed to them, and 'bring forth fruits meet for' [5] damnation!

I am delighted by Coomaz Hioang's [6] good opinion and will strive to deserve it. The news of Lord Milton's marriage [7] pains me, hold-

1. "Regret," in the Sep. number of the *Fortnightly Review*, reprinted, with re-visions and additions, as "Pastiche" (Bonchurch, *3*, 81) in *PB2;* and "A Wasted Vigil."

2. "Matthew Arnold's 'New Poems' " (Bonchurch, *15*, 62–119), in the Oct. number, reprinted in *ES.*

3. George Powell (see above, Letter 212).

4. Petrarch's sonnet "Valle, che de' lamenti miei se' piena": "Sweet path . . . little hill that I once delighted in . . . where Love by habit leads me still" (Swin-burne omits two half-lines).

5. Matthew 3:8.

6. Probably Sir Mutu Coomara Swamy (1834–79), a Hindu barrister. He translated into English a drama from the Tamil and two Buddhist texts from the Pali. Accord-ing to Frederic Boase, *Modern English Biography* (6 vols. Truro, 1892–1921), "He was the first Hindoo (not being a Christian) called to the English bar, and the first among the Tamils to receive the honor of knighthood" (1874). Pope-Hennessy, p. 142, notes that he and Swinburne met at Fryston in Dec. 1862, and suggests that "Juggonath Chundango" in Laurence Oliphant's satire *Piccadilly* (serialized in 1865) was based on Coomara Swamy.

7. William, Viscount Milton (1839–77), eldest son of the 6th Earl Fitzwilliam, was married Aug. 10, 1867, to Laura Maria Theresa, granddaughter of the 8th Duke of St. Albans.

ing as I do that the act is immoral and desiring myself to follow in thought word and deed the strait and narrow way of morality and religion.

I am so glad Lady Houghton is well enough to accompany you,[8] and trust she is better than when you last gave me news; please make all my remembrances to her. I have told Hotten to send Lord Broughton a copy of my Byron essay and shall be delighted if it pleases him; thanks for the hint.

Have you seen how our names are taken in vain together by some scribe in Blackwood?[9] The liber*ties* of the Press etc. etc. (vide Rouher [10] et Cie passim).

As you from Ceylon, I have heard from Brazil. H. M. Consul at Santos [11] (whom I ought to answer today) writes me renewed congratulations on my success in bruising the head [12] of British virtue. I *hope* Mrs. Burton did *not* read 'Richard's' remarks on 'Faustine'—et pour cause!

Yours affectionately,
A. C. Swinburne

215. TO GEORGE POWELL

MS: National Library of Wales.

Holmwood, August 13 [1867]

Dear Powell

A thousand thanks for your gift which is trebly valuable for interest and external belongings and as the seal of friendship. I long to thank you in person and to enjoy the sight and touch of the birch that has been used. I don't think I ever more dreaded the entrance of the swishing room than I now desire a sight of it. To assist unseen

8. To the Continent, where he remained for nearly three months.

9. In "The Easter Trip of Two Ochlophobists by One of Themselves," a mock book of travel that ran (but not very fast) in *Blackwood's* in July and Aug.; reprinted in *Tales from "Blackwood,"* Second Series, 9 (1878–80). In chap. 17 occurs this passage: " 'Well,' said Granville [to 'Lord Fryston'], 'I hear you had Cora Pearl, the Emperor, Montalembert, and Swinburne to breakfast yesterday.' "

10. Eugène Rouher (1814–84), Minister of State under Napoleon III, was so notably hegemonic that *The Times* on Aug. 3 printed an article denying that the Emperor was his tool.

11. Burton.

12. Genesis 3:15; *Paradise Lost*, Bk. X. 181, 498.

at the holy ceremony some after twelve I would give *any* of my poems. The locket is exquisite, worthy of the relic. How on earth did Giles [1] manage to procure you the latter? it must have been a mysterious adventure of knight errantry. What fun it would be to enact (I did once with another fellow—) the whole process, exchanging the parts of active and passive in turn. The Russians with their daily use of it at meals and baths are more delicately civilized than we. Do let us some day get up the scene. I dream of it and wake to laugh. I should like to have seen your cousin and heard his account. How often has he been swished? In the words once addressed to me when at school by a younger cousin at home, 'please write again soon and tell me a Lot more about a lott more swishings, it's such a *joly* spree' (*sic*). I *did* with a vengeance, and the seed fell on good ground.[2] I wish you could send me a representation of the ceremony with text appended as in a realistic romance. I long to run over to you for two days, but my mother is very urgent with me not to move or make the least change in my habits for some time yet. You see my last attack was, they say, of a really dangerous kind, and I am prescribed a *torpor* of mind and body for months. I don't think *this* would hurt me, but cannot resist her pressing request. It is awfully slow in spite of their kindness, and it is a real and great charity to write to me now and amuse me: pray do when you can. I hope you will be back before the holidays are over, I am very curious to see the place empty, and should like of all things to run over to you as soon as I may. I am truly sorry to hear of Charner's renewed illness and its causes. Pray, whenever you write, remember me to him most kindly with all wishes for his better health. Ill health and weakness even among the kindest nurses are damnable things.

I am very sorry there are no more (literally) procurable photographs of my family. I must try and get some reproduced. Were there any we should all have been delighted to send you some. Meantime with kindest regards and from me especial thanks

I am ever

Yours affectionately,
A. C. Swinburne

1. Unidentified.

2. Matthew 13:8 (etc.).

216. TO GEORGE POWELL

MS: National Library of Wales.

[Early September 1867]

My dear Powell

I should like of all things to run over for a few days if I can *get leave*. Write and tell me if you *are* de retour. We also have had infinite wasps here. You will see a song of mine in the Fortnightly and next month an essay.[1] I hope Charner will keep up.

Ever yours affectionately,
A. C. Swinburne

217. TO CHARLES AUGUSTUS HOWELL

MS: British Museum.

September 9 [? 1867][1]

My dear Howell

Forgive, as you are (or are not) a Christian: it wasn't my fault. I left word especially for you, to excuse myself and say that I *must* be out before twelve, but hoped you would come on to the places indicated if not inconvenient. I am quite sorry you lost an hour and wasted a journey for my sake. Write a line of pardon, and come to me before I leave.

Your affectionate,
A. C. Swinburne

What I deserve, you must judge; I leave it to the Marquis (*not* Townshend)[2] to decide!

218. TO EDMUND GOSSE[1]

MS: British Museum. Published: Bonchurch, *18*, 54–55*.

Holmwood, Henley on Thames,
September 14, 1867

Sir

I have received your letter and its enclosure. I have not much time

1. "Regret" and "Matthew Arnold's 'New Poems.' "

1. The date is a mere guess. The paper is watermarked: "[JOYN]SON / [186]5."

2. John Villiers Stuart (1831–99) succeeded as 5th Marquis Townshend in Sep. 1863. He had been at Eton for three terms in 1845, served as M.P. for Tamworth, 1856–63, and was J.P. and D.L. for Norfolk and Middlesex.

1. (1849–1928), knighted in 1925. His father, hearing that he had sought Swin-

for correspondance, but I answer it at once, as you desire my advice. I certainly do not urge you to resign the habit of writing if it gives you pleasure without interfering with other things; I have no right to give such counsel. What prospect of growth and advance in the art you may have is impossible to say. Less promising verses than yours have perhaps been the forerunners of success, and more promising ones of ultimate failure. A man's first attempts can never possibly afford reasonable ground for pronouncing decisively whether he is qualified or disqualified for the attainment of his hope. One thing, while sympathizing with your wishes, I do advise you against; too much thinking and working in one channel. Neither you nor I can tell what kind of work you will in the long run be able to accomplish; but it is certain that good or ill success in this matter of poetry need neither make nor mar a man's work in life. I understand the impulse to write of which you speak and the pain of checking or suppressing it; nor do I tell you to suppress or check it; only not to build upon it overmuch. To fret yourself in the meantime with alternations of hope and fear is useless if you are to succeed, and more than useless if you are not: I always thought so for myself, before I had sent anything to press. One wishes of course for success as for other pleasant things; but the readier we hold ourselves to dispense with it if necessary, the better. I am not old enough to preach, but I am old enough to tell you how I thought at your age of this matter, which of course was to me as serious an aspiration as to you now. To encourage or discourage another is a responsibility I cannot undertake, especially as I think one ought to need or heed neither encouragement nor discouragement.

With good wishes

Yours truly,
A. C. Swinburne

219. TO GEORGE POWELL

MS: National Library of Wales.

Holmwood, Henley on Thames,
September 16, 1867

My dear Powell

I shall hope to be at Slough on Wednesday at 4 P.M. exactly and

---

burne's counsel, is reported to have said (Evan Charteris, *The Life and Letters of Sir Edmund Gosse*, 1931, p. 20), "How *could* you as a Christian seek Swinburne's acquaintance?"

shall I suppose have no difficulty in finding you. I shall like of all things to share your lodging till Saturday. Thanks for answering at once. I have just seen the doctor who let me go, but says I must be regular as here.

Yours affectionately,
A. C. Swinburne

220. TO WILLIAM MICHAEL ROSSETTI

MS: Rutgers. Brief extract in Lafourcade, *Biography*, p. 186 n.

Holmwood, Henley on Thames,
September 17, 1867

My dear Rossetti

I send you a little book on Whitman [1] which an American friend has sent me. I think it will interest you, presuming as I do that you have not seen it, for it seems quite new there. The extracts from his (Whitman's) letters on the hospital work of the war are beautiful; I think of noticing the book in print, to get a chance of demanding that the whole should be collected and published: so I shall in time—say a month or two—want this book back: but in no haste. I think Scott might like to see it, if you will pass it on to him when you have done with it. Whether I do or not, perhaps (it struck me) you might take this occasion to say a short and seasonable word on Whitman in the British ear. If you can conveniently, would you do me a service by asking Hotten when you pass 1) How Blake goes on—I asked a month since without answer—and 2) why my friend Lorimer Graham never (as he writes to me from Saxony in a note accompanying this book) received to order the copy of my Poems he wrote for, de-signed as a present for a Hamburg poet and Professor, who wants to translate me bodily into German, that the young male of the Federalie may look to Dolores as an ideal (objective *and* subjective according to position) and the young female to Anactoria. Cette idée vraiment piquante ferait b - - der un cadavre: le v - - d'un b - - - - - allemand se dresserait à moins. Unless indeed the jungfrau Germany is a per-fect Justine for virtue—inébranlable, literally.

You will see there is some awful rot—des chimères révoltantes comme Dieu et sa fille la vertu—in this book at p. 69 etc. about poetry as an art, such as and worse than Whitman allows himself here and

1. *Notes on Walt Whitman, as Poet and Person* (New York, 1867), by John Bur-roughs (1837–1921), essayist and friend of Whitman. But M. D. Conway had lent Rossetti a copy of the pamphlet in proof on Apr. 30 (see *Rossetti Papers*, p. 230).

there—de la merde, enfin: 'oh monsieur! ca me soulève le cœur'—but, like 'suffering virtue,' one has to swallow it, and on the whole the tone of the book is good. In the next Fortnightly there will be an article of mine on Arnold—curtailed of much I had written, to get it squeezed into shape for a periodical which it would otherwise have overweighted (which is a bore, for the part I have to reserve contained an eloquent exposition of the real nature of Urizen and his crucified son—mais ils ne perdront rien pour attendre)—but, as I expect, retaining two fierce puffs, by way of separate notes, of your sister and of Scotus—'Year of the World'—as enthusiastic if not as beautifully worded as the note to a certain romance where the author, reminded of a friendly doctor who had once proposed to poison the whole of a female hospital in Naples for erotic purposes, breaks out—'Homme aimable! reçois d'un ami loin de toi ce témoignage d'un souvenir que' etc. As the occasion is different, so is the form of the present tribute— but it really is *not* dragged in head and ears, and I hope may 'give satisfaction.' Don't tell Scotus till it *is* out, please, *in case*. I have been very well and comfortable here—Deo non obstante—this last month and more. Love to Gabriel and all our friends. I heard from Howell at St. Leonards. This and W.W. are sent to Cheyne Walk because I don't know the address which I suppose you have now changed to.

Ever yours affectionately,

[A. C. Swinburne] [2]

By the by could you find out for me where and at what price one can get Teulet's Lettres de Marie Stuart (one volume) and Knox's History of the Reformation? [3] there *is* a private Club edition of this, but I suppose costly. I think of tackling Bothwell. Item—if it is not overcharging your kindness with requests—would you ask Ned to get back from Furnivall my father's old book [4] lent to him through me long since, as my father wants it? I don't know F.'s address and would gladly eschew his correspondance which is as tedious and offensive as St. Paul's must have been to the Corinthians. *And*—would you [also mind send]ing me the new issue of the Percy Ballads edited by the said F. (which I know is out) and see if he has put my name down (as I told him) as a *subscriber's*, which is cheapest and surest? He is not over attentive, and it will be a good deed to *prod* him:

2. The signature has been cut off.

3. John Knox, *The Historie of the reformation of religioun within the realm of Scotland* (1586). It was included in David Laing's six-volume Bannatyne Club edition of Knox's works (Edinburgh, 1846–64).

4. See above, Letter 102.

and is it not, don't you think, *oddish* to hear nothing of sales or editions of any of my books? I have only had the money agreed on for 1,000 copies of the Poems—£200 and £50 more on account: and I know he has sold more than the first edition, without changing title pages as I should think he ought—qu'en dites vous? I never thought of troubling you with all this when I began, but I know you can help me just where I am helpless in arrangements, and so it strikes me as *the thing* to tax your good nature.

I am writing—I add it to fill up—a poem (among others) on Siena,[5] of a discursive sort (lyrical) which I rather like and hope you will: and I have one or two projects I should like to talk over with friends when I go to town. How is Whistler, and has the Burlington matter been wound up in any way? [6]

221. TO GEORGE POWELL

MS: National Library of Wales. One sentence in Lafourcade, *Biography*, p. 167 n.

Holmwood, Henley on Thames,
Saturday [October 5, 1867]

My dear Powell

Many thanks for the photograph, which is most interesting. I should like of all things to have a large one, but what a pity the scene is imperfect, a stage without actors, a hearth without fire, a harp without cords, a church without worshippers, a song without music, a day without sunlight, a garden without flowers, a tree without fruit! I would give anything for a good photograph taken at the right minute—say the tenth cut or so—and doing justice to *all sides* of the question. As it is the block is just at the right angle for such a representation. If I were but a painter—! I would do dozens of different fellows diversely suffering. There *can* be no subject fuller of incident, character, interest—realistic, modern, dramatic, intense,

5. "Siena" (Bonchurch, 2, 222–32), published as a pamphlet (for copyright) and then in *Lippincott's Magazine* (June 1868); reprinted in *SBS*.

6. After an altercation in Paris between Whistler and his brother, on one hand, and their brother-in-law, Seymour Haden, on the other ("Haden said that he fell through a plate glass window, Whistler that he knocked him through"), Haden printed an explanatory pamphlet and "threatened to resign from the Burlington Fine Arts Club . . . unless Whistler was expelled." Finally, he *was* expelled on Dec. 13, and both William and Gabriel Rossetti resigned in protest. See E. R. and J. Pennell, *The Life of James McNeill Whistler* (2 vols. London and Phila., 1908), 2, 141–43, and *Rossetti Papers*, pp. 234–35, 245.

and vividly pictorial, palpitant d'actualité. Do get some fellow with a turn for drawing to try it.

I am quite well and have written a poem on this check of Garibaldi's expedition,[1] which (the poem, *not* the check) pleases me more than most things I have done. I shall run over some day and shew it you. I have had time and thought for nothing not Italian these ten days; you will see the result. I think the Roman song will please Mazzini.

I have just read a novel called 'Margaret's Engagement'[2] in which I am bodily introduced with only a difference of height etc. but my looks and ways reproduced unblushingly. C'est un peu fort; but it has amused too much to irritate me.

I suppose you have seen the Fortnightly;[3] tell me what you think. I send you George Meredith's opinion, as I think you wished for a sample of his handwriting!

I shall run over to him soon for a day.

With best regards to Tarver.[4]

Ever yours affectionately,
A. C. Swinburne

222. TO WILLIAM MICHAEL ROSSETTI

MS: British Museum. Extracts in *Modern Language Review*, 22 (1927), 86; *The Ashley Library, A Catalogue, 9* (1927), 137–38; *Revue anglo-américaine, 9* (1931–32), 49–50.

Holmwood, Henley on Thames,
October 6 [1867]

Dear Rossetti

I heard with much delight of your Whitman projects, and on getting your letter sent at once to town for the number of the Chronicle

1. "The Halt before Rome, September, 1867" (Bonchurch, 2, 108–18), published in the *Fortnightly Review* (Nov. 1867), and reprinted in *SBS*.

2. By Catherine A. Simpson Wynne, published (anonymously) in Aug. 1867. Mrs. Wynne, who also wrote *A Life in a Love* (1865) and possibly *Story of a Kiss* (1887), was the daughter of Counsellor Jessopp, of Albany Place, Cheshunt, and Clifton, Bristol. Her husband was a partner in a firm of Liverpool shipbuilders. (I am indebted for this information to Mrs. Paull F. Baum, whose authority was Mrs. Richard Bentley, of the firm that published Mrs. Wynne's works.)

3. "Matthew Arnold's 'New Poems.'"

4. William Henry Tarver (1822–1909), French master at Eton 1851–84.

containing your article,[1] which I read and I need not say enjoyed. I don't think you quite put strength enough into your blame on one side, while you make at least enough of minor faults or eccentricities. To me it seems always that his great flaw is a fault of debility, not an excess of strength—I mean his bluster. His own personal and national self-reliance and arrogance I need not tell you I applaud and sympathize and rejoice in; but the frothy and blatant ebullience of feeling and speech at times is very feeble for so great a poet of so great a people. He is in part, certainly, the prophet of democracy; but not wholly, because he tries so openly to be, and asserts so violently that he is: always as if he was fighting the case out on a platform. This is the only thing I really or gravely dislike and revolt from. On the whole, my admiration and enjoyment of his greatness grows keener and warmer every time I think of him. This harvest carol [2] has fine bits, but is hardly up to his mark, do you think? In spite of glorious verses. How *did* it get into such English company?

Of course your dedication would have been a great delight and honour to me, but I think your precaution quite just and necessary, if only because, little as you or I might care for the yelp of mangy anonymous curs, it might impair the success of the thing we want done. I am very glad it is to be, and think it does credit to Hotten and will repay him. When will it be out? I hunger for the first squeak of the gelded pigs of criticism as they sniff it. That it should be inscribed to Scotus is an additional excellence in my eyes; he of all men is the right one to receive this tribute, and I shall be honestly proud of being cited as a witness to the honour of which we others who know left from right in poetic matters hold so admirable a fellow soldier and leader as Whitman. I have no doubt your course as to selection will be the justest possible, but I must ask if for instance you have rejected the lovely and most pleasurable poem on night and sleep and sleepers because of the ugly or obtrusive words and phrases in it? [3] Of course you give the 'Voice out of the Sea' and the 'Lilacs'? I

1. July 6. *Poems by Walt Whitman*, selected and edited by W. M. Rossetti, was published in 1868.

2. "A Carol of Harvest for 1867," in the *Galaxy* (Sep. 1867), was retitled "The Return of the Heroes" in the pamphlet *Passage to India* (1871).

3. See below, Letter 223. Rossetti said that his "principle of selection would be to miss out entirely any poem, though otherwise fine and unobjectionable, which contains any of his extreme crudities of expression in the way of indecency: I would not expurgate any such poems, but simply exclude them" (*Rossetti Papers*, pp. 239–40). See also Horace Traubel, *With Walt Whitman in Camden* (3 vols. Boston and New York, 1906–14), *3*, 296–308.

hope too to see the 'Camps of Green' from 'Drum Taps' which is a great idol of mine for its perfect classic (*not* academic but purely classic) beauty. I send back Burroughs' letter [4] with thanks for the sight of it: keep his book for me till we meet if you please, I hope it will not be long first. Could you get me that letter of Mazzini on the Congress? [5] I missed it if it was in the Times, and on getting your letter toiled after it in a vain hunt backwards.

I may tell you between ourselves that I have now done enough to enable me to speak with some hope of a design which must come either to nothing or to much, much (that is) for me, if I may so speak of my own aims, and achievements. I think I may some time accomplish a book of political and national poems [6] as complete and coherent in its way as the Châtiments or Drum Taps. This, as you know, Mazzini asked me to attempt—'for us,' [7] as he said. Phantoms and skeletons of national songs I have for some time seen floating in the future before me in plenty, but now I have also done one or two into words and so embodied them that I think they will turn out in good marching order—des soldats *viables!* This week I have worked off one on the news of Garibaldi's arrest which I am tempted to think my best lyric ever written; although as a rule I always feel discouraged at first with any work I have strongly desired and laboured to do well for any outer reason such as moves one in these matters. But this time I am thus far satisfied; and I am hopeful that it will seriously please Mazzini—rather confident that it must. I thought of sending you a sample, but will wait till we meet. It is all up with our Monarchico-constitutional Savoyard friends this time I suspect. There is I think room for a book of songs of the European revolution, and if sung as thoroughly as Hugo or as Whitman would sing them, they ought to ring for some time to some distance of echo. The only fear is that one may be disabled by one's desire—made impotent by excess of strain.

I see by the means of my sweet friends of the Spectator of yester-

4. "Conway sends me a letter from Burroughs relative to my Whitman article in the *Chronicle*," Rossetti wrote in his diary on Sep. 9 (*Rossetti Papers*, p. 240; for the letter see p. 270).

5. "Ai Membri del Congresso della Pace [Geneva]," in *Unità Italiana*, Sep. 11, 1867; reprinted in *Scritti editi ed inediti di Giuseppe Mazzini* (94 vols. Imola, 1906–43), *86* (1940), 81–89 (and in a French translation, pp. liii-lix).

6. *SBS.*

7. See above, Letter 191.

day that the Chronicle has recently been pitching into me.[8] Can you tell me the number? I shall send for the week's before last on the chance. Let me hear what you think of my last essay when you read it. I should like some day to see this book on Robespierre.[9] I think it did once pass under my eyes, at Houghton's.

With love to all friends,
Ever affectionately yours,
A. C. Swinburne

I am of course very desirous to see a copy of Whitman's last edition; I conclude you have one. Were I in your place as English editor I should reprint the great passage on Liberty literally from the preface to the first edition, not as afterwards recast and served up separately.

223. MATTHEW ARNOLD TO SWINBURNE

Text: *Times Literary Supplement* (Aug. 12, 1920), p. 517.

The Athenaeum, October 10 [1867]

Dear Mr. Swinburne,

I am rather proud of my discernment in having grasped and said that you were yourself the French critic; [1] not that the French is not worthy of the best of French critics, but something in the way you brought the quotations in gave me a suspicion; and then they were to the point in a manner I did not think a foreigner could exactly, under the circumstances, have managed. But I write now to beg you some day to let me see the suppressed paper, if you still have it by you; I have the greatest curiosity to read it, after reading the others.

You will own I at least have a conscience, when I tell you I have refused to lecture at Edinburgh on the litterature [*sic*] of the grand siècle, or on any other period of French litterature, alleging that my knowledge was too imperfect.

8. "Mr. Swinburne as Critic," *Spectator* (Oct. 6, 1867), pp. 1109–11. Quoting the *Chronicle's* remark that Swinburne's poetry was marked by "barren poverty of thought," the article asserted that "there is no intellectual thread in any single poem of his that we can remember."

9. Probably E. Hamel, *Histoire de Robespierre d'après des papiers de famille, les sources originales et des documents entièrement inédits,* published in Paris in three volumes, 1865–67.

1. In his essay on Arnold's *New Poems* Swinburne introduced a three-page quotation in French with "A French critic has expressed this in words which I may quote here, torn out from their context."

Sainte Beuve wrote me word that he had set a M. Lacaussade, whom perhaps you know by name, to translate Obermann's preachment, and that he was going to make use of it. But he will keep himself to the Obermann ground, which he knows; the hands which in general *do* English litterature for the révue [*sic*] des 2 mondes—Émile Montégut, your friend Louis Étienne and so on—are not very satisfactory.[2]

I am just giving up my house in London—driven into the wilderness by those young ravens, or cormorants, my sons: but some day I hope to have the pleasure of coming to see you and talk to you.

Ever sincerely yours,
Matthew Arnold

224. TO WILLIAM MICHAEL ROSSETTI

MS: Rutgers. Brief extract in Lafourcade, *Biography*, p. 187.

Holmwood, Henley on Thames,
October 11 [1867]

Dear Rossetti

Thanks for two letters and the enclosures from Hotten. I am glad you agree with what I said of Whitman in my last and flattered by your making use of it [1]—glad too that it should be softened as one would not like even to seem unfriendly or unenthusiastic even towards such a man. I was confident we should be found agreed upon the particular poems in question. I wail over the 'Sleep' but I suppose it must be. Aussi c'est bien un peu sa faute à lui. I hope to be in town

2. The allusions are to Charles Augustin Sainte-Beuve (1804–69), the famous critic; Auguste Lacaussade (1817–97), critic, translator, poet, and librarian; Emile Montégut (1825–95), critic and author; and Louis Etienne (died 1875). Etienne is called "your friend" because of Swinburne's allusion to him (Bonchurch, *15*, 115) in the essay on Arnold (referring to Etienne's article "Le Paganisme poétique en Angleterre," *Revue des deux mondes*, May 15, 1867, pp. 291–317). "Obermann's preachment" is Arnold's poem "Obermann Once More," first published in *New Poems* (1867). Sainte-Beuve and Lacaussade together had translated Arnold's earlier poem, "Stanzas in Memory of the Author of 'Obermann'" (1852), into French prose. Lacaussade's translation of "Obermann Once More" was never published and cannot now be traced (see Louis Bonnerot, *Matthew Arnold poète, essai de biographie psychologique*, Paris, 1947, p. 538).

1. Rossetti quoted (without naming the author) most of the first paragraph of Swinburne's Letter 222, above, in the preface to *Poems by Walt Whitman*. The quotation was first identified by Lafourcade. See his articles on Swinburne and Whitman in *Modern Language Review*, 22 (1927), 84–86, and *Revue anglo-américaine* 9 (1931), 49–50.

next week and see you and talk things over. Henry Kingsley has just been here: [2] I never met him before and like him—especially as in a minute's talk on Italy I found him of one mind with me. (My poem on Rome is in type for next Fortnightly.) He is also excited about the very gross insolence and scurrility of the Spectator and we both think the polecat's nest wants smoking out. For Urizen's sake—or rather Orc's—*hasten* the Whitman work if you can—for I see advertised in a thing called the 'Broadway'—this! 'Walt Whitman: by Robert Buchanan:' [3] the word 'polecat' reminded me.

The 'Page' [4] spoken of as a probable sympathizer by Burroughs is if I remember his article on literary morals 'un bougre tout confit en merde,' to use the happy and classic expression of a great literary moralist.

Very glad you like my essay. I have had two very courteous and pleasant letters from Arnold since it appeared. As to all said in the Notes, I nail my colours to the mast and defy any charge of exaggeration. Thanks for the excerpt about Mazzini's letter. I should like to see the Unità and shall try to get it out of *him*. In haste

Your affectionate,
A. C. Swinburne

225. TO GEORGE POWELL

MS: National Library of Wales.

[? November 1867] [1]

My dear Powell

Very sorry to have missed you and to hear of the reason. I have just come from Mornington Crescent where I went for news and was glad to hear *you* were all right as of course I was rather alarmed by *possibilities*.

I will be with you at six-thirty.

Yours affectionately,
A. C. Swinburne

2. According to S. M. Ellis (*Henry Kingsley 1830–1876*, 1931, p. 83), Kingsley "became friendly with the new poet, and Swinburne was a frequent guest of the Kingsleys at Wargrave, when he was staying near by at Holmwood, Shiplake."

3. In *David Gray, and Other Essays, Chiefly on Poetry* (1868).

4. Probably A. H. Japp (see below, Letter 1232).

1. The date is a mere guess. The paper is watermarked "1867."

226. TO KARL BLIND

MS: British Museum.

22a Dorset Street, W., November 2 [1867]

My dear Sir

I shall be most glad to accept your kind invitation for Friday. For three days past I have been in London—and have been wishing to call on you—but withheld by feeling that you might be just now occupied with immediate and too precious business to allow of my intrusion. I am quite well now, though in the early summer I was so constantly unwell.

Let me tell you that (in consequence of my bad expression) I have unwittingly given you—to my regret—a quite wrong impression in my little article in the 'Fortnightly.' [1] The 'anti-German' words were quoted *ironically* from the writing of another man—whom I meant to 'persifler' or (if you prefer the word) to 'chaff'—by citing them. What I meant was *this*—'*You* say "perhaps we cannot appreciate French verse—we English—we are too *German*." Permit me to assure you that *that* is *not* the reason.' This is what I meant to say—if you look again at the passage, you will see the persiflage. The journals have abused me for attacking England in the same essay. That I meant to do. But pray do not suspect me of any further malice—and believe me, with all thanks and kindest regards to you and yours

Yours very sincerely,
A. C. Swinburne

I hope, as you see the 'Fortnightly,' that you have seen and not disapproved of my last contribution [2]—it was at least written off at a heat for the sake of the subject.

A C S

227. TO GEORGE POWELL

MS: National Library of Wales.

Arts Club, Hanover Square,
November 2 [1867]

My dear Powell

Very glad you will be up on Wednesday and shall be the same to meet you any day we can arrange. I have been at Kingston with George Meredith for two days and will try if I can coax him up to

1. "Matthew Arnold's 'New Poems.'"

2. "The Halt before Rome."

a bad dinner here that you and he may meet. I am sorry you suffered so much in the process of cure; mais que veux-tu? Voilà bien ton bon Dieu, ma chère Justine. It is well you have anyhow evaded for this time the claws of Providence. I hope the same luck awaits Zwecker,[1] and am doubly sorry to hear of his illness. Voilà encore—etc. etc. Could you have come up on Thursday, I had asked Jones to join and he had promised, so we might have had a jolly evening. I hope we shall yet.

Ever yours,
A. C. Swinburne

228. TO GEORGE POWELL

MS: National Library of Wales.

[ca. November 4, 1867]

My dear Powell

Let it be Saturday—and dine with me at seven at the 'Arts'—17 Hanover Square. On Friday I dine at Karl Blind's—you will have heard the bad rumours of defeat [1] this morning and understand we are in trouble about Italy.

Ever yours sincerely,
(in haste),
A. C. Swinburne

229. TO FREDERICK LOCKER [1]

MS: Harvard.

22a Dorset Street, W.,
Monday [November 11, 1867] [2]

Dear Locker

I shall be delighted to meet Mr. Arnold on Monday next, and to

1. Johann Baptist Zwecker (1814–76), German-born painter and illustrator.

1. Garibaldi's, by French and Papal troops, at Mentana on Nov. 3, 1867.

1. Frederick Locker (1821–95), known as Locker-Lampson from 1885, when he added his second wife's name to his own. He wrote light, graceful verse (*London Lyrics,* his only original volume, was published in 1857), and collected it as well (*Lyra Elegantiarum,* his anthology, was first issued in 1867); he is also noted as the creator of the Rowfant Library.

2. The envelope is postmarked Nov. 12.

accept your invitation with thanks.[3] I have been prostrate these two days with influenza but hope to be about tomorrow.

Truly yours,
A. C. Swinburne

230. TO WILLIAM MICHAEL ROSSETTI

MS: Rutgers. Published: Bonchurch, *18*, 55–57.

22a Dorset Street, November 28 [1867]

Dear Rossetti

Thanks for sending on my Broadway letter [1]—and thanks for what you say of my verses of Appeal [2]—which have drawn down on my head (pass for public abuse, but—what I *do* mind—) the devil's own correspondance. O Justine! tu voulais faire une bonne action—tu devais souffrir! I know I deserve all—from Rodin to Ste. Marie! Could I not be warned by the wisest of men or books? Il faudra pour me relever que je fasse quelque chose d'éxécrable.

Meantime I once more want your advice on a confidential matter. I wrote those verses on Wednesday afternoon—on Thursday morning I took them to my friend Dr. Bird,[3] with whom two days before I had

3. "I am to meet Swinburne at dinner on Monday, at the Lockers' . . . ," Arnold wrote to his mother on Nov. 16 (*Letters of Matthew Arnold 1848–1888*, ed. G. W. E. Russell, 2 vols. New York and London, 1896, *1*, 375–76). "He expresses a great desire to meet me, and I should like to do him some good, but I am afraid he has taken some bent. His praise has, as was natural, inclined the religious world to look out in my writings for a crusade against religion, and the *Contemporary Review*, the *Christian World*, and other similar periodicals, fix on the speeches of Empedocles and Obermann, and calmly say, dropping all mention of the real speakers, 'Mr. Arnold here professes his Pantheism,' or 'Mr. Arnold here disowns Christianity.' "

1. Edmund Routledge (1843–99), editor of the *Broadway*, had accepted William Rossetti's poem *Mrs. Holmes Grey* (published in Feb. 1868), and had contracted with him for two articles. Rossetti and he called at Swinburne's on Dec. 14, and Swinburne offered him (*Rossetti Papers*, p. 245) "various things, and handed over a short Boccacciesque tale, *Monna Lisa.*" See below, Letter 234.

2. "An Appeal to England" (Bonchurch, *2*, 272–75) in the *Morning Star* (Nov. 22, 1867); it was reprinted as a broadside in the same year and included in *SBS*.

3. Dr. George Bird, a physician, who lived with his sister, Alice Bird, in Welbeck Street. Swinburne doubtless met them through the Burtons, with whom they had long been intimate, and it was Miss Bird to whom Admiral Swinburne is said to have lamented, "God has endowed my son with genius, but He has not vouchsafed to grant him self-control" (Bonchurch, *20*, 130). Bird was born in 1817, or thereabouts, and survived at least until 1899. As physician for Mrs. Leigh Hunt in the fifties, whom he described as "an intemperate woman and sodden from drink," he

talked of the thing as to be done, if possible—left them with him, as a man knowing in the matter, for insertion where he thought best—and found them in the *Star* on Friday. Now, the manager writes to him, first thanks to me etc., then *confidentially*—'in sending a contribution of so much intrinsic value to a newspaper, would Mr. S. wish it to be treated as purely complimentary, or be prepared to accept a pecuniary acknowledgment for it?' Now my own idea was that for unsolicited contributions newspapers never did pay—let alone for verses—any more than for letters to the editor; so the question was new to me. 'I am equally afraid of wounding his sensitiveness by offering or by acting unfairly by withholding the fee. I need hardly say that an affirmative reply would not in the least lessen our estimate of the compliment paid to the Star by the poet;' who alas! paid none—said only 'Any paper, Daily News, Star, any that would insert it, being on the side of justice and freedom.' Now—what am I to say? 1) I have no a priori objection to their money—and *have* unwittingly earned it, as Bird tells me that within two hours of issue neither Morning nor Evening Star of Friday could be had for love or money. 2) Is it the thing to take money for what was done with any thought but that in my head? 3) Even were I without bills etc. to pay, the money might be taken—as for my Cretan Ode [4]—to give to some Fund or other—say for the widows and orphans of the law's making, or some other nearer to me—Italian or such—never I should think timelier than now. Mind I don't say, if I take any, the money *is* to go so, but it might. Please write one line at once—Do or Don't—I have no first dominant impulse, and that only can decide.

Pardon the trouble and believe me

Yours always,

A. C. Swinburne

I congratulate you on Whitman's letter,[5] and long to see it. I was much distressed to hear from Ned that *his* last news of your sister's health had been bad. I trust they are now better, if not good.

Routledge wants to come here and *talk* things with me. Would you mind being here to see fair play for me—*in case,* and what day, if you can, that I may appoint him? I dread the 'privy paw' [6] of publishers.

---

assuredly acquired a knowledge that stood him in good stead later. See Edmund Blunden, *Leigh Hunt and His Circle* (New York and London, 1930), pp. 328–29.

4. See above, Letter 185.

5. See *Rossetti Papers,* p. 243.

6. "Lycidas," l. 128.

I have been in bed three days and shut up five with influenza and bile: which I take as just judgments on a virtuous attempt. Accomplis tes décrets, Etre Suprême.

231. TO THOMAS PURNELL

MS: Yale.

[December 1867]

My dear Purnell

Here is Trübner's [1] note. I must I suppose take £20 *if I can get no more* under the circumstances. I have spent the day in writing out the 36 stanzas [2] and am half dead—now I must get someone to make me another fair copy. Let me hear from you tomorrow.

With all thanks for your kind offices.

Ever yours sincerely,
A. C. Swinburne

232. TO THOMAS PURNELL

MS: Yale. Published: Bonchurch, *18*, 57–58*.

December 9 [1867]

Dear Purnell

Come when you please and take me to Trübner (say *Wednesday* at *any* hour). This week I am probably—*not* certainly—disengaged every day and evening. Let me know as soon as may be. If you see Dolores [1] before I do, tell her with my love that I would not shew my-

1. Nicholas Trübner (1817–84), the publisher.

2. "Siena."

1. It is impossible to separate fact from fancy in the romance of Swinburne and Adah Isaacs Menken, here called Dolores. That she was born is a fact; when, nobody knows, but perhaps in 1835. She was a robust, handsome, bosomy vaudevillian who worked hard for notoriety, onstage and off, achieving her finest effects, in the first instance, in *Mazeppa* wearing flesh-colored tights and strapped on the back of a "steed," and in the second by providing Dumas *père* (aged 64) with an Indian summer and Swinburne (aged 29) with a Pierian spring. The degree of her *liaison* with the latter has inflamed curiosity since 1867, but, though conjecture has been rampant, the only *fact* is that on hearing of her death in Aug. 1868, Swinburne remarked explicitly (in a private letter to a close friend) that she was "most lovable as a friend as well as a mistress" (see below, Letter 272).

That her affair with Swinburne was notorious is another fact. Purnell wrote (*A Swinburne Library*, p. 266) to the poet on Dec. 4: "To-day I have had a letter from

self sick and disfigured in her eyes. I was spilt last week out of a hansom, and my nose and forehead cut to rags—was seedy for four days, and hideous. Are the poor *boys* to be left much longer tingling in expectation? they would rather have it over.

Ever yours,

A. C. Swinburne

233. TO WILLIAM BELL SCOTT

MS: Yale.

22a Dorset Street, W., December 11 [1867]

My dear Scott

I am going to ask you for something which I shall not be at all put out if you refuse; but if you grant my asking I shall be really obliged. It is for two copies of the 'Year of the World' [1] which cannot be bought and which I know you have in hand. Two friends of mine—one is Mr. Arnold, who has a most enthusiastic admiration of your 'Rosabel' or

---

Dolores—such a letter! She fears you are ill; she is unable to think of anything but you; she wishes me to telegraph to her if you are in danger, and she will fly on the wings of the wind to nurse you. She has become a soft-throated serpent, strangling prayers on her white lips to kiss the poet, whose absence leaves her with ghosts and shadows. She concludes:

" 'Tell him all—say out my despairing nature to him—take care of his precious life. Write at once; believe in me and my holy love for him. Let him write one word in your letter. He will, for he is so good.'

"What do you think of this? It is Cleopatra over again." Around the *"Punch* Table" in Bouverie Street Swinburne's name had often occasioned casual ribaldry, and on Dec. 4, according to Henry Silver's unpublished diary in the *Punch* offices, Du Maurier told "of Swinburne and Menken! queer lech she hath, the Animal." But Shirley Brooks, in the same crowd, wrote to William Hardman in Feb. 1868: "Mrs. Sothern took me to see Ada Menken, and I am my own no longer, *nor my wife's neither.* . . . I am Ada's. . . . She lives at No. 26, Norfolk Street, W. C. Swinburne is the only rival I dread—he knew her first. But I shall sit upon his corpse. He boasts—but he lies!" (S. M. Ellis, ed., *The Hardman Papers*, p. 320). Burne-Jones drew and sent to Swinburne a series of eleven cartoons celebrating the affair titled "Ye Treue and Pitifulle Historie of ye Poet and ye Ancient Dame."

Incomparably the worst thing about the Menken legend is the silly sentimentality of her memorialists, who have one and all sought to aggrandize her by cheapening others, going so far, occasionally, as to praise her poetry, which is appalling. Adah Menken was frankly vulgar, and frank vulgarity is a refreshing quality to find in English literary history in the eighteen-sixties. The fullest study of her, to date, is Bernard Falk's *The Naked Lady; or Storm over Adah* (1934).

1. Scott's poem (1846), which Swinburne had praised in his essay on Arnold (see above, Letter 220).

'Morganne' and knows lots of it by heart—as much I think as I do—
want to see it and can't buy it and knowing I know you have thrown
themselves on my goodnature as I throw myself on yours. 'Blake' is
as good as out—I have the only bound copy except the 'trade' one.

Tell Mrs. Scott that I met yesterday her friend in the Church, and
my former senior at college, Mr. Maconochie,[2] looking very well and
priestly, and in very good spirits.

Ever yours,
A. C. Swinburne

234. TO WILLIAM MICHAEL ROSSETTI

MS: Rutgers.

[December 12, 1867][1]

Dear Rossetti

Can you be here on Saturday evening at eight or a little before?
I have arranged, if you can, to meet Routledge then.[2]

I have received a message from Mazzini of which I cannot trust
myself to write.[3] After this, the British public seems not over important. He is ill and weak, but can read and write.

Ever yours,
A. C. Swinburne

235. TO LADY JANE HENRIETTA SWINBURNE

Text: Leith, pp. 86–87.

December 16 [1867]

. . . Though you may not look at it with the same eyes as I do,
I think you will sympathize with me—knowing what it is to me—when
I tell you that I have had a *most* kind message from Mazzini, sent from
his sick-bed, only making too much of my poor attempts to serve his

2. James MacConechy (1833–71), that is. A native of Glasgow, he entered Balliol
in 1854; B.A. 1858, exhibitioner 1859–64, M.A. 1861. From 1868 to 1871 he was vicar
of Christ Church, Watney Street, St. George's-in-the-East, and in 1871 of All Saints,
Paddington.

1. Supplied by William Rossetti.

2. See above, Letter 230.

3. Mazzini wrote to Emilie Venturi on Dec. 3 (*Mazzini's Letters to an English
Family, 1861–1872*, p. 192): "Do write yourself to Swinburne that I am ill, *cannot*
write, but read, mark each step of his, feel grateful and admiring and touched."

cause by writing. He is getting better, and I suppose may leave Switzerland for England.

236. TO WILLIAM MICHAEL ROSSETTI

MS: Rutgers.

December 19, i.e. 20, 2.30 A.M. [1867]

My dear Rossetti

Whitman's letter [1] is so thoroughly noble and *stimulating* that instead of going to bed as I might and ought I sit down by a dead fire to thank you for a sight of it and send it back at once for fear of accident. I don't *quite* understand on a second reading whether he does object or not to the excision of a word or two in the original Preface. His tone is so worthy of his work at its highest, and so duly and justly appreciative of your position and of his real debt to you, as to reassure me in my previous view of his personal character. I am on all grounds glad that he has shown himself so worthy (personally) of your admiration and of the furtherance of your work.

As to my Blake [2]—first I have to thank you for the intention, then for the sort of choice you give me—and then, to say that I would rather leave it wholly to your judgment. You know the book, and what to say of it, and how. I need not say how much store I should set by any review of yours, nor that, the fuller it was, the more interest and pleasure I should expect from it. *Cela posé,* I may add that I do not at all like Routledge's message—and if that is going to be the style and tone in that quarter, instead of grateful and respectful acceptance of any assistance or patronage from you or me, I seriously think the sooner we drop him and it the better.

Hotten showed me the proof of your dedicatory note to Scott [3]—I need not say the reference to me gave me great pleasure.

I hoped to have met you as well as Gabriel yesterday, but can tell you now by pen instead of mouth the good news brought me by Mme. Venturi, that Mazzini is so far really improved in health as to talk hopefully of arriving here *before* the New Year: when I am to have an early sight of him. He does not think he ought to attempt that just yet; and he says his illness was quite brought on by mental suffering

1. To William Rossetti (printed in *Rossetti Papers*, pp. 285–87).

2. *William Blake A Critical Essay,* though dated 1868, was actually issued this month. It was dedicated to William Rossetti.

3. See above, Letter 222.

and (he was much better before) especially by Garibaldi's personal conduct to him—not only turning a deaf ear to his most earnest expostulations, but ending in a positive quarrel. She says my verses give him real comfort and pleasure: I can hardly imagine them capable. And you know I am not mock-modest.

Write a line in answer if only to say that Whitman has returned safe.

Yours affectionately,
A. C. Swinburne

237. TO JAMES HAIN FRISWELL [1] [?]

Text: Bonchurch, *18*, 62*.

22a Dorset Street, W.,
December 21, 1868 [for 1867]

My dear Sir

I shall be happy to undertake the *Coleridge* [2] on the terms proposed. I presume I shall also have the selection and arrangement of the poems in my hands. It will be a more congenial labour to me than the Selection from Byron, who is not made for selection—Coleridge is. In my eyes his good poems have no fault, his bad poems no merit; and to disengage these from those will be a pleasure to me.

I can let you have the work in less than three months if you like; I shall only have to put other work aside and give my whole attention to this for a time; and this may as well be done now as later.

Believe me

Very truly yours,
A. C. Swinburne

238. TO LORD HOUGHTON

MS: The Marchioness of Crewe.

22a Dorset Street, W., December 21 [1867]

Dear Lord Houghton

I was sorry to have been out when you called, and should have liked

1. (1825–75), journalist, essayist, novelist, and editor of the "Bayard Series, a Collection of Pleasure Books of Literature," for which Swinburne wrote his essay on Coleridge (see below). In 1870 Friswell's *Modern Men of Letters* provoked the wrath of Sala, who sued the publishers (Hodder and Stoughton) and was awarded £500 damages. According to Gosse and Wise, the letter was addressed to Sampson Low (1797–1886), publisher of the "Bayard Series," but Friswell seems a better nomination.

2. *Christabel and the Lyrical and Imaginative Poems of S. T. Coleridge* (1869). Swinburne's introductory essay (Bonchurch, *15*, 140–54) was reprinted in *ES*.

a sight of the 'horrors' in your company. I am very well and have laid to heart the lesson not to get out of hansoms till the beast has definitely drawn up. In my case it *had* stopped, and moved suddenly on just as I had sprung out, catching and pitching me headlong.

I should much like to write an essay on your Keats[1] (you *have* given me a copy if you remember, and I read the new parts with great interest): but I am just now engaged on Coleridge—attempting the same for him as for Byron—essay and select poems: of all such tasks the one I should have chosen, for more than any *great* poet he not only bears, but imperiously demands, the test of selection. It will make one of the 'Bayard series,' and probably be out early in the year.

You will receive, if it has not arrived before this note, in a day or two a copy of my 'Blake,' which but for you could not have been what it now is, a tolerably adequate and complete monograph. I told Hotten to send you in my name an early copy, and shall be curious to hear what you think of it.

I am glad you found Milton enjoying even the immoral and illegitimate bonds of unholy matrimony, though I deplore the perversity which induces young men so far to forget themselves and nature. I also enjoy (certainly) not less the bonds of a somewhat riotous concubinage.[2] I don't know many *husbands* who could exact or expect from a *wife* such indulgences as are hourly laid at my feet!

Yours ever,

A. C. Swinburne

239. TO GEORGE POWELL

MS: National Library of Wales.

22a Dorset Street, W., December 24 [1867]

My dear Powell

I need not try to do what I cannot—to express in words my sympathy with your sorrow.[1] I will trust you to believe how sincere and earnest it is. There are no further words adequate to give comfort or help. If the knowledge that your friend does truly and deeply feel with you can be of any, you may be assured of having that.

I ought before this to have thanked you for your former letter and the photographs enclosed. I came to overlook it in the pressure of

1. A new edition of Houghton's *Life, Letters, and Literary Remains of John Keats* (first published in 1848).

2. See above, Letter 232.

1. Doubtless for the death of "Charner" (see above, Letters 215 and 216).

business of one kind or other, and in the ill health following on a rather bad accident—being flung out of a hansom in motion, face foremost on the kerbstone. I will not write to you now of other things, nor disturb you in a time of trouble with matters of every day; I will only ask you again to believe in the sorrow I feel for your sorrow and the true friendship with which I am always

Affectionately yours,

Algernon Ch. Swinburne

240. TO WILLIAM MICHAEL ROSSETTI

MS: Rutgers. Published: Bonchurch, *18*, 58–59.

December 24 [1867]

Dear Rossetti

I send you a note received this morning from Routledge [1]—with my answer. I forwarded your note to him yesterday at once. If you think my reply in any way wrong or questionable, I will ask you as a friend to withhold it till we can talk the matter over. I can only add that it is not a momentary *spurt*—I have taken twelve hours to think over it. But 'sans mentir' I set so much store by your judgment, that if you bid me withhold or modify it I will.

Now—for better news of better men and things than me and my doings: but this is in confidence (so much so that Mme. Venturi's brother,[2] at whose house I have been dining and supping, is not in the secret—so if I take you into it you must really be—as I have shown myself—discreet). Mazzini is so much better as to write in a 'healthy' handwriting and say—in confidence to his adopted daughter—that if alive he *will* be here in a few days. If he keeps his word—and you know in this Buonapartesque age he has an absurd and inexplicable weakness for keeping his word—I have a promise to see the first of him. You know they say that when Mirabeau was dying a young fellow with healthy blood came and asked if it could not be transfused into *his* veins out of his own—so as to restore life *there* by degrees as it was exhausted *here*. I wish it were true, and might (if necessary—I don't want to die or live superfluously) do that office for a greater and better than Mirabeau. But he wants no alien blood—his spirit supports him, and will.

1. See above, Letter 236.

2. William A. Ashurst.

I have no end of things to write about, and to *show* you, of Mazzini's. I hope *that* will draw you hither soon.

Shall I see you Saturday at 16 Cheyne Walk? And *have* you got your 'presentation copy' of my Blake? Gabriel has written a most jolly note about *his*.

Your affectionate,
A. C. Swinburne

P.S. I have got such a lovely *profile,* first I ever saw in profile, photograph of Mazzini 'as never was' [3]—and the image of him—come and see it.

241. TO LORD HOUGHTON

MS: The Marchioness of Crewe.

Christmas Day, 1867

Cher Monsieur Rodin

I have read—in Southey's Miscellanies—a mediaeval legend to this effect: that a schoolboy flying from punishment took sanctuary in church and clung to a figure of the Blessed Virgin. Even thither, his breeches being down, his master followed, birch in hand; but in recompense of the child's faith, the master's lifted arm was stricken with paralysis, and only released at the boy's intervention. Were I in *that* boy's place, I should fly and cling to a living and fleshly statue of the Venus Callipyge (doubly appropriate)—which I think as competent *without a miracle,* to stiffen any man's—arm.

Your devoted pupil,
A C S

242. TO GEORGE POWELL

MS: National Library of Wales.

[? *ca.* December 30, 1867] [1]

Dear Powell

Come to Jones with me or meet me there if you can on Thursday evening—he will be charmed to see you then or earlier if you please.

Yours in bed with influenza but hoping to be up soon,

A. C. Swinburne

3. Perhaps (not inappropriately) Daniel 12:1 or Wordsworth's "Elegiac Stanzas," l. 15.

1. The paper is watermarked 1867.

243. TO WILLIAM MICHAEL ROSSETTI

MS: Rutgers.

Arts Club, Hanover Square,
New Year's Day [1868]

Dear Rossetti

Mazzini is safe in England, in spite of illness, weather, and all dangers of the one route open to him. It is a thing to begin the year with thanking heaven for. On the third he will be in London.

Many thanks for your note and enclosures. It is tiresome about Blake,[1] but well settled; I was very glad to feel myself as much in your confidence as you in mine throughout the matter. I trust for my sake and Blake's you may touch on the book yet somewhere. Your poem [2] I reread with renewed admiration and quite intense interest. Whitman I have looked at—fine and full of truth and spirit, but again somewhat violent and restless, as I must maintain the seriously strong work of the world is not.—Returning after a most pleasant evening at Howell's the day I left you, I got such a chill on the way back, though quite early in a close cab, that I have been in bed with violent influenza two days and a half, and am only able to write now.

With all seasonable and sincere wishes for you and yours

Ever your affectionate,
A. C. Swinburne

Your papers shall return at once,—with many thanks.

What abject and vomitorial rot of Tennyson's is this in Once a Week! [3]

244. TO FORD MADOX BROWN

Text: Photostat (of MS) in Library of Congress.

Arts Club, Hanover Square,
New Year's Day [1868]

My dear Brown

I was so chilled on the way from Howell's last Sunday night that I have been two days in bed with *streaming* and sickening influenza—excluding all worship either of Love or Friendship, to which latter deity I should have been happy to devote last evening—but I really

1. See above, Letter 236.

2. "Mrs. Holmes Grey."

3. "On a Spiteful Letter," *Once a Week*, Jan. 4.

had to postpone letters as well as visits. I am greatly vexed at missing you again. Be forgiving—as this time it *was* '*no* fault but God's': [1] and give me another chance soon. I met Ned at Brixton,[2] looking admirably well I thought.

You will [be] glad to hear that the safe arrival of Mazzini in England was telegraphed to me today—good news for a new year. With as good wishes

Ever yours,
A. C. Swinburne

Of course like my other friends you have got *your* Blake by this time?

245. TO KARL BLIND

MS: British Museum.

22a Dorset Street, W.,
Friday, January 3 [1868]

My dear Sir

I shall be happy to avail myself of your kind invitation for Sunday, unless the violent influenza which has kept me three days in bed this week should return and knock me up: I trust it will not.

I read with great admiration and interest the report of your splendid speech at Bradford.

You will doubtless have heard when I did of Mazzini's safe arrival in England. In haste,

Believe me ever sincerely yours,
A. C. Swinburne

246. TO GEORGE POWELL

MS: National Library of Wales.

[? *ca.* January 6, 1868] [1]

My dear Powell

So sorry—but when your letter came I was too ill to read, much less write—being replunged for days into the hell of influenza and indigestion. The day *was* Thursday last,[2] but it seems we didn't disappoint

1. *Chastelard*, III. i (Bonchurch, *8*, 66).

2. Where Howell lived.

1. The paper is watermarked 1866.

2. See above, Letter 242.

Jones, as he also forgot. Let us make another appointment—and keep it.

Have you got well on with the study of sacred literature?

Ever yours,
A. C. Swinburne

247. TO JAMES HAIN FRISWELL

MS: John S. Mayfield.

22a Dorset Street, January 23 [1868]

Dear Mr. Friswell

I am so laid (or knocked) up by influenza that for a day or two I shall be unfit, I fear, for society, or I should be happy to accept your invitation. Early next week, if better, I shall hope to see you and arrange plans.[1]

In haste

Yours sincerely,
A. C. Swinburne

248. TO GEORGE POWELL

MS: National Library of Wales. Brief extracts in Lafourcade, *Biography*, pp. 191, 195.

22a Dorset Street, W., January 26 [1868]

My dear Powell

I am ashamed to have left your last note so long unanswered—but I have been so worried of late with influenza, love-making, and other unwholesome things—such as business, money, etc.—that I have 'left undone all that I should have done.' [1] I must send you in a day or two a photograph of my present possessor—known to Britannia as Miss Menken, to me as Dolores (her real Christian name)—and myself taken together.[2] We both come out very well. Of course it's *private*. I hope you are better than I am, or you are not much in the way of health. Jones always asks after you and hopes to meet you again. Do you never mean to come to London for a little?

Ever sincerely yours,
A. C. Swinburne

1. See above, Letter 237.

1. "A General Confession" in *The Book of Common Prayer.*

2. See above, Letter 232. The photograph is reproduced in Bernard Falk's *The Naked Lady,* facing p. 224.

Thanks for photograph and news—but I trust you are better now? L's note [3] is curious—mais! I have done nothing for an age but run at the nose with sickening influenza.

249. GEORGE MEREDITH TO SWINBURNE

Text: *Letters of George Meredith, 1,* 190.

Garrick Club, January 27, 1868

My dear Swinburne

The 'Fortnightly' is no longer in the hands of a company but of a publisher, who tries to diminish the expenses as much as he can; the editor being the chief sufferer. I had to pay for the two poems.[1] 'The Halt before Rome' has evidently been omitted from the list of what is due to you. When I see Morley I will state your complaints to him: but from the sum he gets it's scarcely possible to pay more, without doing so out of his own pocket. It will grieve him as it does me to hear that you are dissatisfied.[2] —I received for my 'Phaethon' (about 150 lines) £5.

Do,—if it's not possible, as I suppose, to buy a copy of Hugo's poem, lend it to me for a day or two. They say that Garibaldi has replied to it in verse.

I propose to come and lunch with you some afternoon. Will you have me? I will stay from two or three to six, and if we are alone, we will give and take, though I shall take ten times the worth of what I give. —I have just got your 'Blake.' M. Conway's notice of it in the 'Fortnightly' [3] is eulogistic, but whether sufficient and closely and

3. In a letter to Powell on Dec. 15 (the original is in the National Library of Wales) Longfellow wrote: "Of Mr. Swinburne's poetic gifts I think very highly; and admire particularly the power of his lyric poems. His theory of Art I do not admire. He too often, like some of the old artists, paints the Devil with a nimbus round his head."

1. "A Wasted Vigil" and "Ave atque Vale. In Memory of Charles Baudelaire."

2. On Mar. 4, after seeing Swinburne at the Joneses' party in their new house, William Rossetti wrote in his diary (*Rossetti Papers*, p. 301): "Swinburne says that his writing in *The Fortnightly Review* has come to a stand for the present. Payment for his *Halt before Rome, Baudelaire,* and another poem, being outstanding, the *Fortnightly* people sent him £12 for the latter two, not as yet settling at all for the first. He considers this £12 altogether below the mark; wrote about the matter more than a month ago, and has as yet received no reply."

3. Feb. 1868, pp. 216–20.

warmly critical I can't yet say. My wife and Willie hope to greet you in the warm Spring days.

Yours ever faithfully,
George Meredith

250. TO J. FREDERICK COLLINGWOOD [?] [1]

MS: John S. Mayfield (who supplied the transcript).

Arts Club, Hanover Square,
January 31 [? 1868]

Dear Brother
By the grace of Satan I will be with you—Deo Nolente—*with* a friend—on Tuesday

Yours in the faith,
✠ A. C. Swinburne

251. TO WILLIAM MICHAEL ROSSETTI

MS: Rutgers.

Arts Club, Hanover Square,
February 1 [1868]

My dear Rossetti
I *can't* get that blessed poem of yours out of my head. It's all very well, but you beginning in that way ought to have knocked us all out of sight. I can't tell you—not what I think of the poem done—but what I think of the poem feasible. Do write something more in my line and I'll be the first to admit your superiority. I'm not writing 'chaff'—but I have today re-read your poem—and I *can't* hold my tongue, or my fingers.

1. See below, Letter 256. Collingwood translated and edited (1863) Theodor Waitz, *Introduction to Anthropology* and also (1870) Louis Büchner, *Force and Matter*. Along with James Hunt (who shared his address), Nicholas Trübner, Charles Carter Blake, Richard Burton, Thomas Bendyshe, Charles Duncan Cameron, and Winwood Reade, all of whom were (or have been called) friends of Swinburne's, Collingwood was a member of the Anthropological Society of London, of which the Cannibal Club, which Swinburne alludes to in this note, was a frivolous and lusty offshoot (see Lafourcade, *La Jeunesse, 1,* 230–31). On Mar. 18 William Rossetti wrote in his diary (*Rossetti Papers,* p. 303): "[A. C.] Lyster tells me that last night at the Anthropological Society a discussion arose as to the races now in America, and the view was maintained that they had no distinctive originating powers, as e.g. in poetry. On this Swinburne spoke to the contrary, citing Poe (and I should presume Whitman, though Lyster doesn't say so)." Swinburne's remarks are printed in the *Journal of the Anthropological Society of London, 6* (1868), cxxv–cxlvi.

That idea [1] of yours in 'Mrs. Holmes Gray' beats everything but Balzac. I can't tell you how its choice impresses and excites me.

Will you let me keep your sheets of Whitman's 'Democracy' a little longer? I want to lay them before Mazzini, whom I hope to see tomorrow. He has been far from well lately, and so I haven't gone and knocked him up.

Ever yours affectionately,
A. C. Swinburne

P.S. Excuse the *scribble*—it isn't because of late hours—but simply because of bad pen and ink. (Vide—first page)   Have you seen the Saturday on me and Blake? [2] Of course I'm dead.

252. TO F. J. FURNIVALL

MS: Yale.

22a Dorset Street, W., February 7 [1868]

My dear Sir

I should have thanked you before for your present,[1] but I wanted to read something of it first, and was laid up in bed for days unable to read or write. Being now able, I do wish to thank you. The other copy was at once forwarded to Ashburnham Place. I am charmed with the book, but particularly and personally with The Birched Schoolboy,[2] who is delicious; it makes one tingle again to read, as one tingled at thirteen. But how *can* you say that boys of this era don't know what a good birching is? I can tell you I did some twelve years since—I could have once or twice matched Tom Tusser's experience to the full. (How like a boy to remember the exact number of 'cuts' he received!) And I shewed the poem and your note to a schoolboy who scouted the idea—said he could give ocular and tangible disproof of

1. Of a coroner's inquest.

2. The *Saturday Review* (Feb. 1, 1868), pp. 148–49. The reviewer, J. R. Green (identified in M. M. Bevington's book, *The Saturday Review 1855–1868*, pp. 223–24), said that *William Blake* revealed Swinburne's "frivolous incapacity as a critic either of poetry or of art; his inability to think consecutively for five minutes together; his powerlessness to express even his gleams of momentary intelligence in intelligible speech."

1. *The Babees Book*. The volume was inscribed "Algernon Swinburne, Esq. with the Editor's compts. and Thanks, 28 Jany. 1868" (Lot 211 in Sotheby's *Catalogue* of Swinburne's library, June 1916). See above, Letter 102.

2. In *The Babees Book*, pp. 403–4.

your assertion that sound flogging was obsolete—but I did not make him shew his honourable scars. I am sure I might have quoted

'He would not leave till it did bleed' [3]

—(and not always then)—often enough. Pray rectify this error. By the by, there is another at p. 83 of the preface to Rhodes. The comedy cited in the note is by Samuel Rowley—'When you see me you know me, or the Life of King Henry VIII' (1608)—whom S. R. seems to like as well as Mr. Froude does. Dr. Christopher Tye appears in the play as music-master to the prince, and the whipping boy's name there is Edward Browne. The whole scene of his flogging is immense fun. Not only Cramer and Tye appear in it, but after his flagellation young Browne comes out blubbering and tying up his breeches, and Will Summers the king's fool chaffing him unmercifully. Then Prince Edward returns from play and makes the boy a Knight as 'having many times shed his blood for me'—which the king confirms. It is a most lifelike bit of schoolboy dialogue, and the best thing in the play. I would send you my copy, bought at Lord Charlemont's unlucky sale [4] when so much good old poetry and prose was burnt, but I have mislaid it.

What a charming book a History of the Birch-rod in England would be. I must get sight of the passage in Caxton about a 'breechless feast.' Any one who has been—is—or will be a schoolboy ought to relish any allusion to birch. I wonder did they use a flogging-block as at Eton, or simply horse one boy on another's back.

I send you three rarities to look at—Lupton [5] I dare say you know—the others I think you said were new to you. Please let me know if they come safe to hand, and whether I may keep your romances longer. I have not had time to read them yet.

Ever yours sincerely,
Algernon Ch. Swinburne

I am glad the Noble Lyf was so useful for extracts.

By the by I have been canvassing a little for the Percy MS and expect to net a subscription or two at least.

3. "The Birched School-Boy," l. 20.

4. See above, Letter 82.

5. Thomas Lupton's *A Thousand Notable Things of Sundry Sortes*, 1586 (Lot 592 in Sotheby's *Catalogue*, June 1916).

253. TO GEORGE POWELL

MS: National Library of Wales.

Arts Club, Hanover Square,
February 11 [1868]

My dear Powell

I am still in town as you see—so don't go to Holmwood—come to Dorset Street. I have been detained 1) by money troubles 2) by teeth. I am fresh from the dentist's—and must be there again tomorrow—my teeth are—GOD who made them for torture knows in what a state of dental chaos. I keep thinking of the young lady 'que l'on enculait tandis que le P. Chrysostôm lui arrachait les dents.'[1] The recollection of that *sweet bit* made me laugh this morning even in the dentist's chair. 'Voilà bien ton b - - - - - de Dieu, ma chère Justine—s'il existe!'

Adieu—I expect you, and shall call myself—perhaps (if alive, like J., après des supplices aussi prolongés) tomorrow night or next day.

Tout à toi,
A.C.S.

254. TO F. J. FURNIVALL

MS: Yale.

22a Dorset Street, W., February 13 [1868]

My dear Sir

Many thanks for your proofs—which interested me much at my first spare time. If you want them back at once, tell me. I hope the 'Post with a Pacquet'[1] will amuse you as far as it goes. Pray observe the letter 'To a faire proud Tit.' Do you remember, in the 'Lamentation of boys burning pricksong' cited by Mr. Halliwell for the Shakespeare Society, the two thrilling lines

'We have so many lashes to learn this peeled song
That out of our buttocks we may pluck the stumps *thus* long'?

I can tell you it is still a matter of daily schoolboy experience. Birching is better than the cursed system of impositions—'poenas' as the Eton phrase is—manlier and wholesomer. The other makes all writing hateful and tedious and gives hours of discomfort instead of minutes of torture.

Yours sincerely,
A. C. Swinburne

1. A rare lapse for Swinburne, who usually seems to know Sade by heart: it was not Chrysostôme but Bonifacio—*La Nouvelle Justine* (4 vols. Sceaux, 1953), *3*, 35.

1. By Nicholas Breton (1545?–1626?).

255. TO J. FREDERICK COLLINGWOOD [?]

MS: John S. Mayfield.

[? February 14, 1868] [1]

Dear Brother

When is the next feast of human flesh to come off? I will attend if possible. I hope it is not on Wednesday as I am engaged that evening.

Yours fraternally,
A. C. Swinburne

256. TO J. FREDERICK COLLINGWOOD [1]

MS: John S. Mayfield.

[February 17, 1868]

Brother

By the grace of the Devil I trust to be with you tomorrow—unaccompanied.

Yours in the faith,
A. C. Swinburne

257. TO JAMES HAIN FRISWELL

MS: John S. Mayfield.

22a Dorset Street, W., March 2 [? 1868] [1]

My dear Sir

I have just received your note inviting me to take part in a public dinner to be given to Mr. Disraeli. [2] I am sorry that I shall not be able to join you.

Yours truly,
A. C. Swinburne

J. Hain Friswell, Esq.

1. The paper is watermarked 1865. I have no idea when this letter was written, and no proof, indeed, that it was addressed to J. Frederick Collingwood. I have merely for convenience dated it thus and assumed it was written to him. See below, Letter 256.

1. The envelope is addressed: "Brother" Collingwood C.C. / 4 St. Martin's Place / W.C. The postmarks are: LONDON W/6/FE 17/68 and LONDON WC/LM/FE 17/ 68. The paper is watermarked 1866. See above, Letter 250.

1. The paper is watermarked 1866.

2. Disraeli succeeded Gladstone as Prime Minister on Feb. 25.

258. TO LORD HOUGHTON

MS: The Marchioness of Crewe.

Arts Club, Hanover Square,
March 28 [1868]

My dear Lord Houghton

I meant to have written in answer to your last note, ages ago—but naturally, being good, the intention came to nothing. —I am *désespéré* to have missed my dear and venerated friend M. Rodin—and I tremble to think what retribution that excellent man may (justifiably) exact, at our next meeting, from a pupil who was twice out of bounds when called for (being already, I fear, under sentence of punishment). Will you—if you should meet him while in Italy—intercede for the offender—as far, that is, as your conscience will allow you? I see by the newspapers that you have moved from the Riviera to Rome—and congratulate you on the change. Whatever you or any one may say, I maintain that the Nizza-Mentone province is unpleasant, angular, arid, sharp-edged, stony, *frowzy*—neither grand nor sweet—and landscape must be one or the other, if it is not to be (as Shelley says) 'damnable—and damned.' [1] I have about twenty poetical irons in the fire (perhaps they had better remain there) but have finished one which I think as good as anything I have yet done. It is sent off to an American magazine, but I intend it to reappear here before it can be pirated. [2] Àpropos des vers—cannot you, as a friend of Mr. Tennyson, prevent his making such a hideous exhibition of himself as he has been doing for the last three months? [3] I thought there was a law against 'indecent exposure'? It was put in force, you remember, against Mr. Robert Browning when, for the second time, he ran stark naked at noonday through the Marble Arch. [4] But *he* is not Laureate. Altogether, these elder poets are too bad. *I* blush, and avert my eyes with disgust and pity.

Have you seen Arnold's new book on continental schools? [5] I lament to observe that he does not touch on the radical—I might say the

1. *Peter Bell the Third,* III. 218.

2. "Siena."

3. According to William Rossetti (*Rossetti Papers,* p. 302), Browning, who called on Mar. 15, "greatly deprecates the publication by Tennyson of the trifling affairs which are now appearing in *Good Words* and *Once a Week* etc.: he says that T[enny-son]'s books are declining in sale within this year or two (perhaps the influence of Swinburne)."

4. See also Letter 1090 below.

5. *Schools and Universities on the Continent* (1868).

fundamental—flaw in foreign education—the absence of that stimulant which the great Keate [6] and the greater Rodin would have supplied. —The English edition of Walt Whitman [7] is a decided success. W.W. (by the by they are Wordsworth's initials—c'est joli) has sent me a copy of his last poems with inscription; [8] they are very fine.

Toujours à vous,
A. C. Swinburne

259. TO SEYMOUR KIRKUP

Text: Bonchurch, *18*, 59–60*.

22a Dorset Street, Portman Square, London, W.,
March 28 [1868]

My dear Kirkup

I have waited long, but only because I was not ready with the right words, to answer your letter about my book on Blake. I was especially desirous to know what you would think of it, and sure that if it [seemed] to you satisfactory, it must be, howe[ver] inadequate, a step in the right dir[ection]. Hotten—the publisher of my book—intends to 'issue' copies done by hand of Blake's mystic works from the first to the last. I of course encourage him in the enterprise, though I doubt if it will *pay* in this 'ultima [Thule?]' of damp, snow, rain, hail and all that Dante found in the nethermost hell, *i.e.* in England.

If, like Shakespeare's Richard 3rd [1] 'I were myself alone,' would not I live out my life in Italy? But there are ties. (This reminds me that my Mother desired, when I wrote, to be 'kindly remembered' to you—she was, and is always, pleased by your recollection.)

Do you know Dr. Garth Wilkinson,[2] the biographer [and trans]lator

6. John Keate (1773–1852), headmaster of Eton 1809–34.

7. Edited by William Rossetti (see above, Letter 222).

8. The fourth edition of *Leaves of Grass* (1867), which was bound together with *Drum-Taps, Sequel to Drum-Taps,* and eight new poems. It was inscribed "Algernon Charles Swinburne from Walt Whitman" (Lot 848 in Sotheby's *Catalogue* of Swinburne's library, June 1916).

1. *III Henry VI*, V. vi. 83.

2. J. J. Garth Wilkinson (1812–99), who edited Blake's *Songs of Innocence and Experience* in 1839. Gosse's note to this letter says that Wilkinson "sent Swinburne a collection of his own philosophic poems, *Improvisations from the Spirit*, which Emerson had praised. I remember Swinburne's irreverent fun over these verses, which he found quite unintelligible, and said should have been 'dictated to Blake by the Soul of a Flea.'"

of Swedenborg? He has written [to me] about this essay on Blake, and since [calle]d on me, having received an answer to his first note. It rather surprised me to find the most eminent disciple of Swedenborg a convert to the worship of Blake. (Blake being so very heretical a Swedenborgian?) He says that my book has shown him a quite new outlet of revelation. . . .

260. TO GEORGE POWELL

MS: National Library of Wales. Brief extracts in Bonchurch, *19*, 153–64, and in Lafourcade, *Biography*, pp. 170, 192.

22a Dorset Street, Portman Square, W.,
April 17 [1868]

My dear Powell

You will excuse my delay in sending the enclosed when you hear the *two* reasons: 1) illness hardly intermittent during weeks and months of weather which would have disgraced hell and raised a new revolution among the devils: 2) that today only have I been able to get for myself one copy of either photograph.[1] There has been a *damned* row about it; paper after paper has flung pellets of dirt at me, assuming or asserting the falsehood that its publication and sale all over London were things authorized or permitted or even foreseen by the sitters: whereas of course it was a private affair, to be known (or shewn) to friends only. The circulation has of course been stopped as far as possible, but not without much irritating worry. The one *signed* I think good—the other not, except for the pose of her shoulder and bosom. I am keeping for you three others just out of myself alone which are thought on all hands excellent, and are certainly the best out. Come and receive them.

So we are promised Lohengrin this season at last and after all! Will the promise be kept? tell me.

I hope you have had no more pains or trouble; for me, I am well enough on warm spring days like this, and sick to death on the foul damp reeky stenchy wintry inferno-anglican days. I have lots of work in embryo, and some already born. I have such a subject before me, untouched—Tiresias at the grave of Antigone—i.e. (understand) Dante at the grave of Italia.[2] I do not say the living heir and successor of Dante as a patriot, for *he* sees her slowly but hopefully rising, though with pain and shame and labour. My beloved chief is still with

1. See above, Letter 248.

2. "Tiresias" (Bonchurch, 2, 235–47), published in *SBS*.

us, very ill and indomitable, and sad and kind as ever. I have worked
much at *his* book since we met. In 'Lippincott's Magazine' (American)
for May (i.e. about mid-May), will be a long poem of mine called
'Siena' which will make part of it. I am going to Holmwood in a day
or two if I can get free. Write me a word if you get this, and believe me

Ever yours faithfully,
A. C. Swinburne

I can't get a foreign envelope that will hold the photos.

261. TO WILLIAM MICHAEL ROSSETTI

MS: Rutgers.

Sunday [May 3, 1868] [1]

Dear Rossetti

Tuesday last—the day after we met at Hotten's—I had a painful and
what might have been a dangerous accident which has laid me up ever
since. I was carrying my lamp (unlit) in the dark (having already in
looking for it smashed a looking glass to begin with) when I fell over
something, smashed the lamp (it was very dark and the curtains close
drawn) and cut open my head, my right knee and (in rising barefoot)
my left foot. I could get no help or plaster till morning and by then
had lost a lot of blood. This is my first attempt at writing. Dr. Bird
has been with me, dressed, and prescribed etc.[2] I am going on very
well, quite strong and healthy otherwise, but of course disabled from
locomotion as yet. I do hope it won't cut me off from my chance of
being your coadjutor, but I can't go to the R.A. tomorrow, and, when
I can, shall probably want some one with me in the crowd, being lame
in both legs. I assure you the bed and floor of my room next morning
looked as if M. de Sade had had a few friends to a small and select
supper party the night before, and had enjoyed himself thoroughly
on the festive occasion.

I return your paper *at last*—I think it admirable—just enough said,
and that just the right thing. I was going to send a mere verbal message
with it, telling you of my disablement and asking you to come and
talk over things, but thought I might as well not bother you except
by writing—as I now can write, and am indeed all right but for a cut

1. William Rossetti's diary reveals (*Rossetti Papers*, pp. 305–6) that he and Swinburne met with Hotten on Monday, Apr. 27, to discuss their combined operation,
conceived by Hotten, "Notes on the Royal Academy Exhibition, 1868" (Bonchurch,
15, 196–216). Swinburne's portion was reprinted, with deletions, in *ES*.

2. See below, Letters 263.

or two. Plût à Dieu que notre orpheline n'eût jamais plus souffert! ce sont là les moindres malheurs de la vertu.

How very fine Tennyson's 'Lucretius' [3] is—all but the last lines. I read it last evening with quite surprised admiration.

Yours ever,
A. C. Swinburne

262. MATTHEW ARNOLD TO SWINBURNE

Text: *Times Literary Supplement* (Aug. 12, 1920), p. 517.

The Athenaeum, May 11 [1868]

My dear Mr. Swinburne

I had hoped to have seen you before we left London, but we lost our youngest child in January [1] and from that time till March, when we went into the country to live, we saw no one. So I take the opportunity of the new edition of my Poems [2] to send them to one who has been so splendidly their friend, and to say at the same time how I regret not having been able to see you in Chester-square. There are a few slight alterations and additions in some of the poems, and I have put a note about Obermann which perhaps will interest you.

As from time to time I have come across the bad effects of that Peter Bayne who persecuted us both,[3] I have felt tempted, as you said you were, to say something in answer; but as Goethe says, 'die Hauptsache ist das[s] man lerne sich selbst zu beherrschen' [4]—and to answer our persecutor, though tempting, would not really be the best way of meeting him.

Believe me,

Sincerely yours,
Matthew Arnold

3. *Macmillan's Magazine,* May 1868.

1. Basil Arnold died Jan. 4. See below, Letter 266 for Swinburne's answer to this letter.

2. A second edition of *New Poems* (1867).

3. "Mr. Arnold and Mr. Swinburne," *Contemporary Review* (Nov. 1867), 337–56. Peter Bayne (1830–96), a Scot, had studied for the ministry, and though he became a journalist, essayist, critic, and historian, he remained a preacher at heart.

4. "The chief thing is to learn to govern oneself" (*Goethes Gespräche mit J. P. Eckermann,* Mar. 21, 1830).

P.S.—May 13th.

This has just been returned to me from a *wrong* Charles A. Swinburne,[5] so I send it to your publishers.

263. DR. GEORGE BIRD TO GIUSEPPE MAZZINI

Text: *Mazzini's Letters to an English Family, 1861–72*, p. 199.

> 19 Welbeck Street, Cavendish Square, W.,
> May 12 [1868]

Dr. Bird presents his compliments to Signor Ernesti[1] and by request
of Mrs. Venturi begs to report on Mr. Swinburne's case.

Dr. Bird is most glad to say that for five days past Mr. Swinburne has
avoided 'the perilous stuff' and is consequently very much improved in
body and mind. No doubt Signor Ernesti will agree with Dr. Bird that
under these circumstances it is better to postpone writing to Mr. Swinburne's family. Mr. —— the artist (a staunch friend of Swinburne)
undertook to write to his father, but Dr. B has taken steps—he hopes
in time—to prevent him for the present at least carrying out this in-
tent.

264. TO WILLIAM MICHAEL ROSSETTI

MS: Rutgers.

[May 18, 1868] [1]

Dear Rossetti

I have today received a very civil and friendly note from J. Morley
(editor of Fortnightly Review) setting things hitherto square 'and
hoping' that I will yet allow them to print my notes on Florentine
drawings,[2] *if* I will reconsider the demand of a pound per page—I
must say, that demand seemed to me very reasonable as things go—
and yet, for reasons which you know and which *I* know that you sympathize with me in respecting—I should like to do what lies in me to
prop the apparently decadent Fortnightly. I don't ask you to take
any trouble about it—but will you just tell me what you would do in

5. Charles Alfred Swinburne, Esq., a barrister, who, in 1868, lived at 37 Bedford
Row, W.C.

1. Mazzini.

1. Supplied by William Rossetti.

2. "Notes on Designs of the Old Masters at Florence" (Bonchurch, *15*, 155–95) appeared in the *Fortnightly Review* (July 1868), and was reprinted in *ES*.

my place, and I will be guided by that. My impulse is to 'kiss and be friends like children being chid' (A. Tennyson) [3] i.e. to leave the MS. with him and give him what I think seriously my best detached or detachable poems for the Fortnightly Review [4] (the Republican canzoni). If you can spare two minutes just to say that you have received and read this and what you would do under the circumstances it will oblige.

Your affectionate,
A. C. Swinburne

265. J. C. HOTTEN TO SWINBURNE

Text: Chatto and Windus Letter-books.

June 18, 1868

Dear Sir

I have drawn up the advertisements, LOST, *etc.,* and forwarded to the *Times, Daily Telegraph.*[1]

I forgot to speak to you about that fellow Friswell's attack upon yourself, W. Rossetti, and W. Whitman in a recent number of his new paper, *The Censor.*[2]

I think it would be well that you should inform your solicitor of your having seen me, and of the arrangement that the a/c shall be gone into upon the return of Mr. W. M. Rossetti, that gentleman having had to do with the arrangement under which I published your books.

Yours truly,
John Camden Hotten

To
A. C. Swinburne Esq.

3. *The Princess,* VI. 271.

4. "A Watch in the Night" (Bonchurch, 2, 96–101) appeared in the *Fortnightly Review* (Dec. 1868), and was reprinted in *SBS.*

1. "LOST, 10 to 20 BLUE FOOLSCAP LEAVES of PAPER, roughly written upon in verse (partly dialogue). Missed between April 15–May 10. May have been left in a cab. Of no use to anybody but the owner. Small REWARD will be given upon restoration by Mr. Hotten, 74 Piccadilly, W." *The Times* (June 20, 1867), p. 1. The manuscripts, according to William Rossetti, were "of *Bothwell* and of *Tristram and Yseult*" (*Rossetti Papers,* p. 319).

2. Friswell edited the *Censor* in 1868 from May 23 to Nov. 7.

266. TO MATTHEW ARNOLD

MS: Richard L. Purdy.

22a Dorset Street, Portman Square,
July 3 [1868]

My dear Mr. Arnold

I ought to have answered your letter of May 11th [1] long since, but have been here and there—and in London chronically (*not* in Mr. Pecksniff's sense [2]—à Dieu ne plaise!) ill—since receiving it. Now that we have something like Italian weather here—an English translation of Dante—heat *minus* light—I have strength to scribble. I have never received your new edition, which I suppose ought to have reached me when your letter did. I didn't like to write and say so at once—but I am sure, now, it never was sent to my address or to my publisher's: and I am—apart from the pleasure of receiving a copy from your hands (you will know I mean this that I say)—desirous to see the additions and the note on Obermann.

Long before your letter reached me, Mr. Locker had told me *why* I could not expect to meet you again this spring.

As to what you say of our excellent friend Mr. P. Bayne—I *do not* think, whatever you may do, that I can keep my hands off him altogether. 'Il est des morts qu'il faut qu'on tue' [3]—I have always thought that a better and more significant axiom than any of La Rochefoucauld's—I had wellnigh said of Chamfort's—though the latter cynic is an idol of mine. His (P.B.'s) insolent stolidity and rampant mendacity call aloud on heaven, earth, and his native and natural place, for chastisement. [4]—If ever I seemed to say a word depreciatory of your friend M. Ste. Beuve, I recant, now that he has made so good a stand, and so practically useful, in the cause of free thought. [5] I must say, from his literary work, I should not have thought it was in him (excuse the rather schoolboyish turn of the sentence as I am scribbling in schoolboy-like haste).

1. See above, Letter 262.

2. *Martin Chuzzlewit*, chap. 9.

3. The last line of a verse written by Fernand Desnoyers (1828–69) and said to have been posted on the statue, at Le Havre, of Casimir Delavigne (1790–1868), whom he loathed (Othon Guerlac, *Les Citations françaises*, Paris, 1931, p. 230).

4. He got his revenge in "Notes on the Text of Shelley" (see Letter 291).

5. "De la loi sur la presse discours prononcé au sénat le 7 mai 1868" (reprinted from *Le Moniteur* by Michel Lévy, Paris, 1868).

Your letter went wrong through misplacing of initials. There is it seems some objectionable and (on optimistic principles) unaccountable being whose surname is mine and whose Christian initials are 'C.A.' Mine are 'A.C.' A French relative once explained to me why his surname now and then turned up among 'roturiers,' thus conclusively— 'Mais, mon cher, depuis huit ou dix siècles, nous devons avoir fait un *énorme* tas de bâtards!' [6]

I trust you won't think this *too* 'Barbarian' an anecdote. I couldn't resist it, apropos of nomenclature. And again, apropos of 'Barbarian,' let me take the liberty of asking (with all sincere enjoyment of your late prose, and gratitude for it, implied) when you will give us more verse? I, and my betters, are athirst for a larger and clearer draught in these Tennysonian times (*the* Laureate is of course delicious at his best—but one can't live, even chez Tortoni, on sorbets—it isn't digestible without bread and wine).

If you should see the Fortnightly (July number) you will find a grand rough poem of W. B. Scott's [7] which I got him to send, and a paper of mine on some unclassed drawings at Florence by the old Masters, which cost me some time and care to draw up. If you care for such things, the article may interest you—I can only answer for its cautious and literal accuracy.

Believe me

Yours very sincerely,
A. C. Swinburne

I direct to the Athenaeum as your last note is dated from there.

267. TO WILLIAM MICHAEL ROSSETTI

MS: Rutgers.

Tuesday evening [July 14, 1868] [1]

Dear Rossetti

On reading over your pencil notes I see they are insufficient for a lawyer's purpose without explanation.[2] I am ashamed to ask you to give any more of your time and trouble to my affairs—but until this is settled I cannot well leave town as I want to do very soon. Thus the

6. This entire sentence is heavily marked through with black ink over Swinburne's brown ink. (See below, Letter 1279.)

7. "Anthony."

1. William Rossetti added the date July 15, 1868, which was a Wednesday.

2. See above, Letter 265.

affair stands: 1) Longbourne—my family solicitor—has received Hotten's statement of accounts pro and con: I cannot check it; till it is checked, L. of course cannot proceed. 2) Hotten requested me while you were away to await your return, professing himself ready to abide by your verdict—if need be, by your *recollections and impressions*— as to the first arrangement between me and him; having first laid before you his view and compared it with yours. By the result, he said, he would gladly abide. 'Then' L. said 'we can do nothing till Mr. Rossetti comes to our help.' And indeed—I say it to my shame—my own ideas are confused as to what was to have been as well as to what has been. As for accounts—you know how I keep them.

If you can do me this one last kind office, we may then leave L. and H. to fight it out 'devil or baker.' If you would once see and tackle H. (it is useless *my* tackling him—the b. refers to you *always*—) as to how many editions of how many copies each he has (by his own count) sold—*and* as to what were the original terms—and let me have these, together with your own remarks and corrections, to lay once for all before L. and bolt from the field of battle—relictâ non *malè* parmulâ ³—it would be as great a kindness as could be done to

Your affectionate,
A. C. Swinburne

268. TO JOHN NICHOL

Text: *Early Letters.*

22a Dorset Street, W., July 22 [1868]

My dear Nichol

Of course I should have written before, but I have really been overwhelmed with notes, calls, etc., let alone lawyers' business. I send now my somewhat tardy thanks, and the assurance that I am none the worse for a fainting fit brought on by the damnable unventilated air of the Museum, of which I am too well aware the thrice-accursed penny-a-liners made up a tragic event.

This was the fact, if you care to know; I went early to the Brit. Mus. to look up certain references—met a man I know, about to leave— and agreed to wait till he could return at 1 or 1.30, when we were to go and lunch together—began to feel giddy and faint in an hour or so (no wonder, you would say, if you had breathed the atmosphere

---

3. For Horace's "relicta non bene parmula"—"my little shield left ingloriously behind" (*Odes* 2. 7. 10).

that day) but thought I would hold out and keep my promise, and consequently after some twenty minutes' struggle fainted right out, and in falling cut my forehead slightly. I was walking about paying calls next morning, ignorant that all the penny screamers were crying out my fearful fate! Of course my first thought was to send off word to my mother that I was all right, and next *per* Mme. Venturi to Mazzini, on hearing that he was distressed by reports of some serious accident.[1]

I am now quite well and strong, and my doctors tell me I am thoroughly sound and healthy inside and out. Jowett [2] has written me a really kind and friendly letter, on the hypothesis that I have been injuring my natural health by intemperate and irregular ways, offering even pecuniary help if needed, to set me straight. Of course I wrote at once my very sincere acknowledgments of such real friendliness, coupled with 'my physician's report'—he being also my familiar friend [3]—to the effect that I hadn't a sign of any illness or weakness induced by any habits of mine, and tho' I should be the better for tonics and sea-bathing (I should think so as to the latter—I am dying for it—there is no lust or appetite comparable!) I was thoroughly well and sound —as aforesaid.

1. The "accident" occurred at the British Museum on July 10, according to the diary of William Rossetti, who upon hearing the news went at once to investigate. On July 13 he and his brother called and found Swinburne "in capital spirits, with health apparently to correspond: a little plaistering on his forehead. He says that the closeness of the Museum Reading-Room on that exceptionally hot day quite overcame him. He had to bear it a long while, awaiting a friend with whom he had an appointment: but at last, rising to go, he was taken with instant faintness, and fell. Everybody on the spot showed him the greatest attention: and he receives most cordially Browning's attention in calling yesterday" (*Rossetti Papers*, pp. 318–19).

2. Benjamin Jowett (1817–93), tutor and Regius Professor of Greek when Swinburne was at Oxford, became Master of Balliol in 1870. As a churchman, he was vigorously Broad, and was one of the contributors to *Essays and Reviews* (1860). Beyond parochial limits he is remembered now primarily as the translator of Plato. Swinburne was proud of his friendship with Jowett, whom he respected highly (see below, Letter 1632). Jowett's estimate of Swinburne is more elusive, and Shelley's treatment at Oxford seems always hovering in the distance. Jowett is quoted as having called Swinburne, in the very early sixties, "a most curious young man. He used to bring me long and eloquent essays. He had a very remarkable power of language; but it was all language. I could never find that he was following any line of thought." On the other hand, Jowett is also quoted as observing: "When I don't say anything, people fancy I am thinking about something. Generally I am thinking about nothing at all." Horatio F. Brown, *John Addington Symonds* (2 vols. 1895), 2, 227.

3. Psalm 41:9 (also, in "The Psalter," Psalm 55:14).

I do not ask you to excuse this egotism—at least as tedious to write as read—for I know you will like to receive a genuine bulletin—*not* journalistic or Napoleonic.

Write me a word at your leisure to Holmwood, Henley-on-Thames, where I shall be for some few weeks *en famille,* before crossing to Étretat in Normandy. I hope and expect to be back here in time to see you in October or even earlier (if you pass thro' London earlier on your philoparthenic mission).

I hope you *will* review me—but it's rather late in the day for moral flagellation—even Mr. Ed. Yates (*cochon sublime*) is flat now (*vide* his last *Tinsley's Mag.*),[4] and where he fails in abusive morality, who can hope to succeed (. . . especially if not gifted with the immense advantage of being a blackguard)? . . . I would back myself to beat *Saturday's Spectator* and the whole crew at their own weapons of religion and morality. Do you see that in a review of Socrates and his school the *Sat. Rev.*[5] backs Théophile Gautier and me—alone against 'Catholicism and Puritanism,' as the representatives of the Cyrenaic philosophy versus the Cynic—Aristippus *v.* Antisthenes? Clearly, at least, we two, in France and England, have fluttered their Volscians in Corioli (in Jerusalem, Montrouge or Lambeth), *alone* we have done it.[6] 'Bah!' I may say now, I hope.

I (more seriously) hope we may achieve an excursion next year— vaporer [7] le Pic du Midi. I know its dear old *nose* (rather than head) so well, and we'll get a swim (bar cramps) in the Lac de Gaube. I wish I were in it now—six in the morning! (There's virtue! and mind, I've been in bed.) Tho' the furnace has not begun to boil.

I hope you like, in the last *Fortnightly,* my pictorial, Morley's political, and W. B. Scott's poetical articles; [8] I should like to have your opinion on each. Hoping to hear soon of Mrs. Nichol's complete recovery, I am always,

Very sincerely yours,
A. C. Swinburne

4. Aug. 1868, Edmund H. Yates (1831–94), a third-rate novelist and a second-rate, but enterprising, editor. He edited *Town Talk* in 1858–59, *Temple-Bar,* 1863–67, *Tinsley's Magazine,* 1867–70, and in 1874 he created the *World* in his own image. His chief claim to fame today is as the igniter of the notorious quarrel between Thackeray and Dickens.

5. July 18, pp. 93–95.

6. *Coriolanus,* V. vi. 115–16.

7. No doubt a misreading of some such word as *vaincre* or *attaquer.*

8. See above, Letter 266. Morley's article was "The Political Prelude."

269. TO GEORGE POWELL

MS: National Library of Wales. Brief extract in Lafourcade, *Biography*, p. 196.

22a Dorset Street,
Tuesday, July 28 [1868]

My dear Powell

I fully thought I had answered your kind first note before your second came to hand. I am sure you will pardon me when you know this. My 'accident' was merely a fainting fit brought on by heat and bad ventilation—I was out next day—the cut on my forehead is nearly healed.[1] I too am suffering from diarrhoea—which be damned —and when I move—say on Monday—I *must* go first for some little time to Holmwood at my mother's urgent request. Then—oh! shan't I be glad to accept your invitation! 1) to see you and cheer and be cheered if ill or worried 2) to satiate my craving (ultra Sapphic and plusquàm-Sadic) lust after the sea. I must go by Boulogne, having a commission there; tell me how to manage the journey as to times and places. Many thanks for your last gift—I send for your collection a curious little double autograph (George Augustus Sala's and D. G. Rossetti's together) and am always

Yours affectionately,
A. C. Swinburne

My life has been enlivened of late by a fair friend who keeps a maison de supplices à la Rodin—There is occasional balm in Gilead! [2]

I do hope you are better and flourishing. Write again—though I don't deserve it.

1. F. M. Brown wrote to Frederic Shields on Aug. 10 (Ernestine Mills, *The Life and Letters of Frederic Shields*, London and New York, 1912, p. 121): "The accident was not severe, and in spite of all the penny-a-liner could say, he was out the next day. But the worst of it is that the accident was caused by a *fit*—a slight one, no doubt, still a fit, which is not the first of the kind he has had. He is now with his parents in Oxfordshire and quiet and safe for a time."

2. Jeremiah 8:22.—See below, Letter 276.

270. TO J. C. HOTTEN

MS: Yale.

[? Late July 1868] [1]

Dear Sir

Here is your list annotated.[2] My quartos are at your service if you will be responsible for them—one or two are *very* rare and valuable. I should say modern print, as in Mr. Dyce's editions—but people are open-eyed now to faulty reprints, and you *must* have thorough and accurate collation of *all* old texts. I should advise an additional volume or half-volume to contain his poems. Of two of these I could lend you original copies. The reprint will then be complete—and I hope successful as it should be.

Yours truly,
A. C. Swinburne
T.O.

Thanks for the Art Journal extract. Will you get back and send me *at once* the photograph I lent long ago of the 'Eton block' [3] etc.? *today if possible* I want it.

A.C.S.

271. TO LADY JANE HENRIETTA SWINBURNE

Text: Leith, pp. 97–98.

[August 1868]

It has been one thing after another in the way of engagements that has kept me back—but nothing in the way of illness. Only you can't think how I get flooded with letters and invitations and that sort of thing (and some from people who are real friends to me) that I don't like to leave town without answering either by a call or by a note. You must take my word for it when I say I'll come down the very first day I can—even if only for a day or two before you start north. What kept me from coming to Holmwood a week since was really serious—the offer of a seat in Parliament next session if I would only

1. The paper is watermarked 1867.

2. In the Chatto and Windus Letter-books is a letter from Hotten, dated July 25, 1868, saying he had adopted Swinburne's suggestion of an edition of Chapman's plays, with an introduction by Swinburne, and asking Swinburne's advice about orthography, ancient or modern.

3. See above, Letter 221.

allow my name to be put up.[1] Of course I felt myself flattered, but at first objected on the grounds that I was not fit or properly trained, and might be taking a better man's place—but most of my friends have been day after day urging and pressing me to accept. Still I don't think it is my line. But you will understand this has detained me and given me a great deal to think about. . . . Of course this business is rather *upsetting* altogether. I know I don't want the 'honour'—but a friend said to me the other day, 'If you believe what you say and write you ought to sacrifice your time and comfort to your country.' But I don't think I will—in that way. . . .

272. TO GEORGE POWELL

MS: National Library of Wales. Brief extract in Lafourcade, *Biography*, p. 193.

22a Dorset Street, W., August 26 [1868]

My dear Powell

At last I am free to accept your repeated summons—and shall be *very* glad when I find myself with you again by the sea. I have been at Holmwood for a week—my father has been far from well, but is better. They are going on a visit to relations in Scotland. I am sure you were sorry on my account to hear of the death of my poor dear Menken [1]—it was a great shock to me and a real grief—I was ill for some days. She was most lovable as a friend as well as a mistress.

I have a commission to do in Boulogne [2] so must move out of the straight way either now or on my return. If it is much out of the way I shall put it off and go over from Etretat some day. Will you write me a word by return as to how to come by the best and quickest way—what line, boats, etc.? You know how stupid I am as a traveller without directions.

I hope you are well by this time and at peace.

Ever yours affectionately,
A. C. Swinburne

1. William Rossetti's diary for Sep. 7 (*Rossetti Papers*, p. 326): "Brown called in Euston Square. He says that Swinburne was lately invited to stand for Parliament, for some place in or near the Isle of Wight, but that he declined. I suppose this must have been an invitation from the extreme Democrats: all his expenses were to be paid." Six days later (p. 330) Brown told him that the invitation "came from the Reform-League, and was declined by S[winburne] on the express advice of Mazzini."

1. Adah Isaacs Menken died on Aug. 10 in Paris.

2. See below, Letter 276.

273. TO B. W. PROCTER

Text: Bonchurch, *18*, 60–61*.

22a Dorset Street, W., September 1, 1868

My dear Sir

I send you some verses[1] written a day since on reading Charles Lamb's Sonnet[2] to you, and remembering what you said (in jest) to Mr. Bayard Taylor and myself the other day about your poetry being less well known than it had been. My tribute is less worth having, but not less sincere; so perhaps you will take it, and excuse it, as what it is, an impromptu.

Yours very truly,
Algernon Charles Swinburne

274. TO LADY JANE HENRIETTA SWINBURNE

Text: Leith, pp. 198–99.

Etretât, September 14 [1868][1]

I am here safe and *so* well and fresh, thanks to the mere sight and smell of sea. *Such* a lovely passage on Saturday—hard due east wind, alternate roll sideways, and plunge forward and splashing—that I was wild with pleasure and others with sickness—*I* had left that behind on shore. I *must* hail the Flying Dutchman and get taken on board in some capacity—then, never stopping or landing, I shall always be well and happy. To get here is an awful labour—endless changes of line (with excessive confusion, stupidity, insolence)—and at last no beds anywhere and two hours' drive by starlight and one antediluvian gig-lamp only—no hotel open—an hour's helpless and hopeless shivering—at last an improvised bed (at 2 A.M. our hotel was roused)—but to-day all right. Powell has got the sweetest little old farmhouse fitted up inside with music, books, drawings, etc.—and of course *pokes* me into *the* nicest room. Do tell M.[2] the place belonged

1. "Barry Cornwall," published in the *Pall Mall Gazette* (Oct. 20, 1874), and reprinted as "Age and Song. To Barry Cornwall" (Bonchurch, *3*, 61–62) in *PB2*.

2. "Commendatory Verses to the Author of Poems Published under the Name of Barry Cornwall."

1. A typographical error made the date 1894 in Leith's version of this letter.

2. Presumably Mary Gordon Leith.

last to the late M. René Favarger.[3] . . . There is a wild little garden all uphill, and avenues of trees about. The sea is splendid, and the cliffs very like the Isle of Wight—two arches of rock each side of the bay, and *one* Needle only, exactly like *half* the Freshwater pair. We are going to Rouen soon to see the Cathedral—a cousin of P.'s lives there (*not* in the cathedral!). I must stop and save postage in time, so with best love and 'the best of lucks to all'. . . .

275. TO LADY JANE HENRIETTA SWINBURNE

Text: Leith, p. 110.

Arts Club, Hanover Square,
October 24 [1868]

I was very glad to find your letter waiting for me—but you might quite as well have sent me a line to Etretât, for in a little bit of a place like that one is known in a day or two. I had a real sea adventure there which I will tell you about when we meet. I had to swim (Powell says) over two miles out to sea and was picked up by a fishing boat; but luckily I was all right though very tired, and the result was I made immense friends with all the fishermen and sailors about—who are quite the nicest people I ever knew. . . .[1]

276. TO LORD HOUGHTON

MS: The Marchioness of Crewe. Published (with deletions): Bonchurch, *18*, 61*.

Arts Club, Hanover Square,
November 9, 1868

Dear Lord Houghton

I am ashamed to have been so long in answering your note. On my return from Normandy—where I received no letters—I found it

3. French pianist and composer, born about 1815, who died at Etretât in 1865. His compositions for the piano had a great vogue in England, where he spent much of his later life.

1. Swinburne's account of this story for his friends does not differ substantially from the version here (see *Rossetti Papers*, p. 335). His poem "Ex-Voto" (Bonchurch, *3*, 74–77; published in the *Athenaeum*, June 2, 1877, and reprinted in *PB2*) memorializes the adventure, and to a printed copy of the poem now in the library of University College, Wales, George Powell, his host, appended this account: "During one of Mr. Swinburne's visits to me at Etretat, he was, whilst bathing, carried out to

waiting for me. I will tell Hotten to send you Siena. It is no end of a work to wring an instalment of my money from his 'throat and maw' [1] though he admits an outstanding debt of hundreds.

I have met Mrs. Burton lately and found her very well and bright —pleasant and friendly of course: but I fear her late family loss [2] will have cut her up much.

Did any common friend tell you of my adventure at Étretât last month when I had to swim between two and three miles in an equinoctial sea for my life and at last was picked up by a passing fisher-boat? that was a lark, and I found place and people charming.

Our fair friend of the grove of the Beloved Disciple [3] has also returned from France and is in high feather. I always find her delicious dans son genre.

Ever yours,
A. C. Swinburne

I leave town for Holmwood, Henley on Thames in a day or two— in case you write.

277. TO GEORGE POWELL

MS: National Library of Wales.

Holmwood, Henley-on-Thames,
November 9 [1868]

My dear Powell

I have been suffering from business and ill health combined and

sea through a rocky archway, and entirely out of my sight, by one of the treacherous undercurrents so prevalent and so dreaded on that dangerous coast. After I had lost sight of him for about 10 minutes, I heard shouts on the cliffs above me to the effect that 'a man was drowning.' Guessing what had occurred, I gathered up Mr. Swinburne's clothes by which I had been sitting, and running with them through the ankle-deep shingle to where some boats lay, sent them off to the rescue. In but a few minutes, however, a boat coming *from* the point at which I feared a catastrophe had taken place, brought us the welcome news that my friend had been picked up by a fishing smack bound for Yport, a few miles distant. I therefore took a carriage and galloped off at fullest speed, with the clothes of the rescued man to the village of Yport, whence we returned to Etretat, in the smack which had picked up Mr. Swinburne, he declining to use the carriage."

Maupassant (aged 18), who was an eyewitness and was present in the "rescue-boat," described the episode in a short story, "L'anglais d'Etretat" (1882) and in the preface to Gabriel Mourey's translation (1891) of *Poems and Ballads*.

1. *Henry V*, II. i. 52(?).

2. The death of her half-brother, Theodore Arundell (1828–68).

3. St. John's Wood, that is—see above, Letters 269, 272.

alternating. Voilà bien ton dieu mon cher Dolmancé,[1] s'il existe. I am sorry, very, you were still suffering so much at his hands, but I hope they are no longer so heavy on you.

Your narrative of the nuptials was amusing, but the reality must have been disgusting—and still more the results. I condole with everyone present except the songster uncle.

Thanks for sending the photos: and things to Holmwood, whither I at once follow them, so please still direct thither when you write. I hope if you have to come we may meet and have a little fun before the year is out. I have found far from dry or chilling the Sadice-Paphian spring of St. John's Wood whereof I once spoke to you.

Ever yours affectionately,
A. C. Swinburne

278. TO LORD HOUGHTON

MS: The Marchioness of Crewe.

Holmwood, Henley on Thames,
[ca. November 16, 1868]

Dear Lord Houghton

I wish I could have accompanied Mrs. Burton, but found it impossible at the last minute. I could not disregard the summons hither and had to be off in a hurry—to my no small vexation.[1] Pray make my excuses to Mrs. Burton and tell her my servant never even told me of her having called till hours later. I write now by the first post I can catch to express my regret. On Friday I hoped against hope that I might be able to escort her—but I should be a rather poor guest—I have the usual November influenza so badly that I am all nose (weeping) and throat (coughing). Excuse the haste and late advent of this scrawl. I am hardly let out of bed, *or* to write.

Ever yours,
A. C. Swinburne

1. Dolmancé is a character in Sade's *La Philosophie dans le boudoir*.

1. He apparently went to Holmwood on Saturday, Nov. 14 (see *Rossetti Papers,* p. 335).

279. TO KARL BLIND

MS: British Museum.

Holmwood, Henley on Thames,
November 20 [1868]

My dear Sir

I am very sorry to be just now in the country and unable to enjoy the pleasure of hearing you lecture. The card of invitation—for
which many thanks—has at this instant been forwarded to me from
London. I have only just heard, to my infinite relief, that Dr. Bertani [1]
has pronounced Mazzini to be decidedly improving—date, the fourteenth. The telegram in the Times of Tuesday made me sick almost
with fear till I got this report from headquarters.

I hope you will give us who lose the hearing of your lecture, a
chance of seeing it in print.

With best remembrances to all your family

Believe me ever

Yours very faithfully,
A. C. Swinburne

280. TO GEORGE POWELL

MS: National Library of Wales.

Holmwood, December 2, 1868

My dear Powell

This day (twice and doubly disastrous to France and the world) [1]
is the 54th anniversary of the death—or shall I say the translation?—
of that great and good man, the Marquis de Sade. I wish we were together and could devise some appropriate ceremony to celebrate the
festival of that apostle and confessor of the faith as it is in Priapus.
If I were even in London I would observe it by a partial reproduction (with female aid) of the rites of Artemis Orthia, mixed with those
of the Europian Cotytto and the Asiatic Aphrodite of Aphaca. M.
Dolmancé I feel sure would find something to suggest. Can you think
of anything against next time? The photos of Étretât are now I think

1. Agostino Bertani (1812–86), surgeon and friend of Mazzini and fellow-
revolutionary.

1. He no doubt refers rather to Louis Napoleon's *coup d'état*, Dec. 2, 1851, than
to Napoleon's victory at Austerlitz, Dec. 2, 1805.

in London whither I have written to have them sent on. Many thanks too for the last of yourself and of the cat—excellent both, as we all think. Perhaps you will keep my sea-breeches till you come to London, and bring them—among your things if not too inconvenient?

I have written Rossetti about the Eau Hess, and he replies thus: 'I find the address is

Mme Hess

64 Rue Neuve des Petit Champs

There is no shop but you go up to some private rooms. The case we got cost 100 francs, and I should think you should get as much as this to give it a fair trial. It is frightfully dear. —F.[2] says the water did her no good, but I knew a case where it did much.'

It *is* dear—what do you think? I *half* think it might on the *whole* be worth trying. My hair was always so proverbially thick and curly that I don't want it thinned before its time. I owe you already—n'est ce pas?—that exact sum, and could if you pleased get a fellow to send you an order for both in French money—or keep it till you appear 'on your native heath' [3] or mud (the main component of England at present) that you may be impelled to hurry over and present yourself in the new part of Shylock.

My mother and sisters were enchanted with the beauty of the exquisite fabrics you gave me. I am very glad you are well again; I too am quite fresh and strong, despite frost and fog both.

You should read the first volume (all yet published) of Browning's new poem; [4] if it is not poetry proper, it is quite wonderfully interesting as a story and a study. I devoured it with the old boyish enjoyment.

I have just got the beginning of Lefanu's new book.[5] It does not promise at all well, though to prop it up he has resuscitated the perennial Larkin and Levi. I half begin to fear he is worked out.

I have had a very pleasant letter of the admiring and sympathetic sort from a French poet at Orleans, Emmanuel des Essarts,[6] which I shall have to answer. Here have I written you quite a long one for me.

2. Fanny Cornforth, Gabriel Rossetti's model and mistress.

3. "My foot is on my native heath, and my name is MacGregor" (Scott's *Rob Roy*, chap. 34) [?].

4. *The Ring and the Book.*

5. *Haunted Lives.*

6. (1839–1909), poet, scholar, teacher.

Hope it will not bore you; write me one in return, a good letter is a luxury in the country.

With kindest regards from all here

Ever yours affectionately,
A. C. Swinburne

280A. TO JAMES ABBOTT McNEILL WHISTLER

MS: Glasgow University.

Holmwood, December 2 [1868]

Cher père

Behold the British journalist! I could not resist cutting out the enclosed to send you. Has your mother heard from Mme Venturi?[1] she was going to write, I know, but her hands are very full. Her last report of Mazzini was still good, and should there be danger (as there is now none) I have her promise to let me know before the newspapers. Tell Wm. Rossetti this, as I know the false reports of M.'s death or danger forged in Paris will have alarmed him if he has not heard to the contrary.

I am very well and strong, quite an anti-Sadique example of the prosperities of virtue. By the by, this day is the 54th anniversary of the death of that great and good man, the Marquis de Sade. Consacrons-lui quelques larmes. Hélas! il lui faudrait plutôt du sang!

Love to all friends

Tons fils dévoué,
A. C. Swinburne

281. TO JOHN THOMSON [1]

MS: Robert G. Hopkins (who supplied the transcript).

Holmwood, December 8, 1868

Dear Thomson

I shall be much obliged if you will take charge of the Coleridge ms. for me and forward proofs hither: the cheque had better be sent

1. Emilie Venturi was an intimate friend of Mazzini, and acted as his literary editor and secretary in England. Born an Ashurst and educated by a father with advanced ideas about the equality of the sexes, she married Carlo Venturi in 1861, immediately after the termination of her first marriage (to Sydney Hawkes) by legal decree. She was widowed in 1866.

1. John Thomson is one of the mysteries in Swinburne's life. Most of what is known about him appears in George R. Sims' *My Life; Sixty Years' Recollections of*

also to this address. This will save trouble to Mr. Friswell as well as myself. I shall want the ms. back to correct the proofs by.

Ever yours truly,
A. C. Swinburne

Bohemian London (1917), which is dedicated to his memory and which is (at least) unreliable in details. According to Sims (p. 42), "Thomson's mother had an apartment house in Bloomsbury, and at one time Swinburne and Savile Clark lodged there. . . . Swinburne took an interest in the boy and had him constantly with him, and it was while he was Swinburne's secretary that poor John first met Adah Isaacs Menken, the actress and poetess, with whom he fell madly in love." Later, he became drama critic for the *Weekly Dispatch*. "There was a good deal of mystery about poor John Thomson," Sims writes (p. 44). "He lived in one of the side roads of St. John's Wood, then playfully referred to as 'The Grove of the Evangelist,' and the house in which he lived was rather sumptuously furnished." See above, Letters 269 and 276. Thomson's intimacy with Swinburne and with Hotten, Swinburne's publisher, is proved by two documents in the British Museum. The first one, dated Nov. 6, 1868, reads: "Received the sum of ten pounds, by cheque, for A. C. Swinburne, Esqr the said amt. not to be appropriated to the purpose of WHORING. [signed] John Thomson / To Mr. J. C. Hotten." This receipt bears a one-penny inland revenue stamp superscribed "£10.0.0," and is accompanied by a canceled cheque from Hotten to Swinburne dated the same day. Another receipt, dated July 19, 1869, reads: "Received on account of A. C. Swinburne, Esqr., Fifty pounds sterling, £50:0:0 [signed] John Thomson."